CITIES ON A FINITE PLANET

Cities on a Finite Planet: Towards transformative responses to climate change shows how cities can combine high quality living conditions, resilience to climate change, disaster risk reduction and contributions to mitigation/low carbon development. It also covers the current and potential contribution of cities to avoiding dangerous climate change and is the first book with an in-depth coverage of how cities and their governments, citizens and civil society organizations can combine these different agendas, based on careful city-level analyses.

The foundation for the book is detailed city case studies on Bangalore, Bangkok, Dar es Salaam, Durban, London, Manizales, Mexico City, New York and Rosario. Each of these was led by authors who contributed to the IPCC's Fifth Assessment and are thus acknowledged as among the world's top specialists in this field.

This book highlights where there is innovation and progress in cities and how this was achieved, also where there is little progress and no action and where there is no capacity to act. It assesses the extent to which cities can address the Sustainable Development Goals within commitments to dramatically reduce greenhouse gas emissions. In this, it highlights how much progress on these different agendas depends on local governments and their capacities to work with their low income populations.

Sheridan Bartlett is a research associate at the Children's Environments Research Group at CUNY Graduate Center in New York, USA. She works primarily on issues of urban poverty as they affect children in low income countries, bridging the gaps between the work of child-focused agencies and the broader development context.

David Satterthwaite is a senior fellow at the International Institute for Environment and Development (IIED) and a visiting professor at University College London, UK. He was a coordinating lead author of the chapter on urban areas in the IPCC's Fifth Assessment (Working Group II) and contributed to the IPCC's Third and Fourth Assessments.

"The contributors to this volume have already inspired generations of scholars and practitioners in development planning. With this book they demonstrate that urban governance is key to deliver a sustainable urban future for all. They do so by engaging with rich empirical evidence of actual cases of cities that have worked actively to deliver sustainability outcomes. A must-read for anyone seeking to make transformative change from within cities and urban areas."

Vanesa Castán Broto, *Bartlett Development Planning Unit, University College London, UK*

"Never before has a book assembled such evidence of the successes and struggles of cities in their quest for preparing for a world with climate change. It promotes the importance of learning from the experience of cities, unifying a deep drill of nine case studies that distil the essence of what works, what does not work, and why."

Diana Reckien, *University of Twente, the Netherlands*

CITIES ON A FINITE PLANET

Towards transformative responses to climate change

Edited by
Sheridan Bartlett and David Satterthwaite

Routledge
Taylor & Francis Group
LONDON AND NEW YORK

earthscan
from Routledge

First published 2016
by Routledge
2 Park Square, Milton Park, Abingdon, Oxon, OX14 4RN

and by Routledge
711 Third Avenue, New York, NY 10017

Routledge is an imprint of the Taylor & Francis Group, an informa business

British Library Cataloguing-in-Publication Data
A catalogue record for this book is available from the British Library

Library of Congress Cataloging in Publication Data
Names: Bartlett, Sheridan, editor. | Satterthwaite, David, editor.
Title: Cities on a finite planet : towards transformative responses to climate change / edited by Sheridan Bartlett and David Satterthwaite.
Description: Abingdon, Oxon ; New York, NY : Earthscan, Routledge, 2016. | Includes bibliographical references and index.
Identifiers: LCCN 2015042080 | ISBN 9781138184091 (hardback) | ISBN 9781138184107 (pbk.) | ISBN 9781315645421 (ebook)
Subjects: LCSH: Climate change mitigation. | Climatic changes--Risk management. | Climatic changes--Political aspects. | Land use, Urban. | Urban ecology (Sociology) | Urban policy.
Classification: LCC QC903 .C4344 2016 | DDC 363.738/746091732--dc23
LC record available at http://lccn.loc.gov/2015042080

ISBN: 978-1-138-18409-1 (hbk)
ISBN: 978-1-138-18410-7 (pbk)
ISBN: 978-1-315-64542-1 (ebk)

Typeset in Bembo
by HWA Text and Data Management, London
Printed by Ashford Colour Press Ltd.

MIX
Paper from responsible sources
FSC® C011748
FSC www.fsc.org

CONTENTS

FIGURES

TABLES

BOXES

CONTRIBUTORS

Fernando Aragón-Durand is a researcher and independent consultant on climate change and disaster risk management. He was a lead author for the chapter on urban areas in the IPCC's Fifth Assessment Report *Climate Change 2014: Impacts, Adaptation, and Vulnerability*. E-mail: fernando.aragon@colmex.mx

Sheridan Bartlett is a research associate at the Children's Environments Research Group at CUNY Graduate Center in New York, USA, and co-editor of the journal *Environment and Urbanization* at the International Institute for Environment and Development in London, UK. She works primarily on issues of urban poverty as they affect children in low income countries, bridging the gaps between the work of child-focused agencies and the broader development context. E-mail: sheridan.bartlett@gmail.com

Ritwika Basu is a research assistant at the Indian Institute for Human Settlements in Bangalore, India, and is working on "Collaborative Adaptation Research Initiative in Africa and Asia (CARIAA)", a climate change and adaptation project, focused on select semi-arid regions. E-mail: rbasu@iihs.ac.in

Amir B. Bazaz is a consultant (practice) at the Indian Institute for Human Settlements in Bangalore. His current research interests are low carbon societies/infrastructure, climate change adaptation, urban–climate change linkages. E-mail: abazaz@iihs.ac.in

Jörn Birkmann is a professor and director of the Institute of Spatial and Regional Planning, University of Stuttgart, Germany. His research interests are concerned with issues of vulnerability and risk research in the context of natural hazards and climate change, focusing also on spatial planning and governance. He was lead author for the IPCC's Fifth Assessment Report (IPCC 2014) and the Special Report on Managing the Risks of Extreme Events and Disasters to Advance Climate Change Adaptation (SREX). He is the editor of the first and second editions of *Measuring Vulnerability to Natural Hazards – Towards Disaster Resilient Societies*. E-mail: joern.birkmann@ireus.uni-stuttgart.de

Jan Corfee-Morlot heads the Climate, Environment and Development Unit at the OECD and she was a lead author for the chapter on urban areas in the IPCC's Fifth Assessment Report *Climate Change 2014: Impacts, Adaptation, and Vulnerability*. E-mail: Jan.CORFEE-MORLOT@oecd.org

Gian Carlo Delgado-Ramos is a researcher at the program "City, management, land and environment" of the Interdisciplinary Research Centre on Sciences and Humanities, National Autonomous University of Mexico. He was a lead author in the Inter-governmental Panel on Climate Change (IPCC) for its Fifth Assessment Report on *Climate Change 2014: Mitigation of Climate Change* for the chapter on human settlements, infrastructure and spatial planning. He received the Mexican Academy of Sciences research prize 2014 for Social Sciences. E-mail: giandelgado@unam.mx

Shobhakar Dhakal is an associate professor at the Energy Field of Study, Asian Institute of Technology, Thailand. His teaching, research and international activities comprise energy and climate policy, energy system analysis, accounting of energy and carbon emissions and mitigation opportunities, and low carbon cities. He was a Coordinating Lead Author with the Inter-governmental Panel on Climate Change (IPCC) for its Fifth Assessment Report on *Climate Change 2014: Mitigation of Climate Change* for the chapter on human settlements, infrastructure and spatial planning. E-mail: shobhakar@ait.ac.th or shobhakar.dhakal@gmail.com

David Dodman is a principal researcher in the Human Settlements Group at the International Institute for Environment and Development (IIED). He has co-edited *Global Change and Caribbean Vulnerability* and *Adapting Cities to Climate Change*, and has contributed to international reports including the UN Habitat Global Report on Human Settlements and the Inter-governmental Panel on Climate Change Fifth Assessment Report, *Climate Change 2014: Impacts, Adaptation, and Vulnerability*. E-mail: david.dodman@iied.org

Michael Dorsch works at the Graduate Center, City University of New York, USA. His research focuses on urban climate resiliency, adaptation and mitigation, especially in New York and other US cities. E-mail: mdorsch@gc.cuny.edu

Arabella Fraser is a research associate in the Geography Department at King's College London, UK. A political scientist by background, she has worked on climate change adaptation research projects for international organizations including the World Bank, IIED and Oxfam. Email: arabella.fraser@kcl.ac.uk

Sumetee Pahwa Gajjar is lead-practice at the Indian Institute for Human Settlements in Bangalore. She leads the "Collaborative Adaptation Research Initiative in Africa and Asia (CARIAA)", a climate change and adaptation project, focused on select semi-arid regions. She was a contributing author for the chapter on urban areas in the IPCC's Fifth Assessment Report *Climate Change 2014: Impacts, Adaptation, and Vulnerability*. E-mail: spgajjar@iihs.ac.in

Lisa Guastella is a researcher and independent environmental consultant, specializing in air quality, meteorology, oceanography, coastal processes and climate change impacts. She has co-authored a book chapter on the 2006–2007 coastal erosion events in *Observations on Environmental Change in South Africa* and authored a chapter on physical oceanography in *Ugu Lwethu – Our Coast: A profile of coastal KwaZulu-Natal*. E-mail: lisagus@telkomsa.net

Jorgelina Hardoy is a senior researcher at IIED–América Latina, an NGO working on issues of housing, access to infrastructure and services, vulnerability, social inclusion, risk reduction and adaptation. E-mail: jhardoy@iied-al.org.ar

Vanessa Herrera is a lawyer and has a Masters in Local Public Management. She is technical advisor at the Environmental Planning technical coordination office of the Under-Secretariat of Environment, Municipality of Rosario. E-mail: vherrer0@rosario.gov.ar

Nongcebo Hlongwa is a climate protection scientist at the Environmental Planning and Climate Protection Department of eThekwini Municipality. She leads the community-based adaptation work for the department as well the Central KwaZulu-Natal Climate Change Compact. E-mail: nongcebo.hlongwa@durban.gov.za

Radley Horton is an associate research scientist at the Center for Climate Systems Research, Columbia University, USA. He works on climate modeling including sea level rise projections and urban climate impacts. He is the lead technical climate scientist for the New York City for Panel Change. E-mail: rh142@columbia.edu

Garima Jain is a consultant-practice at the Indian Institute for Human Settlements in Bangalore, India. Her research areas include issues of vulnerabilities and risks particularly in urban areas, migration, climate change and multi-dimensional urban poverty. She also contributes to the curriculum-building exercise for

Quantitative and Empirical Methods, Urban Management and Urban Planning. E-mail: gjain@iihs.ac.in

Robert Kiunsi is a physical planner and an associate professor in the School of Environmental Science and Technology at Ardhi University Tanzania. He teaches and does research on environmental planning, land degradation environmental impact and strategic assessments, disaster risk reduction, climate change impacts, adaptation and mitigation focusing on urban areas, and was a lead author for the chapter on urban areas in the IPCC's Fifth Assessment Report *Climate Change 2014: Impacts, Adaptation, and Vulnerability*. E-mail: robertkiunsi@yahoo.com

Markella Koniordou is a scientific officer at the London School of Hygiene and Tropical Medicine, UK. She is currently working on novel drugs against the vector-borne disease Leishmaniasis and pursuing her research interests in the crossovers between environmental change and health. E-mail: markella.koniordou@lshtm.ac.uk or mkoniordou@gmail.com

Sari Kovats is a senior lecturer at the London School of Hygiene and Tropical Medicine, the leading research institution on public health in the UK. Her research interests are primarily on methods to assess the human health impacts of weather, climate and climate change. She is also Director of the NIHR Health Protection Research Unit in Environmental Change and Health, a five-year research programme in partnership with Public Health England, and was coordinating lead author for Chapter 23 on Europe in the Fifth Assessment Report for the Inter-governmental Panel on Climate Change (IPCC) (2014). E-mail: sari.kovats@lshtm.ac.uk

Daniela Mastrángelo is a chemical engineer. She is director of Office of Innovation and Environmental Management of the Under-Secretariat of Environment, Municipality of Rosario, Argentina. E-mail: dmastra0@rosario.gov.ar

Derek Morgan is currently an independent environmental consultant and was previously at the Energy Office of the eThekwini Municipality in Durban, South Africa. His research interests are in climate change mitigation, distributed alternative energy and low carbon transport systems. Email: morgan.derek@gmail.com

Sean O'Donoghue is at the Environmental Planning and Climate Protection Department of eThekwini Municipality and an honorary research associate, School of Life Sciences, Westville Campus, University Road, Westville, Durban, South Africa. E-mail: Sean.ODonoghue@durban.gov.za

Lesley Patrick works at the Science and Resilience Institute at Jamaica Bay, Brooklyn College, City University of New York, USA. Her research interests include urban climate vulnerability and exposure mapping with a specific focus on coastal storm surge inundation. E-mail: patrick@hunter.cuny.edu

Mark Pelling is professor of geography at King's College London, UK. His research interests are in the institutions and social relationships that shape vulnerability and adaptation to natural disasters, including those associated with climate change, and in the ways in which conflicting values and practices of development inform resilience and transformation in the face of environmental change. He has served as a coordinating lead author for the Intergovernmental Panel on Climate Change Special Report on Managing the Risks of Extreme Events and Disasters to Advance Climate Change Adaptation (SREX) and a lead author for the chapter on urban areas in the IPCC's Fifth Assessment Report *Climate Change 2014: Impacts, Adaptation, and Vulnerability*. E-mail: mark.pelling@kcl.ac.uk

Penny Price is a consultant in Cape Town, South Africa, specializing in climate adaptation, monitoring and evaluation, governance, co-production and climate knowledge networks. She has worked in local and provincial government on issues related to climate change adaptation policy, planning and practice. E-mail: Penylopeprice@gmail.com

Aromar Revi is the director of the Indian Institute for Human Settlements (IIHS) and a co-chair of the UN Sustainable Development Solutions Network (SDSN). He was a coordinating lead author for the chapter on urban areas in the IPCC's Fifth Assessment Report *Climate Change 2014: Impacts, Adaptation, and Vulnerability* and is co-principal investigator in an International Climate Adaptation research programme that spans India and sub-Saharan Africa. E-mail: arevi@iihs.co.in

Debra Roberts is deputy head of the Environmental Planning and Climate Protection Department (EPCPD) of eThekwini Municipality, Durban, and honorary professor at the School of Life Sciences, University of KwaZulu-Natal, South Africa. She was a lead author for the chapter on urban areas in the IPCC's Fifth Assessment Report *Climate Change 2014: Impacts, Adaptation, and Vulnerability*. In October 2015, she was appointed co-chair of the IPCC's Working Group II. E-mail: debra.roberts@durban.gov.za

Cynthia Rosenzweig works at the Goddard Institute for Space Studies, NASA, Columbia University USA. Her research interests focus on climate science and impacts, urban climate impacts assessment, and climate modelling. She is the co-chair of the New York City Panel on Climate Change, and is the co-founder of the Urban Climate Change Research Network (UCCRN). E-mail: crr2@columbia.edu

David Satterthwaite is a senior fellow at the International Institute for Environment and Development (IIED) and visiting professor, University

College London, UK. He is also editor of the international journal *Environment and Urbanization*. His main interest is in how to get the SDGs acted on in each locality in ways that involve and support the organizations and federations formed by slum/shack dwellers. He was a coordinating lead author of the chapter on urban areas in the IPCC's Fifth Assessment (Working Group II) and contributed to the IPCC's Third and Fourth Assessments. In 2004, he was awarded the Volvo Environment Prize. E-mail: david@iied.org

Ashish Shrestha is a research associate at the Energy Field of Study, Asian Institute of Technology, Thailand, involved in the research project on the water–energy–carbon nexus in Asian cities. His research areas and interests include the water–energy nexus, urban water systems, urban hydrology, climate change modeling and environmental engineering. E-mail: ashish@ait.ac.th or ashish.shrs@gmail.com

Stephen Solecki is an enverionmental scientist and planner and a graduate student at New York University Wagner School of Public Service, USA. He is currently working as a disaster planning and services managers at the American Red Cross, Greater New Area. E-mail: Stephen.solecki@gmail.com

William Solecki is professor of geography at Hunter College–CUNY, USA. His research focuses on urban environmental change and transition, and climate change and cities. He has contributed to several New York City area climate assessment studies and was a lead author for the chapter on urban areas (Chapter 8) in the IPCC's Fifth Assessment Report *Climate Change 2014: Impacts, Adaptation, and Vulnerability*. E-mail: wsolecki@hunter.cuny.edu

Alice Sverdlik is a PhD student in city planning at the University of California, Berkeley, USA. Previously, she worked at IIED in London and served as a voluntary chapter scientist for Chapter 8 on Urban Areas of the IPCC's Fifth Assessment. Her other research has explored sanitation, food vendors and electricity provision in Nairobi's informal settlements. E-mail: sverdlik@berkeley.edu

Luz Stella Velásquez Barrero is an architect and a senior researcher and independent consultant for the Institute of Environmental Studies (IDEA) at the National University of Colombia in Manizales, the Universidad Autónoma de Barcelona, Spain, and the Universitat Politécnica de Catalunya, Spain. E-mail: bioluzve@hotmail.com

Torsten Welle is a senior researcher at the Institute of Spatial and Regional Planning, University of Stuttgart, Germany. His research focus is on method development for risk and vulnerability assessments and resilience approaches in the context of natural hazards and climate change. E-mail: torsten.welle@ireus.uni-stuttgart.de

FOREWORD

> The illiterate of the twenty-first century will not be those who cannot read and write, but those who cannot learn, unlearn, and relearn.
>
> (adapted from Alvin Toffler 1970)

In the spirit of Toffler, this book questions what we have learned about the relationship between cities and climate change and offers the opportunity to reflect (and perhaps unlearn and relearn) how local level urban action might transform the world.

Ironically, both cities and climate change are artefacts of human endeavor. At one end of the spectrum, cities are hailed as humankind's greatest creation (Glaeser 2011), creating economies of scale and the possibility and opportunity of a better quality of life. At the other end of the spectrum, human transformation of global land and energy systems has literally fueled a level of global climate change that has contributed to the emergence of what is being proposed as the "Anthropocene". This is a new geological period in which the very different and uncertain state of the Earth system (compared to the relative stability of the Holocene during which our civilization evolved) is likely to provide a much less hospitable context for human development (Steffen et al. 2015). Global leaders as diverse as President Obama, Professor Stephen Hawking and Pope Francis have thus all characterized climate change as one of the greatest threats to humanity.

At the same time the Earth system is being transformed, we ourselves are transitioning. We are increasingly an urban species; already 55 per cent of us are urban dwellers. Over the last 60 years, we have lived through the most rapid urbanization in our species' history (and between 2015 and 2050, the world's urban population is projected to grow by another 2.3 billion). We are thus beginning to see global leaders speaking out about the unique opportunity offered by cities to counter this global threat with coordinated local action capable of creating a new, equitable, resilient and sustainable world. Pope Francis, President Obama, Rockefeller Foundation President Judith Rodin and United Nations Secretary General Ban Ki-Moon are all early promoters of this new urban understanding of the planet.

This book is an important contribution to that emerging urban vision and represents another step in the ongoing campaign by the urban scientists involved in the production of the Inter-governmental Panel on Climate Change's (IPCC) Fifth Assessment report (AR5) to highlight and articulate the agency of cities (and their governments) in addressing climate change. It is perhaps hard to imagine that anything more needs to be said by these authors after the thousands of pages that make up AR5. But a careful reading of the two urban chapters in that assessment indicates that the existing discourse could benefit from a more thorough reflection on how the climate change adaptation and mitigation agendas of the world's cities could be more effectively aligned and coordinated with growing needs for poverty reduction, sustainable development and equity.

Responding to that challenge, this book offers new insights into transformative adaptation pathways and how they can increase societal resilience and offer mitigation co-benefits through local, context appropriate climate action that respects both planetary and societal boundaries. This upscaling of local evidence (as opposed to the usual downscaling of global evidence) is extremely timeous as there are now increasingly calls for a stronger regional focus in the work of the IPCC's Sixth Assessment cycle (AR6). This book therefore provides one of the first bridges between AR5 and AR6. It gives a voice to those on the urban front lines and examines the agency of multiple stakeholders in the world's cities. It also talks to the needs of the post-2015 Sustainable Development Agenda which includes, for the first time, a global urban goal focused on making cities and human settlements inclusive, safe, resilient and sustainable, and acknowledges the need to "substantially increase the number of cities and human settlements adopting and implementing integrated policies and plans towards … mitigation and adaptation to climate change" by 2020.[1] The nine city case studies presented in this book show that if we are to 'leave no one behind' then we need to rethink the role of the world's cities in creating a more resilient and climate-smart world. In many cases this will require that we dispense with the traditional urban rule book and focus on transgressive and transformative change in our cities. As is so wryly observed by my favourite street artist, Banksy, who hails from the city of Bristol in the United Kingdom, "The greatest crimes in the world are not committed by people breaking the rules but by people following the rules". This is our contribution to that urban rule-breaking agenda.

Debra Roberts
IPCC Co-Chair, Working Group II, AR6

Note

1 https://sustainabledevelopment.un.org/?menu=1300

References

Glaeser, Edward (2011), *Triumph of the City: How Our Greatest Invention Makes Us Richer, Smarter, Greener, Healthier and Happier*, Basingstoke: Macmillan.

Steffen, Will, Katherine Richardson, Johan Rockström, Sarah E. Cornell, Ingo Fetzer, Elena M. Bennett, Reinette Biggs, Stephen R. Carpenter, Wim de Vries, Cynthia A. de Wit, Carl Folke, Dieter Gerten, Jens Heinke, Georgina M. Mace, Linn M. Persson, Veerabhadran Ramanathan, Belinda Reyers and Sverker Sörlin (2015), "Planetary boundaries: Guiding human development" *Science* 347(6223). DOI: 10.1126/science.1259855.

Toffler, Alvin (1970), *Future Shock*, New York: Random House.

PREFACE

David Satterthwaite

Building on the IPCC's Fifth Assessment

The Fifth Assessment of the Inter-governmental Panel on Climate Change had three working groups, each of which produced a detailed report: Working Group I on the Physical Science Basis (IPCC 2013), Working Group II on Impacts Adaptation and Vulnerability (IPCC 2014a), and Working Group III on Mitigation of Climate Change (IPCC 2014b).

This book, *Cities on a Finite Planet*, is prepared by the team that wrote the chapter on urban areas in the IPCC Working Group II report: *Climate Change 2014: Impacts, Adaptation, and Vulnerability* (IPCC 2014a). Aromar Revi and David Satterthwaite were what the IPCC calls coordinating lead authors (CLAs) for this chapter and they had responsibilities for ensuring the production of the chapter and responses to the many comments from reviewers. Fernando Aragón-Durand, Jan Corfee-Morlot, Robert B.R. Kiunsi, Mark Pelling, Debra Roberts and William Solecki were lead authors – all of whom attended the IPCC chapter meetings and who drafted different sections of the IPCC urban chapter. They also helped respond to reviewer comments. Alice Sverdlik was the chapter scientist and she also attended the IPCC chapter meetings and supported all the authors in drafting and reviewing texts. Jorgelina Hardoy managed the preparation of three detailed city case studies for the IPCC and the chapters in this volume on Rosario and Manizales. The book also draws in other IPCC chapter authors who have an interest in urban areas: Shobhakar Dhakal who was one of the coordinating lead authors of the chapter on human settlements in IPCC 2014b; Sari Kovats who was one of the coordinating lead authors for the chapter on Europe in IPCC 2014c and had been a lead author on the chapter on human health in IPCC 2007; and David Dodman who was a lead author in the chapter on rural areas in IPCC 2014a. Our goal was to produce a book that would be essential reading for those working on urban issues, development issues and climate change issues (and their intersections), providing a more detailed account than was possible in the IPCC's Fifth Assessment, but that could also be read with interest by non-specialists.

The book explores the ways that cities can address their local needs around climate change adaptation, as well as development and disaster risk reduction, while at the same time contributing to the global goals of climate change mitigation. There is a need for this kind of city focus. Most discussions about development and about climate change adaptation and mitigation focus on the roles of national government and international agencies, rather than the roles of local governments, local civil society organizations and city residents.

To undertake this task, the book builds on evidence from nine city case studies, which show how each of these cities is addressing its own specific local needs, and the extent to which climate change issues are being addressed. It makes a strong case for the importance of city government, both in what they have achieved and in what they still need to address. These case studies also demonstrate the importance of getting it right in cities if we hope to address global concerns. The authors consider how cities can combine high quality living conditions and resilience to climate change (and to non-climate related disasters) and, at the same time, contribute to mitigation and to avoiding dangerous climate change.[1] They do this based on in-depth local analysis of how these cities and their governments and citizens and civil society organizations can integrate or combine these different agendas. Cities may concentrate populations at risk from climate change – but many cities also demonstrate effective paths to a high level of resilience. Almost all wealthy cities have high per capita greenhouse gas emissions, especially with consumption-based accounting. But there are also wealthy cities that have low average emissions per person. Less affluent cities have far lower emissions on the whole, but many of them are contributing nonetheless to this global mitigation effort, as well as to a repertoire of adaptive responses. We need to understand and act on trajectories for wealthy cities that delink quality of life from high emissions and trajectories for less affluent cities to delink development (including a high quality of life) from increases in GHG emissions.

In bringing more attention to local capacity and action, this discussion also contributes not only to the tortuous process of trying to reach global agreement on mitigation, but also to the global debates about the Sustainable Development Goals, which give little attention to the local level and in general are poorly articulated if they are to be translated to the local level. We demonstrate here the limits of national and global discussions in the absence of a strong focus on cities and city governance. The book also locates the role of cities and urban systems within current debates on climate justice, urban resilience and transformative adaptation by illustrating the range of pathways now being built within the case study cities and where the gaps in these approaches are emerging.

Why city case studies?

The nine careful, detailed city case studies that form the foundation of this book are each prepared by authors with very detailed knowledge of their particular city. The emphases are somewhat different, but all the case studies have much that we can learn from. From Durban, for instance, we hear how a small group of committed civil servants pushed for innovation and continuity. From Manizales, with its long history of location-based disasters, we learn how a good environmental policy and commitment to disaster risk reduction provided a base from which to build a strong adaptation strategy. From Rosario, we see how a conventional development agenda with a commitment to improving living conditions and a history of land use planning provided another basis for adaptation and for the beginning of a mitigation agenda.

Looking at the cities covered in this book, the value of a cross-city comparison may be questioned. How can a vast metropolis like Mexico City be compared with Manizales? What do New York or London have in common with Dar es Salaam? New York has generated almost all the funding for climate change action itself (although even here there has been the need for significant federal funding to complement this); in Dar es Salaam, what is needed far exceeds local budgets. In London and New York, almost everyone has sewer connections and water piped to their homes. Most of Dar es Salaam's residents have neither of these. Every city is unique – formed or shaped by local economic, social, political and environmental circumstances, as well as national and often global influences. We have to pay attention to how each city is formed by a unique mix of factors, and we can't assume that what worked well in one city can be duplicated in others.

Of course there are elements that all cities, these nine among them, have in common. They all represent concentrations of human populations and investments, with institutions elected or delegated to govern them. All nine cities face new or heightened risks from climate change, many of them driven or exacerbated by what their city government is or is not addressing. But this book is not really intended as a cross-city comparison. We are not seeking to compare the performance of each city in climate change adaptation and mitigation (e.g. comparing transport systems, electricity generation and distribution or buildings performance). These are nine quite different examples considering what commitments their governments have brought to address climate change, what they have managed to do and what they have been unable to do.

All the contributors to this book agree that too little attention is paid to understanding how to catalyse action by city and municipal authorities on climate change adaptation and mitigation and how to integrate these into the development agenda and disaster risk reduction. How is it possible to achieve this integrated, coordinated response when these responsibilities fall to different departments or sectors? How is it possible in cities that rely on national government for much of their budget – especially where national governments have yet to develop the legislative and financial base to support local governments? How is it possible for city or municipal governments to manage where the list of their responsibilities goes far beyond their capacities? How can climate change get attention, when the focus of both the city and higher levels of government is on economic growth? City governments may see a focus on climate change as highlighting risk and discouraging investment. The growing literature on city and municipal innovations for climate change often shows that what is being done is the easy bits – low cost and good returns – or merely relabelling what was being done already.

Moving beyond the IPCC and its coverage of urban areas

This book seeks to move beyond the IPCC's Fifth Assessment focus on city case studies that address adaptation and mitigation, with an analysis that addresses the connection between urban, development and disaster risk reduction.

The IPCC's Fifth Assessment gave far more detailed coverage to cities than previous assessments did, both in the Working Group II (adaptation) and the Working Group III (mitigation) reports. But the contributors who worked on this coverage recognized the need for greater depth and detail on this topic and a better integration of mitigation and adaptation. They also agreed on the importance of considering policies and practices that go beyond the bounds of the IPCC's Fifth Assessment in defining an agenda for action. The IPCC has to avoid being policy prescriptive. It is the *Inter-governmental* Panel on Climate Change and it is national governments that send their representatives to IPCC meetings. They do not want the IPCC to tell them what policies are needed, but to provide a summary of the evidence on climate change that will help them develop their own policies.

So we chose for this book to pick a small number of cities where IPCC chapter authors and those who supported them had strong contacts with the city governments, or where they had actually worked. The chosen cities include at least one in each global region (Africa, Asia, Latin America, North America, Europe). But the list was also influenced by cities that are addressing climate change issues on one level or another. If we had wanted to focus primarily on innovation, the list of cities would have been somewhat different. But we felt it important to concentrate on cities we knew in order to get more insight into their actual workings. In most of the cities, one or more of the IPCC team has advised city government on climate change issues, or was engaged in some way with city government; in Durban, one of the authors (Debra Roberts) is actually part of city government. The author team that prepared Chapter 6 on Durban were all local government staff from the Climate Change Adaptation branch that Debra Roberts heads.

One of the most interesting issues to come out of the city case studies is how misleading it can be to review a city's performance from afar, based on official policies. Rosario is interesting here. As the authors of Chapter 11 note, "The city of Rosario is not an international frontrunner or a recognized leader in the field of climate change. It has no explicit climate change strategy or program, nor any office coordinating initiatives that contribute to mitigation or adaptation." But the city has actually done a great deal in meeting needs and reducing poverty, and in the course of that has built greater resilience to extreme weather and a strong environment programme with many elements that contribute to adaptation and/or mitigation.

We also wanted to assess each city's performance across development, disaster risk reduction, climate change adaptation and mitigation and to do so with a strong local perspective. Here, we come across a common paradox: in many cities, there are innovations and progress that attract the admiration of outsiders and suggest that city is doing well in comparison with other cities. Yet large sections of its population may still have unmet needs. Durban illustrates this paradox. This city is an important innovator on climate change adaptation and mitigation, as described in Chapter 6, and it has worked to increase the proportion of the population with piped water, good sanitation, drainage and other developmental needs, with measures to provide free basic water and electricity to low income households. But these successes mean nothing to those who still lack that provision and struggle to survive on inadequate incomes. There is also the disagreement in Durban on the appropriateness of large-scale infrastructure projects as the means to meet growing human development needs. So again, what we seek to provide in this book is a better, deeper understanding of the actual, mostly local, processes by which progress is being made (or not) in combining development, disaster risk reduction, climate change adaptation and mitigation.

This book is also evidence of how much the team responsible for the urban chapter in *Climate Change 2014: Impacts, Adaptation, and Vulnerability* (IPCC 2014a) wanted to promote more attention to urban areas. At the IPCC'S final Working Group II Fifth Assessment meeting in Bled in October 2013, we agreed to meet again to see what more we could do to stimulate attention to adaptation and mitigation at city and municipal levels. We then met in Bellagio in July 2014 and agreed to prepare this book, drawing in a few IPCC authors who had worked on other chapters, including Sari Kovats and Shobhakar Dhakal, and Sheridan Bartlett was to edit the volume.

As mentioned above, the IPCC's Fifth Assessment was the first of the five IPCC assessments to focus in detail on urban areas. The Third and Fourth Assessments included excellent, but very succinct, discussions of urban areas within other chapters. The first was part of a 36-page chapter on "Human Settlements, Energy and Industry"; the second was included in a 34-page chapter on "Industry, Settlement and Society". Both these chapters are excellent summaries of what was known at that time, but they also noted the limited available literature.[2] Between the publication of the Fourth Assessment in 2007 and work on the Fifth Assessment, the literature had grown dramatically. The Fifth Assessment included not only the full chapter on adaptation in urban areas (75 pages), but also a strong, detailed concern for urban areas within a 78-page chapter ("Human Settlements, Infrastructure and Spatial Planning") in the mitigation report. Both ended up being considerably longer than originally planned. (The urban chapter in the adaptation report runs to 75 pages, including 14 and a half pages of references, even though the intention was to keep it to under 30 pages.)

During the IPCC's planning phase for the Fifth Assessment, there was a recognition that a greater focus on urban areas was needed. The need for a stand-alone chapter on urban areas had in fact been one of the recommendations of an IPCC AR5 Scoping Meeting in Venice in July 2009, and was approved at the 31st Session of the IPCC in Bali in October 2009. In part, this recognition was because of the concentration of risks and vulnerabilities in urban areas, and an awareness of the importance of urban governments to action on both adaptation and mitigation. But also the rapidly expanding literature on adaptation and resilience included many more case studies of cities, some of them in a rich "grey" literature whose use was permitted as long as the original was lodged with the IPCC Working Group II technical secretariat.

This is not to say that urban issues only receive attention in the Urban Areas chapter – or that the Urban Areas chapter does not consider connections with other agendas (for instance in relation to ecosystem services). But for the first time, those who are concerned with urban areas (including local governments) had a chapter that directly addressed their concerns.

Assembling the authors for the urban chapter

Authors for IPCC Assessments are recommended by their national governments, and these recommendations are drawn on by the IPCC Technical Support Unit for each Working Group to form chapter teams. Those chosen for the Working Group II Urban Areas Chapter team were happily diverse in both geographic and disciplinary terms, and all the lead authors had relevant experience – many with an engagement with climate change adaptation or disaster risk reduction for specific cities. They were also committed to coming to all the working group meetings (no easy task as there was no remuneration for time) and to contributing to drafting the chapter. This is not always the case with chapter teams.

The team was fortunate to include Debra Roberts, who heads the Environmental Planning and Climate Protection Department of eThekwini (Durban). Since government recommendations for chapter specialists are made by national government ministries or secretariats, her inclusion was surprising. But she brought to the chapter not only her knowledge of climate change and ecosystem services but also long experience working in city government and knowledge of where and how to advance a climate change adaptation and mitigation agendas. Combined with the insights of other lead authors who have worked with city government (William Solecki on New York, Fernando Aragon-Durand for various cities in Latin America and Robert B.R. Kiunsi for Dar es

Salaam), this provided a strong on-the-ground focus, and the chapter included very detailed profiles of risks and potential for adaptation for their cities. Added to this was the expertise of Mark Pelling on disaster risk reduction and links with climate change adaptation, of Jan Corfee-Morlot for financing adaptation and of Aromar Revi on adaptation and mitigation at national, regional and local scales. We also had a very knowledgeable set of contributing authors (Jo da Silva, David Dodman, Andrew Maskrey, Sumetee Pahwa Gajjar and Raf Tuts), two rigorous, careful but supportive review editors (John Balbus and Omar-Dario Cardona) and an exceptional volunteer chapter scientist in Alice Sverdlik.

The chapter teams worked together in four meetings: in Tsukuba in January 2011, in San Francisco in December 2011, in Buenos Aires in October 2012 and in Bled in July 2013. The two coordinating lead authors of the urban chapter (Aromar Revi and David Satterthwaite) also attended the March 2014 meeting in Yokohama where the summary for policy makers was approved and the rest of the Assessment Report accepted. Support from the Rockefeller Foundation allowed seminars to be added to the meetings in Buenos Aires and San Francisco, which drew in some of the contributing authors and other specialists. As noted earlier, it was in the meeting in Bled that the idea of preparing this book was hatched.

A meeting focused specifically on the development of the book followed in Bellagio in July 2014 (courtesy of the Rockefeller Foundation), and the process was set in place. All the authors recognized the importance of an expanded version of the Fifth Assessment texts, with more attention to policy and to the potential for integrating adaptation and mitigation, and for the kind of socially and ecologically transformative action that attention to climate change, at its best, can imply. But these authors are also all extremely busy people, and were adding this volunteer effort to the already heavy demands on their time that had been made by their work for the Fifth Assessment. In the end, it has taken more than a year to realize a task that was planned for completion far earlier. There were a few scary moments when it seemed that not all the chapters would come in. We all owe a huge debt to Sheridan Bartlett for how much her editing improved the chapters and how her tenacity kept us on track; also to Helen Bell at Routledge for all her support, helpful advice and management of the manuscript. But the fact that this book exists at all is also testament to the dedication of researchers and officials around the world who contributed their energies and expertise to this daunting challenge.

Notes

1 See Chapter 1 for more detail.
2 I was a lead author for the "Human settlements…." chapter in the Third Assessment and a Review Editor for the Fourth Assessment. But what needs acknowledgement is the outstanding contributions of the coordinating lead authors for these chapters – for the Third Assessment Michael Scott and Sujata Gupta, for the Fourth Assessment Tom Wilbanks and Patricia Romero Lankao.

References

IPCC (2007), *Climate Change 2007: Impacts, Adaptation and Vulnerability*. Contribution of Working Group II to the Fourth Assessment Report of the Intergovernmental Panel on Climate Change, M. L. Parry, O. F. Canziani, J. P. Palutikof, P.. J. van der Linden and C. E. Hanson (eds.,) Cambridge University Press, Cambridge, UK, 976 pp.

IPCC (2013), *Climate Change 2013: The Physical Science Basis*. Contribution of Working Group I to the Fifth Assessment Report of the Intergovernmental Panel on Climate Change, T. F. Stocker, D. Qin, G.-K. Plattner, M. Tignor, S. K. Allen, J. Boschung, A. Nauels, Y. Xia, V. Bex and P. M. Midgley (eds). Cambridge University Press, Cambridge, UK and New York, USA, 1535 pp.

IPCC (2014a), *Climate Change 2014: Impacts, Adaptation, and Vulnerability. Part A: Global and Sectoral Aspects*. Contribution of Working Group II to the Fifth Assessment Report of the Inter-governmental Panel on Climate Change, C. B. Field, V. R. Barros, D. J. Dokken, K. J. Mach, M. D. Mastrandrea, T. E. Bilir, M. Chatterjee, K. L. Ebi, Y. O. Estrada, R. C. Genova, B. Girma, E. S. Kissel, A. N. Levy, S. MacCracken, P. R. Mastrandrea and L. L. White (eds). Cambridge University Press, Cambridge, UK and New York, USA, 1132 pp.

IPCC (2014b), *Climate Change 2014: Mitigation of Climate Change*. Contribution of Working Group III to the Fifth Assessment Report of the Intergovernmental Panel on Climate Change. O. Edenhofer, R. Pichs-Madruga, Y. Sokona, E. Farahani, S. Kadner, K. Seyboth, A. Adler, I. Baum, S. Brunner, P. Eickemeier, B. Kriemann, J. Savolainen, S. Schlömer, C. von Stechow, T. Zwickel and J. C. Minx (eds). Cambridge University Press, Cambridge, UK and New York, USA.

IPCC (2014c), *Climate Change 2014: Impacts, Adaptation, and Vulnerability. Part B: Regional Aspects*. Contribution of Working Group II to the Fifth Assessment Report of the Intergovernmental Panel on Climate Change. V. R. Barros, C. B. Field, D. J. Dokken, M. D. Mastrandrea, K. J. Mach, T. E. Bilir, M. Chatterjee, K. L. Ebi, Y. O. Estrada, R. C. Genova, B. Girma, E. S. Kissel, A. N. Levy, S. MacCracken, P. R. Mastrandrea and L. L. White (eds). Cambridge University Press, Cambridge, UK and New York, USA, 688 pp.

ACRONYMS

AAG	Adaptation Assessment Guidebook (New York)
ACC DAR	Adapting to Climate Change in Coastal Dar es Salaam
AICE	Association Internationale de Ciudades Educadoras (International Association of Educating Cities)
BBMP	Bruhat Bangalore Mahanagara Palike (Greater Bangalore City Corporation)
BMA	Bangkok Metropolitan Authority
BMR	Bangalore Metropolitan Region
BRT	Bus rapid transit
C40	Cities Climate Leadership Group
CCAPMC	Climate Change Action Program of Mexico City
CCIAM	Climate change impacts, adaptation and mitigation
CCP	Cities for Climate Protection campaign of ICLEI (Local Governments for Sustainability)
cCR	Carbon*n* Climate Registry
CDM	Clean Development Mechanism
CDP	Comprehensive Development Plan (Bangalore)
CERs	Certified emission reductions
CFCBP	Carbon Finance Capacity-Building Programme (Tanzania)
CIBSE	Chartered Institution of Building Services Engineers (UK)
CIDEU	El Centro Iberoamericano de Desarrollo Estratégico Urbano (Iberoamerican Centre of Urban Development)
CKZNCCC	Central KwaZulu-Natal Climate Change Compact
CLUVA	Climate Change and Urban Vulnerability in Africa

CMP7	7th Session of the Conference of the Parties to the Kyoto Protocol
CO	Carbon monoxide
CO_2	Carbon dioxide
COEM	Central de operaciones de emergencias (Municipal Emergency Operations Centre, Rosario)
COP	Conference of the Parties (governing body for an international convention). For this book, the COP is for the UN Framework Convention on Climate Change
CORPOCALDAS	Corporación Autónoma Regional del Caldas (Autonomous Regional Corporation of Caldas)
CSUPPU	Citywide Slum Upgrading and Prevention Programme Unit (Tanzania)
DANIDA	Danish International Development Assistance
DART	Dar Rapid Transit project
DE	Decentralization of energy
DICCPP	Durban Industry Climate Change Partnership Project
D'MOSS	Durban Metropolitan Open Space System
DPP	Disaster prevention policy
DRM	Disaster risk management
DRR	Disaster risk reduction
ECBC	Energy Conservation Building Code (a national code in India)
ECO	Energy company obligation
EEDSM	Energy efficiency and demand side management
EGAT	Electricity Generation Authority of Thailand
ELCITA	Electronic City's Industrial Township Authority (Bangalore)
EMA	Environmental Management Act (Tanzania)
ENSO	El Niño southern oscillation
EPM	Environmental Planning and Management (being applied in Dar es Salaam)
FEMA	Federal Emergency Management Agency (USA)
FINAGRO	Fondo para el Financiamiento del Sector Agropecuario (Agricultural Financial Fund)
FIRM	Flood insurance rate maps
FITS	Feed-in tariffs
GDP	Gross domestic product
GGBP	Greener, Greater Buildings Plan (New York)
GHG	Greenhouse gas
GLA	Greater London Authority
GNI	Gross national income
GoK	Government of Karnataka (India)
GRIHA	Green Rating for Integrated Habitat Assessment (India)

HAI	Human Achievement Index
ICLEI	Local Governments for Sustainability
ICMA	International city/county management association
IDP	Independent domestic producers
IPCC	Inter-governmental Panel on Climate Change
IT/ITeS	Information technology/information technology enabled services
JNNURM	Jawaharlal Nehru National Urban Renewal Mission (India)
KSNDMC	Karnataka State Natural Disaster Monitoring Centre
KSPCB	Karnataka State Pollution Control Board
LCCSMC	Local Climate Change Strategy of Mexico City
LDA	Lake Development Authority (Bangalore)
LEAP	Long-range energy alternatives planning system
LEED	Leadership in Energy and Environmental Design (certification system covering different aspects of green buildings and neighbourhoods)
LNR	Local nature reserve (as applied in London)
LPG	Liquified petroleum gas
LULU	Locally unwanted land use
MCPP	Municipal Climate Protection Programme (in Durban)
MCVCCC	Mexico City Virtual Center of Climate Change
MDGs	Millennium development goals
MEA	Metropolitan Electricity Authority (Bangkok)
MoEF	Ministry of Environment and Forests (India)
MTA	Metropolitan Transportation Authority (New York)
MWA	Metropolitan Waterworks Authority (Bangkok)
NAPA	National adaptation programme of action
NAPCC	National Action Plan on Climate Change (India)
NNR	National nature reserve (as applied in London)
NPCC	New York City Panel on Climate Change
NUTP	National Urban Transport Policy (India)
NYCEEC	New York City Energy Efficiency Corporation
NYSERDA	New York State Energy Research and Development Authority
OLTPS	Office of Long-Term Planning and Sustainability (New York)
PCP	Power Conservation Program (Durban)
PERM + 10	Plan Estratégico Rosario Metropolitana (Metropolitan Strategic Plan for Rosario)
PIECAS-DP	Plan Estratégico Integral para la Conservación y Aprovechamiento Sostenible en el Delta del Paraná (Strategic plan for the conservation and sustainable use of the Paraná Delta)

PIM	Plan Integral de Movilidad (Integrated Mobility Plan of Rosario)
PM_{10}	Particulate matter up to 10 micrometres in size
PNACC	Plan Nacional de Adaptación al Cambio Clímatico (National Climate Change Adaptation Plan, Colombia)
PONCAS/POMAS	Environmental protection plans for catchment areas
POT	Plan de Ordenamiento Territoria (Land Use Plan)
PUR	Plan Urbano de Rosario (Urban Plan of Rosario)
PV	Photovoltaic
PWA	Provincial Waterworks Authority
RAMCC	Red Argentina de Municipios frente el Cambio Climatico (Argentine Network of Municipalities for Climate Change)
REDD programme	Reducing Emissions from Deforestation and Forest Degradation
RE:FIT	Scheme to reduce carbon emissions in Greater London.
RE:NEW	Programme to help make London's homes more energy efficient.
RHI	Renewable heat incentive
RICCLISA	Red Interinstitucional de Cambio Climático y Seguridad Alimentaria (Inter-institutional Network on Climate Change and Food Security)
SAC	Special area of conservation (as applied in London)
SAPCC	State Action Plan on Climate Change (India)
SDGs	Sustainable development goals
SDI	Slum/Shack Dwellers International
SDP	Sustainable Dar es Salaam Project
SDSN	Sustainable Development Solutions Network
SELCO	Solar Electric Light Company of India
SIGAM	Sistemas de Gestion Ambiental Municipal (Municipal Environmental Management System)
SIMAP	Sistema Municipal de Áreas Protegidas (Municipal System of Protected Areas)
SISCLIMA	Sistema Nacional de Cambio Climático (National Climate Change System, Colombia)
SLA	Special local administration
SNPD	Sistema Nacional para la Prevención y Atención de Desastres (National System for the Prevention and Attention to Disasters in Colombia)
SPA	Special protection area (as applied in London)
SREX	Special IPCC Report on Managing the Risks of Extreme Events and Disasters to Advance Climate Change Adaptation
SSSI	Site of special scientific interest (as applied in London)

SUDS	Sustainable drainage systems
TANESCO	Tanzania Electric Supply Company Limited
tCO2e	tonnes of carbon dioxide equivalent
TE2100	Thames Estuary 2100 Plan
TMA	Tanzania Meteorological Agency
Tshs	Tanzanian shillings
TZED	Zero Emissions Development Project (Bangalore)
UBN	Unsatisfied basic needs
UCLG	United Cities and Local Governments
UEMP	Environmental Management Programme (in South Africa)
UHI	Urban heat island
UNFCCC	United Nations Framework Convention on Climate Change
UNIDO	United Nations Industrial Development Organisation
UNISDR	United Nations International Strategy for Disaster Reduction
UPFI	Urban Poor Fund International (managed by Slum/Shack Dwellers International)
USAID	United States Agency for International Development
VOC	Volatile organic compound
WRMP	Water resource management plan
WWTP	Waste water treatment plant

1

URBANIZATION, DEVELOPMENT AND THE SUSTAINABLE DEVELOPMENT GOALS

David Satterthwaite and Sheridan Bartlett

Introduction

Cities have always been important for their concentration of people, investment and ideas. At their best they are centres of vitality, diversity and aspiration; also places where the ideal of the common good can be most fully realized. In the absence of effective governance, they can, of course, also be places where the common good is most dramatically violated, locally and globally. The dominant processes that drive cities' economic success, especially investments in new or expanding businesses, do not of themselves produce healthy or sustainable or inclusive cities. Nor do they produce cities adapted to climate change, or cities that are keeping their greenhouse gas emissions low.

Climate change presents critical new governance challenges to achieving the common good, but also perhaps new opportunities to consider the kinds of fundamental transformation that could address the impacts of climate change along with other inequities.

What happens in cities and other urban centres in the next few decades will be the defining influence on whether or not dangerous climate change is avoided. While many urban centres have high levels of greenhouse gas emissions, it is also in urban centres that much potential for reducing such emissions is concentrated. There are so many examples of cities with ambitious targets for emissions reduction (Seto, Dhakal et al. 2014), along with particular cities that have achieved a great deal in reducing emissions. But for this to happen on the scale that is needed to avoid dangerous climate change, national governments will have to commit to ambitious and equitable global agreements and then actually follow through by delivering the promised emissions reductions as well as reductions in other drivers of climate change. This will require buy in from local governments and, in some nations, buy in from national government to what city governments have done or are doing.

Even with this national support for mitigation, however, most urban centres will also require very substantial investments in adaptation for the climate change impacts they can expect. This is even the case if global agreement is reached on the needed emissions reduction to stop global warming. These impacts will include more, or more intense, extreme weather events, sea level rise and, for many, such challenges as freshwater resource constraints and drought. A particular concern is the time-lag between emissions reduction and the slowing and then halting of sea-level rise. There are also worries about whether the current targets for emissions reduction will keep sea-level rise to levels that can be adapted to.

Also of great concern is the fact that the world's cities need to deal with the climate change challenges at a time of global environmental crisis. Scientists have identified and quantified nine planetary boundaries within which humanity can continue to develop and ensure well-being for all. Crossing these boundaries could generate abrupt or irreversible environmental changes. Four of the nine planetary boundaries have already been crossed: climate change, loss of biosphere integrity, land-system change and altered biogeochemical cycles (phosphorus and nitrogen) (Steffen et al. 2015). This means that climate change is not the only urgent (local and global) environmental issue and that cities will increasingly be called upon to integrate responses to climate changes with other global environmental change agendas such as the loss of biodiversity.

Municipal, city and metropolitan governments around the world already face the challenges of their conventional development agenda, which includes human development and poverty reduction. To this must now be added three others: climate change adaptation, climate change mitigation (especially the reduction of greenhouse gas emissions) and the reworking of disaster risk reduction both to make it more effective and to include within it the necessary attention to new or enhanced risks from climate change. This requires changes to policies, plans, regulatory frameworks and budgets. This is one of the key messages from the 5th Assessment of the Intergovernmental Panel on Climate Change (IPCC). Yet climate change adaptation and mitigation, and often even disaster response, fall outside the realm of local government roles and responsibilities. Even if this changes, so many city and municipal governments have little or no capacity to act on these added responsibilities. Most cannot even meet the long-standing challenge of ensuring provision of basic infrastructure and services to most of their inhabitants. The scale of their failure on this front can be seen in the one billion urban dwellers who live in informal settlements, who lack provision for risk-reducing infrastructure and basic services, and whose homes and livelihoods are often those most at risk from climate change impacts.

It seems patently unfair to add these new responsibilities for urban centres in low- and middle-income nations. Most have little or no investment capacity (UCLG 2014, Cabannes 2015). The increasing risks and uncertainties they have to respond to have been driven mostly by wealthier nations and people. Yet the need to reduce greenhouse gas emissions is so urgent that even cities with very low per capita emissions are being asked to contribute. For most cities, these added burdens will require transformational change to their very underpinnings – their economies, buildings, infrastructure and services, consumption patterns and land-use management – to serve both adaptation and mitigation. Effective action on the part of urban governments will also require support from politicians and political parties, citizens and civil society organizations – and at least the acquiescence of private sector interests. Given that almost all the growth in the world's population is expected to take place in urban areas in what are currently low- and middle-income nations (United Nations 2014), there is the additional issue of meeting the needs of another two billion urban dwellers without overstretching local resources and damaging local eco-systems, all while responding to the concerns raised by climate change.

The core of this book consists of case studies of nine cities, and how they are managing to add climate change adaptation and mitigation to their other agendas. The reasons for choosing these nine cities are explained in more detail in the preface. They were chosen in part to have at least one city from each of the world's regions, and in part because the IPCC 5th Assessment chapter team on urban adaptation that decided to prepare this book knew these cities and worked in them. Most of these nine cities have seen little or no support from national government or international agencies for any of their actions and investments in their more routine agendas, let alone climate change adaptation and mitigation. The steps they have taken – or not taken – provide some practical evidence of

Box 1.1 Preventing dangerous climate change

The ultimate objective of the United Nations Framework Convention on Climate Change (UNFCCC) that was signed at the 1992 UN Earth Summit in Rio de Janeiro by more than 150 countries and the European Community is the "stabilisation of greenhouse gas concentrations in the atmosphere at a level that would prevent dangerous anthropogenic interference with the climate system". At present, the goal of the UNFCCC is to get international agreement among all countries to stabilize global temperatures below 2 degrees above pre-industrial levels, although there are still considerable risks even if this is achieved and "the precise levels of climate change sufficient to trigger abrupt and irreversible change remain uncertain" (IPCC 2014 page 13).

To prevent dangerous climate change, the UNFCCC has adopted the principle of "common but differentiated responsibilities" which is intended to recognize the need for all countries to act to address climate change, while accepting their different contributions to causing it and different levels of responsibility for responding. This approach could also be used as a guiding principle for considering the role of city and local governments in responding to climate change.

what cities and their governments and people are able to do on their own, and how far greater national and global attention could go to enhance their efforts.

Growing interest in urbanization but not in urban governance

When the United Nations announced in 2008 that more than half the world's population lived in urban centres, this helped to generate more attention to urban issues from governments and some international agencies. Now, according to the UN's latest datasets, 55 per cent of the world's population lives in urban areas (United Nations 2014). These areas contain most of the world's economy, private investment and innovation. They also house most of the world's high-consumers whose consumption patterns underlie so much anthropogenic climate change. They are also home to an ever-growing proportion of the world's poor. A perhaps surprising and influential ally in demanding more attention to urban development, poverty and climate change is Pope Francis. This can be seen in his 2015 encyclical entitled "Care for our Common Home" which discusses in detail the common good – and climate as a common good.[1] His references to the planet as "our common home" and his discussion of "the common good" in his speech to the United Nations in September 2015 also resonate strongly with the objectives of this book.

But the increased interest in urban issues on the part of most national governments and international agencies has little to do with measures to ensure the common good. It is primarily focused on the key role that cities have in economic growth. It usually involves little interest in poverty reduction other than the hope that economic growth will help. This lack of interest is reflected in a global literature on development priorities that greatly underplays the scale and depth of poverty in urban areas (Mitlin and Satterthwaite 2013). There is also too little interest among national governments and international agencies in disaster risk reduction, climate change adaptation and mitigation in cities.

Definitions of urban

There is no international agreement as to the definition of a city, so despite the UN figures, it is not possible to specify exactly what proportion of the world's population lives in cities. All cities may be urban centres, but there are also many urban centres with only a few thousand (and in some countries a few hundred) inhabitants, which lack the size, economic importance or government administrative rank to be considered cities. If we accept that cities are distinguished from urban centres based on these characteristics, what are the appropriate thresholds – how large a population, what indicator of economic importance, what administrative rank?

The United Nations Population Division has figures for all cities with over 300,000 inhabitants. If we take this as our definition for cities, then 57 per cent

TABLE 1.1 Distribution of the world's large city population in different population size categories in 2015

Population	*Number of urban centres*	*Population (million)*	*Percent of global urban population*
Under 300,000	100,000? (estimated number)	1,710.5	43.2
300,000–499,999	653	250.4	6.3
500,000–999,999	538	371.0	9.4
1–1.99 million	269	367.6	9.3
2–4.99 million	159	479.6	12.1
5–9.99 million	44	306.9	7.8
10–20 million	21	280.1	7.1
20+ million	8	191.2	4.8

NB: The total urban population in 2015 was 3,957.3 million. Interpret this table with caution – and note the differences in the range of city populations in the columns. Based on figures in United Nations (2014).

of the world's urban population and 31 per cent of its total population live in cities in 2015 (see Table 1.1).

But many urban centres that are considered to be cities have less than 300,000 inhabitants. These include many long-established cities that had great importance historically but that have not had rapidly growing populations or economies for many decades.

The definition of "urban areas" also varies a lot between countries. Within most nations, there are settlements that are unambiguously rural, and a range of settlements that are unambiguously urban. But there are also settlements that could be considered either large villages (and thus rural) or small urban centres (and thus urban). Then there are also the rural populations that live within city boundaries – this is especially common for cities with boundaries that encompass large areas beyond the built up area, as in Bangkok Metropolitan Area (see Chapter 4) or Durban (see Chapter 6). It is also common for urban populations to live in districts classified as rural – for instance, as a city's population spreads beyond the city boundary into a neighbouring (rural) area. In many cities, large numbers of "rural" dwellers also commute to urban areas, so their homes are rural but their livelihoods are urban, and the urban centre they commute to has a larger day-time than night-time population.

The lack of agreement on designations is one reason why we do not know precisely how many people live and/or work in cities – or urban areas. Another reason is that not enough attention has been given to analysing census data on the distribution of the urban population between urban centres of different size. Also, for some nations there are no recent census data.

The nine case study cities in this book are all unambiguously "cities", and there is clearly a need for more attention to the issues that we raise in this book to be applied to the very substantial proportion of the world's population that lives in small urban centres.

The importance of cities

We know that cities concentrate much of the world's economic activity (and new investments) and the GHG emissions that accompany this. Cities also concentrate the need for more equitable development, for disaster risk reduction and for climate change adaptation. We need to understand how their governments grapple with these agendas, why they often ignore them and what supports them to act effectively. While climate impacts could negatively affect urban economies, at the same time, more compact urban growth, connected infrastructure and coordinated governance could respond to the need for climate change mitigation and adaptation at the same time that they reduce long-term urban infrastructure capital requirements, and allow for more equitable development (Global Commission on the Economy and Climate 2014).

Although much of the literature focuses on cities needing to change, it is actually particular groups that need to change. Acting on climate change does not depend on cities but on the people who live and work there, on the institutions set up to govern them and on what the private sector does and accepts there. Cities bring opportunities, along with many agglomeration economies, for climate change adaptation and mitigation, as well as for human development and disaster risk reduction. But these opportunities have to be identified and acted on by institutions that have the capacity to act and are accountable to their populations.

One characteristic of the global development enterprise is an increasingly lengthy list of goals and targets that national government delegations within the United Nations produce and then commit to. But national governments do this without involving local governments, despite the fact that the achievement of so many of these goals and targets fall within the responsibilities of local governments. This has been going on for several decades – a case in point is the commitments made for the universal provision for water, sanitation and health care in the 1970s that still have not been met. This is still happening today. If we assess changes in provision for water (piped on premises) and sanitation for urban areas, there are many nations that are far from the MDG targets in 2015, even though these targets were far more modest than universal provision (they only required a halving of the proportion without provision). There is even a substantial list of nations where the percentage of the urban population with water piped to premises and "improved sanitation" was lower in 2015 than it had been in 1990 (Satterthwaite 2016).

With climate change adaptation and mitigation, it is even stranger. Addressing these issues depends heavily on urban governments, yet they are not explicitly recognized as local government responsibilities and little or no funding is available to support them. This is the context within which we review attention to climate change adaptation and mitigation in nine cities, and the linkages (if any) with development and disaster risk reduction. How will most city and municipal governments act on climate change and a growing range of other global environmental change issues when they are already struggling to implement conventional urban agendas? How can they possibly add climate change adaptation and mitigation and enhanced disaster risk reduction to planning, regulation, poverty reduction and provision of infrastructure and services?

Two important issues provide some guidance. The first is that good *local* development (with local governments able and willing to meet their responsibilities and respond to the needs of their citizens) provides the framework for adaptation and enhanced disaster risk reduction. A city where most or all of the population have water piped to their home, connections to sewers and storm drains, a regular solid waste collection service (critical for keeping drains clear too) and good quality housing served by all-weather roads has a good base from which to adapt to climate change and to reduce disaster risk. A well-functioning system for providing health care and emergency services also provides a base from which to build greater effectiveness in responding to extreme weather and other potential catalysts for disasters. Land-use planning and management, implemented to guide city expansion, provides the base for adjusting to changing patterns of risk. Achieving all of this requires a functioning local authority and an adequate funding base. It also requires mandates. Even if local government has the competence, capacity and funding to act, it is still hard to tackle issues for which it has no legislated responsibility.

Table 1.2, drawn from the IPCC's 5th Assessment, illustrates the differences in adaptive capacity between cities and the many factors that influence this. "It indicates how each urban centre falls within a spectrum in at least four key factors that influence adaptation: local government capacity; the proportion of residents served with risk-reducing infrastructure and services; the proportion living in housing built to appropriate health and safety standards; and the levels of risk from climate change's direct and indirect impacts" (Revi, Satterthwaite et al. 2014, page 545).

As Table 1.2 suggests, there are urban indicators that are relevant for assessing the resilience to climate change impacts that urban areas have acquired (including the proportion of the population living in legal housing that meets health and safety standards, with water piped to their homes, sewers, drains, health care, and emergency services); it is more of a challenge to find indicators for climate change related risks and for the quality and capacity of government.

The second important issue that provides some guidance for action is that human development, disaster risk reduction and climate change adaptation are all about understanding and acting on local risks. Even if they have different risk-lenses, there is much overlap – for instance inadequate drainage can be seen as a development, adaptation and disaster risk issue.

TABLE 1.2 The large spectrum in the capacity of urban governments to adapt to climate change

City characteristics	*Very little adaptive capacity or resilience/ "bounce-back"capacity*	*Some adaptive capacity and resilience/ "bounce-back" capacity*	*Adequate capacity for adaptation and resilience/ "bounce-back" but needs to be acted on*	*Climate resilience and capacity to bounce forward*	*Transformative adaptation*
The proportion of the population served with risk-reducing infrastructure (paved roads, storm and surface drainage, piped water, provision for sanitation ....) and services relevant to resilience (including health care, emergency services, policing/rule of law) and the institutions needed for such provision	0–30% of the urban centre's population served; most of those unserved or inadequately served living in informal settlements	30–80% of the urban centre's population served; most of those unserved or inadequately served living in informal settlements	80–100% of the urban centre's population served; most of those unserved or inadequately served living in informal settlements	Most/all of the urban centre's population with these and with an active adaptation policy identifying current and probable future risks and with an institutional structure to encourage and support action by all sectors and agencies. In many cities, also upgrade ageing infrastructure	Urban centres that have integrated their development and adaptation policies and investments within an understanding of the need for mitigation and sustainable ecological footprints
The proportion of the population living in legal housing built with permanent materials (meeting health and safety standards)				Active programme to improve conditions, infrastructure and services to informal settlements and low-income areas. Identify and act on areas with higher/increasing risks. Revise building standards	Land use planning and management successfully providing safe land for housing, avoiding areas at risk and taking account of mitigation

Proportion of urban centres covered	Most urban centres in low-income and many in middle-income nations	Many urban centres in many low-income nations; most urban centres in most middle-income nations	Virtually all urban centres in high-income nations, many in middle-income nations	A small proportion of cities in high-income and upper-middle income nations	Some innovative city governments thinking of this and taking some initial steps
Estimated number of people living in such urban centres	1 billion	1.5 billion	1 billion	Very small	
Infrastructure deficit	Much of the built up area lacking infrastructure			Most or all the built up area with infrastructure (paved roads, covered drains, piped water…..)	
Local government investment capacity	Very little or no local investment capacity			Substantial local investment capacity	
Occurrence of disasters from extreme weather – see text in regard to disasters and extensive risk (United Nations 2011)	Very common			Uncommon (mostly due to risk-reducing infrastructure, service and good quality buildings available to almost all the population)	
Examples	Dar es Salaam, Dhaka	Nairobi, Mumbai	Most cities in high-income nations. Rosario and Mexico City	Cities such as New York; London, Durban and Manizales with some progress	

continued …

Table 1.2 continued

City characteristics	*Very little adaptive capacity or resilience/ "bounce-back" capacity*	*Some adaptive capacity and resilience/ "bounce-back" capacity*	*Adequate capacity for adaptation and resilience/ "bounce-back" but needs to be acted on*	*Climate resilience and capacity to bounce forward*	*Transformative adaptation*
Implications for climate change adaptation	Very limited capacity to adapt. Very large deficits in infrastructure and in institutional capacity. Very large numbers exposed to risk if these are also in locations with high levels of risk from climate change	Some capacity to adapt, especially if this can be combined with development but difficult to get city governments to act. Particular problems for those urban centres in locations with high levels of risk from climate change	Strong basis for adaptation but needs to be acted on and to influence city government and many of its sectoral agencies.	City government that is managing land-use changes as well as having adaptation integrated into all sectors	City government with capacity to influence and work with neighbouring local government units. Also with land-use changes managed to protect eco-system services and support mitigation

NB: For cities that are made up of different local government areas, it would be possible to apply these categories at an intra-city or intra-metropolitan scale. For instance, within many large Latin American, Asian and African cities, there are different local government areas that would fit in each of the first three categories.

There is little direct overlap with mitigation, but there are many measures that city governments can take that are good environmental practice and that also contribute to mitigation – for instance solid waste collection and management (enhancing re-use and recycle, capturing and using methane emissions), water and waste water management (reducing water and energy use), the promotion and implementation of energy efficiency (lowering CO_2 emissions), improving public transport and provision for bicyclists and pedestrians (lowering CO_2 emissions), air pollution reduction (often linked to fuel switches or less fuel use) and the management and expansion of parks and other public spaces (with contribution to carbon capture). We return to this issue in Chapter 13.

Cities and the UN Framework Convention on Climate Change

The international agreement that sets the objectives for action on climate change, the UN Framework Convention on Climate Change (UNFCCC), has been around since 1992, and has been signed by 196 parties. Since 1995, annual Conferences of the Parties (COPs) have been held to negotiate the terms of the convention and the mechanisms that can support adaptation and mitigation.

Because this is an international treaty, all the signatories to the UNFCCC are nation states – which means that the perspectives of local governments are frequently ignored and their potential to act is not fully tapped. Despite the fact that they are not central to the negotiations, however, a range of efforts have been made over the intervening years to include local and municipal governments in and alongside the negotiations, and to recognize the contribution that they can make to adaptation and mitigation. The Cities Climate Registry was initiated in the run-up to COP16 in Cancún in 2010, and provides a mechanism for local governments to publicly and regularly report on their emissions. The following year, the Durban Adaptation Charter was launched alongside COP17 in South Africa as a framework for sub-national governments to make commitments for adaptation. COP19 in Warsaw saw the first "Cities Day" as part of the Conference of Parties, involving sub-national governments formally within the UNFCCC. However, the formal negotiating texts still make relatively little reference to the responsibilities of local governments, or to mechanisms to fund adaptation in cities – with mention limited to rather vague statements of intention around "facilitating the sharing among Parties of experiences and best practices of cities and subnational authorities" (COP19 – Decision 1/CP19).

The Sustainable Development Goals

Although not focused specifically on climate change, the most recent international agreement, the Sustainable Development Goals (SDGs), endorsed by national governments in September 2015 at the United Nations Summit, are also integral to addressing climate change. They also recognize the importance of cities and urban areas, and of the four agendas discussed in this book and their integration (United Nations 2015). The first of these agendas, human development, is central to the SDGs, which stress the elimination of extreme poverty and hunger, reduction of all poverty and "leaving no-one behind". But the SDGs also include goals and targets relevant to disaster risk reduction, climate change adaptation and climate change mitigation in urban areas and even a recommendation that responses to these need to be integrated.

The SDGs relevant to human development and poverty reduction are mostly national goals – and so are assumed to include urban populations. They include:

- *Universal provision for risk-reducing infrastructure:* 6.1 By 2030, achieve universal and equitable access to safe and affordable drinking water for all; 6.2 By 2030, achieve access to adequate and equitable sanitation and hygiene for all and end open defecation, paying special attention to the needs of women and girls and those in vulnerable situations.
- *Universal provision for services:* 7.1 By 2030, ensure universal access to affordable, reliable and modern energy services; 1.3 Implement nationally appropriate social protection systems and measures for all, including floors, and by 2030 achieve substantial coverage of the poor and the vulnerable; 1.4 By 2030, ensure that all men and women, in particular the poor and the vulnerable, have equal rights to economic resources, as well as access to basic services…; 3.8 Achieve universal health coverage, including financial risk protection, access to quality essential health-care services and access to safe, effective, quality and affordable essential medicines and vaccines for all; 4.1 By 2030, ensure that all girls and boys complete free, equitable and quality primary and secondary education; 11.2 By 2030, provide access to safe, affordable, accessible and sustainable transport systems for all.
- *Universal housing:* 11.1 By 2030, ensure access for all to adequate, safe and affordable housing and basic services and upgrade slums.
- *The rule of law:* 16. Promote peaceful and inclusive societies for sustainable development, provide access to justice for all and build effective, accountable and inclusive institutions at all levels; 16.3 Promote the rule of law at the national and international levels and ensure equal access to justice for all; 16.9 By 2030, provide legal identity for all, including birth registration.
- *Voice/participation/government accountability to citizens:* 11.3 By 2030, enhance inclusive and sustainable urbanization and capacity for participatory, integrated and sustainable human settlement planning and management in all countries; 16.6 Develop effective, accountable and transparent institutions at all levels; 16.7 Ensure responsive, inclusive, participatory and representative decision-making at all levels; 16.10 Ensure public access

to information and protect fundamental freedoms, in accordance with national legislation and international agreements.

There is also one goal in the SDGs that specifically mentions cities, and its full text is presented in Box 1.2. Some of its sub-goals are mentioned above as they are part of poverty reduction/human development. The text for goal 11.b, which includes integrated attention to mitigation and adaptation to climate change and resilience to disasters, is not a bad summary of the four agendas that are the focus of this book and their integration. Other goals also highlight the importance of climate change adaptation and mitigation – for instance 1.5 ("By 2030, build the resilience of the poor and those in vulnerable situations and reduce their exposure and vulnerability to climate-related extreme events and other economic, social and environmental shocks and disasters") and text in goal 12 on ensuring sustainable consumption and production patterns. Goal 13 is on taking urgent action to combat climate change and its impacts.

If all or even most of these SDG commitments were actually implemented in low- and middle-income countries, they would represent enormous progress towards the common good – a transformation in health and living conditions and in the reduction of risk including disaster risk. It would also mean great progress in building the resilience of cities (including climate change adaptation) and in getting much needed mitigation. But as will become evident in the nine city cases studies and in the cross-city discussions, we are missing the framework, both within each nation and globally, to guide and support local governments in taking action on all this. The SDGs are clear and explicit as to what needs to be achieved, but not on how, by whom and with what funding. The final chapter of this book goes more deeply into this.

The common good

We have referred here to the common good, a concept that is familiar to all, but that can be defined in ways that serve very different political and philosophical interests. It's not uncommon, for instance, for "the common good" or "the public good" to be invoked to support moneyed interests, as they evict informal settlers from desirable land or privatize what should in fact be for the shared benefit of all. We are using the concept in its broader sense here, as an ideal or a value that underlies democracy and good governance, that is implicit in the notion of social justice, that implies that the planet is in fact, as Pope Francis would have it, "our common home". The SDGs, from this perspective, might well be thought of as an attempt to operationalize the concept of the common or public good.

For the purposes of this book, and in the context of addressing climate change within cities, we see the common good as a shorthand term for the values that ideally inform this endeavour. As is more fully explained in the following chapter, responses to the impacts of climate change have increasingly been

Box 1.2 SDG Goal 11. Make cities and human settlements inclusive, safe, resilient and sustainable

11.1 By 2030, ensure access for all to adequate, safe and affordable housing and basic services and upgrade slums

11.2 By 2030, provide access to safe, affordable, accessible and sustainable transport systems for all, improving road safety, notably by expanding public transport, with special attention to the needs of those in vulnerable situations, women, children, persons with disabilities and older persons

11.3 By 2030, enhance inclusive and sustainable urbanization and capacity for participatory, integrated and sustainable human settlement planning and management in all countries

11.4 Strengthen efforts to protect and safeguard the world's cultural and natural heritage

11.5 By 2030, significantly reduce the number of deaths and the number of people affected and substantially decrease the direct economic losses relative to global gross domestic product caused by disasters, including water-related disasters, with a focus on protecting the poor and people in vulnerable situations

11.6 By 2030, reduce the adverse per capita environmental impact of cities, including by paying special attention to air quality and municipal and other waste management

11.7 By 2030, provide universal access to safe, inclusive and accessible, green and public spaces, in particular for women and children, older persons and persons with disabilities

11.a Support positive economic, social and environmental links between urban, peri-urban and rural areas by strengthening national and regional development planning

11.b By 2020, substantially increase the number of cities and human settlements adopting and implementing integrated policies and plans towards inclusion, resource efficiency, mitigation and adaptation to climate change, resilience to disasters, and develop and implement, in line with Sendai Framework for Disaster Risk Reduction 2015–2030, holistic disaster risk management at all levels

11.c Support least developed countries, including through financial and technical assistance, in building sustainable and resilient buildings utilizing local materials

framed in terms of resilience. Resilience itself is being framed not just in terms of the capacity to "bounce back" after an external shock but also an opportunity to "bounce forward" toward something that works better for all.

The development paradigm that created anthropogenic climate change – one that has economic growth as its primary driver – has not in fact worked out that well for us. Addressing the impacts of this global emergency has to mean not simply responding to the upheaval it is creating, but working at the same time to radically change course. Building the kind of resilience that allows us to bounce forward towards a saner more equitable future requires, as Chapter 2 explains, a transformation in our way of doing business. This transformation is implicitly underpinned and steered by notions of social justice and the common good. Cities are the main stage for this human endeavour – the places where much of our problematic activity has been centred, where many of the impacts are being most sorely felt, and where the most promising solutions are being thrashed out. These cities are the product of local struggles and aspirations, and while their agendas may be shaped by national and international policies and agreements, what happens there remains intensely local and must be understood and responded to in those terms.

Note

1 Encyclical Letter Laudato Si' of the Holy Father Francis on Care For Our Common Home; 24 May 2015, http://w2.vatican.va/content/francesco/en/encyclicals/documents/papa-francesco_20150524_enciclica-laudato-si.html

References

Cabannes, Yves (2015), "The impact of participatory budgeting on basic services; municipal practices and evidence from the field", *Environment and Urbanization* Vol 27, no. 1, pages 257–284.

Global Commission on the Economy and Climate (2014), *Better Growth; Better Climate; The New Climate Economy Report*, World Resources Institute, Washington DC.

IPCC (2014), *Climate Change 2014: Synthesis Report.* Contribution of Working Groups I, II and III to the Fifth Assessment Report of the Intergovernmental Panel on Climate Change. Core Writing Team, R. K. Pachauri and L. A. Meyer (eds), IPCC, Geneva, Switzerland, page 13.

Mitlin, Diana and David Satterthwaite (2013), *Urban Poverty in the Global South: Scale and Nature*, Routledge, London.

Revi, Aromar, David Satterthwaite, Fernando Aragón-Durand, Jan Corfee-Morlot, Robert B. R. Kiunsi, Mark Pelling, Debra Roberts, William Solecki, Sumetee Pahwa Gajjar and Alice Sverdlik (2014), Chapter 8: Urban Areas in C. . Field, V. R. Barros, D. J. Dokken, K .J. Mach, M. D. Mastrandrea, T. E. Bilir, M. Chatterjee, K. Ebi, Y. O. Estrada, R. C. Genova, B. Girma, E. S. Kissel, A. N. Levy, S. MacCracken, P. R. Mastrandrea, and L. L. White (eds), *Climate Change 2014: Impacts, Adaptation, and Vulnerability. Part A: Global and Sectoral Aspects.* Contribution of Working Group II to the Fifth Assessment Report of the Intergovernmental Panel on Climate Change, Cambridge University Press, Cambridge and New York, pages 535–612.

Satterthwaite, David (2016), "Missing the Millennium Development Goal targets for water and sanitation in urban areas", *Environment and Urbanization*, Vol. 27, no. 1. DOI:10.1177/0956247816628435

Seto, Karen C., S. Dhakal, A. Bigio, H. Blanco, G. C. Delgado, D. Dewar, L. Huang, A. Inaba, A. Kansal, S. Lwasa, J. E. McMahon, D. B. Müller, J. Murakami, H. Nagendra and A. Ramaswami (2014), Chapter 12: Human Settlements, Infrastructure, and Spatial Planning in O. Edenhofer, R. Pichs-Madruga, Y. Sokona, E. Farahani, S. Kadner, K. Seyboth, A. Adler, I. Baum, S. Brunner, P. Eickemeier, B. Kriemann, J. Savolainen, S. Schlömer, C. von Stechow, T. Zwickel and J. C. Minx (eds), *Climate Change 2014: Mitigation of Climate Change*. Contribution of Working Group III to the Fifth Assessment Report of the Intergovernmental Panel on Climate Change, Cambridge University Press, Cambridge and New York, pages 923–1000.

Steffen, Will, Katherine Richardson, Johan Rockström, Sarah E. Cornell, Ingo Fetzer, Elena M. Bennett, Reinette Biggs, Stephen R. Carpenter, Wim de Vries, Cynthia A. de Wit, Carl Folke, Dieter Gerten, Jens Heinke, Georgina M. Mace, Linn M. Persson, Veerabhadran Ramanathan, Belinda Reyers and Sverker Sörlin (2015), "Planetary boundaries: guiding human development." *Science* Vol. 347, no. 6223. DOI: 10.1126/science.1259855

UCLG (United Cities and Local Governments) (2014), *Basic Services for All in an Urbanizing World; the Third Global Report on Local Democracy and Decentralization*, Routledge, London.

United Nations (2011), *Revealing Risk, Redefining Development: The 2011 Global Assessment Report on Disaster Risk Reduction*, United Nations International Strategy for Disaster Reduction, Geneva, 178 pages.

United Nations (2014) *World Urbanization Prospects: The 2014 Revision*, POP/DB/WUP/Rev.2014/1/F09, Population Division, Department of Economic and Social Affairs, New York.

United Nations (2015) *Transforming our World: The 2030 Agenda for Sustainable Development*, Draft outcome document of the United Nations Summit for the adoption of the post-2015 development agenda agreed by consensus by the member states on Sunday 2 August 2015, United Nations, New York, 29 pages.

2

UNDERSTANDING RISK IN THE CONTEXT OF URBAN DEVELOPMENT

Definitions, concepts and pathways

Arabella Fraser, Mark Pelling and William Solecki

Introduction

This chapter presents the conceptual landscape used in this book to analyse urban disaster and climate change risk. As well as providing working definitions to be taken forward in subsequent chapters, it discusses the implications for urban adaptation and mitigation agendas of current debates surrounding the concepts of risk, vulnerability, resilience, transformation and development. Each term brings its own challenges, manifest in urban contexts (Bulkeley and Tuts 2013). Further, this chapter examines how different modes of thinking about risk may be framed and harnessed to promote socially and ecologically effective and just urban responses to climate change. In this sense, the objective is normative: the chapter outlines concepts of risk that can be applied in cities in order to promote particular social and environmental ends (Klein et al. 2003), and against which current efforts to reduce climate-change-related risks and impacts can be benchmarked.

The following section unpacks conceptual debates about risk, vulnerability, resilience, transformation and development. After that, we discuss pathways to achieving risk reduction as seen through these different conceptual lenses. We then examine how the agency of urban actors may be best understood through these perspectives. The conclusion reflects on how these definitions, concepts and analytic trajectories can be taken forward to promote socially just and environmentally sustainable outcomes in urban contexts.

Box 2.1 Definitions

- *Risk:* The potential for consequences where something of human value (including humans themselves) is at stake and where the outcome is uncertain. (IPCC 2014)
- *Vulnerability:* The propensity or predisposition to be adversely affected. Vulnerability encompasses a variety of concepts including sensitivity or susceptibility to harm and lack of capacity to cope and adapt. (IPCC 2014)
- *Resilience:* The capacity of a social-ecological system to cope with a hazardous event or disturbance, responding or reorganizing in ways that maintain its essential function, identity and structure, while also maintaining the capacity for adaptation, learning and transformation. (IPCC 2014)
- *Transformation:* A change in the fundamental attributes of a system, often based on altered paradigms, goals or values. (IPCC 2014)
- *Urban development:* The social, economic, cultural and physical improvement of urban areas. Sustainable development refers to processes of improvement that meet the needs of the present with social justice and ecological sustainability, without compromising the ability of future generations to meet their own needs. (World Commission on Environment and Development 1987)

Sources: IPCC 2014; World Commission on Environment and Development 1987.

Analytic terms

Risk

As Box 2.1 shows, the IPCC associates the term "risk" with the potential for harm to something of human value, where the outcome is uncertain.

There is a core difference between understandings of disaster risk and climate change risk. The focus in the climate change adaptation field is on the future impacts of anthropogenic climatic change (climate variation and extremes), and how adaptation (or a process of adjustment in behaviour or characteristics) might occur in response to this perceived sub-set of risk based on future scenarios (Brooks 2003). In disaster risk management, risks have classically been described by projecting past events into the future – an empirical rather than a modelled assessment. This difference between fields is expressed through different forms of hazard assessment. In disaster planning, assessments tend to be based on probabilistic analysis, or the likelihood of a particular hazard or a consequence from a particular hazard (with consequence encompassing various dimensions) based on historical trends and experience (IPCC 2012; Brooks 2003). These approaches are rooted in local, empirical contexts and connect directly to policy agendas, but need to take better account of changing baselines driven by climate change. In contrast, climate change-oriented assessments are derived from climate modelling, not past observation. Modelling provides future, imagined predictions of climatic trends over the medium and long term (Dickson et al. 2010). Increasingly, risk analysis has tried to bring together climate change modelling and disaster risk assessment approaches to provide empirically robust but futures-oriented risk assessment.

Risk, and loss and damages, are experienced along a spectrum of severity. Risks range from the intensive to the extensive. Intensive risk is related to infrequently occurring events affecting a small number of geographic areas with high impact on mortality and economic loss (such as hurricanes); extensive risk is related to low to moderate but persistent events that are individually minor but that in aggregation (e.g., small floods or building collapses) can have a larger impact on development opportunities than rare, intensive risk or loss events (Bull-Kamanga et al. 2003; UNISDR 2011).

The relationship between extensive and intensive risk and loss depends on local conditions. In some cases, exposure to extensive loss can lead to the build-up of practical experience and policy momentum to reduce risk and in turn potentially avoid the consequences of intensive events. Elsewhere a lack of information, capacity or institutional frameworks can lead to risk accumulation and an increase in intensive risk. Research has also shown that after intensive events, local economies and physical infrastructure can be made more resilient to future risk, whether extensive and intensive. This can come about through the updating of physical infrastructure through reconstruction efforts (Solecki and Rozensweig 2014). More commonly however, reconstruction is incomplete and can increase risk through poor design and delivery or by contributing to, rather than challenging, underlying patterns of social inequality (Pelling 2011).

Alongside this broad definition of risk, specific interests have led to debates about how to define risk that have important implications for how we analyse and act upon climate change. In its narrowest sense, risk is the likelihood of a hazard event occurring, where hazard is the physical manifestation of climate change or variability in the "natural" system (Brooks 2003). The risk to human life, health and property is therefore a function of the hazard and the human asset exposure, defined as "The presence of people; livelihoods; environmental services and resources; infrastructure; or economic, social, or cultural assets in places that could be adversely affected" (IPCC 2012). Approaches to tackling risk according to this paradigm focus on physical protection against risk and the reduction of exposure through resettlement policies, or by changing behaviour through risk communication. The emphasis is on the robustness of individual components of a system (Tyler and Moench 2012). This understanding of, and paradigm for, approaching risk has, however, been expanded over the 2000s to include the concepts of vulnerability, resilience and transformation. These in turn emphasise the social production of risk and the opportunities for risk reduction that come from a greater emphasis on social and economic policy and governance (or "development"). This is especially significant in urban cases where the governance of multiple and conflicting stakeholder groups, along with civic engagement, determines the processes leading to, as well as the distributional outcomes of, access to basic services and critical infrastructure.

Vulnerability

As Box 2.1 indicates, a general definition of vulnerability to climate change refers to "the propensity or predisposition to be adversely affected" (IPCC 2014). The notion of social vulnerability emphasizes the social properties of an affected system that make it susceptible to that hazard, beyond understanding the exposure of affected populations and infrastructure (Brooks 2003). This is also referred to as the "contextual" or "inherent" vulnerability approach – and it places the primary emphasis on altering social arrangements in an affected place or system (Brooks 2003; Romero Lankao and Qin 2011). Vulnerability theorists in this vein therefore see climate-related disasters as the product not only of physical phenomena but also of social, economic and political processes that leave particular populations physically exposed and economically and socially sensitive to such events (Blaikie et al. 1994; Brooks 2003; Adger 2006), including application to urban contexts (Pelling 2003). Whereas the emphasis of a hazards-focused or impacts-based approach is on identifying, defining and preventing the impacts of historic or modelled changes to physical phenomena, "Vulnerability analysis turns impact analysis on its head by examining the multiple causes of critical outcomes rather than the multiple outcomes of a single event" (Ribot 1995, p. 119). Vulnerability analysis can therefore better explain the adaptive potential of particular urban groups.

Vulnerability depends on sensitivity to the impacts of climate change but also the capacity to prepare for, cope with and respond to this impact. Whereas sensitivity refers to the predisposition to be affected owing to an ability to resist effectively (IPCC 2012), capacity can be thought of as the set of perceptions, knowledge and skills as well as entitlements to resources that facilitate people's abilities to prepare for, cope with, resist and recover from climate-related shocks and stresses (Wisner and Fordham 2014). Without acknowledgement of the potential for such agency, interventions to reduce vulnerability can be both patronising and disempowering (ibid.). The agency in question relates both to adaptive capacity, or the capacity for long-term, sustained adjustments, and coping capacity, which refers to the resources for survival and the fulfilment of basic needs in the face of an immediate stress (IPCC 2012). Adaptive and coping capacity varies considerably in urban areas (Pelling 2003; Baker 2012), and by social group. Children may be particularly vulnerable to the health impacts of contaminated water supply, for example, and the elderly to heat waves (Bartlett 2008).

Different, overlapping strands of this socially contextual approach to vulnerability have emerged in urban climate change research, but all stress how social differentiation and inequality within urban areas shapes vulnerability. The first strand groups around household-based livelihoods studies that stress how climate change impacts are affected by what people have and what they do (Moser et al. 2010; Wamsler 2007; Jabeen, Johnson and Allen 2010; Douglas et al. 2008; Braun and Abheuer 2011; Roy, Hulme and Jahan 2013). Work in low income urban settings highlights the impact of a highly monetised economy, where households depend more starkly than rural households on their labour, their housing (as an asset for rental or enterprise) and (related) financial assets and social capital, and less directly on natural resources (although land for housing may also be considered a critical "natural" capital) (see Moser 1998; Moser and Satterthwaite 2008; Pelling 2003). However, the potential for adaptations at this household scale may be limited, and will depend on actions at higher levels to be effective (in providing drainage services, for instance) (Romero Lankao and Qin 2011). The second strand of urban social vulnerability research groups around structural-entitlements approaches, which seek to understand how the distribution of entitlements through the economic, political and social structures operating across society facilitates or constrains the ability of affected populations to respond to climate change impacts. For example, social organizations may be co-opted or maintained in dependent and clientelist relationships by political regimes in ways that limit the engagement and the flow of opportunities for the most vulnerable households in particular communities (Pelling 2003). A further strand of urban vulnerability research is concerned with how urban discourses and forms of knowledge influence the distribution of entitlements for affected communities, such as services and infrastructure, and the effect of this on vulnerability. For example, these studies highlight how framings of disaster that present it as a natural event to be managed through technical solutions hide the socio-political and structural processes underpinning the construction of risks and vulnerabilities and justify inaction in this domain (Pelling 1999; Aragon-Durand 2007; Rebotier 2012; Mustafa 2005).

These different approaches to urban vulnerability move from a concern with the material aspects of what people have and do to one that analyses the social and political relations and processes that influence the ability of different urban groups to prepare, cope and respond. By taking this more relational and dynamic perspective, vulnerability research can highlight important questions about the role of social equity and power relations in shaping risk, exposure and vulnerability, and who wins and who loses from climate change policy responses (Taylor 2013). What represents an adaptation for one urban group may well exacerbate exposure and vulnerability for another – where wealthier households build boundary walls around their houses to protect themselves from flooding, for example, adjacent households which cannot afford boundary walls may face greater risks (Bahadur and Tanner 2014). This perspective is also important to understanding the local governance processes that are critical to risk reduction, and the relationships between local government and non-governmental actors that, ultimately, determine the success of risk reduction goals (Satterthwaite 2013).

Resilience

The term resilience is often used to mean the opposite of vulnerability, or the capacity to cope with shocks and stresses. In relation to urban disaster risk and climate change adaptation, resilience increasingly denotes a conceptual field that draws on multiple disciplinary perspectives. It is a field that continues to evolve and be debated. Further, it has been taken up in multiple ways in scholarship on urban climate change.

As the IPCC definition in Box 2.1 shows, the concept of resilience provides a way of thinking about the urban context as a system in which the social and ecological dimensions of urban life are intertwined. This definition emphasizes the capacities of this system and the actions taken within it to accommodate the impacts of climate change, beyond the ability to respond to a specific event or impact (IPCC 2014; Ensor et al. 2013). Achieving urban resilience requires more than the installation of particular system components, such as sea walls to avoid flooding events, for example, but relates rather to the ability of an overall system to reinstate its functions even if one component fails (Tyler and Moench 2012; Béné et al. 2014). This framing highlights differentials in the quality of governance, access to information and freedom to act – alongside resource access – and the need to consider procedural as well as distributional aspects of justice in the management of climate change impacts.

The inherent systems property of resilience frameworks is usefully applied in urban contexts, where complex and dense interconnections exist between infrastructures and institutions, which in turn face a variety of social and ecological stressors and shocks (Revi et al. 2014; Romero Lankao and Qin 2011). Cities are also linked into other systems at multiple scales (Cutter et al. 2009; Tyler and Moench 2012). The notion of resilience therefore allows for the analysis of urban spaces in the context of the linkages with the regions and hinterlands in which they are embedded (Revi et al. 2014; Leichenko 2011); global supply chains within which they are inserted (Tyler and Moench 2012); and across the rural–urban divide (especially important for peri-urban areas, where rural–urban dynamics intersect most manifestly, and which are sites of rapid urbanization) (Béné et al. 2014). Urban poverty and well-being depends on access to critical infrastructure systems, embedded in these linkages of scale, while the urban system itself is dense and dynamic and creates new systemic risks (Friend and Moench 2013). Analysis in this vein highlights the challenges to the urban governance of climate change risk, where urban boundaries are not static and where coordination and management is required across urban-regional boundaries. Food or electricity production, for example, may be rural in origin, but nevertheless influence the functioning of urban systems (Revi et al. 2014; Tyler and Moench 2012). Resilience thinking stresses not only the complexity of these types of inter-linkages across scales and timeframes, but also the uncertainty inherent in the ongoing processes of change between different system components (Ensor et al. 2013). This includes the additional element of uncertainty induced by downscaling predictive global climate models at local scales for use by city decision-makers (Jha, Bloch and Lamond 2012).

Within the concept of an urban area as a socio-ecological system, resilience thinking can be used to illuminate the mechanisms of change that occur within the system (Romero Lankao and Qin 2011). As systems change, they may reach critical points or thresholds beyond which return is not feasible (Ensor et al. 2013; Pelling 2011; Miller et al. 2010). Understanding when and how thresholds emerge is important as beyond certain thresholds, processes of change, such as ecological deterioration, may become irreversible. However, in complex non-linear systems – such as cities, and neighbourhoods – thresholds are difficult to identify and predict (ibid.). The characteristics that determine how resilient a system is and the processes of change that need to occur within the system, and therefore what should be prioritized in order to build resilience, vary across studies and contexts but cluster around three central features described in Box 2.2: flexibility and diversity, redundancy and modularity, and safe failure.

As an analytic framework therefore, resilience thinking overlaps with vulnerability perspectives on urban risk but also introduces new, critical elements. Where vulnerability analysis concentrates predominantly on the social conditions of particular population groups, resilience theory focuses on the co-constitution of social-ecological systems in which particular populations

Box 2.2 The resilience-enhancing characteristics of an urban system

The characteristics of an urban system said to enhance resilience, as summarised by Tyler and Moench (2012), include:

- *Flexibility and diversity:* The ability to perform essential tasks under a wide range of conditions, and to convert assets or modify structures (which are spatially and functionally diverse) to introduce new ways of performing these tasks.
- *Redundancy, modularity:* Spare capacity for contingency situations; multiple pathways and a variety of options for service delivery; or interacting components composed of similar parts that can replace each other if one, or even many, fail. Redundancy is also supported by the presence of buffer stocks within systems (e.g. local water or food supplies to supplement imports).
- *Safe failure:* Ability to absorb sudden shocks or the cumulative effects of slow-onset stress in ways that make it possible to avoid catastrophic failure. Safe failure also refers to the interdependence of various systems which support each other – failures in one structure or linkage being unlikely to result in cascading impacts across other systems.

Source: Tyler and Moench 2012.

are affected (Adger 2006; Miller et al. 2010; Romero Lankao and Qin 2011). Vulnerability analyses and assessments often overlook long-run analysis of the dynamic linkages affecting urban systems, although more recent vulnerability frameworks do underline the need to view vulnerability within a process, and give due account to environmental conditions (Miller et al. 2010; Birkmann et al. 2013). Resilience perspectives can also be applied independent of hazard events, while the occurrence and nature of hazard is intrinsic to the conception of vulnerability (Tyler and Moench 2012).

Resilience in practice

Different strands of resilience thinking emerge when we consider the goals of a resilient urban system. A more closed perspective stresses the characteristics and actions of a system that allow it to maintain its desired functions, identity and structure. This view is often associated with the idea of "bouncing back" after a climate disturbance or shock or returning to "normal", or to the state of affairs prior to a climate event. Yet writers on resilience have become increasingly uncomfortable with the social justice implications of this view, especially where actions to achieve resilience might reinforce or even exacerbate pre-existing social inequities (Pelling 2011; Miller et al. 2010). The IPCC definition used here opens up the possibility for social change and transformation to occur, in which systems "bounce back better" or "bounce forward". This broadens the analysis of urban socio-ecological systems and aligns the terminology of resilience with the goal of achieving socially just urban adaptation and mitigation. The definition provided here as a frame through which to discuss urban resilience also makes explicit reference to the capacity for adaptation and learning as a core feature of a resilient system. This dimension of resilience also moves us beyond more "closed" interpretations of resilience (in which systems retain spare capacity to maintain the same function) to allow for the ways in which systems must change in order to adjust to future external shocks and stressors (Béné et al. 2014). However, the term transformation is also separated off from resilience in this chapter – the reasons for this and the relationship of transformation to resilience is discussed further below.

As a conceptual paradigm, the notion of resilience has expanded from an exclusive focus on biophysical and ecological change to one that encompasses social change. Resilience thinking, however, faces challenges in its conceptualization of the social world which affect its application in urban contexts (Béné et al. 2014). While social elements of power, governance, politics, equity and social justice have been increasingly accommodated in theoretical resilience frameworks, they tend to remain on the margins of the practicalities of resilience policy and analysis (Béné et al. 2014; Bahadur and Tanner 2014; Romero Lankao and Qin 2011; Leichenko 2011). As applied to urban areas, resilience thinking has lacked a focus on urban politics and the political and economic networks that reproduce patterns of risk management and urban development decision-making (Pelling and Manuel-Navarrete, 2011), and that shape critical relationships between local governments and urban citizens (Satterthwaite 2013) and undergird patterns of resource access (Bahadur and Tanner 2014). These questions of power and distribution are inherent to the operation of urban systems, and also to how resilience itself becomes defined within such systems (Friend and Moench 2013). With its roots in a positivist tradition, resilience thinking has also been less adept at capturing the role of emotions, values and culture (Pelling 2011; Miller et al. 2010) and the ways in which conceptions of risk held by different actors may become subject to political and social contests across different scales of governance (Rebotier 2012; Boyd et al. 2014). These questions about agent behaviour are not easily translated into systems attributes, and require different techniques of investigation (Romero Lankao and Qin 2011; Tyler and Moench 2012). Finally, where resilience thinking remains oriented towards the city as a resilient system, and less focused on its constituent social groups, it lacks a normative focus on advancing the needs and interests of the most marginalized – and most vulnerable (Béné et al. 2014). These questions about the focus of resilience work demand explicit recognition of social values, but also the stronger uptake within resilience thinking of wider theoretical frameworks concerned with human development and rights (ibid.).

Attention to resilience may lead to transformation if changes to parts of the system are scaled up or replicated (Pelling 2011). However, the imperative of avoiding outcomes that are socially and environmentally harmful and that might simply accommodate an unjust status quo leads us to analyse transformation in a separate discussion (Béné et al. 2014; Pelling 2011). This also allows for aspects of socio-political change not discussed under existing resilience frameworks to come to the fore.

Transformation

Addressing climate change in urban areas requires, ideally, fundamental change in urban systems. The concept of transformation that is implied here builds upon the objectives of the vulnerability and systems-resilience approaches, but goes beyond these to facilitate a more profound vision of socio-ecological change. Within this conceptual framing, transformation demarcates a new – and challenging – policy domain, discussed further below. Transformation is well established in mitigation discourses, for example in academic thinking and policy development around social-technological transitions, transitions to sustainability and low or no carbon economies. It has only more recently emerged as an innovative goal for adaptive responses, featuring in both the IPCC Special Report on Managing the Risks of Extreme Events and Disasters to Advance Climate Change Adaptation (SREX) (2012) and the IPCC Working Group Two contribution to the IPCC Fifth Assessment Report (2014) (Pelling 2014). Indeed, the IPCC Fifth Assessment Report makes a useful distinction between incremental and transformational adaptation, discussed further below

(IPCC 2014). The concept potentially unites the climate change mitigation and adaptation agendas with the development agenda, calling for adaptive planning and action that aims to facilitate climate change mitigation efforts and to support socially just and ecologically sustainable development. This may not be possible, but aiming for transformation requires a clear stance and a rationale for alternative policy objectives and outcomes that until now have been missing.

The definition of transformation in Box 2.1 conveys an occurrence of profound system change, which entails not only structural and behavioural changes but also a realignment of the values and goals espoused by collective and individual actors within a system. This can be contrasted with incremental adaptation actions, which maintain the integrity of a system at a given scale (IPCC 2014). Transformation has been referred to as "the deepest form of adaptation" (Pelling 2011, p. 50), expressed through reforms within political and economic regimes as well as within the broader cultural discourse on questions of development, security and risk. It implies, for instance, moving away from the paradigm of national security to a paradigm of human security, based on respect for human rights and basic needs (Pelling 2011). Other uses of the term refer to transformation as the extension of existing actions at bigger scales, or as the kinds of adaptation needed when incremental adaptation to preserve a given system reaches its limits (Pelling 2014). These interpretations do not necessarily imply the sense of fundamental change and normative direction which we consider here to be integral to the term.

Where transformation becomes the goal of systems change, our lens on urban vulnerability and adaptation shifts away from its local and proximate causes to wider and less easily visible root causes. Dominant development practices and pathways may knowingly or unknowingly reproduce these underlying reasons for vulnerability. As a policy arena, therefore, transformative adaptation aims to address these causes and not just the proximate triggers of climate change impacts (Pelling 2011). This goes beyond the narrower sense of adaptation as "coping". It also challenges existing incremental adaptation practices, focused on local conditions of endangerment, and seeking to preserve a given systems element (Wise et al. 2014). For transformative adaptation to be realized, urban planning must be rethought. It will require different ways of conceptualizing how cities grow and develop and new modes of engagement with urban citizens (Bulkeley and Tuts 2013). Lessons already learned in pro-poor urban development planning are valuable here. Mitlin (2012) presents the network Slum/Shack Dwellers International as one example of a poor-led governance system that has been able to exert influence, gain resource and reduce risk within an alternative development paradigm that emphasizes social justice. This is just one example of transformation at scale that can reduce risk and achieve progressive social change.

Transformation in practice

The actual or potential emergence of the new political regimes implied by transformation requires new distributions of rights and responsibilities between state and citizens that support risk reduction along with human development. The notion of social contract – or the balance of rights, responsibilities and authority in a consent-based political system – brings to the fore the institutional arrangements that support particular development pathways and risk management structures (Pelling 2011). Where social contracts are incomplete, political marginalization can drive people's vulnerability to risk. Existing empirical work illustrates how the nature of contemporary social contracts shapes the expectations and willingness of different actors to act on risk (Adger et al. 2013). Other current work outside the climate change field, but with bearing on it, illustrates that informal urban dwellers lack the forms of formalized social contract open to other social groups and are left reliant on contingent bargaining processes in the political system to gain access to resources (Chatterjee 2006). Social contracts are not static or necessarily stable, and can alter with the impacts of climate-related shocks (O'Brien, Hayward and Berkes 2009; Adger et al. 2013; Pelling and Dill 2010). The challenge is to understand how new social contracts might be forged outside such "extraordinary" moments in acts of "deliberate transformation", and in preparation for disasters, rather than in their aftermath. Here, normative work supports our understanding of the kinds of social contracts that might be envisaged to support equity and justice (discussed below). Of course, continuous system change could be harmful in itself and might bring unforeseen costs (Pelling 2011). Further, the lens of the classical social contract requires development to encompass the full range of contemporary governance regimes, including private sector actors and international non-governmental bodies. Social contract theory alone is also limited in telling us how power and authority operate, indicating scope for integration with a range of potential theoretical and analytical frames. Nevertheless, it is an important device through which existing failures to address risk, transformative potential and processes of transformation can be understood.

An immediate challenge is how to identify and operationalize transformative adaptation. This raises questions about the time scales over which transformative adaptation might occur, and the spatial scales over which it would operate, both in terms of levels of governance and orders of magnitude with regard to population groups. Different interpretations of these questions lead us to different examples of what transformation might look like for urban areas. There are few known "complete" and deliberate transformations at the city scale beyond historical examples, such as the sub-urbanization of cities driven by rail and road transport (with the environmental and social costs only now being realized), or the sanitation revolution of the 19th century which affected urban design, architecture, health aspirations and outcomes. Work by urban political-ecologists opens up analysis of the ways in which urban environmental transformations are contingent on wider national and international political-economic shifts (Swyngedouw, Moulaert and Rodriguez 2003).

However, visions of transformation are manifest in the ideas and social experiments of urban citizens and community groups too, even if these have not always achieved wide success in terms of population coverage or political change. It may be that in Southern cities, where citizen networks have a greater stake in the direct shaping of neighbourhoods, local actors can be a realistic driver for urban transformation within adaptation agendas. Examples might include the initiatives supported by the Orangi-Pilot Project-Research and Training Institute, initiatives by the federations of shack and slum dwellers that are part of Slum/Shack Dwellers International, community-based housing co-operatives and local alternative development schemes, networks of informal waste recyclers and the support given by local governments to community initiatives and citizen engagement within the Asian Coalition for Community Action (Revi et al. 2014). Less clear is the scope for creative synergy between community, municipal and national level drivers for transformation instigated through adaptation and mitigation in the city.

Important questions also remain about what drives transformation and when, where and how it occurs (Pelling and Manuel-Navarrete 2011). This affects our analysis of whether systems have the capacity for transformation. What resilience frameworks may fail to capture is how opportunities for development may in fact emerge from structural collapse (Matyas and Pelling 2014). Transformation can emerge across multiple activity spheres as a precursor to this collapse (Pelling et al. 2015). Climate-related disasters and other extreme events themselves may become tipping points for transformation, as a point in time at which underlying development failures in a regime become evident, generating instability and allowing alternative visions of society to emerge. Historical analysis of regime changes following disaster events illustrates both how this might open up democratic space but also how the status quo may be maintained even in the face of strong civil society and organized opposition (Pelling 2011).

Development

The concept of transformation therefore encourages us to place risk management in the broader context of development, to understand the development pathways that lead to disasters and to see risk management as a window through which to understand contemporary development failures (Pelling 2014). This leads us to discuss the notion of development itself – and specifically urban development. The term development is often used to refer both to current processes of development (i.e. with a descriptive purpose) and also to what development should be (i.e. with a normative purpose). In defining development we need to consider, on the one hand, how risks are embedded in current processes of development and, on the other, how alternative visions of development might support actions to promote risk reduction and transformation.

In the context of climate change, the term sustainable development, as defined in Box 2.1, provides a normative view of development. Arising out of the World Commission on Environment and Development in 1987, this term was a corrective to the conventional view of development as economic growth or "modernity", adding an environmental perspective. Key to this notion of sustainable development is the idea that development in the present should not compromise development for future generations. This has been built upon in recent discussions around the formulation of the Sustainable Development Goals (or SDGs), the successor goals to the UN Millennium Development Goals. The proposed definition here refers to meeting a "just balance among the economic, social and environmental needs of present and future generations" (United Nations 2014, p. 2). In urban contexts, the reduction of risk is to be realized through poverty eradication, including the provision of safe, accessible and affordable urban infrastructure, and an increase in the number of cities and human settlements adopting and integrating plans for adaptation, mitigation and resilience to disasters, backed by national commitments to mitigate and adapt to climate change through the United Nations Framework Convention on Climate Change. The Goals themselves are viewed as integrated across their social, economic and environmental dimensions, with risk reduction therefore embedded in broader sets of actions to promote sustainable development.

The term sustainable development has a long pedigree, however, and has been critiqued for its appropriation by the same conventional paradigm it attempted to replace (Pelling 2011). Sustaining existing levels of environmental degradation also potentially compromises the needs of future generations, and some commentators prefer to talk of "regenerative urban development", which would restore the ecological functions of cities (World Future Council 2010). This could occur as part of urban regeneration projects and in planning for growing cities of the global South, where it is possible to establish regenerative systems from the outset, thereby "leapfrogging" conventional, modernist development pathways.

As outlined in Chapter 1, current urban development patterns can contribute to increased exposure and vulnerability to climate risks as well as increased carbon emissions. The location of large concentrations of people and economic activities in hazard-prone areas heightens exposure, while the inability of planning systems and services to keep pace with rapid urbanization leaves populations sensitive to climate change impacts. Disaster and climate change risks also negatively affect contemporary development processes, and investment in development without consideration of these risks can lead to the accumulation rather than the reduction of risk.

Putting these trends into a conceptual context, post-war theories of development assumed that "less developed" nations would follow "more developed" nations, essentially pursuing a market-led approach to growth and development (McGranahan et al. 2001). This view was later critiqued for ignoring the power relations that maintained the dependence of "less developed" nations and cities on their "more developed" counterparts (Hayter 1971), and for neglecting the basic needs of the poorest groups (Overseas Development Institute 1978). The conventional growth model of development has also become increasingly problematic as a frame for urban development (Robinson 2006). It associated the global cities of the North with innovation and progress, and other "less developed" cities with imitation only (ibid.). Cities across the world are testing new institutional arrangements and experimenting with new policies (Anguelovski and Carmin 2011), and the call to learn from these diverse innovations, rather than categorizing them on a "development ladder", is highly relevant to understanding urban climate change mitigation and adaptation.

Urban risk, resilience, transformation and social justice

Within the landscape of debates about select climate risk-related terms, definitions have emerged that influence the support of just and effective responses to climate change. This chapter has highlighted the evolution of recent debates towards stronger conceptualizations of the social and political relations that underpin existing development trajectories and their impact upon risk, and how realignment of these relations might lead to more sustainable futures. This brings to the fore questions about the social contracts on which existing development pathways rest, and the institutional processes that support such contracts. As well as taking these questions into our analysis of urban responses to climate change, there is a need for policy responses to address these elements as an integral part of risk assessment and management.

Thinking of adaptation and mitigation through the frame of transformation restores the analytic focus on "people, politics and power" missing in resilience thinking, and imbues systems thinking with normative direction (Bahadur and Tanner 2014; Pelling 2011). The question remains, however, how appropriate normative goals should be specified and agreed. Here, the lens of social justice is integral to our understanding of risk, and informs debates about vulnerability, resilience and transformation.

Discussions around climate change and justice distinguish between the distributive and procedural aspects of justice. Distributive justice refers to the distribution of outcomes across different groups (Adger and Paavola 2002). It is broadly concerned with equity and fairness, but may be pluralist in its objectives, including aspects such as human welfare and ecological sustainability (ibid.). In the context of climate change, it elicits a concern with intra-generational justice (i.e. between existing social groups) and inter-generational justice (i.e. between current and future generations). Distinctions can also be made between egalitarian frameworks that seek to reduce risk amongst the most vulnerable, and utilitarian frameworks that would seek to raise the largest number of people from positions of vulnerability – leading to the targeting of the least vulnerable first (Pelling 2011). Procedural justice concerns how and by whom decisions on adaptive responses are made, and is influenced by power distributions, social recognition and political representation (Adger and Paavola 2002; Fraser 2005). However, as Forsyth writes, neither aspect of justice should overlook the question of who decides what is to be distributed and what limits are appropriate for whom (Forsyth 2014). A singular focus on carbon reduction, for example, may lead to projects that actually increase vulnerabilities for local communities (ibid.). Approaches that incorporate climate change mitigation with actions that increase the adaptive capacity of individuals – such as waste management that provides livelihoods to local waste sorters – offer a more promising way forward (ibid.).

In thinking about urban adaptation and social justice, we are broadly concerned with equity and fairness in the mobilization and allocation of resources for adaptation; in the opportunities for actions that support adaptation to occur, ensuring that adaptation for one group does not jeopardize adaptation for another; and in the adaptive process, including how risks are defined by affected people themselves. However, as this chapter aims to illustrate, a narrow focus on mitigation and adaptation actions alone may not be enough to sustain a just response to climate change but may need to accompany broader social and political change. The potential that adaptation and mitigation offer not only to reduce risk but also to open dialogue and new action and policy to address underlying development failures is yet to be harnessed.

Critical pathways for adaptation

The terrain for analysing urban adaptation laid out in the sections above highlights how different framings of risk carry different normative ideals that determine different pathways for adaptation. Conservative framings of risk as resilience, with their emphasis on self-organization, can lend themselves to the ideal of self-reliance, and the withdrawal of state support for adaptation (Abeling and Huq 2015; Friend and Moench 2013). The section above, however, indicated that conceptualizations of risk are increasingly couched within a stronger emphasis on a paradigm of social justice and a concern for social and political change. It showed how normative concerns might orient the analysis of urban adaptation. This framing brings to the fore the need for analysis of relational and dynamic human vulnerabilities situated in an understanding of complex urban systems and shifting urban ecologies and shaped by structurally and historically embedded sets of power relations. It also makes explicit the social values and normative goals that lie within debates about how to conceptualize risk, and how debates about these end-points – in practice as much as in theory – might guide the analysis of urban adaptation. This section moves from debates about analytic frames to discuss what forms of policy and practical engagement might emerge from these conceptual insights.

The challenge posed by resilience thinking – how to live with uncertainty and complexity – requires a mind shift in current modes of urban risk management (Ensor et al. 2013). Existing analysis highlights two important features of current regimes. First, the way that resilience has entered policy discourses and practices is often loosely rooted in analytic debates, often more as a "buzzword" than as a set of principles to be operationalized (Béné et al. 2014; Friend and Moench 2013). As an all-encompassing catchword, the concept is unlikely to leverage new, and necessary, action (Matyas and Pelling 2014). Second, technical modes of management continue to predominate, with a focus on "predicting and preventing" risk through the development of climate models and the undertaking of structural measures (Birkmann et al. 2010; Taylor 2013). As discussed above, vulnerability scholars have long highlighted the fact that such an approach fails to address – and may even exacerbate – the causes of vulnerability and also fails to acknowledge the adaptation capacities of different groups. Further, interpretations of resilience that centre on learning and experimentation as key to enhancing adaptive capacity highlight the differences between a "conventional" management paradigm and "adaptive" governance. The former centralizes power rather than sharing it, and depends on technical rather than procedural knowledge systems and on generalized rather than contextualized experimentation and testing (Ensor et al. 2013). As discussed above, a number of other contrasting features might also characterize resilient systems (depending on the interpretation of resilience). However, a more important approach than transplanting abstract (and inferred) criteria into the policy context (while retaining the functionality of key institutions and structures) is one that works from an understanding of the scope of options in a given political, historical and cultural context (Cote and Nightingale 2012). Different strategies – whether managing impacts, returning to pre-disaster conditions or embracing transformation – may also all be necessary at different points (Matyas and Pelling 2014).

Building on critiques of hazard management and resilience to incorporate the demand for the transformation of urban systems, the concept of transformation has two further implications for existing adaptation pathways. The first is the need to root actions for addressing risk more firmly within broader efforts to promote development and well-being, understanding the mutual influence between the two. In the context of disaster risk reduction, it is indeed claimed by Lewis and Kelman that "[…] the greatest failing of top-down institutionalised DRR is that it has been, and continues to be, separated from the reality of its contexts, whereas it is those contexts that actively contribute to the causes of disasters. By separating DRR from other separated sectors of government, the causes of people's vulnerability to disasters must prevail" (Lewis and Kelman 2012, p. 16). As climate change adaptation policies and programmes become institutionalized in the apparatus of urban government, often harnessed to disaster risk reduction agendas, there is a danger of a similar separation. Beyond "mainstreaming" adaptation into sectoral policies, however, transformation implies a more fundamental shift in policy to address long-term, structural change, which may require changes to institutions themselves (Pelling 2011; Friend and Moench 2013). The issues to be addressed – or the root causes discussed above – relate to why people are vulnerable, and how to support both their access to institutions and their empowerment to uphold their rights and freedoms. This contrasts with policies that target support to the most poor and vulnerable in times of crisis, but often simply maintain the status quo (ibid.). While local governments may not have the resources to implement all that this agenda implies, they are nevertheless important for setting the frameworks through which vulnerable populations can be supported to reduce risk, implying changes to existing social contracts (Satterthwaite 2013).

This raises the question of who is to be supported to adapt. Here, there are possible trade-offs between the needs of the urban system as a whole and the needs of vulnerable groups, which need to be recognized. While clearing flood plains of inhabitants might lead to more effective ecological management that reduces flood risk for the city, for example, such a move may dislocate people whose livelihoods depend on them inhabiting such areas (Friend and Moench 2013). Further, in considering the needs of vulnerable groups, it is necessary to acknowledge that poverty and vulnerability are not the same (Adger and Kelly 1999). Measures to reduce poverty will not necessarily reduce vulnerability to climate change, and adaptation measures do not necessarily reduce poverty (Erikson and Brown 2007). There is a need too for a better understanding of how vulnerability is distributed across groups and across time and to grapple with the relative nature of vulnerability, as well as to assess how changes to urban systems may create fragilities for people and communities who may not be asset poor (Friend and Moench 2013).

In this paradigm for adaptation, process is important as well as outcome, both intrinsically and instrumentally (Matyas and Pelling 2014). The participation of all relevant actors is intrinsic to definitions of well-being as freedom, embedded in human security approaches and manifest in the idea of transformation. Resilience thinking also brings an added emphasis on knowledge and learning (Pelling 2011; Taylor 2013). Two critical pathways for adaptation in resilient systems are social learning and self-organization (Pelling 2011). Social learning emphasizes the need for linkages within and between individual sites, actors and sectors, and for experimentation and testing to be always present in order for learning to take place as systems and conditions change (Ensor et al. 2013). Taken together, self-organization and social learning imply a governance arrangement that supports localism and decentralization within a rich framework of inter-organizational and cross-sectoral learning and exchange (Hordjik, Sutherland and Miranda Sara 2014). There are many ways in which such a system might exhibit itself and no one ideal model. One characteristic is support for the movement of resources as well as information to support risk reduction and response. The goals of such arrangements – such as prioritization of the most or least vulnerable, and of efforts to tackle social and physical vulnerability as a lever for building resilience – will depend upon the development preferences of individual actors and urban governance regimes. In effect, the nature of a given strategy for adaptation is secondary to the development of capacity for deliberation and reflexivity among actors, in order to assess trade-offs and thresholds and come to politically and socially acceptable solutions (Matyas and Pelling 2014). Here, it may be necessary to recognize that processes of learning and innovation in formal institutional settings, such as in local urban government, rest not only on formal rules and interactions but also on informal networks, or the "shadow" systems of urban government (Pelling and High 2005; Leck and Roberts 2015). These systems may nurture the introduction and sustaining of new ideas, but they may also be exclusionary and fragile – depending on personalities and power relations (ibid.).

This impetus in theory for promoting learning between a diversity of actors, in particular in the context of urban poverty and informality, is echoed in recent IPCC reports. The urban chapter of the 2014 IPCC Working Group II states that effective urban adaptation strategies require local governments to work in partnership with low-income groups and vulnerable communities (Revi et al. 2014). There is a lack of experience in implementing such partnerships, however (Ensor et al. 2013), and deep challenges to doing so. As Ensor et al. show for adaptation policy in the city of Maputo, Mozambique, local communities may be consulted and informed but there is a lack of real engagement (ibid.). Securing opportunities for power and knowledge sharing is a process complicated by the ways in which power is mediated through formal and informal channels, which make decision-making opaque and outcomes difficult to predict (ibid.). Other cases illustrate the danger of co-option of less powerful actors in such fora (Boyd et al. 2014). The unequal power and political struggles that characterize the urbanization process therefore challenge such experiments; but there is also evidence that resilience-building projects can build civil awareness and can function as a challenge to accountability structures and to existing forms of social and political relations (Ensor et al. 2013; Friend and Moench 2013; Archer et al. 2014). Some cities – such as Durban, Rosario and New York – have begun to grapple with the need for adaptation, and with concepts of resilience and transformation in their new planning efforts, despite deep challenges to these explorations (Satterthwaite and Dodman 2013).

Actors and agency

As the analysis above has discussed, resilience theory – with its focus on systems and socio-ecological linkages – has often lacked a consideration of actors and agency and their power relationships. Concepts of vulnerability and transformation, however, place actors and agency centre stage, examining the human drivers of risk and the possibilities for deliberate action for adaptation. Without neglecting the role of institutional and organizational structures, and the (non-intentional) agency of environmental forces in determining risk, the ensuing analysis of urban mitigation and adaptation focuses on the role of actors and their agency in defining responses to climate change. Following Dietz et al., human agency refers to the capacity of both individual and corporate actors, with the diverse cultural meanings that they espouse, to play an independent causal role in history (Dietz and McLaughlin 2008). More holistic definitions of agency – with greater power to capture the different dimensions of behaviour – look beyond resource- and infrastructure-based explanations of human action, to cultural and psychosocial motivations (Brown and Westaway 2011). An actor-oriented approach performs a number of important functions. First, it constitutes a human-centred approach to environmental change (ibid.). Second, it ensures that vulnerable groups are not portrayed simply as passive, but as active agents, and recognizes that they have their own priorities that may diverge from those of external, and more powerful, actors (Dietz and McLaughlin 2008). Third, in analysing the policy environment for urban adaptation and mitigation, the focus on actors allows for the role of individuals to emerge. Here, policy "entrepreneurs" or "champions" may be critical in enabling decision-making in favour of more resilient, or even transformative, pathways (Bahadur and Tanner 2014). In analysing the broader governance networks and relations that support responses to environmental change beyond the formal climate change policy-making arena, an actor-based focus allows us to investigate the practices and everyday actions that constitute "governance", beyond the formal rules and structures of government (Leach, Scoones and Stirling 2010).

Conclusion

This chapter sets the stage for the subsequent case studies and their analysis by providing a set of definitions and concepts which help to clarify discussion of urban disaster and climate change risk. Arguing that the concepts of vulnerability, resilience and transformation provide important lenses for the study of urban risk, the chapter has discussed ways in which these terms may be used, first, in a way that allows us to understand the current production of urban risks as complex, relational and political across actors and spaces and, second, in a way that allows us to analyse how deeper changes may be realized to promote sustainable development and social justice as key to effective and equitable risk reduction. Analysis of urban risk therefore needs to be attentive to the actors that drive risk reduction or accumulation pathways and the power relations between them, in particular at the local level between citizens and urban governments. The normative goal inherent in the conceptual definitions adopted here makes for a challenging policy paradigm that goes beyond existing pathways to integrate risk reduction and sustainable development goals, but that is necessary to achieve just and sustainable objectives.

References

Abeling, T and N Huq (2015), "Building resilience among communities in Europe", Deliverable Report, UNU-EHS for the emBRACE Consortium.

Adger, N (2006), "Vulnerability", *Global Environmental Change* Vol 16, pages 268–81.

Adger, N, and PM Kelly (1999), "Social vulnerability to climate change and the architecture of entitlements", *Mitigation and Adaptation Strategies to Global Change* no 4, pages 253–6.

Adger, N, and J Paavola (2002), "Justice and adaptation to climate change", Working Paper 23, Tyndall Centre.

Adger, N, T Quinn, I Lorenzoni, C Murphy, and J Sweeney (2013), "Changing social contracts in climate change adaptation", *Nature Climate Change* Vol 3, pages 330–3.

Anguelovski, I, and J Carmin (2011), "Something borrowed, everything new: innovation and institutionalization in urban climate governance", *Current Opinion in Environmental Sustainability* Vol 3, no 3, pages 169–75.

Aragon-Durand, Fernando (2007), "Urbanisation and flood vulnerability in the peri-urban interface of Mexico City", *Disasters* Vol 31, no 4, pages 477–94.

Archer, D, F Almansi, M DiGregorio, D Roberts, D Sharma, and D Syam (2014), "Moving towards inclusive urban adaptation: approaches to integrating community-based adaptation to climate change at city and national scale", *Climate and Development* Vol 6, no 4, pages 345–56.

Bahadur, A, and T Tanner (2014), "Policy climates and climate policies: analysing the politics of building urban climate change resilience", *Urban Climate* 7, pages 20–32.

Baker, Judy L (2012), *Climate Change, Disaster Risk, and the Urban Poor: Cities Building Resilience for a Changing World*, World Bank Publications.

Bartlett, S (2008), "Climate change and urban children: impacts and implications for adaptation in low- and middle-income countries", Human Settlements Discussion Paper Series: Theme: Climate Change and Cities 2, IIED, London.

Béné, C, T Cannon, J Gupte, L Mehta, and T Tanner (2014), "Exploring the potential and limits of the resilience agenda in rapidly urbanising contexts", IDS Evidence Report 63, Brighton, UK, IDS.

Birkmann, J, OD Cardona, L Carreno, A Barbat, M Pelling, S Schneiderbauer, S Kienberger et al. (2013), "Framing vulnerability, risk and societal responses: The MOVE Framework", *Natural Hazards* Vol 67, no 2, pages 192–211.

Birkmann, J, M Garschagen, F Kraas, and N Quang (2010), "Adaptive urban governance: new challenges for the second generation of urban adaptation strategies to climate change", *Sustainability Science* Vol 5, no 2, pages 185–206. doi:10.1007/s11625-010-0111-3.

Blaikie, Piers M, T Cannon, I Davis, and B Wisner (1994), *At Risk: Natural Hazards, People's Vulnerability, and Disasters*, London and New York, Routledge.

Boyd, Emily, J Ensor, V Castan-Broto, and S Juhola (2014), "Environmentalities of urban climate governance in Maputo, Mozambique", *Global Environmental Change* Vol 26, pages 140–51.

Braun, B, and T Abheuer (2011), "Floods in megacity environments: vulnerability and coping strategies of slum dwellers in Dhaka, Bangladesh", *Natural Hazards* Vol 58, pages 771–87.

Brooks, N (2003), "Vulnerability, risk and adaptation: a conceptual framework", Working Paper 38, Tyndall Centre for Climate Change Research.

Brown, K, and E Westaway (2011), "Agency, capacity, and resilience to environmental change: lessons from human development, well-being, and disasters", *Annual Review of Environment and Resources* Vol 36, pages 321–42.

Bulkeley, Harriet, and R Tuts (2013), "Understanding urban vulnerability, adaptation and resilience in the context of climate change", *Local Environment* Vol 18, no 6, pages 646–62.

Bull-Kamanga, L, K Diagne, A Lavell, F Lertise, H MacGregor, A Maskrey, M Meshack et al. (2003), "From everyday hazard to disasters: the accumulation of risk in urban areas", *Environment and Urbanization* Vol 15, no 1, pages 193–204.

Chatterjee, P (2006), *The Politics of the Governed: Reflections on Popular Politics in Most of the World*, Columbia University Press, New York.

Cote, M, and A Nightingale (2012), "Resilience thinking meets social theory situating social change in Socio-Ecological Systems (SES) Research", *Progress in Human Geography* Vol 36, no 4, pages 475–89.

Cutter, S, Christopher T Emrich, Jennifer Webb, and Daniel Morath (2009), "Social vulnerability to climate variability hazards: a review of the literature", Report for Oxfam America, Hazards and Vulnerability Research Institute, University of South Carolina.

Dickson, E, A Tiwari, J Baker, and D Hoornweg (2010), "Understanding urban risk: an approach for assessing disaster and climate risk in cities", Washington DC, World Bank Urban Development and Local Government Unit.

Dietz, T, and P McLaughlin (2008), "Structure, agency and environment: towards an integrated perspective on vulnerability", *Global Environmental Change* Vol 18, no 1, pages 99–111.

Douglas, I, K Alam, M Maghenda, Y Mcdonnell, L Mclean, and J Campbell (2008), "Unjust waters: climate change, flooding and the urban poor in Africa", *Environment and Urbanization* Vol 20, no 1, pages 187–205.

Ensor, J, E Boyd, S Juhola, and V Castan-Broto (2013), "Building adaptive capacity in the informal settlements of Maputo: lessons for development from a resilience perspective", in T H Inderberg, S Eriksen, K O'Brien, and L Synga (editors), *Social Adaptation to Climate Change in Developing Countries: Development as Usual Is Not Enough*, London, Routledge.

Erikson, S, and K Brown (2007), "Vulnerability, poverty and the need for sustainable adaptation measures", *Climate Policy* Vol 7, pages 337–52.

Forsyth, T (2014), "Climate justice is not just ice", *Geoforum* 54, pages 230–2.

Fraser, N (2005), "Mapping the feminist imagination: from redistribution to recognition to representation", *Constellations* Vol 12, no 3, pages 295–307.

Friend, R, and M Moench (2013), "What is the purpose of urban climate resilience? implications for addressing poverty and vulnerability", *Urban Climate* Vol 6, pages 98–113.

Hayter, T (1971), *Aid as Imperialism*, Harmondsworth, Penguin.

Hordjik, M, C Sutherland, and L Miranda Sara (2014), "Resilience, transition or transformation: a comparative analysis of changing water governance systems in four southern cities", *Environment and Urbanization* Vol 26, pages 130–46.

IPCC (2012), *Managing the Risks of Extreme Events and Disasters to Advance Climate Change Adaptation. A Special Report of Working Groups I and II of the Intergovernmental Panel on Climate Change.* Edited by C B Field, V Barros, T F Stocker, D Qin, K L Dokken, M D Ebi, K J Mastrandrea et al., Cambridge, UK, and New York, USA, Cambridge University Press.

IPCC (2014), *Climate Change 2014: Impacts, Adaptation, and Vulnerability, Annex II: Glossary*, Cambridge, UK, and New York, USA, Cambridge University Press.

Jabeen, H, C Johnson, and A Allen (2010), "Built-in resilience: learning from grassroots coping strategies for climate variability", *Environment and Urbanization* Vol 22, no 2, pages 415–31.

Jha, A, R Bloch, and J Lamond (2012), *Cities and Flooding: A Guide to Integrated Urban Flood Risk Management for the 21st Century*, Washington DC, World Bank and GFDRR.

Klein, R J T, R J Nicholls and F Thomalla (2003), "The resilience of coastal megacities to weather-related hazards: a review", in A Kreimer, M Arnold and A Carlin (editors), *Building Safer Cities: The Future of Disaster Risk*, Disaster Risk Management Series No 3, World Bank, Washington DC, USA, pages 101–20.

Leach, M, I Scoones, and A Stirling (2010), *Dynamic Sustainabilities: Technology, Environment, Social Justice*, London, Earthscan.

Leck, H, and D Roberts (2015), "What lies beneath: understanding the invisible aspects of municipal climate change governance", *Current Opinion in Environmental Sustainability*, no 13, pages 61–7.

Leichenko, R (2011), "Climate change and urban resilience", *Current Opinion in Environmental Sustainability* Vol 3, pages 164–8.

Lewis, J, and I Kelman (2012), "The good, the bad and the ugly: disaster risk reduction (DRR) versus disaster risk creation (DRC)", *PLOS Currents Disasters*. http://currents.plos.org/disasters/article/the-good-the-bad-and-the-ugly-disaster-risk-reduction-drr-versus-disaster-risk-creation-drc/ DOI: 10.1371/4f8d4eaec6af8.

Matyas, D, and M Pelling (2014), "Positioning resilience for 2015: the role of resistance, incremental adjustment and transformation in disaster risk management policy", *Disasters* Vol 39, pages 1–18.

McGranahan, G, P Jacobi, J Songsore, C Surjadi, and M Kjellen (2001), *The Citizens at Risk: From Urban Sanitation to Sustainable Cities*, London, Earthscan.

Miller, Fiona, Henny Osbahr, Jochen Hinkel, Tom Downing, Carl Folke, Donald Nelson, Emily Boyd et al. (2010), "Resilience and vulnerability : complementary or conflicting concepts?" *Ecology and Society* Vol 15, no 3, pages 1–25.

Mitlin, D (2012), "Lessons from the urban poor: collective action and the rethinking of development", in M Pelling, D Manuel-Navarrete, and M Redclift, (editors), *Climate Change and the Crisis of Capitalism*, Routledge, London.

Moser, C (1998), "The asset vulnerability framework: reassessing urban poverty reduction strategies", *World Development* Vol 26, no 1, pages 1–19.

Moser, C, and D Satterthwaite (2008), "Towards pro-poor adaptation to climate change in the urban centres of low and middle income countries", Human Settlements Discussion Paper 3, Climate Change and Cities, London, IIED.

Moser, C, A Norton, A Stein, and S Georgieva (2010), "Pro-poor adaptation to climate change in urban centres: case studies of vulnerability and resilience in Kenya and Nicaragua", Social Development Department Report 54947-GLB. Washington, World Bank.

Mustafa, Daanish (2005), "The production of an urban hazardscape in Pakistan: modernity, vulnerability and the range of choice", *Annals of the Association of American Geographers* Vol 95, no 3, pages 566–86.

O'Brien, K, B Hayward, and F Berkes (2009), "Rethinking social contracts: building resilience in a changing climate", *Ecology and Society* Vol 14, no 2. www.ecologyandsociety.org/vol14/iss2/art12/

Overseas Development Institute (1978), "Briefing paper: basic needs", Briefing Paper 5, London, Overseas Development Institute.

Pelling, M (1999), "The political ecology of flood hazard in urban Guyana", *Geoforum* Vol 30, pages 249–61.

Pelling, M (2003), *The Vulnerability of Cities: Natural Disasters and Social Resilience*, London and New York, Routledge, 1st edn.

Pelling, M (2011), *Adaptation to Climate Change: From Resilience to Transformation*, London and New York, Routledge.

Pelling, M (2014), "Transformation: a renewed window on development responsibility for risk management", *Journal of Extreme Events* Vol 1, no 1. DOI: 10.1142/S2345737614020035

Pelling, M, and K Dill (2010), "Disaster politics: tipping points for change in the adaptation of sociopolitical regimes", *Progress in Human Geography* Vol 34, no 1, pages 21–37.

Pelling, M, and C High (2005), "Understanding adaptation: what can social capital offer assessments of adaptive capacity?" *Global Environmental Change* Vol 15, no 4, pages 308–19.

Pelling, M, and D Manuel-Navarrete (2011), "From resilience to transformation: the adaptive cycle in two Mexican urban centres", *Ecology and Society* Vol 16, no 2. www.ecologyandsociety.org/vol16/iss2/art11/

Pelling M, K O'Brien, and D Matyas (2015), "Adaptation and transformation", *Climatic Change*, doi: 10.1007/s10584-014-1303-0.

Rebotier, Julien (2012), "Vulnerability conditions and risk representations in Latin-America: framing the territorializing urban risk", *Global Environmental Change* Vol 22, pages 391–8.

Revi, A, D Satterthwaite, F Aragon-Durand, J Coffee-Morlot, R Kiunsi, M Pelling, D Roberts, and W Solecki (2014), "Chapter 8. Urban Areas", In *Climate Change 2014: Impacts, Adaptation and Vulnerability*, Assessment Report 5, IPCC.

Ribot, J C (1995), "The causal structure of vulnerability: its application to climate impact analysis", *Geojournal* Vol 35, no 2, pages 119–22.

Robinson, J (2006), *Ordinary Cities: Between Modernity and Development,* London, Routledge.

Romero Lankao, Patricia, and Hua Qin (2011), "Conceptualizing urban vulnerability to global climate and environmental change", *Current Opinion in Environmental Sustainability* Vol 3, no 3, pages 142–9, doi:10.1016/j.cosust.2010.12.016.

Roy, David Hulme, and Ferdous Jahan (2013), "Contrasting adaptation responses by squatters and low-income tenants in Khulna, Bangladesh", *Environment and Urbanization* Vol 25, no 1, pages 157–76.

Satterthwaite, D (2013), "A future urban poor groups want: addressing inequalities and governance post-2015", IIED Briefing, London, IIED.

Satterthwaite, D, and D Dodman (2013), "Editorial: towards resilience and transformation for cities within a finite planet", *Environment and Urbanization* Vol 25 no 2, pages 291–7.

Solecki, W, and C Rozensweig (2014), "Hurricane Sandy and adaptation pathways in New York: lessons from a first-responder city", *Global Environmental Change* Vol 28, pages 395–408.

Swyngedouw, E, F Moulaert, and A Rodriguez (2003), "The world in a grain of sand: large-scale urban development projects and the dynamics of 'glocal' transformations", in *The Globalized City – Economic Restructuring and Social Polarization in European Cities*, Oxford, UK, Oxford University Press.

Taylor, M (2013), "Climate change, relational vulnerability and human security: rethinking sustainable adaptation in agrarian environments", *Climate and Development* Vol 5, no 4, pages 318–27.

Tyler, S, and M Moench (2012), "A framework for urban climate resilience", *Climate and Development* Vol 4, no 4, pages 311–26.

UNISDR (2011), *Revealing Risk, Redefining Development. Global Assessment Report on Disaster Risk Reduction*, Geneva, Switzerland, United Nations International Strategy for Disaster Reduction.

United Nations (2014), *Report of the Open Working Group of the General Assembly on Sustainable Development Goals*, United Nations.

Wamsler, C (2007), "Bridging the gaps: stakeholder-based strategies for risk reduction and financing for the urban poor", *Environment and Urbanization* Vol 19, no 1, pages 115–42.

Wise, R M, I Fazey, M Stafford Smith, S E Park, H C Eakin, E R M Archer van Garderen, and B Campbell (2014), "Reconceptualising adaptation to climate change as part of pathways of change and response", *Global Environmental Change* Vol 28, pages 325–36.

Wisner, B, and M Fordham (2014), "Vulnerability and capacity", *Handbook of Global Environmental Pollution* Vol 1, pages 857–63.

World Commission on Environment and Development (1987), *Report of the World Commission on Environment and Development: Our Common Future*, New York, United Nations.

World Future Council (2010), *Regenerative Cities*, World Future Council.

3

BANGALORE, INDIA

Aromar Revi, Sumetee Pahwa Gajjar, Ritwika Basu, Garima Jain and Amir B. Bazaz

Introduction

The drought-prone city of Bangalore[1] is inhabited by ever-growing numbers of people, spurred by an expanding service economy. The city's economic and physical growth has made it vital to the region's economic development – nearly 34 per cent of the economic output of Karnataka state comes from this one city. At the same time, Bangalore's growth has also put tremendous pressure on its natural environment, contributing to the degradation of the local eco-system and affecting the city's spatial structure and character. Its growth is accompanied by an increasing demand for water, yet it remains totally dependent on supplies piped in from the river Cauvery, over 100 km away. At the same time, the number and intensity of floods is increasing because of poorly managed development, including the blockage of natural drainage channels. These problems, intensified by a changing climate, challenge the city and its people now and pose serious questions about its sustainability in the future and that of the region that depends on its economy. Bangalore's fragmented governance, with its multiplicity of institutions and jurisdictions, complicates its sound development and impedes a holistic approach towards mitigation of and adaptation to the growing impacts of climate variability being experienced by the city. The limited understanding of climate change and its implications further constrains attention to what must become the city's priorities.

Physical context and land use

Bangalore, which had its origins as a modern city in the 1500s, is located in southeast Karnataka state on the Deccan plateau on a mix of level land and undulating hills and valleys. It has a dry tropical savanna climate with generally moderate temperatures, and experiences both the southwest monsoon (June to September) and the northeast monsoon (October through November) which together yield about 860 mm of rainfall. The city's landscape was dry and scrubby prior to the mid-19th century, when extensive tree plantations were undertaken to provide shade, greenery and visual relief (CDP 2009).

One of the most rapidly growing cities in India, Bangalore has a built-up area that has increased more than six-fold since the 1970s, driven by large-scale construction that has transformed the rural economy, landscape and culture. By 2011, the city jurisdiction (the Bruhat Bangalore Mahanagara Palike or BBMP) covered 741 km^2 and it continues to grow. The larger Bangalore Metropolitan Region (BMR), 1,307 km^2, also includes the peripheral rural district's villages and towns and the Bangalore–Mysore infrastructure corridor project area (CDP 2009). New development has typically taken place away from the low-density city core, leading to extensive sprawl, and the city's physical footprint increased by over 100 per cent between 1992 and 2009 (IIHS 2014). Reasons for the extent of the growth include preferential investments in the periphery (in housing and commercial activities), greater personal mobility as middle class incomes rise, and limited ability to change designated land-uses in the core, resulting in the proliferation of new settlements – legal and illegal – in the periphery.

Bangalore's "mega-city problems" started emerging distinctly in the 1990s, manifesting through slum proliferation, severe water supply and sewage problems, extreme road congestion, pollution and associated health issues, as well as rapidly escalating social inequality. Initially slum development centered on industrial areas, but over time, spread to multiple sites across the city (Goldman 2011).

Growth on the city's expanding peripheries has put considerable pressure on the natural surroundings, resulting in a sharp decline in water bodies and natural vegetation. Bangalore has long depended on a system of wetlands and constructed lakes, ponds and water tanks, many built in the 16th century by damming springs and streams for drinking water and irrigation. These constituted a vital ecosystem, serving multiple livelihood and domestic purposes, and also capturing rainfall, helping replenish groundwater and modulating the city's microclimate. However, the almost 300 such water bodies counted in the 1960s have mostly dried up or vanished as the city has grown and densified, and more than 70 per cent of the wetlands have disappeared since the 1970s, the result of cascading development pressures – encroachment and construction, pollution, illegal mining and quarrying (SoER 2008).

Social context

Bangalore's extensive spatial growth has been accompanied by rapid population increase, primarily from a massive inflow of migrants. A quiet city of under a million in the 1950s, it grew to 5.1 million in 2001 and to 8.4 million in 2011, a 65 per cent increase over that one decade (Census 2011). The estimated

TABLE 3.1 Bangalore's changing demography, economy, area and land-use area and use

	1991	*2001*	*2011*
Population (millions)	3.3	4.3	8.5
Decadal population growth (per cent)	30%	31%	98%
Proportion of state population (per cent)	7%	11%	14%
Literacy (per cent)	41%	75%	80%
Sex ratio (females per 1,000 males)	913	918	914
Mean life expectancy at birth (years)	63	66	67
City GDP (US$ billion PPP)	0.1	5	10
City per capita income (US$ PPP/year)	106	235	531
Proportion of national GDP (US$ PPP/year)	0.02%	0.4%	0.4%
Area (km^2)	226	276	741
Population density (people / km^2)	11,948	19,065	11,371

population for 2015 is almost 11 million, making it the third most populous city in India (IIHS 2014). The primary reason for the city's rapid growth is the expanding service sector economy, ably supported by adequate education and technical skill infrastructure. A snapshot of the changes is provided in Table 3.1.

While the large numbers of migrants from all over the country were attracted by the promise of the city's livelihood opportunities and quality of life, the distribution of these benefits has been highly unequal (Benjamin 2000; CDP 2009). About 43 per cent of the city's population lives in multi-dimensional poverty, and there are growing disparities, especially around living conditions. The rising prices of land and rentals have made housing a major issue, and although a lower percentage of the population lives in slums than in other large cities in India, the number of informal settlements has grown significantly, housing more than half a million people (Sudhira et al. 2007). The informal economy also employs far more people than all the formal sectors put together. Most of this informal economy functions outside the purview of formal planning mechanisms, and the recognition of slums and informal settlements as legitimate parts of the city is still problematic. Especially in peri-urban areas, unclear jurisdictions create neglect and pockets of settlements at high risk. There are, for instance, major disparities regarding access to potable water. The city core is generally well connected, but in some more peripheral areas fewer than 10 per cent of households are connected to the main system. Irregular water supply has created problems of hygiene, with the highest risks in poor residential areas and informal settlements. Although water supply is especially critical (Ranganathan et al. 2009), weaknesses in provision extend to other services as well.

The city has a reasonably good provision of healthcare and education, but has underscored in its development plans the importance of strengthening both. Some of the pressing health-related issues are linked to deteriorating air and water quality; various programs and initiatives have been undertaken in the past to address these issues, and they have been prioritized for the future. The city boasts some of the country's best academic and research institutes, but here too there is an identified need to strengthen capacity to support the emerging high-technology industry in the city, as well as continuing to strengthen basic primary and secondary education.

Economic context

Bangalore's economy has grown significantly over the past 20 years. GDP reached $10 billion in 2011, and per capita income increased from $106 in 1990 to $531 in 2011 (PPP). Bangalore serves as a magnet for investment and employment in Karnataka, contributing almost 34 per cent to the state's GDP with only 14 per cent of its population (Directorate of Economics and Statistics 2015). Long a stronghold of domestic textiles and other light manufacturing, Bangalore has emerged over the last two decades as a global center for new service sector economies, such as information technology and biotechnology, attracted in part by its academic institutions and skilled workforce (Sudhira et al. 2007).

Despite its international reputation on this front, however, and the flow of resources to support this sector, a greater share of the city's formal employment actually remains in manufacturing (43 per cent as opposed to 32 per cent in the services sector, including IT/ITES (CDP 2009; Mahadevia 2008)). A large number of jobs are also provided by the government and its parastatal agencies, and employment in retail and real estate has also grown, driven by the area's upward economic mobility.

What most catches attention, however, is the colossal expansion of the city's informal economy, resulting from the limitations of the formal sector in creating formal jobs for the influx of migrants. An important factor influencing these economies is the city's location, on the border of two states (Andhra Pradesh and Tamil Nadu), and in proximity to a third (Kerala). This results in an "agglomeration of people from different ethnic backgrounds; with diverse skills, traditions, capital and most importantly access to markets" (Benjamin 2000, p.36; Benjamin et al. 2006). These jobs, mostly poorly paid, are critical, as noted, in generating livelihoods for the greater part of the population. These local economies grew in the late 1970s to mid-1980s, spurred by the inflow of investment in the formally planned manufacturing sector, which outsourced jobs to these ancillary support units (Benjamin 2000). The informal sector also includes construction and transport activities, waste collection, the food industry, handicrafts, home-based textile industry and domestic support activities for the residential sector (Mahadevia 2008). This informal economy is unregulated and keeps expanding rapidly, but has trouble providing sufficient jobs to a growing number of migrants, especially to seasonal migrants.

While the 1950s to 1980s were characterized by public sector investment, the 1990s saw rapid growth in private sector investment in industry and the service sector. To entice businesses, the state government offered land and tax incentives and built infrastructure, including elevated roads, a new metro and a new airport. The rapid growth of new economic sectors (IT/ITES, Biotechnology) in Bangalore boosted the real estate market, both locally and regionally (Nair 2005; Benjamin et al. 2006), specifically that aimed at serving high-income groups, both investors from outside and the local elite. The 1990s simultaneously exposed the Indian economy to liberalization, which played an enormous role in shaping Bangalore's corporate identity. By the late 1990s, however, industrial stagnation had set in, primarily in formal manufacturing. The major impact was in the construction industry, and the slowdown severely affected employment. At the same time, the IT sector was on a rising trajectory. It made a noteworthy contribution to the city's employment situation, but had serious distributional implications. Disparities between the rich and the poor became sharper, as visibly observed in growing inequality in access to services, especially water and sanitation (Benjamin 2000). Indeed, the growth of inequality and poverty in the city is considered in part to be the result of the skewed focus of public policy on the globalized hi-tech growth sector (CDP 2009; Benjamin et al. 2006).

Governance

In 2007, the Greater Bangalore City Corporation (BBMP) was established by merging the existing corporation with several neighboring municipal councils and over 100 surrounding villages (ULBs or urban local bodies) (CDP 2009). The BBMP is primarily responsible for all city-based functions and service delivery, assisted by a range of statutory organizations/authorities (Table 3.2). These multiple agencies, with their overlapping administrative boundaries and jurisdictions, contribute to fragmented and often conflictual governance processes which undermine the management of climatic and non-climatic risks. The municipal government is often financially strapped, understaffed and lacks capacity to tackle problems associated with planning and development (IIHS 2014). There are pockets spatially distant from the central core, especially, with little or no governance or public service. Presently, the BBMP is building a case for splitting the jurisdiction into three parts. This is projected to complicate governance further, particularly in the context of a range of risks.

A critical aspect of Bangalore's governance is its land-use management. The rapid transformation of the peripheral rural landscape has, as noted, put tremendous pressure on peri-urban ecosystems. Ecological commons such as lakes, wetlands and community gardens, providing livelihoods and social and cultural services, used to be managed through community oversight systems (Sundaresan 2011). Much of the city's transformation has also resulted not from

TABLE 3.2 Governance structure in Bangalore

Government institution	*Roles*
Bangalore Development Authority (BDA)	Develops plans, controls, monitors, facilitates urban; development and urban environmental improvement
Bangalore Metropolitan Transport Corporation (BMTC)	Operates bus transport service in the Bangalore Metropolitan Region, extending to the nearby villages (in a 25-km radius)
Bangalore Water Supply and Sewerage Board (BWSSB)	Drinking water supply to the city and nearby village areas, maintains the water distribution network and sewerage lines
Lake Development Authority (LDA)	Regeneration and conservation of lakes
Karnataka Urban Infrastructure Development and Finance Corporation (KUIDFC)	Assists urban agencies in development of infrastructure; nodal agency for externally aided projects and mega city schemes
Karnataka Slum Clearance Board (KSCB)	Rehabilitation of declared slum areas within city corporation
Bangalore Metropolitan Region Development Authority (BMRDA)	Planning, co-ordination, supervision of development in larger BMR (comprising both urban and rural districts)
Bangalore Metropolitan Land Transport Authority (BMLTA)	Co-ordinates land transport in BMR, regulates implementation of KUIDFC traffic and transportation plans (CTTP)

Source: Adapted from CDP 2009.

planned interventions, but from the activity of the private sector, civil society and poor inhabitants (Goldman 2011). Informal settlements expanded without oversight, and even the transfer of agricultural land to real estate developers, starting in the mid-1990s, often took place without legal approval or attention to basic standards on access roads or sewer lines.

All this is now the purview of the Bangalore Development Authority, through plans drafted every ten years, as well as the decisions and actions of various other agencies and departments. In the context of rapid growth and change, a transition to planned management was essential, but it has not been successful on the whole. Implementation has often been ineffective, and the process is inaccessible to most residents. While formal mechanisms exist for more strategic long-term planning, actual plans focus more on opportunities for land development than on the kind of zoning and management that is responsive to the full range of the city's development needs. For instance, while the administration has clearly identified the importance of sustaining the industrial structure and has underscored the importance of unlocking land in the city core and the periphery (CDP 2009), there are weaknesses in the policy-implementation space with regards to, for example, safeguarding areas at risk from flooding or protecting water bodies from encroachment. The lack of an effective mechanism for distributing serviced land to both citizens and industry also reduces the city's effectiveness in meeting its development needs and impedes sensible growth (IIHS 2014). The city's vision for its development seems in effect to be driven by processes which for the most part conform to pressures for economic growth rather than to the objective of long-term sustainability.

GHG emissions profile and mitigation goals

Bangalore's rapid urban development contributes to growing greenhouse gas emissions. Under a Business As Usual (BAU) scenario, per capita emissions are expected to more than double between 2007 and 2030, driven by demand increase across all sectors – building, transport and most of all industry.[2] While there have been no official estimates for GHG inventory in the city, several researchers have attempted to quantify the extent of GHG emissions. A recent study found Bangalore's carbon emission footprint to be 19.8 $mtCO_2e$ for 2009. Major contributors were road transport (44 per cent) followed by domestic use (37 per cent) and industry (12 per cent). Primary drivers of emissions are fossil-generated electricity consumption and consumption of liquid fuels in transport and industry. Other contributing sectors are waste, agriculture and emissions from auxiliary consumption and transmission loss (in the electricity sector). Per capita GHG emissions were 2.23 CO_2e in 2009, placing Bangalore fifth among India's major cities (Ramachandra and Aithal 2015).

Power generation in the BMR is minimal and the principal source is the regional and national grid. Electricity is procured from coal, hydroelectric, oil and even wind power plants, located mostly outside Bangalore. Fossil fuels are the major energy source across all sectors, although 21 per cent of Bangalore's electricity comes from hydro and renewable sources (SoER 2008) (Figure 3.1). The use of biomass is only a small part of this, generally restricted to cooking in poorer households, and some small-scale industries. Understandably estimates around biomass consumption are under-reported.

With the expected demand increase, existing resources will need to be supplemented. Despite the relatively high green share of Bangalore's power sector, this would still need to be much improved in the context of an emergent mitigation pathways. Reforms would need to include improved energy efficiency and a switch from fossil fuels to a lower grid emission electricity. The most intense use currently is by commercial buildings, completely glazed structures reliant on air conditioning tied to the service sector boom in the city. Decreasing consumption depends heavily on efficiency gains in this sector.

The increase of population and economic growth in Bangalore has meant an exponential growth in transportation needs. During the last two decades the vehicular population in Bangalore has increased three-fold, mostly in two-

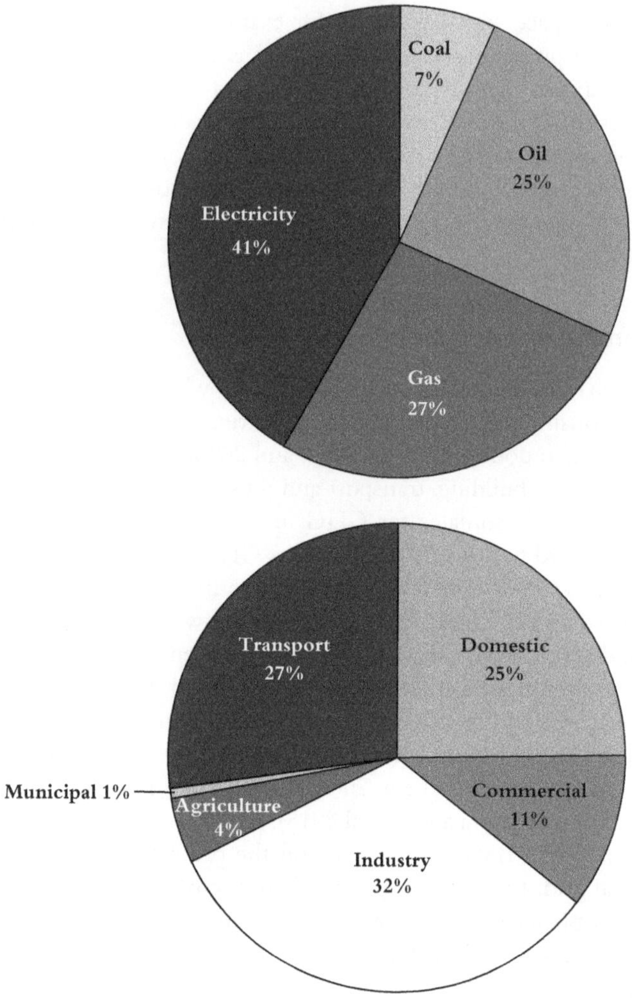

FIGURE 3.1 Energy source and consumption profile of Bangalore, 2007 (data source: SoER, 2008)

wheelers (CDP 2009). Nearly 99 per cent of the petrol and 80 per cent of the diesel used in Bangalore is consumed by the transport sector. The shift to LPG in the intermediate public transport category (like three-wheelers) has slightly reduced consumption.

The BMR region accommodates around 70,000 industries and many industry types, led by general engineering and textiles (SoER, 2008). Energy consumption is high, primarily of electricity but also diesel and bulk LPG. Figure 3.1 highlights the small percentage of coal consumption in Bangalore, essentially for brick manufacturing connected to real-estate growth (UNDP 2009).

Key climate risks – multiple, interlinked and growing

Bangalore's economic and physical growth has, as noted, put tremendous pressure on the natural environment of the city, affecting the city's geographic spread and spatial structure. These challenges, in combination with the pressures imposed by a changing climate, are increasing the vulnerability of people and infrastructure, and aggravating the challenges and risks to growth prospects, including attempts to offset urban poverty (CDP 2009).

The changes in climate are especially notable in precipitation and temperature. Average annual rainfall in Bangalore has been increasing in frequency and intensity since 1900, and particularly since 1950 (Guhathakurta et al. 2011). At the same time, unplanned urbanization has significantly reduced the drainage potential of both natural catchments and manmade lakes, increasing still further the volume and rate of surface runoff. There is direct and indirect damage, including infrastructure and property losses with considerable social consequences, a decrease in property values, production losses and a higher incidence of disease (Ramachandra and Kumar 2010). The rise of 2 to 2.5°C in the mean temperature in the last decade can be attributed to both climate change as well as the increasing urban heat island effect, associated with expansion in the built-up area (ibid.). While not as destructive of property, this trend has serious health and productivity implications, as well as feeding back into more irregular weather patterns.

Despite increased rainfall, water scarcity is a key challenge in the city and, in interaction with other socio-economic vulnerabilities, creates a huge accumulation of risk. The newly developed peripheries of Bangalore rely heavily on groundwater through private self-supply as a result of the absence of public supply. This unregulated and indiscriminate use has caused the water table in many areas to drop to dangerous levels. The pumped extraction of groundwater is also very energy intensive, adding to carbon emissions. Even where groundwater is more plentiful, there can be problems with contamination from inadequate sanitation and sewerage infrastructure, from leaking sewer lines and wastewater.

Land use management issues greatly intensify the potential impact of projected climate change. Increasing density means the accumulation and concentration of risk. The significant reduction in water bodies and vegetation cover exacerbates heat impacts, creates ecological imbalances and reduces buffers for managing extreme events like rainfall or drought. According to one study, "Impacts are likely to affect a range of sectors – food and water, health, buildings, transport and natural ecosystems. Evident already are a decline in the water table, urban flooding, increasing air pollution and the significant heat island effect" (IIHS 2014, p.15; Guhathakurta et al. 2011).

The incidence of urban flooding has increased substantially in recent years, causing damage to low lying areas of the city and severely affecting transportation systems. Many low lying areas were formerly water reservoirs, but through a systemic process of encroachment are now dry and inhabited, which causes challenges to drainage patterns. Critical infrastructure for water, sanitation and drainage is prone to flooding. Recently, 1077 areas were identified as flood prone, of which 85 per cent were categorized as critical by the BBMP. Flooding risk is expected to be further aggravated by micro-climate changes (UHI), leading to intensified localized water cycles and precipitation, which may be high for short intervals of time (ibid.). Table 3.3 summarizes the climate and non-climate risks in Bangalore and the prospects for action.

The City Development Plan (2009) recognized the imperative of disaster management, and in 2010 Karnataka's first Disaster Management Plan identified urban flooding as a key risk in Bangalore. Some initiatives that have gathered momentum within this framework include monitoring of natural disasters through the Karnataka State Natural Disaster Monitoring Centre (KSNDMC) and enhancement of weather monitoring stations. As of 2014, 86 telemetric rain gauges were installed across the BMR, generating daily rainfall data, sending necessary alerts and creating an infrastructure of early warning. There is still not a comprehensive response to disaster risk reduction in the city, including a range of extensive and intensive risks, but the Disaster Management Plan provides a framework for a progressive implementation of disaster risk reduction.

Climate change adaptation and mitigation in Bangalore

The larger context

In India, policy and action on climate change are heavily driven by the government and to a lesser extent from the state level. There are no official climate plans at city level, nor even any official estimates of GHG emissions. Understanding what is happening in Bangalore means understanding this larger context.

For India, the global challenge of climate change must, in turn, be understood within its development context (Economic Survey of India 2014). India is still grappling with the challenges of poverty reduction, employment generation, and equitable access to water, sanitation, health services and universal education. Until recently, the government's development initiatives were concentrated in rural areas, but with rapid urbanization, efforts have been made to address the significant urban gaps. The focus has been to merge development objectives (through the National Urban Renewal Missions), with the goals of the National Action Plan on Climate Change (NAPCC) and its state equivalent (State Action Plan on Climate Change – SAPCC) as co-benefits, reducing natural and social vulnerability and buffering cities from climate-induced shocks and stress through strategies embedded in the urban renewal agenda. The national government has repeatedly emphasized the building of ancillary linkages and benefits for adaptation and mitigation through development interventions (NAPCC 2008). However, the national policy for climate change does not explicitly accept that the accumulated and future risks due to climate change need to be addressed (ibid).

TABLE 3.3 Bangalore climate risks and prospects for action

	Key risk	*Observations/evidence*	*Adaptation issues and prospects*	*Mitigation issues and prospects*	*Climatic drivers*
1	Terrestrial ecosystems and ecological infrastructure	Over 70% of Bangalore wetlands have disappeared since the 1970s, the result of cascading anthropogenic pressures and rapid urbanization (e.g. encroachment, diversification, pollution, illegal mining and quarrying). Groundwater levels in newly developed city peripheries without municipal supply have fallen steadily from withdrawal for private use and by private water tankers.	Lack of strong guidelines on wetland buffer zone demarcation is a barrier to wetland restoration and management. Low prospects for protection of green areas, urban wetlands, ground water resources and for more drainage systems. Inadequate zoning and building encroachment on natural drainage pathways means extreme rainfall exerts pressure on the existing ecological infrastructure. Low prospects due to unplanned urbanization.	Managing terrestrial ecosystems would moderate urban surface heat and reduce energy demand. Wetlands would improve groundwater levels, mean less energy consumption for ground water pumping. Energy demand for cooling needs could be addressed through existing laws (like the building code) and a viable market for energy-efficient products/services.	Extreme precipitation and rise in mean temperature. Significant increasing trend in frequency of rainy days per year and in one day extreme rainfall for 1901 to 2005. Mean increase of approximately 2 to 2.5°C during the last decade, attributed both to urban heat island effect and potential early climate signals.
2	Water supply waste water systems	Reduced availability of reliable good quality water supplies; increasing incidence of urban floods. Where groundwater levels are high, supplies are contaminated by wastewater from surface	Improved water resource management and water supply system efficiency. Medium prospects – some measures already being implemented. Increase in spatial coverage	Energy-intensive extraction of groundwater is expensive and generates additional carbon emissions Waste-to-energy conversion interventions affected by the quality of waste – medium prospects.	Drying trend, extreme precipitation Monsoon season and annual rainfall averages show an increasing trend for 1901 to 2000, most pronounced for 1951 to 2000.

continued ...

Table 3.3 continued

	Key risk	*Observations/evidence*	*Adaptation issues and prospects*	*Mitigation issues and prospects*	*Climatic drivers*
		water bodies and leaking sewer lines. Drainage systems unable to cope with increased water volume and blockage from indiscriminate solid waste disposal.	of sewerage (low prospects), improved onsite waste disposal systems (high prospects).		
3	Energy systems	Karnataka's energy intensity lower than the national average, but demand for electricity is likely to grow in Bangalore with expansion of the service sectors. Karnataka faces power deficit, relies heavily on imported energy. Some steps include strategic conservation action plan as per Energy Conservation Act (2001) guidelines through energy efficiency improvement/demand side management programs.	Replace centralized energy source with decentralized solar energy. Very high prospects, huge potential for employment generation, reduced dependence on biomass-based energy, conservation of terrestrial ecosystems. But land may be a critical constraint. Improved solid waste management systems to help maintain existing and new drainage systems. High prospects as new infrastructure is being built.	Need to augment energy-efficient measures, harness cleaner alternative energy sources (biomass, solar). Costly at present, but if resources are secured would provide a quick payback.	Drying and warming trends (leading to more energy demand).

4	Transportation and communications systems	Rising traffic congestion is a key issue; length of roads is good, but widths are restricted. Bus transport is good, but rail-based commuter system is marginal at present.	Design standards and development control in context of climate change. Low prospects – climate change issues yet to be mainstreamed in the sector.	Huge mitigation prospects in developing bus and rail with added benefits for air quality and energy security.	Extreme precipitation.
5	Housing	The number of informal settlements have grown significantly. Most will likely be affected by environmental shocks and stresses. A housing backlog, although a higher percentage of permanent and semi-permanent structures than in many Indian cities.	New building codes, effective development control and upgrading of informal settlements. Some measure already being taken into account; but increasing densities and land prices leave people with limited choice. Many are forced to live in exposed or low lying areas, with minimal access to basic services.	New housing stock could use sustainable energy design, less energy-intensive building material, decentralized energy technology. High prospects with appropriate incentives.	Warming trend, extreme precipitation.
6	Human health	Deteriorating local air quality, poor drainage (in extreme rainfall events), lack of sanitation facilities, settlements in more exposed and low lying areas are all critical for better human health outcomes.	Improvement of water supply, solid waste management, housing, land use planning, food security and provision of health insurance. Medium prospects; these require a lot of financial resources.	Improvement in public transport infrastructure would mean better local air quality and health benefits.	Warming and drying trends, extreme temperature and precipitation.

continued …

Table 3.3 continued

	Key risk	*Observations/evidence*	*Adaptation issues and prospects*	*Mitigation issues and prospects*	*Climatic drivers*
7	Key economic sectors and services	Benefits of Bangalore's rapid growth have not been spread equally across all socio-economic classes. Poor drainage in extreme rainfall events, health risks in unserved settlements may cripple economic activity.	Improvement of storm drains and transportation networks. Use of clean energy for power generation. A mixture of high and low prospects due to availability of technology but huge investment requirements.	New infrastructure provides opportunity to use clean and more efficient energy options – very high prospects in energy efficiency by just implementing good planning procedures/tools.	Drying trend, extreme temperature and precipitation.
8	Poverty and access to basic services	People and households are exposed to a range of risks due to increasing densities, location of habitation and varying degrees of access to basic infrastructure facilities and resources.	Formalizing informal economic sector, upgrading of informal settlements, improving housing conditions, empowering local communities to tackle problems related to climate change. High prospects, already being implemented as a development issue.	Formalizing informal activities, improving basic infrastructure would create market demand for clean energy products. Empowering local communities would create opportunities that utilize economies of scale for clean energy projects and contribute to GHG mitigation. Huge prospects as large market can bring down cost of implementation.	Warming and drying trends and extreme precipitation and temperature.

The Jawaharlal Nehru National Urban Renewal Mission (JNNURM) was launched in 2005 to address infrastructure deficits in cities, reduce urban poverty and improve urban governance. Important objectives included measures addressing water supply, sanitation, storm water drainage, solid waste management, urban transport, and renewal of core urban areas, preservation of heritage sites and water bodies, integrated development of slums and provision of basic services to the urban poor. These same interventions were the primary urban response to emergent risks from climate change. Some notable progress made in the transport sector emerged as a result of the National Urban Transport Policy (NUTP), launched as part of JNNURM, aimed at comprehensive improvements in urban transport infrastructure including public transport to improve mobility and economic opportunities for the urban poor and reduce air pollution. City governments have also been required to reform governance and management, with initiatives including a community participation law, reformed rent control, reasonable user service charges, and secure tenure at affordable prices (NUTP 2006).

The 2008 National Action Plan on Climate Change (NAPCC) has eight missions (including for instance the National Mission on Sustainable Habitat and the National Water Mission) which map out long-term, integrated strategies towards national goals around climate change. It aims to reduce the vulnerabilities of the poor while maintaining high growth for improved living standards through sustainable development pathways that advance both economic and environmental objectives. Strategies include deployment of appropriate technologies, use of innovative markets, regulatory and voluntary mechanisms, and linkages between various governance actors (e.g. civil society, local government institutions and private bodies).

The Eleventh Five Year Plan, commenced in 2007, was marked by special energy-related challenges – a sharp rise in international oil and coal prices and the need for large-scale energy efficiency measures to ensure sustained economic growth and to address global climate change threats through mitigation. Emphasis was on renewable energy and energy efficiency through a mix of policies on incentives/disincentives, regulation and management reform. These measures stayed largely out of the domain of city government (Eleventh Five Year Plan 2007–2012).

In 2009, states and union territories were called on to prepare plans to implement NAPCC missions, aligning them with state and city development priorities in the respective state level plans (referred to as the State Action Plan on Climate Change; SAPCC). Based on Ministry of Environment and Forests (MoEF) guidelines, a common framework emphasized city and state adaptation needs and vulnerabilities that had not received much attention in the national plan. Guiding principles included sustainable pro-poor development strategies, development and growth interventions with mitigation co-benefits, ecologically sustainable practices, promotion of knowledge and research in building climate scenarios, cost-effectiveness and feasibility of various adaptation and mitigation options, and the creation of an enabling environment for NAPCC implementation at state level.

The Government of Karnataka (GoK) also strategized a state urban development policy (KSUDP 2008), guided by the mandate for devolution and the ongoing urban renewal program. The policy adopted a holistic view aimed at improving the economic base of cities with a focus on equity. None of the state provisioning programs (access to basic services and housing, livelihoods) have explicitly addressed either urban vulnerability or risk mitigation (Revi 2008). The GoK did, however, pass legislation in 2005 on disaster management and instituted the Karnataka State Disaster Management Authority (KSDMA) to create frameworks for coping with natural disasters (climate-induced or not), a departure from earlier planning notions and a positive move in preparing settlements and regions for extreme rainfall events.[3]

Adaptation and mitigation activities in Bangalore

Climate change is an agenda that has failed to capture the state and local government imagination in Bangalore. The agreement and buy-in at higher levels of government is not reflected locally. Most climate change-related action here is a function of centrally sponsored schemes and programs or is managed at the state level through dedicated programs that transcend city boundaries.

In some other case study cities, local attention to climate change developed in tandem with higher level processes; but there are a number of reasons for the lack of city-level attention in Bangalore. As in several other Indian cities, the ability of the municipal government to tackle local challenges, including climate change impacts, is very limited. A lack of technical capacity has been a major hindrance to an awareness of climate change as a key concern, and this has been compounded by the pronounced mismatch in the functioning of multiple levels of government. Authority is widely dispersed among several city and other connected para-statal agencies, often leading to problems of jurisdictions and responsibility. While there is a recognition of the enhanced vulnerability of sectors, people and systems due to climate change, an appropriate and structured institutional response at the city level is yet to emerge. The lack of attention to climate change also relates directly to the economic-growth-first development path prioritized by the city over the years, an orientation that does not take into account both adaptation and mitigation concerns.

Another problem has been the lack of clarity within the State Climate Change Action Plan (SAPCC 2012). All states, as noted, were advised to prepare these plans in 2009, and this was the lowest level in India's federal structure at which climate action plans have been initiated. The Government of Karnataka (GoK), through a rapid assessment, found that most local and state-wide actions were responding primarily to development concerns without explicitly responding to climatic challenges. Addressing climate change was considered to derive from development interventions rather than needing to be an explicit consideration in its own right. The Karnataka Climate Change Action Plan is at this point pending approval with the Central Ministry of Environment, Forests and Climate Change. According to the Plan, the "scope and nature of actions were primarily confined to mitigation options" (SAPCC 2012, p.26). Other highlighted priorities focus on the agriculture and water sectors at the regional level and there is much less attention to the specific problems within Bangalore or other urban areas. The proposed actions, in addition, are loosely defined and lack dedicated financial support.

Most city-level interventions in Bangalore (primarily driven by the National Urban Renewal Mission) have been aimed at upgrading city-level infrastructure.[4] However, even here the pace has not been encouraging and changing political regimes mean changes in priorities are inevitable. The new urban renewal mission appears to aim at addressing key city vulnerabilities, improving resource use efficiency and creating robust city economies. However, integration of city development plans with the climate change agenda is clearly missing, and a more explicitly defined response is desirable.

Some key state initiatives related to climate change risks that are being implemented in Bangalore are listed here:

1 *Water resources:* the use of rainwater harvesting is mandatory in residential and commercial buildings in certain areas; the Karnataka Groundwater legislation, enacted in 2011, requires better protection of groundwater resources; in new layouts dual piping is mandatory for use of treated water; the National Lake and River conservation program requires the establishment of decentralized wastewater treatment systems.
2 *Forestry and biodiversity:* there are active plantation drives and development of carbon sinks and potential; protection of forests.
3 *Energy:* there is now mandatory use of solar water heaters, efficient provision of lighting and pumping technology, integration of energy efficiency and renewable energy in new buildings; incentives for the installation of solar water heater through tariff discounts; special tariffs for power purchase from renewable energy sources; decision to introduce a Green Energy Cess of INR 0.05 per kWh on commercial and industrial consumers; Solar Karnataka Program for 25,000 solar rooftops with net metering; CNG pipeline work is in progress and an effort towards pursuing natural gas deployment in Karnataka; the extensive use of solar streetlights in Bangalore.
4 *Specific to urban areas:* waste management in urban local bodies; promotion of public transport through better planning for bicycles and pedestrians in Bangalore; replacement of 2-stroke auto rickshaws with 4-stroke; a proposal for high speed rail to Bangalore International Airport.
5 *A case of evictions for environmental rejuvenation*: on concerns regarding encroachment of common property resources raised by the Supreme Court of India and a Bangalore-based civil society litigation, focused on removing encroachments on the lake bed and restoring the city's hydrological balance,

> the local government initiated the process of eviction in April 2015. These encroachments, over a 34-acre area of the lake bed, included a private dental college, 30 commercial complexes, a BBMP road and over 80 residential buildings. This initiative is expected to contribute to rejuvenating the city's lake system, although the question of who pays and who benefits is still unclear.

These initiatives are being implemented by a range of institutions, both local and parastatal, and their effectiveness has not, on the whole, been gauged.

One significant area for Bangalore that has seen an action by local government and higher levels is attention to lakes and wetlands. Realizing the importance of lakes for the sustenance of the city's water supply and other ecosystem services, in 2002, an autonomous body, the Lake Development Authority (LDA) was established by the Government of Karnataka, to take charge of a previously designed reinvigoration plan guided by the National Lake Conservation Authority and the Karnataka State Pollution Control Board (KSPCB). The local government has embarked on planned initiatives for the development of 17 lakes, at the same time undertaking the maintenance of 11 existing lakes. There are also regulations to promote and manage open spaces and green spaces. The absence of well-defined guidelines on the demarcation of wetland buffer zones has been identified by the local and regional government as a major barrier to wetland restoration and management.

While there has been an increasing recognition of climate change by various civil society groups in the city, the focus on the part of local government has primarily been on ensuring the provision of quality public services. There have been some notable interventions in Bangalore, driven by non-state actors, mostly operating at smaller urban scales but with significant impacts. Most of the initiatives respond to sustainability and environmental challenges, while also addressing key risks to the city. For example, Embarq India[5] has been influencing the statutory processes around interlinked aspects of integrated transport management, economic development, health and well-being in Bangalore. The SELCO Foundation is implementing action research projects targeted at building the adaptive capacities of the urban poor in Bangalore, focusing on energy and livelihood security.[6] Promotion of clean energy has been an important agenda for non-state actors and Bangalore has seen many such initiatives implemented at smaller scales or in pilot. For example, SELCO and Pollinate Energy have been actively engaged in this space.[7] A few emerging cases with potential for scalability are emerging from the "private" space. Such interventions are driven by negligible or no carbon emissions, closely linked with energy and resource use efficiency throughout the building life cycle. Another notable initiative led by a network of private enterprises, NGOs and think tanks (called Fem S3, supported by the ELCITA – Electronic City's Industrial Township Authority) and working within the administrative jurisdiction of the IT park in Bangalore (called the Electronic City) have launched a number of socially relevant business models for better waste management, wastewater treatment and recycling within Electronic City. Such networks are also engaged in risk mitigation activities for the urban poor by participating in various development projects.[8]

The city's water sector has attracted a lot of attention, even on the part of multilateral organizations; and it remains a key priority for the city. Most of the action in the sector is focused on ensuring the creation of sustainable water supply systems, and a consideration of climate change as a distortion on the supply side is yet to take firm root.

The energy efficiency sector has, however, seen a relatively higher degree of focus in the city. The period 2007–2012 saw the initiation of many energy conservation programs at the national level. These initiatives include standards for equipment and appliances, energy efficiency in buildings (a national energy conservation building code (ECBC) has been prepared for the design of new commercial buildings), energy efficiency in industry, and measures related to improving efficiency in residential lighting. The private real-estate sector in Bangalore is required to adhere to the new energy conservation guidelines and is proactively earning building certifications like LEED and GRIHA. The process of obtaining these certifications has yet to gather real momentum, but this augurs well for the future.

Future directions

Bringing together the adaptation and mitigation agendas around climate change has been explicitly highlighted as an objective in the recent IPCC Assessment Report 5 (Revi et al. 2014; Seto et al. 2014). But in order to reach the point where this is a feasible objective within Bangalore, there is still some distance to go. The city, to start with, has no explicit official climate change agenda. Its current development pathway is focused on economic growth, clearly not a conducive foundation for either adaptation or mitigation. Ineffective governance remains a key barrier to addressing the dynamics of risk in the city, and to developing a more comprehensive and integrated response to the complexities of climate change.

While the constraints are significant, the situation also offers an opportunity for city leadership. It is essential to identify the key climatic and non-climatic risks that the city faces, in light of the dynamic changes in the urban structure and form, and to ensure that awareness and understanding within the local government structures are enhanced. A clearly defined response framework to the comprehensive risk context, particularly in the light of current development challenges and social inequities, will be critical in moving Bangalore towards a sounder trajectory. Bringing adaptation, mitigation and development together would offer a constructive lens through which sustainable transitions can be framed and operationalized, with a clear emphasis on effective governance processes as a critical lever.

Notes

1 Bangalore officially became Bengalaru in 2014, but we are referring to it still as Bangalore in this chapter.
2 Authors' calculations – using 2007 fuel-consumption as the base, the authors made a quick calculation of carbon emissions for 2030 from energy use. The underlying technological structure was left unchanged and specific drivers were used to estimate energy use across residential, commercial, industry, transport and agriculture sectors. For residential use, population and household size was used as the driving variable. For commercial, industry and agriculture sectors, value-add from the sector was used as the driver, while population rates were used to estimate energy demand from the transport sector. In the transport sector, the underlying modal split, trip length and trip rates were untouched.
3 Karnataka State Disaster Management Authority (KSDMA) www.ksdma.co.in/
4 National Urban Renewal Mission http://jnnurm.nic.in/
5 World Resource Institute's center for sustainable transport ongoing work http://embarqindia.org/
6 Selco Foundation www.selcofoundation.org/
7 Pollinate Energy is a social business model, involving community volunteers (called energy pollinators in this initiative) who are trained to carry forward the work of distributing clean energy appliances (both for lighting and cooking) and in the process create green jobs for community members. At present more than 250 communities in the city have gained from this venture.
8 Addressing sanitation, affordable housing, micro insurance and financial schemes for the poor in and around the city.

References

Benjamin, Solomon (2000), "Governance, economic settings and poverty in Bangalore", *Environment and Urbanization* Vol 12, No 1, pages 35–56.

Benjamin, Solomon, R Bhuvaneswari, and S Aundhe (2006), "Urban futures of poor groups in Chennai and Bangalore: How these are shaped by the relationships between parastatals and local bodies", in N G Jayal, A Prakash and P K Sharma (editors) *Local Governance in India: Decentralization and Beyond,* New Delhi, 154 pages.

CDP (2009), *Comprehensive Development Plan*, Report prepared for KUIDFC, 183 pages, available at http://218.248.45.169/download/pds/finalcdp.pdf

Census (2011), *Census of India 2011: Karnataka, District Census Handbook: Bangalore, Directorate of Census Operations Karnataka*, available at www.censusindia.gov.in/2011census/dchb/2918_PART_B_DCHB_BANGALORE.pdf

Directorate of Economics and Statistics (2015), Sectoral Composition of GSDP, Policy document, Karnataka, Government of India, available at http://des.kar.nic.in/docs/sip/GSDP_NSDP2015.pdf

Economic Survey of India (2014), Report prepared for Union Government, India, available at http://indiabudget.nic.in/survey.asp

Eleventh Five Year Plan (2007–2012), Policy document, India: Planning Commission, Government of India, available at http://planningcommission.nic.in/plans/planrel/11thf.htm

Goldman, Michael (2011), "Speculative urbanism and the making of the next world city", *International Journal of Urban and Regional Research* Vol 35, No 3, pages 555–581.

Guhathakurta, P, O P Sreejith and P A Menon (2011), "Impact of climate change on extreme rainfall events and flood risk in India", *Journal of Earth System Science* Vol 120, No 3, pages 359–373.

IIHS (2014), "Future proofing Indian cities: Bangalore Action Plan for Green-Blue Infrastructure", in *Future Proofing Indian Cities*, Indian Institute for Human Settlements.

Karnataka State Action Plan on Climate Change (SAPCC) (2012), Policy document. Bangalore: Department of Ecology & Environment, available at www.empri.kar.nic.in/Karnataka-SAPCC-EMPRI-TERI-2012-03-22.pdf

Karnataka State Urban Development Policy (KSUDP) (2008), Policy document. Bangalore: Urban Development, available at http://cistup.iisc.ernet.in/Urban%20Mobility%208th%20March%202012/urban%20development%20policy%20for%20karnataka.pdf

Mahadevia, Darshini (2008), "Metropolitan employment in India", in D Mahadevia (editor), *Inside the Transforming Urban Asia: Policies, Processes and Public Actions*, New Delhi: Concept, 37 pages.

Nair, Janaki (2005), *The Promise of the Metropolis: Bangalore's Twentieth Century*, Oxford University Press, USA.

National Action Plan on Climate Change (NAPCC) (2008), Policy document, India: Ministry of Environment, Forest and Climate Change, available at http://envfor.nic.in/ccd-napcc

National Urban Transport Policy (NUTP) (2006), Report prepared for Ministry of Urban Transport, Karnataka, 22 pages, available at www.urbantransport.kar.gov.in/National%20Urban%20TransportPolicy.pdf

Ramachandra, T V and B H Aithal (2015), "GHG footprint of major cities in India", *Renewable and Sustainable Energy Reviews* Vol 44, No 1, pages 475–495.

Ramachandra, T V and U Kumar (2010),"Greater Bangalore: emerging urban heat island", *GIS Development* Vol 14, No 1, pages 86–104.

Ranganathan, M, L Kamath and V Baindur (2009), "Piped water supply to Greater Bangalore: putting the cart before the horse?", *Economic and Political Weekly,* pages 53–62.

Revi, A (2008), "Climate change risk: an adaptation and mitigation agenda for Indian cities", *Environment and Urbanization* Vol 20, No 1, pages 207–229.

Revi, A, D E Satterthwaite, F Aragón-Durand, J Corfee-Morlot, R B R Kiunsi, M Pelling, D C Roberts and W Solecki (2014), "Urban areas", in *Climate Change 2014: Impacts, Adaptation, and Vulnerability. Part A: Global and Sectoral Aspects. Contribution of Working Group II to the Fifth Assessment Report of the Intergovernmental Panel on Climate Change*, United Kingdom and New York, Cambridge University Press, 77 pages.

Seto K C, S Dhakal, A Bigio, H Blanco, G C Delgado, D Dewar, L Huang, A Inaba, A Kansal, S Lwasa, J E McMahon, D B Müller, J Murakami, H Nagendra and A Ramaswami (2014) "Human settlements, infrastructure and spatial planning", in *Climate Change 2014: Mitigation of Climate Change. Contribution of Working Group III to the Fifth Assessment Report of the Intergovernmental Panel on Climate Change*, United Kingdom and New York, Cambridge University Press, 77 pages.

State Action Plan on Climate Change (SAPCC) (2012), Policy document. Bangalore: Department of Environment and Forest, available at www.moef.nic.in/sites/default/files/sapcc/Karnataka.pdf

State of Environment Report (SoER) (2008), prepared for Ministry of Environment and Forest – Karnataka, 374 pages, available at http://parisaramahiti.kar.nic.in/pubs/State-of-Environment-Report-Bangalore-2008.pdf

Sudhira, H S, T V Ramachandra and M H Bala Subrahmanya (2007), "Bangalore", *Cities* Vol 24, No 5, pages 379–390.
Sundaresan, J (2011), "Planning as commoning: Transformation of a Bangalore lake", *Economic and Political Weekly* Vol 46, No 50, pages 71–79.
United Nations Development Program (UNDP) (2009), Annual Work Plan, Report prepared for Ministry of Environment and Forest, Government of India, available at www.undp.org/content/dam/undp/documents/projects/IND/00047625_Project%20 Document%20-%2057405.pdf

4

BANGKOK, THAILAND

Shobhakar Dhakal and Ashish Shrestha

Introduction

Bangkok, the capital of the Kingdom of Thailand, is a nationally and regionally important coastal city, located in the flat deltaic plain of the Chao Phraya River basin adjacent to the Gulf of Thailand. The area is flat and low-lying, with an average elevation of only 1.5 meters above mean sea level. The city faces considerable environmental management problems, including air and water pollution, solid waste management, flood and storm water management. These problems are being exacerbated by climate change, along with population growth and in-migration, the over-consumption patterns of urbanites, competitive economic growth and globalization. Flooding is a particular concern. Bangkok is expected by 2070 to rank seventh among the world's cities in terms of population exposed to coastal flooding (over 5 million people), and tenth in terms of the assets exposed (around 1,117 billion USD) (OECD 2007).

History of expansion

Bangkok, one of the largest cities of Southeast Asia, started expanding and industrializing in the 1960s and the past two decades have been particularly crucial to its economic and physical growth, as to that of other Southeast Asian megacities. The city, which occupies 1,568.74 km^2, is administered within Greater Bangkok or the Bangkok Metropolitan Region (BMR), an urban agglomeration that includes the city and five provinces (Nonthaburi, Samut Prakan, Pathum Thani, Samut Sakhon and Nakhon Pathom) into which Bangkok expanded in recent decades. Together they cover 7,761.50 km^2 (Figure 4.1). Between 1986 and 2002, residential areas in Bangkok more than doubled from 181 to 366 km^2 and the commercial area from 18 to 61 km^2. Agricultural land at the same time

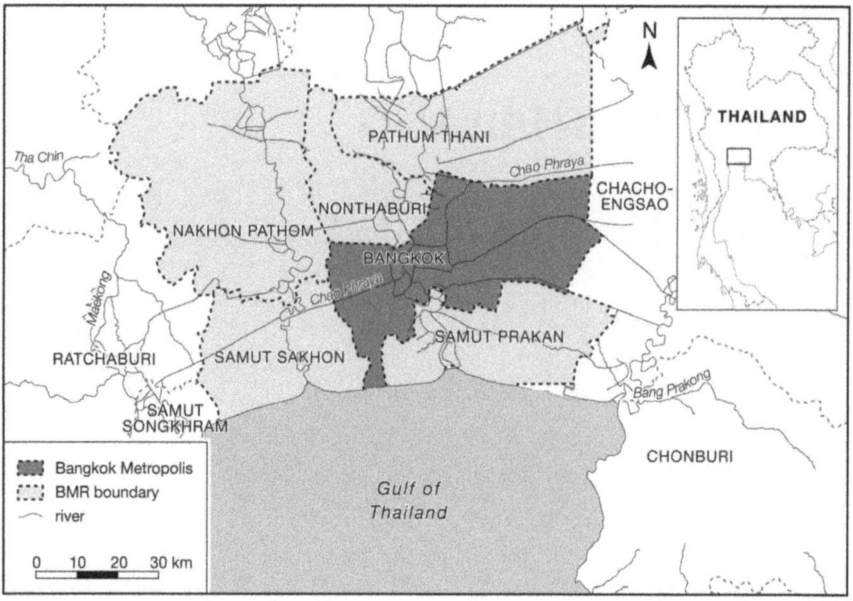

FIGURE 4.1 Map of Bangkok Metropolitan Region (BMR) showing Bangkok city and five adjoining provinces

decreased by 31 per cent and vacant land area by 39 per cent (Klongvessa and Chotpantarat 2015; BMA et al. 2009). Expansion in BMR was still more intense in the 2000s than in the 1990s (Estoque and Murayama 2015), and by 2009 built-up land accounted for approximately 20 per cent of BMR land area, more than 1,550 km^2.

The most recent census in 2010 put the population of the city of Bangkok at about 8.2 million, and that of the BMR at about 14.5 million, up about 30 per cent from 2000 in the city and about 43 per cent in the BMR as a whole.[1] These numbers include the large unregistered population, mostly composed of rural migrants, which makes up about one third of the total population. The formal registered population of Bangkok city peaked at 5.84 million in 2003 and decreased gradually to 5.7 million in 2013, at the same time that population was increasing in the neighboring provinces (BMA 2013). Reasons for higher population growth in vicinity provinces (both for registered and unregistered populations) are the increasing economic activities as the city expands outwards, and heavier in-migration from other provinces due to increasing employment opportunities. Population density (persons per km^2) in the city was 5,259 and 1,877 in the BMR in 2010 (NSO 2010).

Socio-economic context

The economic growth rate in Thailand, 8 to 9 per cent per year during the 1980s and 90s, has slowed down in recent years. It was about 5 per cent from 2002 to 2007, and the global financial crisis in 2008 and serious flooding in 2011 reduced the growth rate much further (World Bank 2015). In 2011, growth increased by only 0.1 per cent, despite projected growth of 3.8 per cent (Okazumi and Nakasu 2015). By 2014, growth was still only 0.7 per cent, but was projected to increase to 3.5 per cent in 2015, and to continue growing (World Bank 2015). Despite the slow recent growth rate, the World Bank upgraded the country to the upper-middle income category in 2011, based on its Gross National Income (GNI). Bangkok is ranked highest within Thailand on the Human Achievement Index (HAI) at 0.6974, placed especially high on sectors like health, education, income and travel/communication (UNDP 2014).

Despite its slower economic growth over the past two decades, the poverty level in Thailand decreased from 42.6 per cent in 2000 to 12.6 per cent in 2012. In BMR, formal poverty rates are low compared with both other developing Asian cities and the rest of Thailand, and only 0.6 per cent here were classified as living below the income poverty level of 51 USD per month in 2007 (World Bank 2009). This absolute poverty line, however, which is the same across Thailand, fails to take into account the high cost of living in the city. In fact, economic disparities are high, and about 20 per cent of the population is estimated to live in slum settlements, defined by the Bangkok Metropolitan Administration (BMA) as, "an overcrowded, non-orderly and dilapidated community with unample environment which can be harmful to health and lives and with a minimum of 15 housing units per 1,600 square meters" (UN Habitat 2003). By 1985, there were 1,020 slum settlements in Bangkok (Shummadtayar et al. 2013) and this had increased to 2,051 by 2013. The slum population, much of it unregistered, numbered 2.08 million in 2013, up from 1.96 million in 2009 (BMA 2009, 2013). Some slum dwellers have benefitted from government-supported upgrading programs, but many still squat on government or private land without the benefit of services (GNESD 2014). Many of these slum settlements are located alongside canals, exposed to flooding and to storm damage, and are especially vulnerable to the impacts because of poor provision for drainage and solid waste removal.

Governance

Thailand's administrative system has three levels: central, provincial and local. There are different types of local government, and Bangkok comes under the Special Local Administrations (SLA) category, which includes only the Bangkok Metropolitan Administration (BMA) and the city of Pattaya. This gives the BMA the same administrative status as a province. While national government is the central decision maker, BMA is authorized to take the lead in some important policy areas, particularly in land use, environment management, transport, water/wastewater and solid waste management. As part of its urban planning function, the BMA developed its Action Plan on Global Warming Mitigation 2007–2012 and has formulated a 10-year Master Plan on Climate Change 2013–2023, which covers both adaptation and mitigation but which has yet to be approved and implemented.

BMR consists of 50 districts under the authority of the BMA. Given its ongoing urban expansion, one of the governance challenges in Bangkok has been the gap between the functionally integrated central economic area and its far-flung administrative boundaries. The insufficient coordination between the city of Bangkok and its vicinity provinces makes it difficult to implement plans and strategies to cover the whole BMR, and highlights the need for better horizontal cooperation between local jurisdictions (OECD 2015).

Service provision

Service provision in Bangkok is generally strong, although there are significant backlogs in some services, and provision is especially poor in slum settlements that have not been upgraded. Accurate current figures are hard to come by for these settlements, however.

Residential and industrial water supplies in BMR are provided with a combination of surface and groundwater, the latter mainly in the outskirts of the city. The Metropolitan Waterworks Authority (MWA), a state-owned enterprise, supplies water primarily from the Chao Phraya and Mae Klong rivers to Bangkok City, Nonthaburi and Samut Prakan, about 81 per cent of the total serviced area (the Provincial Waterworks Authority (PWA) supplies water to the other BMR provinces). In 2006, MWA met about 91 per cent of the total residential, industrial and commercial demand in its coverage area (4.66 million cubic meters per day) from surface water sources. The remaining 9 per cent was met from deep wells (Polprasert 2007), largely extracted by private users and industries, since the Groundwater Act of 1997 prohibits MWA from abstracting groundwater because of the problem of land subsidence (Chiplunkar et al. 2012). It is not clear whether the demand figures include slum settlements, which in 2003 were estimated to be 97 per cent covered (Pornchokchai 2003). Total water consumption per capita water was 440 liters per day in 2013 (OECD 2015).

Coverage for sanitation and wastewater treatment is less comprehensive than for water. BMR currently has seven central wastewater treatment plants (WWTPs), treating almost a million cubic meters per day of domestic wastewater and serving an area of 196 km^2. These are supplemented by 12 additional small community WWTPs. Only 46 per cent of wastewater is treated overall, and the remainder is discharged into canals (OECD 2015). A centralized sanitation service in 1998 served only 2.34 per cent of the population. Coverage has grown rapidly, but still served only 55 per cent by 2008 (Chiplunkar et al. 2012). The remainder of Bangkok's residents make use of on-site solutions such as septic systems.

Solid waste generation in Bangkok was 1.75 kg/capita/day in 2013, up from an average of 1.55 kg/capita/day from 2003–2007, of which 99 per cent was being collected; 10,000 tons of municipal solid waste are collected every day, 89 per cent of which is disposed in sanitary landfills. There is little recycling, and proposals to reduce the per capita amount of waste have not so far been successful (World Bank 2009; OECD 2015). The available figures do not include slum settlements, 58 per cent of which were estimated to be served in 2003 (Pornchokchai 2003).

Bangkok is well served with electricity, the consumption of which has grown very rapidly. Even slum settlements are fully connected (albeit in many cases with illegal connections). Electricity supply for Thailand is the responsibility of the Electricity Generation Authority of Thailand (EGAT), which in 2014 was responsible for 45 per cent of the country's gross energy generation. Electricity is also purchased from independent domestic producers (IDPs) and imported from neighboring countries. EGAT sells electricity to electricity distribution bodies, including the Metropolitan Electricity Authority (MEA) which supplies Bangkok city, and the Provincial Electricity Authority, which is responsible for all other provinces.

Total electricity consumption in the MEA service area increased from 2002 to 2013 by 16 per cent from 41,482 GWh to 47,984 GWh. The residential sector accounted for 24 per cent of total electricity consumed in the MEA service area in 2013 (EPPO 2014), and per capita consumption increased from 4.6 MWh in 2002 to 6 MWh/p in 2012, higher than that in Paris (5.01 MWh) or China (5.9 MWh) (OECD 2015).

GHG emissions

Thailand contributes 1 per cent of the total GHG emission worldwide, and average per capita emissions are lower than the global average. However, total CO_2 emissions in Bangkok (which undertook its first GHG inventory in 2000), are 42.65 million tons per annum, close to that of cities like London (44 million ton per annum) or New York (48 million tons per annum). Per capita CO_2 emissions in Bangkok are 7.1 tons a year, higher than that in New York (5.7 tons) (BMA et al. 2009).

Electricity use is responsible for 33 per cent of Bangkok's CO_2 emissions – as noted above, electricity consumption has increased considerably. The energy mix for generation in Thailand includes natural gas (66.91 per cent), coal (20.11 per cent), hydropower (2.92 per cent), bunker oil and diesel (1.07 per cent), biomass and renewable energy (2.24 per cent) and imported energy (6.91 per cent) (EGAT 2014).

The Bangkok transportation sector has been responsible for about 38 per cent of CO_2 emissions. In 2007 it consumed an estimated 8,948,683 million liters of

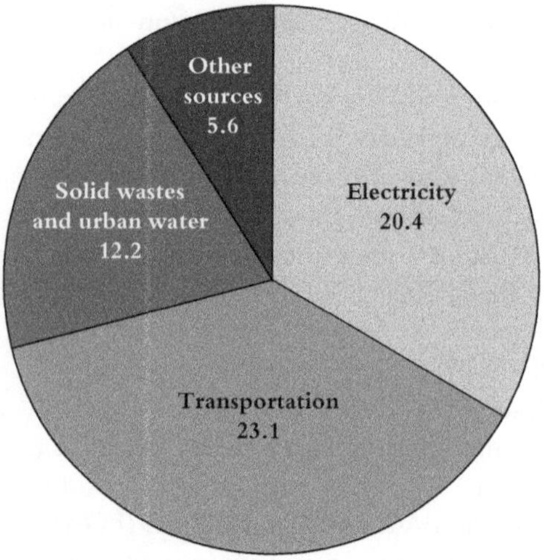

FIGURE 4.2 GHG inventory in Bangkok, 2007, millions tons CO_2 (data source: BMA, 2009)

gasoline and diesel with CO_2 emissions of 23.07 million tons annually (BMA et al. 2009). Methane from solid waste landfill and wastewater is another source of GHG emissions, estimated at 12.16 million tons of CO_2 equivalent annually or almost 20 per cent of total emissions. Solid waste in the city is estimated to have increased from 6,634 tons per day in 1995 to 8,718 tons per day in 2007 (BMA et al. 2009) and to 8,930 tons per day in 2011, with food waste responsible for over 42 per cent and plastics responsible for over 21 per cent of this. Notably after the 2011 flood, the solid waste collected increased to 12,000 tons per day with excess waste damaged furniture and electrical equipment (BMA 2012). A study by the Asian Institute of Technology shows that Bangkok's energy footprint in the urban water sector, which also contributes to CO_2 emissions, is 0.21 to 0.25 kwh/m^3 and for wastewater is 0.09 to 0.2 kwh/m^3 (Dhakal 2015). The remaining 9 per cent of Bangkok's GHG emissions are from miscellaneous sources such as rice fields, canals, etc., totaling 5.58 million tons of CO_2 equivalent annually (Figure 4.2).

Transport, as is the case in many cities, has been responsible for the greatest share of GHG emissions. By the end of 2014, there were over 8,600,000 vehicles in Bangkok city. About 40 per cent of these were sedans, about 38 per cent motorcycles, 18 per cent microbuses, passenger vans and taxis, and the remainder buses, trucks and other vehicles. These numbers represented an overall vehicle increase of about 34 per cent since 2010, mostly in sedans and motorcycles, which increased by 50 per cent and 26 per cent respectively (Department of Land Transport 2014). Cars are the major emitters of carbon monoxide (CO), hydrocarbons, and nitrous oxide (NO_x), while CO and particulate matter (PM) emissions from two-stroke motorcycles are also a source of air pollution, but this type of motorcycle is decreasing in number. Diesel trucks (both heavy and light duty) are responsible for high emissions of PM, NO_x, CO and hydrocarbons.

Around 2006, CO levels were found to have declined slightly, despite a yearly increment of vehicles. Fleet modernization, enforcement of emission standards, reduced traffic congestion and improvements in fuel quality all made a difference. Between 1992 and 2005, roadside measurements of CO levels in Bangkok showed steady reduction, and annual ambient levels in 1992 were not very different from those for 2003 and 2004 (BMA et al. 2009; ADB and CAI-Asia 2006). Air quality, which had been improving in several parts of Thailand up to 2012, worsened again in 2013.

Air pollution conditions in Bangkok are worse than in other parts of Thailand, and air pollutant (ozone) concentration exceeds standards. Particulate matter smaller than 10 microns (PM_{10}) was highest in Bangkok city and in Saraburi Province and the upper Northern provinces. In 2013, annual average PM_{10} concentrations in the metropolitan area were slightly lower than the standard threshold of 50 $\mu g/m^3$. Ozone (O_3) in the lower atmosphere, formed as a chemical reaction from primary air pollutants such as nitrous oxide (NO_x) and volatile organic compounds (VOCs) including formaldehyde and acetaldehyde was found to be increasing in relation to a rise in gasohol consumption. During 2013, the maximum one-hour average of O_3 in the whole BMR area was 140 $\mu g/m^3$, while the standard threshold is 100 $\mu g/m^3$. Similarly, the benzene concentration in the air in different parts of Bangkok from 2009 to 2013 was in the range 1.8 to 5 $\mu g/m^3$, while the standard threshold is 1.7 $\mu g/m^3$. Old automobiles in particular are major emitters of these pollutants. Power plants and factories are also responsible for pollution in nearby provinces (PCD 2014).

Climate trends and future projections

BMR has a tropical monsoon climate with three main seasons: rainy (May–October), cool (November–January), and hot (February–April). Average annual rainfall, occurring primarily between May and October, is approximately 1,500 mm. The river discharge normally increases in October. The temperatures are generally hot year round, ranging from an average low of 20.8°C in December to an average high of 34.9°C in April.

Projections for climate change impacts in Bangkok point primarily to an increase in the frequency and intensity of extreme events. Over recent decades, temperatures have increased relative to long-term averages. From 1991 to 2000, maximum average temperatures of Bangkok in the summer months were found to be significantly higher than the long-term average, and lowest temperatures in the winter months were also warmer than the long-term average (BMA et al. 2009). Between 1982 and 2010, the mean annual temperature in Bangkok was found to have increased at a rate of 0.06°C a year (Klongvessa and Chotpantarat 2015).

The maximum one-day rainfall at different stations in Bangkok was found mostly to have decreased between 1980 and 2010, except in dense commercial areas where the urban heat island effect was observed, and the higher return period rainfall increased (Klongvessa and Chotpantarat 2015). The increased frequency of higher return period rainfall events causes surface flooding in Bangkok.

While extreme rainfall events have increased in both frequency and intensity, Bangkok is also affected by prolonged periods of no precipitation and drought is increasingly becoming a problem. This is exacerbated by upstream river and dam management issues which affect water supply systems and hydropower plants. Based on the IPCC Special Report on Emissions Scenarios (SRES),[2] by 2050 under the A1F1 scenario, the mean (June–August) basin precipitation for Bangkok would increase by 3 per cent, temperature by 1.9°C and sea level by 0.29 meters. Under a B1 scenario, these figures would be 2 per cent, 1.2°C and 0.19 meters respectively (World Bank 2009). Future projections for rainfall in Bangkok city[3] all show average maximum daily rainfall increasing in all months from 2011 to 2065 compared with observed data in 1981 to 2010. In the A2 scenario, the 3-hour rainfall depth for a 20-year return period could increase up to 10–25 per cent in the period from 2046 to 2065 compared with 1981–2010 (Shrestha 2013). During the 2011 flood, the mean annual rainfall peaked, with a 24 per cent increase over normal (Noy 2015).

Climate change vulnerability and risks

The adverse impacts of climate change have been evident in many developmental sectors such as water, energy, health and built infrastructures. Some of the strongest evidence of the direct impacts is with regard to sea level rise, flooding, water availability and public health.

Sea level rise

BMR is located along the Upper Gulf of Thailand where the relative sea level rise is about 1–2 cm per year. The average value is 1.3 cm per year, of which 3 mm is related to actual sea level rise and 1 cm to land subsidence (World Bank 2009). By 2050, this could mean a combined sea level rise of 45 cm. The outcomes of a flood model simulation by BMA show that almost 55 per cent of Bangkok would be affected by floods if the mean sea level were to rise by 50 cm; if it rose by 100 cm, 72 per cent of the city would be affected. These levels are 16 and 34 per cent higher, respectively, than the areas inundated by the severe flooding in 1995 (Dutta 2007).

Flooding

As a coastal city with low elevation, BMR is topographically prone to flooding. Rapid urbanization in recent decades has meant changes in land use which have affected long-existing watercourses, canals and ponds. In the west of BMR, important cultural heritage sites along the river are also at risk. BMR has numerous networks of canals draining into the Chao Phraya River and the Gulf of Thailand. Most of these canals have poor water quality and this, combined with the risk of flooding, carries a significant public health hazard. The backwater flow at high tides can overflow the banks of the Chao Phraya delta during tidal surges and in the event of heavy runoff from upstream.

Severe floods occurred in Bangkok in 1942, 1983, 1995 and 2011. The flood in 2011, resulting from a heavy monsoon and tropical storm, was the worst Thailand had experienced in 50 years. The Chao Phraya River flooded and inundated 15 provinces, killing 744 people. Damage in agriculture, manufacturing and service industries decreased the country's GDP (market value) by about 1.1 billion USD and its economic growth for the year by 3.7 per cent. People living in the affected areas were displaced and educational institutions were closed for months. The city of Bangkok, because of its central importance to the country, benefitted from strong flood protection measures. But even here, 42 out of 50 districts in the city were under water for weeks, 73 per cent of the residents of low income communities were affected, and manufacturing and business sectors were very hard hit. Damage in the city alone was calculated in excess of 9 billion USD (OECD 2015).

Although flood protection projects have continued to be improved after the devastating floods in 1995 and 2011, Bangkok is still at increasing risk of flooding, and the approximately 907,000 people currently at risk is expected to increase to more than 5 million by 2070. The economic losses related to infrastructure that would be caused by such floods, estimated to be $39 billion currently, are expected to grow to a staggering $1.12 trillion by 2070 (BMA et al. 2009; OECD 2007).

Land subsidence plays a key role in increasing flood risks by affecting drainage, pumping efficiency and effectiveness of flood protection measures. The maximum subsidence is now occurring in outlying areas of Bangkok in the southeastern and southwestern industrial zones, where the phenomenon is taking place at the alarming rate of 30 mm per year. One reason for land subsidence is continued over-pumping of groundwater, despite a cabinet resolution in 1983 to regulate its abstraction.

Flood modeling in Sukhumvit, the core commercial area in Bangkok city, shows that under an A2 scenario for 2046–2065,[4] pluvial flood volume could increase by 10 to 11.9 per cent in 2-year return period rainfall events and 9.8 to 24.1 per cent in a 20-year return period, compared with flood volume in 2010 (Shrestha et al. 2014). The risk of fluvial flood from Chao Phraya River is high, and relevant city departments like the Department of Drainage and Sewerage in the BMA have put serious effort into preventive measures to eradicate the risk of possible flood damage to the inner city. However, pluvial flood risks persist here because of the combination of extreme local rainfall and massive built-up areas with impervious surfaces. The stormwater runoff is drained into canals which empty into Chao Phraya River. Depending on the water level in Chao Phraya, canal pumps come into operation. The current system could handle a 10-year return period rainfall event – anything more than that would be likely to result in flooding. In the past, some parts of Bangkok have suffered surface flooding when a 3-hour rainfall event exceeds 100 mm, and the duration of surface flooding lasts from 30 minutes up to 3 hours (Shrestha 2013). The design criteria of infrastructure have not been given high importance in most Thai cities, including Bangkok. The development of Bangkok's present and future Intensity, Duration and Frequency (IDF) curve, an important hydrological design tool, has shown that between 2046 and 2065, the rainfall depth at 3-hour duration could increase between 8.45 and 18.3 per cent in a 5-year event and from 10.76 to 24.09 per cent in a 20-year event, compared with the present-day IDF curve (1981–2010) in use (Shrestha et al. 2014; Shrestha 2013). There is a need to update design criteria for city infrastructure as a possible flood mitigation and adaptation strategy.

Water availability

The river hydrology pattern in Thailand is changing, and is characterized by flooding in the wet season and low flow in the dry season. More frequent and prolonged drought conditions during the dry season will make it impossible to meet even the city's current water demand. Water supply and management in Bangkok is influenced by the huge upstream watershed of Chao Phraya River, which currently supplies water to over 14 million people. In the event of drought, the city can reserve only a 30-day supply. The problems are intensified by the back water flow of seawater, which turns the river brackish. Since Bangkok is expected to grow further in future, water demand is expected to increase, along with problems of water supply and contamination of surface and ground water sources. With the increase in temperature, the water demand for drinking, agriculture and industry will also increase. The implications of climate change for the availability and quality of water will eventually necessitate changes in technology that may have further implications for energy use.

Urban heat island

Waste heat from vehicles, building air conditioners, and a vast increase in impervious built areas are contributing to the urban heat island (UHI) effect in Bangkok. This increase in ambient temperature means in turn increased energy use in air conditioning. The intensity of UHI in Bangkok is strongest during the dry season (November–April); and at night and early morning (Jongtanom et al. 2011). A peak intensity of almost 5°C was found when average hourly temperatures in Bangkok and Pathumthani, a non-urban province within BMR, were compared (Arifwidodo and Tanaka 2015). A 1°C increase in ambient air temperature in Bangkok can result in a 7.49 per cent increase in average monthly electricity consumption (Wangpattarapong et al. 2008), increasing the overall city's energy use and associated GHG emissions. The situation could be expected to worsen in a high global climate change regime.

Health

Climate change has numerous implications for health, both direct and indirect. Bangkok urbanites face exposure to flooding, drought, heat and the potential failure of infrastructure related to water, health care and transport services. Most vulnerable are low income groups and those living in slum settlements along canals, exposed to risk of flooding, and rendered still more vulnerable by their poor access to services. Both flooding and more extreme rainfall, as well as drought conditions, can affect the transmission of water-borne and water-washed disease. Vector-borne disease is also likely to be affected by changing temperatures. Dengue transmission, for example, is favored by high absolute humidity, which increases with high temperatures and rainfall (Campbell-Lendrum and Corvalán 2007). Urban heat island effects also have consequences for health. In addition to the detrimental effects of higher temperatures, there is also the increased demand for cooling, with higher energy consumption, higher emissions and resulting air pollution. One of the important pollutants of concern is PM, also linked (as noted above) to wide use of diesel-fueled vehicles and motorcycles. A study by Li and Crawford-Brown (2011) estimated that total health damage costs due to PM emissions in BMR in 2010 was equivalent to 2.4 per cent of Thailand's GDP, totaling 2,678 million USD. Under a business-as-usual (BAU) scenario, the health damage cost was projected to reach 2.5 times more in 2015. A 25 per cent reduction in PM_{10}, on the other hand, could yield a benefit of 1,484 million USD. A few other indirect health effects may arise, such as ground water contamination due to land subsidence, salt water intrusion, nitrates, coliform and volatile organic compounds.

Mitigation and adaptation strategies

In order to develop Bangkok as a sustainable low carbon and climate resilient metropolis, the Bangkok Metropolitan Administration (BMA) and Japan International Cooperation Agency (JICA) initiated a new study in 2012 to prepare the Bangkok Master Plan on Climate Change 2013–2023. This plan covers environmentally sustainable transport, energy efficiency and alternative energy, efficient solid waste management and wastewater treatment, green urban planning and adaptation planning. Although the plan was initially to take effect in 2013, the implementation has been delayed. But even in advance of the formal initiation of the master plan, the BMA has been engaged in a number of relevant activities, including capacity development for the implementation of the master plan, the Low Carbon Bangkok City Project in 2013, and targeting groups such as office buildings, schools and universities to improve building energy consumption efficiency.

The BMA also operates within the framework of other national level policies and plans including the Energy Efficiency Development Plan 2011–2030 and the Alternative Energy Development Plan, the National Master Plan on Climate

Change and Thailand Nationally Appropriate Mitigation Actions (NAMAs). The new Bangkok master plan aims to expand the scope of BMA activities to focus on adaptation and mitigation plans by partnering with different governance levels, public and private sectors and establishing monitoring and evaluation mechanisms as well as measurement, report and verification mechanisms. New targets for GHG reduction from key sectors in Bangkok (transport, energy, water and wastewater) are to be established.

The institutional arrangement for implementing this master plan consists of a steering committee, working group, task forces, BMA secretariat and external partners. The steering committee members have key roles in providing overall guidance, monitoring and evaluation and reviewing progress. Working groups will handle the technical issues and coordinate different task forces to implement action plans. Task forces are divided into different sub-sectors: transport, energy, water and wastewater, urban green planning and adaptation, to develop action plans and outreach activities. After approval of the draft master plan, yearly regular monitoring and evaluation and a comprehensive five-year review have been proposed. BMA is further prioritizing capacity development for BMA officials, stakeholders and inter-city cooperation in ASEAN.

Mitigation activities

In Bangkok, the mitigation work stream has developed in advance of serious attention to adaptation. Thailand has been a signatory to the United Nations Framework Convention on Climate Change (UNFCCC) since June 1992, and ratified the Convention in March 1995. The convention does not require Thailand to reduce greenhouse gas emissions, given its comparatively lower emissions than other industrialized countries. In the run-up to COP21, Thailand pledged to reduce greenhouse gas emission by 20–25 percent from the projected business-as-usual (BAU) level by 2030. However, comprehending the global impacts of climate change and the threat to the low-lying coastal and inland regions, Thailand has been contributing to international efforts.

Although Thailand's contribution to GHG emissions is relatively low, Bangkok, as indicated above, has high emissions relative to global norms. In 2007, BMA, along with 36 organizations, jointly signed a Declaration of Cooperation on Alleviating Global Warming Problems, highlighting five major strategies to mitigate global warming:

- reducing energy consumption and maximizing efficiencies in resource utilization in all activities to minimize global impacts as well as the considerable local effects of the city's high emissions;
- promoting and supporting all sectors and stakeholders to jointly reduce GHG emissions;
- promoting the sufficiency economy lifestyle to prepare for, and adapt to, global warming;

TABLE 4.1 BMA's Five-Year Action Plan, 2007 to 2012 (BMA 2012)

Initiatives	*Action plans*	*Target 5-year reduction of CO_2 by 2012 (million tons)*	*Total amount of actual CO_2 reduced (million tons)*
Expand mass transit and improve traffic system	• Expand the mass transit rail system within the Bangkok Metropolitan Area • Improve public bus system • Improve traffic system	5.53	1.01
Promote the use of renewable energy	• Promote the use of biofuels	0.61	0.88
Improve electricity consumption efficiency	• Improve building energy consumption efficiency • Electricity conservation campaign for residents	2.25	2.70
Improve solid waste management and wastewater treatment efficiency	• Increase efficiency in solid waste management • Increase efficiency in wastewater treatment	0.46	0.70
Expand park areas	• Plant trees in the Bangkok Metropolitan Area • Plant trees in the neighboring province areas	0.90	1.69

- promoting and supporting activities that lead to GHG absorption;
- promoting and supporting activities that continuously work to mitigate global warming by building public awareness and knowledge.

This declaration led BMA to develop its first five-year action plan on global warming mitigation, with ten actions plans (Table 4.1). The objective was to reduce overall GHG emissions between 2007 and 2012 by 15 per cent. The implemented actions have been crucial for addressing the objectives around climate change issues for other different government levels and organizations as well.

The GHG emission in 2007 of around 42.65 million tCO_2 equivalent was projected to reach 48.69 million by 2012 under a business-as-usual (BAU) scenario. The total targeted reduction of CO_2 for 2012 was 9.75 million tons, and of this, 72 per cent was achieved (BMA 2012).

Some of the issues BMA faced in implementing these actions plans are as follows:

- The mass transit system needed time to implement the project, including undertaking an Environmental Impact Assessment (EIA) report and the budget.
- Construction takes time, and some of the larger projects were not complete by 2012.
- There are constraints in the cost and ease of use of alternative energy, which is not yet widely applied.
- Renovation costs for existing buildings are high.
- There are management and continuity issues, and high costs in waste and wastewater management in the whole of Bangkok.
- Expanding green areas in Bangkok is constrained by the high value of land and the availability of space. However, between 2009 and 2012, the number of public parks increased from 24 to 31, with a total area of 2685 ha, still very low compared to the average Asian city.

Some of the proposed mitigation measures in the new master plan for the transport sector include expansion of public transport infrastructure with improvements in connectivity and promotion of measures, such as common ticket systems to encourage use of public vehicles. The use of low emission vehicles and expansion of bike lanes are also proposed. Energy use in buildings is resulting in huge CO_2 emissions and to address this issue BMA plans to implement such measures as retrofitting and renovation of existing facilities, and improving thermal insulation in government buildings. In commercial and residential buildings, the promotion of energy saving measures is also planned, with a program to conduct cost-benefit analyses and awareness. Although solid waste, water and wastewater sectors are lesser contributors to GHG emissions, reducing their emissions could greatly contribute to achieving the overall city target. BMA has plans to promote reduction of waste at source, fuel efficiency of waste collection/transport systems and energy recovery from waste. Other activities include promoting less water use, expanding wastewater collection systems, improving the efficiency of wastewater treatment equipment and utilizing treatment byproducts. Expansion of the city's green area and its long-term management are being proposed in mitigation plans with effective mechanisms and awareness campaigns.

Adaptation measures

In the adaptation component of the Bangkok Master Plan on Climate Change, the key focus is the looming risks from flooding, coastal erosion and other climate-related disasters. Several flood mitigation strategies have been implemented in BMR. BMA has installed giant pumps and instituted other measures such as dykes along the river and canals, which prevent much of the flooding that used to be an annual event. There are 369 pumping stations with a total capacity of 1,531 m^3, seven drainage tunnels, 19 km long, and 155 m^3 of pumping capacity. Notably,

BMA's "Monkey Cheek" project has the capacity of 12.7 million m^3 for flood water retention. Other coastal areas have planted bamboo along the shoreline for protection against wave action, and have rehabilitated mangrove forests.

The new master plan will implement comprehensive adaptation plans to address flooding and coastal erosion. Measures, both structural and non-structural, include expansion and improvement of retention ponds, dredging canals, installing additional pumps, and improving pumping stations, water gates and flood dykes. Emergency preparedness plans and evacuation plans are also being prepared to minimize flood impacts. Similar adaptation measures for coastal erosion are proposed, involving improvement of dyke systems, and boosting mangrove forest plantation with local level participation.

On the other side of water management, sustainable water management options in Bangkok include increased harvesting of rainwater, decentralizing the wastewater management system, and synergistic interactions among government, private and community sectors (Polprasert 2007). There are as yet no significant actions on these fronts, however. As BMR is downstream of the Chao Phraya river basin, the upstream hydrology determines drought (and flood) conditions for BMR as well as other downstream provinces. The improvement in dam operations could minimize the impacts of drought. BMA has also proposed construction of reservoirs and measures to minimize city water usage.

Challenges and prospects

Bangkok plays a significant role in the regional and national spheres and it will continue to be central to the country's socio-economic development. It has the potential also to be a leading example in the region on developing a sustainable, low carbon and resilient city. Recent studies demonstrate that climate change in Bangkok is already apparent, and this low-lying delta megacity will be under even greater stress in the future. Especially given its ongoing expansion, climate compatible urban development is essential for Bangkok, on the one hand reducing GHG emissions, and on the other, reducing the implication of climate-change impacts through risk management. There are strong opportunities here for simultaneously reducing GHG emissions, improving public health, building positive economic growth, and keeping the population safe from climate-related hazards, through low carbon policies related to transport systems, urban planning, building regulations, household energy supply and environmental management. But all this requires a comprehensive planning response from Bangkok.

Expansion has complicated the administration of this vast metropolitan area, and strong institutional mechanisms will be crucial to implementing mitigation and adaption strategies effectively in BMR. This can be achieved through effective vertical and horizontal coordination among BMA, with central and local government, non-government organization, local stakeholders and other jurisdictions. Bangkok is taking many good initial steps, but it needs to move from this incremental approach to more integrated transformative change. The challenges for such transformative change are institutional arrangements, financial resources and technical challenges – but these are also the opportunities. Current mitigation and adaptation strategies are in place, playing an imperative role, and with new plans in the works, there are entry points for sustainable growth. Favorable policies, right technologies, and strong regulatory mechanisms could lead the city to a future defined by sustainable transport, green energy and low carbon growth. Given the existing challenges, and with experience from implementing the 2007–2012 global warming mitigation plan, the BMA, concerned city planners and other stakeholders will ideally address climate change with robust mitigation measures and adaptation strategies to create a resilient future city for all its citizens.

Notes

1 www.citypopulation.de/php/thailand-prov-admin.php?adm1id=B
2 In the 4th Assessment Report.
3 Using a downscaling tool, Long Ashton Research Station Weather Generator (LARS WG) (Semenov and Stratonovitch, 2010) and 15 GCM data incorporated into LARS WG under IPCC 4th Assessment Report's SRES – SRB1, SRA1B and SRA2 scenarios in the study by Shrestha (2013).
4 Based on output from GFCM21 and HADCM3 GCMs.

References

Arifwidodo, Sigit D and Takahiro Tanaka (2015), "The characteristics of urban heat island in Bangkok, Thailand", *Procedia – Social and Behavioral Sciences* Vol 195, pages 423–428.

Asian Development Bank (ADB) and Clean Air Initiative for Asian Cities (CAI-Asia) (2006), *Country Synthesis Report on Urban Air Quality Management*, Discussion Draft, December, available at www.cleanairnet.org/caiasia/1412/csr/thailand.pdf

Bangkok Metropolitan Administration (BMA) (2009), *Statistical Profile of Bangkok Metropolitan Administration 2009*, available at http://office.bangkok.go.th

Bangkok Metropolitan Administration (BMA) (2012), *Bangkok State of Environment 2012* (Revised Edition), available at http://office.bangkok.go.th

Bangkok Metropolitan Administration (BMA) (2013), *Statistical Profile of Bangkok Metropolitan Administration 2013*, available at http://office.bangkok.go.th

Bangkok Metropolitan Administration, Green Leaf Foundation and United Nations Environment Programme (BMA) (2009), *Bangkok Assessment Report on Climate Change 2009*. Bangkok: BMA, GLF and UNEP, available at http://ipcc-wg2.gov/njlite_download2.php?id=11024

Campbell-Lendrum, Diarmid and Carlos Corvalán (2007), "Climate change and developing-country cities: implications for environmental health and equity", *Journal of Urban Health* Vol 84 (Suppl. 1), 109–117.

Chiplunkar, Anand, Kallidaikurichi Seetharam and Cheon Kheong Tan (2012), *Good Practices in Urban Water Management: Decoding Good Practices for a Successful Future*. Asian Development Bank, Mandaluyong City, Philippines, available at www.adb.org/sites/default/files/publication/29888/good-practices-urban-water-management.pdf

Department of Land Transport (2014), Transport Statistics Sub-Division, Planning Division, Department of Land Transport, www.dlt.go.th/th/

Dhakal, Shobhakar (2015), "Water, energy and carbon nexus in cities", Presented at Scientific Research and Capacity Development Initiatives to Address Adaptation, Mitigation and Climate Resilience in Southeast Asia, APN side event in Regional Forum on Climate Change (RFCC), Asian Institute of Technology, 2 July 2015.

Dutta, Dushmanta (2007), "Flood vulnerability of coastal cities to sea level rise and potential socio-economic impacts: a case study in Bangkok", Paper presented at the Science and Practice of Flood Disaster Management in Urbanizing Monsoon Asia International Workshop, Chiang Mai, Thailand, 4–5 April 2007, available at www.sea-user.org/download_pubdoc.php?doc=3407

Electricity Generation Authority of Thailand (EGAT) (2014), *Annual Report 2014*, available at www.egat.co.th

Energy Policy and Planning Office (EPPO) (2014), *Energy Statistics of Thailand 2014*. Ministry of Energy, Royal Thai Government, available at www.eppo.go.th/info/cd-2014/Energy%20Statistics%20of%20Thailand%202014.pdf

Estoque, Ronald C and Yuji Murayama (2015), "Intensity and spatial pattern of urban land changes in the megacities of Southeast Asia", *Land Use Policy* Vol 8, pages 213–222.

GNESD (2014), *Country Report (Thailand). Energy Poverty in Developing Countries' Urban Poor Communities: Assessments and Recommendations. Urban and Peri-urban Energy Access III*. Report prepared for the Global Network on Energy for Sustainable Development by the Asian Institute of Technology (AIT). Roskilde, Denmark.

Jongtanom, Yenrutai, Charnwit Kositanont and Surat Baulert (2011), "Temporal variations of urban heat island intensity in three major cities, Thailand", *Modern Applied Science* Vol 5, no 5, pages 105–110.

Klongvessa, Pawee and Srilert Chotpantarat (2015), "Statistical analysis of rainfall variations in the Bangkok urban area, Thailand", *Arabian Journal of Geosciences* Vol 8, no 6, pages 4207–4219.

Li, Ying and Douglas J Crawford-Brown (2011), "Assessing the co-benefits of greenhouse gas reduction: Health benefits of particulate matter related inspection and maintenance programs in Bangkok, Thailand", *Science of the Total Environment* Vol 409, no 10, pages 1774–1785.

National Statistical Office Thailand (NSO) (2010), *Population and Housing Census 2010*, available at www.nso.go.th/.

Noy, Illan (2015), "Comparing the direct human impact of natural disasters for two cases in 2011: The Christchurch earthquake and the Bangkok flood", *International Journal of Disaster Risk Reduction* Vol 13, pages 61–65.

Okazumi, Toshio, and Nakasu Tadashi (2015), "Lessons learned from two unprecedented disasters in 2011 – Great East Japan Earthquake and Tsunami in Japan and Chao Phraya River flood in Thailand", *International Journal of Disaster Risk Reduction* Vol 13, pages 200–206.

Organization for Economic Co-operation and Development (OECD) (2007), *Ranking of the World's Cities Most Exposed to Coastal Flooding Today and in the Future*, available at www.oecd.org/env/cc/39721444.pdf

Organization for Economic Co-operation and Development (OECD) (2015), *Green Growth in Bangkok, Thailand,* OECD Green Growth Studies, OECD Publishing, Paris, available at http://dx.doi.org/10.1787/9789264237087-en

Pollution Control Department (PCD) (2014), *Thailand State of Pollution Report 2013. Pollution Control Department, Ministry of Natural Resources and Environment*, PCD. No.

06-053 ISBN 978-616-316-205-2, available at www.pcd.go.th/public/Publications/en_print_report.cfm ?task=en_report2556

Polprasert, Chongrak (2007), "Water environment issues of Bangkok city, Thailand: options for sustainable management", *ScienceAsia* Vol 33, no 1, pages 57–58.

Pornchokchai, Sopon (2003), *Global Report on Human Settlements 2003. City Report: Bangkok*, UN Habitat, Nairobi, available at www.thaiappraisal.org/pdfNew/HABITAT1new.pdf

Semenov, Mikhail A and Pierre Stratonovitch (2010), "The use of multi-model ensembles from global climate models for impact assessments of climate change", *Climate Research* Vol 41, pages 1–14.

Shrestha, Ashish (2013), *Impact of Climate Change on Urban Flooding in Sukhumvit Area of Bangkok*, Master Thesis, Asian Institute of Technology, Thailand.

Shrestha, Ashish, Mukand Singh Babel and Sutat Weesakul (2014), "Integrated modelling of climate change and urban drainage", *Managing Water Resources under Climate Uncertainty*, Springer Water 2015, pages 89–103.

Shummadtayar, Umpiga, Kazunori Hokao and Pawinee Iamtrakul (2013), "Investigating the low-income settlement in an urbanization and urban form a consequences of Bangkok Growing City, Thailand", *Lowland Technology International* Vol 15, no 1, pages 45–54.

United Nations Development Programme (UNDP) (2014), *Thailand Human Development Report: Advancing Human Development Through ASEAN Community*, ISBN: 978-974-680-368-7, Report prepared for UNDP, available at http://hdr.undp.org/sites/default/files/thailand_nhdr_2014_0.pdf

United Nations Human Settlements Programme (UN Habitat) (2003), *The Challenge of Slums: Global Report on Human Settlement*, ISBN: 1-84407-037-9, Report prepared for UN Habitat, available at www.unhabitat.org.jo/pdf/GRHS.2003.pdf

Wangpattarapong, Kiattiporn, Maneewan Somchai, Ketjoy Nipon and Rakwichian Wattanapong (2008), "The impacts of climatic and economic factors on residential electricity consumption of Bangkok Metropolis", *Energy and Buildings* Vol 40, no 8, pages 1419–1425.

World Bank (2009), *Climate Change Impact and Adaptation Study for Bangkok Metropolitan Region*, Final report by Panya Consultants Co. Ltd., available at http://documents.worldbank.org/curated/en/2009/03/11164992/climate-change-impact-adaptation-study-bangkok-metropolitan-region-final-report-vol-1-3

World Bank (2015), *Thailand Overview*, available at www.worldbank.org/en/country/thailand/overview

5

DAR ES SALAAM, TANZANIA

Robert Kiunsi

Introduction

Dar es Salaam, founded in 1860 by Sultan Majid of Zanzibar as a trading port, is located on the coast of the Indian Ocean. It is Tanzania's main port, its largest city and most important political, commercial, administrative and manufacturing centre. The port, an important strategic asset, serves both Tanzania and landlocked countries in East and Southern Africa. Although it has not formally been the capital since 1974, the city houses many government ministries, local and international financial institutions, embassies, political party head offices and international organizations, and plays a major role in the country's development.

Physical context

Dar es Salaam is a sprawling low-rise city, covering 1,691 square kilometres, a considerable expansion over the 1.77 square kilometres it occupied in 1891 (Kiunsi and Lupala 2009; Tanzania Cities Network 2014). Only 22 per cent of the city is built-up, about half of it unplanned. The average population density is relatively low at 24 persons per hectare, but some areas, especially near the city centre, have densities of 300 or more per hectare (Lupala and Kiunsi 2011). Apart from the high-rise structures in the city centre, most buildings are single-storey. The housing in planned areas, and in some medium-density unplanned areas, is of acceptable standard. But in unplanned high-density areas especially, many of them in low-lying areas subject to flooding, most housing is of poor quality. Some of these settlements lack space for provision of public services and there is little adherence to city building codes, which exacerbates their vulnerability to flooding.

Social context

Dar es Salaam's population in 2012 was 4.36 million, having increased rapidly from 2.5 million in 2002 and 1.4 million in 1988, with annual growth rates for these periods more than double the national average (National Bureau of Statistics 2014a). This rapid increase is due primarily to reclassification of urban boundaries and natural growth (83 per cent together) and less to in-migration (17 per cent) (Muzzini and Lindeboon 2008). The population is dominated by young people of between 10 and 29, partly because of high levels of in-migration by this age group (National Bureau of Statistics 2013).

Like many cities in the global South, Dar es Salaam has high levels of both disparity and informality, with unequal access to planned and serviced land, basic services and employment opportunities. Up to 80 per cent of residents live in the city's unplanned settlements, most of them poorly served and characterized by poor living conditions, especially those of high density or located in hazardous areas (Tanzania Cities Network 2014). The needs not met by public provision for water, sanitation, solid waste management and public transport are normally provided through informal means. Formal employment opportunities are also limited, partly due to rapid population growth and a low level of industrial activity. Over 60 per cent depend on the informal sector as their main source of employment with petty trading, urban agriculture, fishing, and such technical jobs as mechanical repairs, carpentry, masonry, plumbing and tailoring as main livelihood activities (Nnkya and Lupala 2010).

The monthly mean expenditure per capita and per household is Tshs 111,237 (US$ 70) and 442,000 (US$ 276) respectively, with on average 43.6 per cent going to food. Extreme poverty levels are low: the basic needs poverty line is Tshs 36,482 (US$ 23) per adult equivalent per month, and the food poverty line is Tshs 26,085 (US$ 16); only 4.2 per cent and 1 per cent respectively are below these poverty lines (National Bureau of Statistics 2014b).

Economy

Dar es Salaam plays a key role in the country's economy, accounting for 45 per cent of gross industrial manufacturing output, 83 per cent of national government domestic revenue and 40 per cent of the country's revenue (UN-Habitat 2009; Tanzania Cities Network 2014). The dominant economic activities are large- and small-scale industry and trading (wholesale and retail), which together employ 80 to 90 per cent of the workforce (Division of Environment 2012). Other activities are tourism, transportation, property development, urban agriculture, fisheries and mining. The GDP of Dar es Salaam in 2013 was Tshs 7.5 trillion (US$ 4.7 billion), 17 per cent of that for the country (*The Citizen* October 3, 2014). The city also has a high concentration of the country's socio-economic services including health and education facilities and financial institutions.

Although cities in Tanzania are required by law to collect 95 per cent of their revenue from their own sources (Tanzania Cities Network 2014), most still depend heavily on central government funding for their budgets. In 2012/13 for example the central government was expected to fund 84 per cent of Dar es Salaam's projected budget of Tshs 22.3 billion (US$ 139 million) (Prime Minister's Office 2010/11). The main revenue sources for the city are property taxes, land rent, service levy, guest house levies, licences and permits, fees and charges.

The national household budget survey for 2011/12 found the employment to population ratio for Dar es Salaam to be 57.9 per cent with only 36.4 per cent in formal occupations (National Bureau of Statistics 2014b).

Governance, planning and public service provision

Dar es Salaam is headed by the city mayor and a city director who is responsible for urban planning, water supply, sanitation, solid and liquid waste management, transportation, engineering and fire services, health, and environmental issues. The city is divided into three municipalities of Kinondoni, Ilala and Temeke, each with its own local government, mayor and municipal director. It has 27 wards, each represented by an elected councillor, and 113 sub-wards.

Spatial development has partly been guided by master and strategic plans, prepared in 1949, in 1968 and most recently in 1997. In the early 1990s the Environmental Planning and Management (EPM) approach was introduced in Dar es Salaam city under the Sustainable Dar es Salaam Project (SDP). EPM focuses on identifying main urban environmental issues and key actors; it seeks political commitment, sets priorities, develops strategies, and plans and implements programmes and projects through participatory processes. This approach was used until the end of the 1990s when external support ended. A new master plan for Dar es Salaam is now under preparation.

Provision for public services – water supply, sanitation, solid and liquid waste management, roads and storm water drainage – is relatively poor, reflecting in part the low capacity of the city to generate revenue for this purpose. Only a small proportion of the city's population has water piped to their homes, sewer connections and adequate storm drainage. The city also has a water deficit. The total water demand for the city is 450,000 cubic metres per day; surface water and boreholes supply around 60 per cent of total demand (Division of Environment 2011). The rest comes from 255 shallow wells (Division of Environment 2011). It is a challenge to get reliable figures on water provision but the National Bureau of Statistics in 2014 showed more than half the city's households are connected to the piped water supply through house connections (20.1 per cent), connections to the yard (12.9 per cent) and public stand pipes (18.8 per cent). The remainder rely on wells, vendors and other sources (National Bureau of Statistics 2014a).

Sanitation systems are still inadequate. Only 5 to 10 per cent of city dwellers are connected to the sewer system which serves only some pockets of the city, including the Central Business District (Division of Environment 2011). Of the remainder, 32 per cent have flush toilets connected to septic tanks and 61.8 per cent have pit latrines; 0.2 per cent have no toilets (National Bureau of Statistics 2014a).

The storm water drainage system, serving only a small part of the city, has 1,100 km of open lined ditches and 600 km of piped storm water drainage, concentrated in planned areas (JICA 2008). This lack of provision contributes to flooding in many parts of the city, including the city centre, and an overloading of the sewer system during the rainy season. Inadequate provision, along with blockages, has led to the destruction of houses built near natural drainage channels. The city generates about 4,000 metric tons of solid waste per day, half of it from households, much of it disposed of in streets, market areas, river channels and storm water drainage channels. Solid waste collection and disposal services, managed jointly by the city authorities and private companies, collect and safely dispose of only about 40 per cent of the waste (Division of Environment 2011).

About 63.4 per cent of residents are connected to the national electric grid, most using electricity for lighting only. Connection and monthly charges are relatively high for low-income households but are expected to go down from mid-2015 when most power will be generated by the utility TANESCO, using gas and hydro power. Fuelwood is still the main energy source for cooking – 73.5 per cent of households use charcoal and 6.6 per cent firewood. The remainder use electricity, paraffin or gas, and less than 1 per cent use coal or solar energy (National Bureau of Statistics 2014a).

The city's road network is inadequate; of the 1,700 km of roads, only 25 per cent are paved and much of this is poorly maintained (JICA 2008). Roads cover only 2.5 per cent of land area compared with the 15–20 per cent recommended in Tanzania's urban planning guidelines, contributing to serious congestion (Mittal 1976; United Republic of Tanzania 1997a). Despite poor conditions, the number of cars has increased from 24,600 in 1997 to 701,521 in 2011 (Kiunsi 2013).

Greenhouse gas emissions

The city authorities have not conducted a formal inventory of GHG emissions, but estimates suggest emissions are still low, amounting to only 1.6 megatons of carbon equivalent and under 0.5 tCO_2e per capita (Sugar 2010; Kennedy, Ibrahim, and Hoornweg 2014). Transportation, including aviation and marine traffic, accounts for an estimated 61 per cent of emissions, waste for 32 per cent and electricity for 7 per cent (Sugar 2010). High transportation emissions are partly due to the preference for private cars by those who can afford them because of poor public transport, while for waste it is due to the use of dumpsites rather than landfills for final disposal of solid waste. Emissions are relatively low for electricity, a large portion of which is generated by hydro power and natural gas. Dar es Salaam emission estimates are likely to be low as emissions from fuelwood, used by most city residents, were not taken into account.

Climate change hazards, exposures and vulnerabilities

Dar es Salaam has a hot humid climate, with an average temperature of 29°C and a bi-modal rainfall system with 1,000–1,300 mm per year (UN–Habitat 2008; Pan-African START Secretariat et al. 2011). Tanzania is projected to become warmer by 2.5–4.5°C by the year 2080 under the A2 scenario. Data show that both minimum and maximum temperatures have been increasing since the 1960s in a trend similar to the global average. Although precipitation is projected to increase in all rainfall seasons (IPCC 2007; Mongi, Majule, and Lyimo 2010), the mean annual rainfall reduction over the last four decades contradicts these projections – records show rather a decrease in the number of rainfall days and mean annual rainfall, and increased variability in rainfall intensity (Pan-African START Secretariat et al. 2011).

Eight per cent of the area of Dar es Salaam lies in the Low Elevation Coastal Zone, less than 10 metres above mean sea level. About 140,000 people live in this zone, and economic assets are worth more than US$ 168 million (Kebede and Nicholls 2011). Even without sea level rise, more than 31,000 people are currently at risk there from a 1-in-100 year storm surge (i.e. a 3.09-metre rise in water level). This number is anticipated to increase by 2030 to 100,000, and the value of assets to more than US$ 400 million (Kebede and Nicholls 2011). Some locations in Dar es Salaam, including Kunduchi/Bahari and Ocean Road beach areas, are already being eroded due to sea level rise and/or storm surges. Rainstorms and sea level rise are likely to lead to increases in frequency and severity of flooding. Figure 5.1 shows the population exposed to flooding in different years under the A1B scenario with no adaptation (Kebede and Nicholls 2011). Those most at risk are communities in unplanned settlements in river valleys and along the coast, where flooding is exacerbated by poor planning, poor drainage and housing conditions, and lack of local capacity to adapt to flooding (Watkiss, Downing, Dyszynski, Pye et al. 2011). Figure 5.2 shows flood-prone areas overlaid on unplanned settlements in the city, and Box 5.1 gives examples of settlements and areas that are flooded regularly.

There are no comprehensive assessments of vulnerability to climate change impacts in the lowlands of Dar es Salaam, but studies conducted by the Pan-African START Secretariat (2011) in unplanned lowland settlements (Msasani Bonde la Mpunga, Msimbazi Valley, Jangwani and Mkocheni B Vigunguti, Mtambani and Mnyamani, and Kizinga River) showed that the top five climate and environmental risks experienced locally were flooding, temperature rise, drought, increases in disease and air pollution.

Drought is a major problem in many regions of the country and contributes directly to water and electricity shortages in cities and to increases in food prices (World Food Program 2010). Dar es Salaam, for instance, is directly affected by

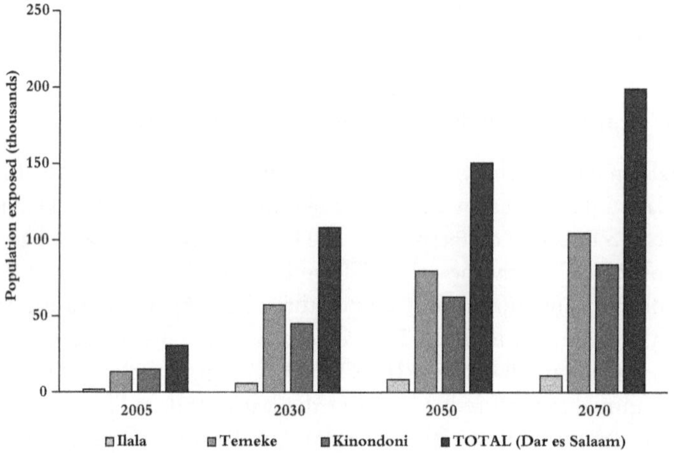

FIGURE 5.1 Population exposed to 1-in-100 year flood event in 2005, 2030, 2050 and 2070 under the A1B mid-range Sea Level Rise scenario, no adaptation (adapted from Kebede and Nicholls 2011)

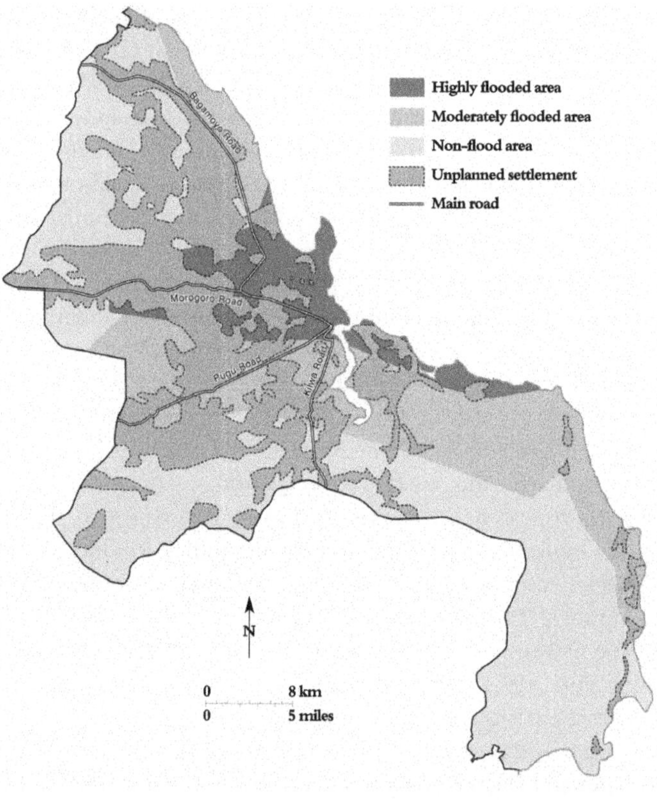

FIGURE 5.2 Flood hazard map overlain on urban unplanned settlements

Box 5.1 Examples of settlements and areas in Dar es Salaam that are flooded regularly

Mkunduge is an unplanned informal settlement with 9,565 inhabitants, located along a river channel. The area floods during the rainy seasons. The settlement lacks roads, drains and sewers. People are dependent on bore-holes for water but it is salty and not safe to drink. There is no solid waste collection service. For sanitation, most people use pit latrines (many of which are shared) and they often open their toilets during heavy rains to flush the waste away. A nearby river channel has been narrowed and partly blocked by solid waste and this has intensified flooding. Residents remain because of the good location within the city and the low rents. Rental accommodation is particularly cheap in the areas that are flooded most often and where housing quality is poor (houses on the road where there is less flooding and that are often of better quality have much higher rents). During periods of flooding, many businesses close and households have many additional tasks such as removing water and mud from homes, increased child care (as schools close) and going further to get water because local sources become contaminated. There is a plan to unblock the river and arrange for solid waste collection through a contribution of 2,000 Tanzania shillings per household. But some community members continue to dump solid waste into the river.

Suna is an informal settlement five kilometres from the city centre with 9,450 inhabitants. Close to half the buildings in the settlement are exposed to flooding because of their proximity to the Jangwani River and the lack of drains and sewers. These buildings are in the unplanned parts of the settlement – the planned areas are less at risk. Floods cause most businesses to stop, including home-based ones. Those who work outside of the home frequently cannot get to work. Of 211 households interviewed following the December 2011 floods, only 15 per cent said that their income had not been affected; 41 per cent had lost home possessions; 34 per cent had lost money; most of the houses had been flooded right up to their roofs; and a few houses had been completely destroyed. Three people had died – a husband, wife and small child – when a wall collapsed. People continue to live here because of the affordable land and rents close to the city centre.

Msasani Bonde la Mpunga: This settlement covers an area of 60 hectares about five kilometres from the city centre, has around 12,000 inhabitants and consists of a mix of residential, commercial and institutional buildings. The residential areas are a mix of poor- and medium-quality buildings and infrastructure. Two main storm water channels pass through the area. The 1979 Master Plan designated the site as hazard prone, yet development continues because of its proximity to the new American Embassy, a private

continued ...

Box 5.1 continued

hospital and hotels, large shopping malls and residences of former senior government officials. Drainage channels are blocked by refuse throughout the year as well as by structures that hinder the flow of wastewater, causing houses to be flooded by sewage-contaminated water.

Msimbazi Valley covers a wide area across both Ilala and Kinondoni municipalities. It floods regularly, even when there is no rainfall in Dar es Salaam, with waters from the Msimbazi River, which is also clogged with waste. Despite the flood risks, the area includes many of the fastest-growing settlements in the city because of easy access to unregulated farming and building plots, proximity to the city centre, poor enforcement of regulations concerning land use, and availability of low-cost housing. This was one of the most seriously affected areas in the December 2011 floods, with many reported deaths and thousands made homeless.

drought as it depends on hydropower for its electricity, surface (river) water for its main water supply, and on food from rural areas.

Policy framework and mandate for action

The 1997 National Environmental Policy provides the overall framework for the management of environmental issues in Tanzania, but does not list climate change as a problem (United Republic of Tanzania 1997b). Section 75 of the Environmental Management Act (EMA) 2004 points to measures that could be taken to address climate change impacts, including adaptation measures, the development of guidelines and strategies for their management (United Republic of Tanzania 2004). This is supported by a number of sectoral laws, some with environmental components. However, many of these laws do not address climate change directly. The Division of the Environment, the main coordinator for climate change issues, issued a draft National Climate Change Strategy and Action Plan in 2012 highlighting adaptation actions to be taken by different sectors (Division of Environment 2012). For the human settlements sector, the proposed interventions are improvement of building standards and land use, the relocation of communities living in flood-prone areas, and promotion of sustainable housing schemes. The National Climate Change Committee, composed of senior government officials from different sectors and research institutions, provides overall guidance on the management of climate change issues. Its main function is to advise the Division of Environment on climate change issues and on mitigation and adaptation measures, working together with sector ministries, research institutions and NGOs. But there is no formal institutional arrangement for climate change management in urban areas.

Development of adaptation and mitigation initiatives

There are two main kinds of adaptation initiatives in Dar es Salaam: those aimed primarily at addressing the development deficit, which in the course of their implementation indirectly contribute to climate change adaptation; and those that are directly related to climate change adapattion.

Programmes to address the development deficit

The government of Tanzania and Dar es Salaam city authorities have introduced a number of programmes focused on improving public services and infrastructure, formalizing existing unplanned settlements and controlling the rapid growth of informal settlements. These include the Community Infrastructure Upgrading Programme (CIUP) (2005–2011), which improved infrastructure and reduced flooding in the project area; the Programme to Formalize Unplanned Areas through Residential Licences (2005–2007); the 20,000 Plots Project (2003–2004); and the Water and Sanitation Improvement Programme (2003–2010). Most recent is the Citywide Action Plan for Upgrading Unplanned Settlements in Dar es Salaam (2010–2020) which seeks to upgrade half the existing unplanned settlements and prevent the formation of new unplanned settlements through several action plans: the land action plan (access to planned areas, increased city revenue from land taxation, increased provision of surveyed plots and control of densification of residential areas); the basic services plan (improved access to drinking water and sanitation, increased road coverage, storm water drains and improved solid waste management); the housing action plan (increased access to housing); and the capacity-building action plan (improved knowledge and skills required to upgrade unplanned settlements and prevent the development of new squatter areas).

Implementation is spearheaded by the Citywide Slum Upgrading and Prevention Programme Unit (CSUPPU) assisted by a steering committee (with members from city government, Dar es Salaam municipal governments, sector ministries, the Prime Minister's office, academic and research institutions and development partners) and a technical committee. Local communities participate through community planning committees, which are mandated to provide inputs in project planning and implementation. The programme is costing US$ 1.2 billion, which is being raised from local communities, the private sector, municipal councils, central government and development partners.

Measures to address climate change mitigation and adaptation directly

There is little knowledge or capacity with regard to climate change mitigation and adaptation in Dar es Salaam, and limited evidence of any planning and implementation of direct measures on these fronts. Measures that focus on mitigation include tree planting; the protection of coral reefs and mangrove vegetation; the use of more efficient cooking stoves; energy-saving street lights; an improved public transport system; methane gas capture at waste disposal sites, and the promotion of natural gas and briquettes instead of oil and coal.

The main sources for electricity generation currently are natural gas (40–45 per cent),[1] hydropower and diesel thermal plants. Two projects are in the works to increase the amount of electricity from natural gas to 80 per cent and to encourage industries to switch to natural gas use (Kiunsi et al. 2009). The first is construction of a new natural gas pipeline from Mtwara to Dar es Salaam; the second is construction of two power plants capable of generating a total of 390 MW in Dar es Salaam. The two projects, to be operational by mid-2015, will lead to a lower unit price for electricity, and enable more households to switch from using fuelwood or charcoal. Another significant measure is the development of bus rapid transit through the DART (Dar Rapid Transit) project, which will introduce large buses on dedicated lanes. Bus lanes and stations are currently under construction (United Republic of Tanzania 2014). It is anticipated that DART will reduce the number of private cars and minibuses in the city (there are now an estimated 5,000–7,000 minibuses), thereby reducing traffic congestion and emissions of greenhouse gases.

The main climate change adaptation measures in the city focus on control of flooding and coastal erosion. They include building sea walls and groynes to protect hotels and beaches, improving or constructing new storm water drainage systems, especially in flood-prone areas like Msasani Bonde la Mpunga; strengthening or constructing new bridges, for example at Mtogole along the main road in Magomeni Mapipa, at Bunju along Mpiji River and in Kinyerezi; constructing new roads with adequate storm water drainage channels; regular cleaning of storm water drainage channels and of rivers, including Sinza and Mlalakuwa Rivers. A good example of community level adaptation comes from Msasani Bonde la Mpunga near the city centre, one of many informal settlements prone to flooding. Residents formed a flooding committee that worked with the city authorities and the Prime Minister's Office. Vulnerable houses are now being replaced by commercial buildings, and storm water drainage is being constructed (Kiunsi et al. 2009). Households also take measures to protect their property. For instance, in Kijiji Cha Wavuvi settlement within Mtoni, an unplanned area on the coast, a large natural drainage channel runs from an industrial compound, directing storm water to the sea. To protect their houses from being washed away by storm water and high sea tides, residents have stacked used tyres along the drainage channel. Other coping mechanisms include putting possessions on high shelves or roofs, hanging furniture and other possessions from hooks high up on walls, and sleeping on tables or roofs.

Dar es Salaam has developed a number of international alliances with regard to climate change, including with the Mayors' Task Force on Climate Change, Disaster Risk and Urban Poor; ICLEI Local Governments for Sustainable Development; and the World Bank. Under the auspices of the Mayors' Task

Force, a study on urban poverty and climate change in Dar es Salaam was conducted (World Bank 2011; Pan-African START Secretariat et al. 2011). Under ICLEI, a capacity-building programme on adaptation was implemented in Temeke municipality, including workshops for municipality staff and other selected key stakeholders and the planting of mangrove trees in a degraded mangrove forest area. As in São Paulo and Jakarta, Dar es Salaam has a Carbon Finance Capacity-Building Programme (CFCBP), which includes distance training and direct learning on developing carbon projects in the city. The city is also implementing a mitigation project at the now-closed Mtoni solid waste dump site, where methane gas is captured to generate 2.5 to 5 MW of electricity.

Synergies with disaster risk response

Disaster risk response in Tanzania is coordinated by the Disaster Management Department located in the Prime Minister's Office. In accordance with policy requirements, disaster management committees have been set up at national, regional, district, ward and village levels, although not in urban areas. Climate change issues, as noted, come under the Division of Environment which is in the Vice President's Office, and at the city level under the Standing Committee on Urban Planning and Environment. Institutional arrangements provide no direct links between disaster management and climate change adaptation, and there has been little coordination among the key institutions in Dar es Salaam. The December 2011 floods that hit the city, causing 20 deaths, and displacing 10,000 people, clearly showed the need for such links, but also the importance of links between disaster risk reduction and physical planning and infrastructure development. The International Federation of Red Cross and Red Crescent reported that the 2011 floods caused 20 deaths, injured more than 200 persons and displaced 10,000.[2] Dar es Salaam is now reportedly preparing a disaster resilience action plan that will include a disaster recovery centre to address the availability of accommodation and other essential facilities after the floods. The floods also highlighted the need for the disaster management policy, which is under review, to include climate change impacts, and mitigation and adaptation issues.

Research activities

Relevant research activities on climate change and its impacts are on the increase. Climate Change Impacts, Adaptation and Mitigation (CCIAM), funded by the government of Norway, is a collaborative programme involving Sokoine University of Agriculture, the University of Dar es Salaam, Ardhi University, the Tanzania Meteorological Agency (TMA) and a number of universities in Norway, including the University of Life Sciences. Its main focus is in rural areas, especially in the REDD programme – Reducing Emissions from Deforestation and Forest Degradation. A second research programme is

Climate Change and Urban Vulnerability in Africa (CLUVA), which involves five universities in Africa and a number of European and African research institutions.[3] Research is taking place in Addis Ababa, Dar es Salaam, Doula, Ouagadougou and Saint Louis with a specific focus in each: in Dar es Salaam on sea level rise, coastal erosion and flooding; in Addis Ababa on drought, desertification and water scarcity; in Doula on sea level rise and flooding; in Ouagadougou on drought and flooding from intense rainfall; and in Saint Louis on sea level rise and flooding. The programme, funded by the European Union, has the goal of developing methods and knowledge for African cities to manage climate change risks, reduce vulnerabilities and improve coping capacity and resilience. Under the Dar es Salaam programme, five PhD research projects are being conducted, namely climate change modelling, impacts of climate change on urban infrastructure, urban heat islands, vulnerability assessments on flood prone areas, and land use development control.

A third research programme is Adapting to Climate Change in Coastal Dar es Salaam (ACC DAR), partly funded by the European Union and implemented by the Inter-university Research Centre Development at the Sapienza University in Rome in collaboration with Ardhi University in Tanzania. It aims to contribute to the implementation of the National Adaptation Programme of Action (NAPA). Initial findings indicate that understanding of climate change issues is low, helping explain the absence of climate change issues in the city's development agenda, and pointing to the need for capacity building of city employees (Kassenga and Mbuligwe 2012).

Conclusions

Dar es Salaam faces a large development deficit as well as current climate change impacts and future impacts that need to be planned for. Planning and implementation of direct climate change mitigation and adaptation in Dar es Salaam still receives very low priority and, to date, there are no significant city level climate change mitigation and adaptation activities. The main indirect mitigation measures are increased generation of electricity from natural gas instead of diesel, and improvement of public transport. Households, communities and businesses impacted by floods or beach loss have taken their own measures, and adaptation measure implemented by the city authorities include cleaning of rivers, building of sea walls and improvement of selected bridges. Limited coordination among government institutions dealing with climate change and disaster management hinders effective planning and implementation of mitigation and adaptation measures.

The implementation of development deficit programmes has a number of outcomes, including overall improvement in living conditions in upgraded planned areas. Improvements include better road accessibility, storm water drainage and solid waste management. Upgrading programmes has reduced flood occurrences in some unplanned areas. To date, the government priority has been to improve the social and economic conditions and infrastructure; the capacity to manage development so that it also addresses climate change issues is low and needs to be improved. Action is needed in five main areas:

- raising awareness of both the general public and the decision makers regarding climate change issues and how these can be incorporated into development activities;
- improving the knowledge base of city employees, especially physical planners and engineers, to enable them to take account of climate change issues when preparing city plans and projects;
- exploring potential synergies between climate change and disaster management communities;
- increasing the financial capacity of the city through improved tax collection or external support;
- mainstreaming climate change mitigation and adaptation into the development plans for upgrading the unplanned areas.

Notes

1 https://24tanzania.com/mtwara-dar-gas-pipeline-commissioning-2014
2 www.ifrc.org/docs/appeals/11/MDRTZ013.pdf
3 www.cluva.eu

References

Centre for Community Initiatives in collaboration with Environmental Protection and Management Service (2012a), "Climate change vulnerability draft report case study: Suna settlement in Magomeni ward, Dar es Salaam, Tanzania", CCI, Dar es Salaam, 28 pages.

Centre for Community Initiatives in collaboration with Environmental Protection and Management Service (2012b), "Report on assessing climate change vulnerability and impacts on the urban poor: case study of Mkunduge informal settlement in Dar es Salaam", CCI, Dar es Salaam, 28 pages.

Division of Environment (2012), *National Climate Change Strategy,* Vice President's Office, Dar es Salaam, 92 pages.

Division of Environment, United Nations Environmental Program (2011), *Dar es Salaam City Environmental Outlook 2011*,Vice President's Office, Dar es Salaam, 95 pages.

IPCC (2007), *Climate Change 2007: Synthesis Report*, Cambridge University Press, Cambridge, UK, 52 pages.

JICA (2008), *Dar es Salaam Transport Policy and System Development Master Plan*, Technical Report 1: Urban and Regional Planning, 88 pages.

Kebede, A S and R J Nicholls (2011), *Population and Assets Exposure to Coastal Flooding in Dar es Salaam (Tanzania): Vulnerability to Climate Extremes*, Report submitted to the Global Climate Adaptation Partnership (GCAP), University of Southampton, School of Civil Engineering and Tyndall Centre for Climate Change Research, UK, 26 pages.

Kennedy, C, A Ibrahim and N Hoornweg (2014), "Low-carbon infrastructure and strategies for cities", *Nature Climate Change* Vol 4, pages 343–346.

Kiunsi, R (2013), "A review of traffic congestion in Dar es Salaam city from the physical planning perspective", *Journal of Sustainable Development* Vol 6, No 2, pages 94–103.
Kiunsi, R and J Lupala (2009), "Building disaster-resilient communities: Dar es Salaam, Tanzania", in Mark Pelling and Ben Wisner (editors), *Disaster Risk Reduction; Cases from Urban Africa*, Earthscan Publications, London, pages 127–146.
Kiunsi, R, G Kassenga, J Lupala, B Malele, G Uhinga and D Rugai (2009), *Mainstreaming Disaster Risk Reduction in Urban Planning Practice in Tanzania,* Research ReportURAN, 44 pages. (*www.preventionweb.net/.../13524_TANZANIAFINALREPORT27OCT0..*)
Lupala, J and R Kiunsi (2011), "Dar es Salaam city, 50 years to come: conceptual considerations", unpublished workshop Working Paper presented during the 50 Years Anniversary of the University of Dar es Salaam, Tanzania.
Mittal, S C (1976), "Space standards for residential development for urban areas of the United Republic of Tanzania", Paper presented at Ardhi Annual Conference, Moshi, Tanzania, December 1976.
Mongi, H, A E Majule and J G Lyimo (2010), "Vulnerability and adaptation of rain-fed agriculture to climate change and variability in semi-arid Tanzania", *African Journal of Environmental Science and Technology* Vol 4, No 6, pages 371–381.
Mtongori, I and P M Innes (2010), "Climate change impacts in East Africa", Paper presented at Second International Conference on Climate, Sustainability and Development in Semi-arid Regions, Fortaleza–Ceara, Brazil, August 16–20.
Muzzini, E and Lindeboon, W (2008), *The Urban Transition in Tanzania: Building the Empirical Base for Policy Dialogue,* International Bank for Reconstruction and Development/World Bank, Washington.
National Bureau of Statistics (2013), *Population Distribution by Age and Sex*, Ministry of Finance, Dar es Salaam, 499 pages.
National Bureau of Statistics (2014a), *Basic Demographic and Socio-Economic Profile,* Ministry of Finance, Dar es Salaam, 245 pages.
National Bureau of Statistics (2014b), Household budget survey main report, 2011/12. Ministry of Finance, Dar es Salaam, 201 pages.
Nnkya, T and J Lupala (2010), "Planning education in Tanzania: the experience of Ardhi University", *Journal of Building and Land Development*, Special Issue, pages 157–173.
Pan-African START Secretariat, International START Secretariat, Tanzania Meteorological Agency and Ardhi University, Tanzania (2011), *Urban Poverty & Climate Change in Dar es Salaam, Tanzania: A Case Study,* 129 pages. (*start.org/download/2011/dar-case-study.pdf)*
Prime Minister's Office Regional Administration and Local Government. Dar es Salaam City Council. Local budget plan FY 2010/11 (www.prmoralg.tz)
Shamdoe, R, G Kassenga and S Mbuligwe (2015), Implementing climate change adaptation and mitigation interventions at the local government levels in Tanzania: Where do we start, *Current Opinion on Environmental Sustainability* Vol 13, pages 32–41.
Sugar, L (2010), Global Cities and their Response to Climate Change, thesis submitted in conformity with the requirements for the degree of Master of Applied Science, Department of Civil Engineering, University of Toronto, 72 pages.
The Citizen newspaper, Friday October 3, 2014 (www.thecitizen.co.tz/News/Dar-tops-wealth-list)
UN-Habitat (2008), *The State of African Cities 2008: A Framework for Addressing Urban Challenges in Africa*, UN–Habitat, Nairobi, 206 pages.
UN-Habitat (2009), *Tanzania: Dar es Salaam City profile,* UNON, Publishing Services Section, Nairobi Kenya, 32 pages.
United Republic of Tanzania (1997a), *The Town and Country Planning (Town Planning Space Standards) Regulations*, Government Notice No 157, Dar es Salaam, 10 pages.

United Republic of Tanzania (1997b) National Environmental Policy, Vice President's Office, Dar es Salaam, 41 pages.

United Republic of Tanzania (2004) Environmental Management Act, Government Notice Vol. 86, No 6 Dar es Salaam, 236 pages.

United Republic of Tanzania (2014), *Dar Rapid Transit (DART) Project: Phase 1,* Project Information Memorandum Final version. Prime Minister's Office for Regional Administration and Local Government (PMO-RALG).

Watkiss, P, T Downing, J Dyszynski, S Pye et al. (2011), *The Economics of Climate Change in the United Republic of Tanzania*, Report to Development Partners Group and the UK Department for International Development, January, available at http://economics-of-cc-in-tanzania.org/, 34 pages.

World Bank (2011), "Climate change, disaster risk and the urban poor: cities building resilience for a changing world (Summary)", World Bank, Washington DC, 33 pages.

World Food Program (2010), *Comprehensive Food Security and Vulnerability Analysis (CFSVA), United Republic of Tanzania*, World Food Program, Rome, 228 pages.

6

DURBAN, SOUTH AFRICA

Debra Roberts, Derek Morgan, Sean O'Donoghue, Lisa Guastella, Nongcebo Hlongwa and Penny Price

Introduction

Durban, like many other African cities, faces serious climate variability and climate change threats. Its climate-related work began in the early 2000s with an externally driven focus on mitigation. As local understanding of climate change improved, Durban emerged as an early leader in the field of climate change adaptation (Roberts 2008, 2010, Leck et al. 2011, Carmin et al. 2012, Diab and Roberts 2012, Roberts et al. 2012, Cartwright et al. 2013, Roberts and O'Donoghue 2013, Walsh et al. 2013, Archer et al. 2014, Ziervogel et al. 2014, Leck and Roberts 2015). There are now increasing attempts to integrate the adaptation and mitigation work-streams of the Municipal Climate Protection Programme (MCPP) in acknowledgement of mitigation's critical contribution to the city's adaptive capacity. These two work-streams, along with a broad range of other issues, are also being integrated into the city's emerging resilience agenda.

Physical context

Durban is the largest city and port on Africa's east coast and the third largest of South Africa's metropolitan areas. Two thirds of the municipality remains rural, but these areas are urbanising rapidly. Located in one of the world's 35 Global Biodiversity Hotspots, Durban contains grassland, savannah and forest areas, all represented in the Durban Metropolitan Open Space System (D'MOSS), which covers a third of the municipality and provides ecosystem services central to its adaptation strategy. Only 7 to 10 per cent of D'MOSS is formally managed or protected, and most key vegetation types are threatened (EThekwini Municipality 2014a).

Durban has a sub-tropical climate, with about 1000 mm annual summer rainfall, average temperatures from 11°C to 28°C and high humidity.[1] Climate change projections include increases in temperature, more variable rainfall, sea-level rise and compounding storm surge (Golder Associates 2011). This puts the city at risk from sudden as well as slow onset disasters, ranging from flash floods and droughts, to coastal erosion and storm surges exacerbated by sea-level rise, which has been calculated to be 2.7 mm per annum (Mather et al. 2009). There are as yet insufficient data to definitively link climate change to any of the hazards currently being experienced by the city (e.g. prolonged drought, flooding etc.). Data systems are, however, being established to collect information that will be used to describe the extent to which the local population is being affected by these hazards. Such long-term data collection systems will also enable the link between these hazards and climate change to be clarified.

Social context

Durban is a melting pot of people and cultures. Most residents (74 per cent) are classified as indigenous African, followed by Indian, White and Coloured (17, 7 and 2 per cent respectively). The population, 3.4 million, has grown by 1.1 per cent per year since 2001 (Statistics South Africa 2012), driven by both natural increase and migration, and affected also by HIV and access to anti-retroviral drugs. The city's population is overwhelmingly young and life expectancy is 53 years for males and 59 for females (Statistics South Africa 2012).

Among South Africa's cities, Durban has the highest percentage of people in poverty (EThekwini Municipality 2013a), and high levels of inequality, with a Gini Coefficient of 0.63 in 2012 (EThekwini Municipality 2015a). In 2013, 28 per cent lived below the food poverty line (USD 142 per capita per month),[2] down from 35 per cent two years earlier (Statistics South Africa 2014). Those unemployed and looking for work declined over the same period from 24 to 20 per cent (EThekwini Municipality 2015b). Ten percent have no education and only 25 per cent complete secondary school (EThekwini Municipality 2013b). Africans experience the highest poverty and unemployment rates.

Economy

Durban's economy is driven by its port, the busiest in southern Africa. It is the country's second largest industrial centre (EThekwini Municipality, 2015b), and draws 3.7 million mostly local tourists each year (EThekwini Municipality, 2014b). Key sectors are finance, manufacturing, community services, trade, transport and construction. The main commercial crop is sugar cane. In 2013, gross domestic product (GDP) was about $21 billion, about two thirds that of the Province (EThekwini Municipality 2015a). Challenges include high levels of poverty and inequality, lagging investment, net imports, infrastructure backlogs and the cost of doing business (EThekwini Municipality 2013a).

Municipal governance and provision

Durban is governed by an elected council of ward and proportional representatives and the administration is headed by a city manager. The total budget (operating and capital) for 2015/16 is USD 3.73 billion (EThekwini Municipality 2015a). The operating budget (USD 3.1 billion) is drawn primarily from service charges (USD 1,581 million), grants and subsidies (USD 590 million) and property taxes (USD 552 million). There is a narrow rates base – only 21 per cent of the population paid property tax in 2012/13 (EThekwini Municipality 2015a).

Durban has considerable backlogs in infrastructure and basic services (Table 6.1). While good progress has been made in electricity supply, refuse removal and sanitation, piped water remains a challenge (Figure 6.1). The diversity of settlement types (formal, informal, rural and urban) necessitates different service level types, such as urine diversion toilets in more remote rural areas, a source of dissatisfaction in some poor communities, despite being regarded as economically and environmentally appropriate (Roma et al. 2013). The supply of adequate housing remains a challenge; as of 30 June 2015, the municipality had delivered 183,537 houses, but a backlog of 391,992 units remains.[3] Over the next three years, capital expenditure, drawing most heavily from grant funding, is expected to focus on housing and infrastructural backlogs.

Safe, efficient public transport is a further challenge, and there are plans for a smart, affordable, accessible public transport network, as well as a new dig-out port, expansion of existing port facilities, and road and rail infrastructure to service the new international airport and trade port north of the city. Detractors see the latter investment as supporting a carbon-intensive growth path, while displacing historically-disadvantaged communities and threatening endangered ecosystems.

Environmental management in Durban is highly decentralised, with specialised environmental issues being dealt with by separate municipal line functions. The city's adaptation work is driven primarily by the Environmental

TABLE 6.1 Existing service delivery backlogs in Durban, as of 30 June 2014, with the exception of housing, which is as of 30 June 2015

Basic service	*Existing backlog (consumer units)*	*Delivery ranges per annum*	*Timeframe based on current funding levels*
Water	68,957	2000–2500	26–34 years
Sanitation	182,271	8000–10,000	18–23 years
Electricity	274,810	8000–13,000	21–34 years
Refuse removal	0	1500–2000	0 years
Roads	1,106.6 km	10–15 km	74–111 years
Housing	391,992	5000–10,000	40–81 years

Source: EThekwini Municipality (2015a, p. 63).

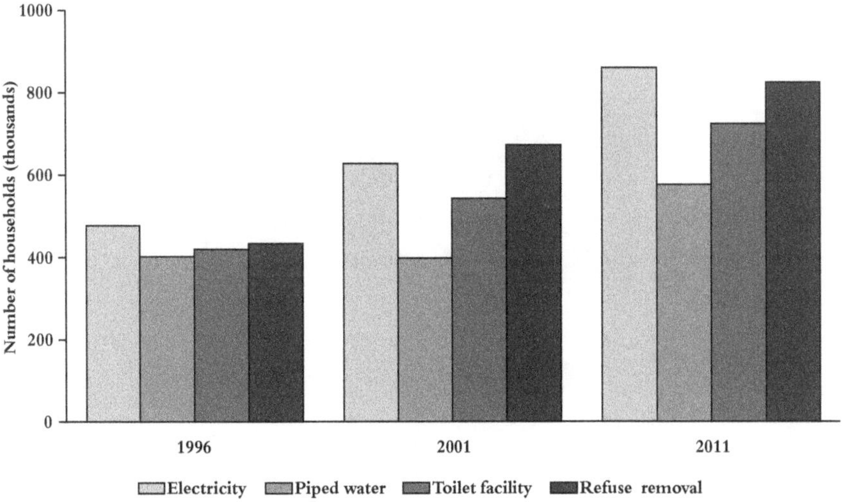

FIGURE 6.1 EThekwini Municipality service delivery in 1996, 2001 and 2011 (source: Stats SA 2012)

Planning and Climate Protection Department, supported by the Coastal, Stormwater and Catchment Management Department; mitigation work comes under the Energy Office. Both work extensively with other departments.

The considerable climate-related hazards in Durban combine with social vulnerability (poor access to basic services, unsafe housing, health threats, poverty and unemployment) to create high levels of risk. The legacy of apartheid planning locates many of the city's poor far from economic opportunities, contributing to migration and the development of informal settlements which house a quarter of the city's residents (EThekwini Municipality 2015a), and are particularly vulnerable to climate change impacts. The Municipal Systems Act (2000) and the Disaster Management Act (2002) require local governments to develop a disaster management plan focused on risk reduction. Durban's Disaster Management Unit has established a Disaster Management Advisory Forum, with a technical task team on adaptation. The Unit is undertaking a city-wide risk assessment, including consideration of climate change and biodiversity loss, which will inform development of the Disaster Management Plan.

GHG inventory

Durban's greenhouse gas emissions according to the 2013 GHG emissions inventory amounted to 28,741,558 tCO_2e (EThekwini Municipality 2015c). The largest contributors were transportation (largely road vehicles, especially heavy trucks for goods transport) and industry (mainly from purchased electricity and stationary fuel combustion) (Figure 6.2). The upward trend in emissions (5.8 per cent since 2010) is due in part to increased methodological rigour.

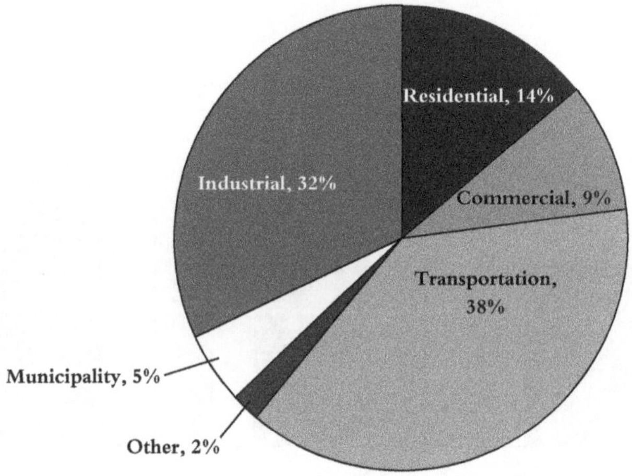

FIGURE 6.2 GHG emissions by sector for Durban (source: EThekwini Municipality 2015c)

The origins of climate protection action in Durban

Work by the Environmental Planning and Climate Protection Department in the early 2000s laid the foundation for both the mitigation and adaptation work-streams of Durban's Municipal Climate Protection Programme (MCPP). (This department has undergone several name and institutional changes over the years and will be referred to in this text by the name in use at the time under discussion.[4]) Three key "trigger" activities have stimulated the majority of work undertaken to date (see Figure 6.3 for a representation of both the adaptation and mitigation work-streams).

First, while climate change was evaluated as a potential work area by the then Environmental Branch in 1999, work began only in 2000 with USAID's funding of the South African pilot of ICLEI's Cities for Climate Protection campaign (CCP). Despite the Branch's lack of relevant capacity (its core business was biodiversity) and its need to deal with other critical development-related issues, upper management insisted that it engage with CCP to avoid the perception that Durban "rejected" the programme. Outputs included the city's first greenhouse gas (GHG) inventory in 2003, and a municipal building energy efficiency programme. Because the core business of the Branch was biodiversity planning, much of the climate work had to be undertaken by external consultants, with municipal staff in an oversight role (Roberts 2008).

Second, over this same period (2002 onwards), Durban's Solid Waste Department initiated a Landfill Gas to Electricity Project at the city's largest landfill sites.[5] This built staff capacity in climate change mitigation and carbon financing. The project remains a key mitigation activity, generating 234,507 tCO_2e Certified Emission Reductions (CERs) in 2010 and 201,601 tCO_2e CERs in 2013 (EThekwini Municipality 2015c). It has also attracted criticism from environmental justice advocates due to the landfill's proximity to residential neighbourhoods and has influenced the way the city's climate work is viewed by some stakeholders.

Third, in 2004, the head of the Environmental Management Department attended an international programme, the first opportunity for in-depth engagement with climate change science which highlighted the potential impacts for the department's biodiversity focus. This was critical in initiating the MCPP in 2004 and underscored the importance of champion-building for institutionalising a focus on climate change (Roberts and O'Donoghue 2013).

The mitigation work-stream

In 2006, the Danish International Development Agency (DANIDA) provided funding for an Urban Environmental Management Programme (UEMP) in South Africa (DANIDA 2005), which in turn funded development of a municipal energy strategy, the need for which had been highlighted during the CCP buildings energy efficiency project. Because of limited interest in the Electricity Unit, this strategy development was also led by the Environmental Management Department. Despite the on-going skills mismatch, the mitigation function stayed anchored here until a more appropriate institutional champion could be found.

Resolution came from an unexpected source. In 2008, energy shortages and rolling black-outs placed energy security at the top of the national agenda, and programmes were initiated by national government, including a rotating load-shedding schedule and the Power Conservation Programme (PCP), with various interventions to reduce the national demand for electricity by 10 per cent. EThekwini Municipality became a critical partner in achieving this PCP target. The energy shortages, along with recommendations in the Energy Strategy (EThekwini Municipality 2008) and DANIDA funding, contributed to the establishment of the Energy Office in 2008. Initially located in the Electricity Unit, it was subsequently relocated to the Treasury Department. Its initial focus was on electricity efficiency in municipal infrastructure, but the Environmental Management Department urged that the climate change mitigation function also be transferred there. Meanwhile, the Department had started to develop a strong climate change adaptation focus, better aligned with its core business of biodiversity planning.

Despite the earlier donor-driven work, mitigation only became institutionally embedded in Durban after the establishment of the Energy Office in 2008 and the appointment of a permanent manager in 2010. A range of factors contributed to development of this function, including the embrace of catalytic projects and donor-funded interventions. For example, in 2009–2010, the UN Industrial Development Organisation (UNIDO) funded the Durban Industry Climate Change Partnership Project (DICCPP)[6] to support industry and the Municipality in responding to climate change, confirming the need to broaden the Energy

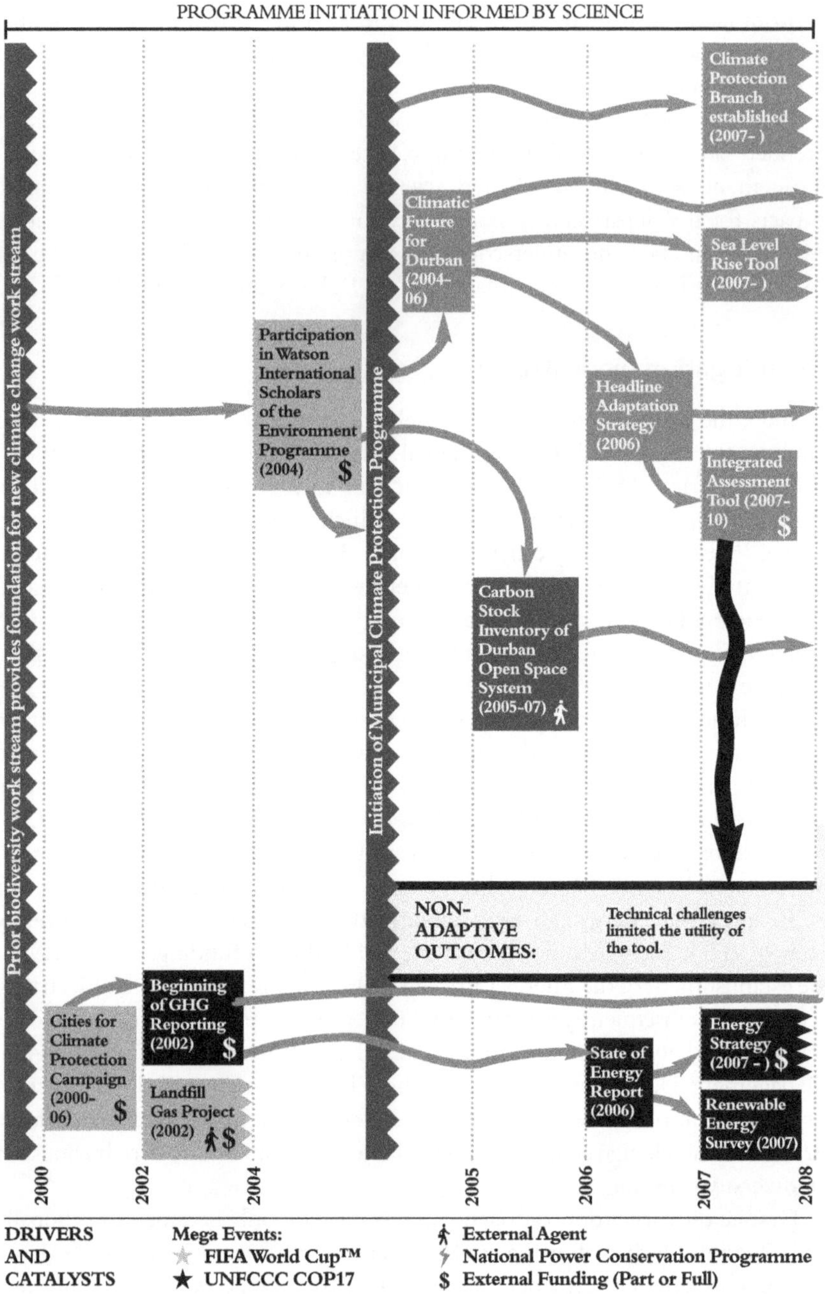

FIGURE 6.3 Flow diagram of project pathways depicting development of the adaptation and mitigation work-streams of the Climate Protection Branch and the Energy Office in eThekwini Municipality

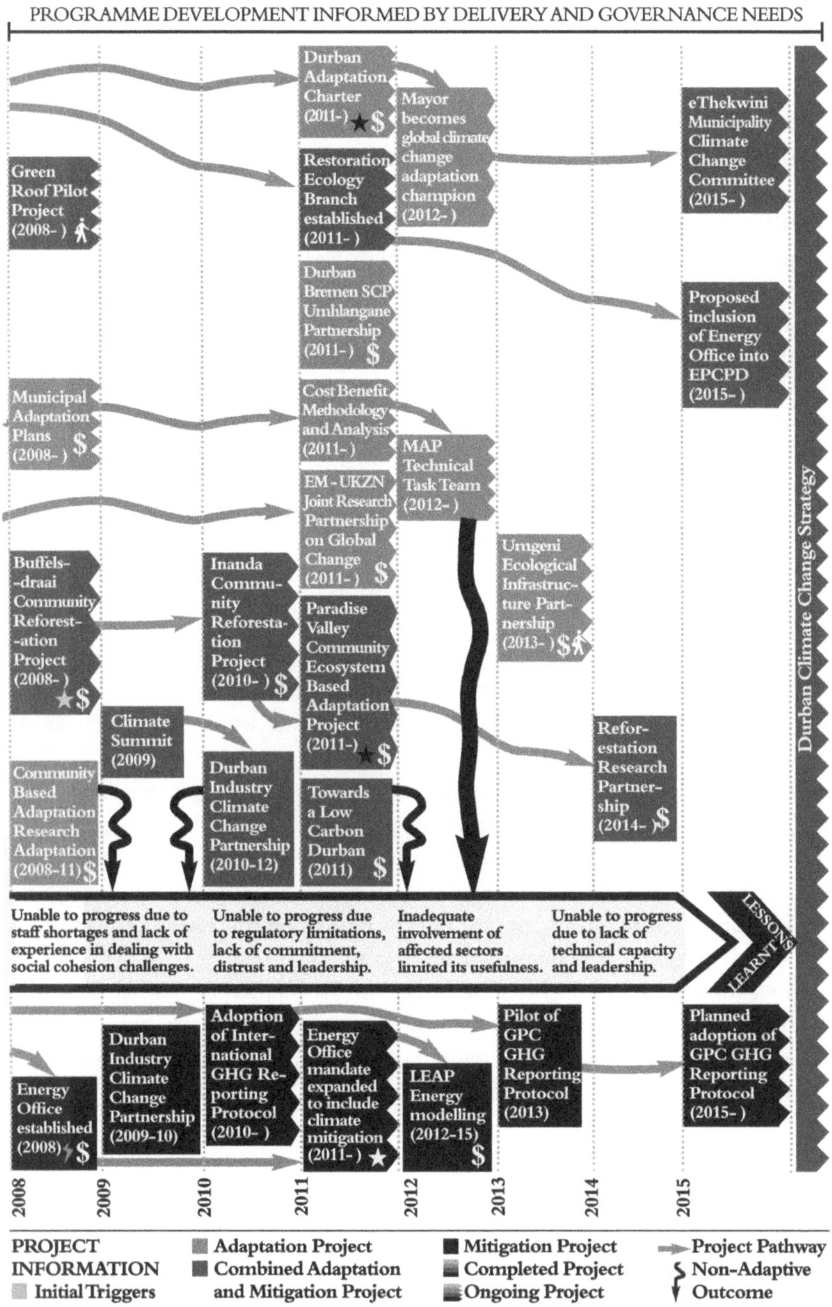

PROGRAMME DEVELOPMENT INFORMED BY DELIVERY AND GOVERNANCE NEEDS
Durban Adaptation Charter (2011-)
Mayor becomes global climate change adaptation champion (2012-)
eThekwini Municipality Climate Change Committee (2015-)
Green Roof Pilot Project (2008-)
Restoration Ecology Branch established (2011-)
Durban Bremen SCP Umhlangane Partnership (2011-)
Proposed inclusion of Energy Office into EPCPD (2015-)
Municipal Adaptation Plans (2008-)
Cost Benefit Methodology and Analysis (2011-)
MAP Technical Task Team (2012-)
EM-UKZN Joint Research Partnership on Global Change (2011-)
Umgeni Ecological Infrastructure Partnership (2013-)
Buffels-draai Community Reforest-ation Project (2008-)
Inanda Community Reforestation Project (2010-)
Paradise Valley Community Ecosystem Based Adaptation Project (2011-)
Climate Summit (2009)
Reforestation Research Partnership (2014-)
Community Based Adaptation Research Adaptation (2008-11)
Durban Industry Climate Change Partnership (2010-12)
Towards a Low Carbon Durban (2011)
Durban Climate Change Strategy
Unable to progress due to staff shortages and lack of experience in dealing with social cohesion challenges.
Unable to progress due to regulatory limitations, lack of commitment, distrust and leadership.
Inadequate involvement of affected sectors limited its usefulness.
Unable to progress due to lack of technical capacity and leadership.
LESSONS LEARNT
Adoption of International GHG Reporting Protocol (2010-)
Pilot of GPC GHG Reporting Protocol (2013)
Planned adoption of GPC GHG Reporting Protocol (2015-)
Durban Industry Climate Change Partnership (2009-10)
Energy Office mandate expanded to include climate mitigation (2011-)
LEAP Energy modelling (2012-15)
Energy Office established (2008)
2008
2009
2010
2011
2012
2013
2014
2015
PROJECT INFORMATION
Initial Triggers
Adaptation Project
Combined Adaptation and Mitigation Project
Mitigation Project
Completed Project
Ongoing Project
Project Pathway
Non-Adaptive Outcome

Office's mandate to include mitigation. Another outcome was the adoption of an internationally recognised protocol[7] for Durban's GHG reporting, allowing standardisation of reporting to such global platforms as the carbon*n* Cities Climate Registry. The city has also pilot tested the recently released Global Protocol for Community-Scale Greenhouse Gas Emission Inventories (GPC).

This expanded Energy Office mandate was also influenced by the lead up to COP17-CMP7,[8] hosted in Durban in 2011. The head of the Environmental Planning and Climate Protection Department had pointed to the incongruity of a city with no formally acknowledged mitigation function hosting a COP focused on the future of the Kyoto Protocol. As a result, the City Manager formally recognised mitigation as an Energy Office responsibility. Within this context, the Energy Office has developed future energy scenarios for Durban using the Long-range Energy Alternatives Planning System (LEAP)[9] to map both business-as-usual and alternative scenarios for the city. One of these scenarios included an emissions reduction decrease in line with the national target of 42 per cent by 2030 (Scenario Building Team 2007), large-scale installation of small-scale embedded solar photo voltaic and significant modal shift to public transport, and identified five short-term priorities:

1. *Energy efficiency:* including capital investment in municipal energy efficiency and demand side management (EEDSM), promotion of solar water heaters and other residential energy campaigns and private sector energy efficiency programmes.
2. *Renewable energy:* including resource assessments, decentralised energy generation and investment in municipal infrastructure pilot projects.
3. *Climate change reporting:* including yearly GHG inventories, development of climate change strategies and reports to national and international agencies.
4. *Transport:* focusing on promotion of non-motorised transport in the city and a municipal city fleet energy efficiency plan.
5. *Economy and outreach:* increasing public awareness of climate change and developing a market for sustainable energy products and services. Programmes include a sustainable energy forum, an incubator for small businesses and on-line awareness campaigns.

Critical next steps are identifying funding mechanisms to bridge the transition to a low carbon future and mainstream energy and GHG reduction throughout the city. This sort of aggressive, low-cost mitigation in cities is the most efficient, cost-effective way to deal with the global climate change challenge. Durban's mitigation function has evolved over 15 years from almost no capacity to an Energy Office with 17 staff posts (not all permanently filled). It will need to build rapidly from this foundation to respond adequately to climate change.

A key mitigation challenge for Durban is the lack of a nationally mandated GHG reduction target, without which it is difficult to push for fundamental changes. A further challenge is the Municipality's reliance on electricity sales for income. Initial research indicates a potential operating budget loss of 8–15 per cent as energy efficiency and renewable energy become more widespread. This income will need to be raised through other taxes, which will mean a negative public response to mitigation. A third challenge is electricity prices. Although they increased rapidly in South Africa from 2010 to 2013, this comes off a very low base, and the cost to the industrial sector is among the lowest in the world (approximately $0.06/kWh) (Thopil and Pouris 2013) – a key barrier for the development of renewable energy, although price parity in terms of kWh has been achieved for certain technologies following electricity price increases since 2013. The up-front capital costs for renewable energy, however, remain an inhibitor.

Development of the adaptation work-stream

This MCPP work-stream was initiated in 2006 following a climate change impact analysis by the Environmental Management Department, which clarified likely local impacts and provided important methodological learning. Key among the latter was the recognition that simple trend analyses (rather than the costly down-scaling of climate models) would have sufficed as a starting point for climate protection planning. The adaptation work-stream is currently made up of several components:

- municipal adaptation (i.e. the development of municipal adaptation plans linked to key line functions in local government);
- community-based adaptation (i.e. activities focused on understanding and improving the adaptive capacity of local communities);
- a strong ecosystem-based component in municipal and community interventions;
- urban management interventions addressing specific climate change challenges (e.g. the urban heat island and increased storm water runoff);
- attempts to develop locally appropriate climate change tools (e.g. sea-level rise models and cost benefit models focused on human benefit and ecological integrity);
- actions to mainstream climate protection (e.g. mega-event greening to raise the profile of climate change and institutional restructuring);
- knowledge and data generation through development of research partnerships;
- networking at the local, sub-national, national and international levels.

The work-stream is supported by five dedicated posts in the Climate Protection Branch (established in 2007 as part of the development of the MCPP) and 43 in the broader Environmental Planning and Climate Protection Department. The lack of skilled and experienced adaptation professionals has, however, substantially delayed filling the posts. The department head, nevertheless, has remained a strong and dedicated champion and ensured continued support for the function. This is significantly different to the prematurely initiated mitigation work-stream which has experienced sporadic and changing leadership.

The development of the adaptation work-stream has been phased and opportunistic because of limited precedents, interest, leadership, institutional support and resources (Roberts and O'Donoghue 2013). The experience and knowledge gained through early interventions has shaped and refined subsequent actions and thinking. The focus has been on "no-regrets" projects that are beneficial under a range of climate change scenarios. These have helped build constantly evolving adaptation pathways (Barnett et al. 2014) composed of manageable steps over time, each triggered by a change in the contextual conditions of the programme (e.g. available resources, knowledge, unexpected opportunities) (see Figure 6.3). The resulting successes and failures have generated a cycle of continuous learning that has helped build a clearer understanding of the complexity of local-level adaptation action and enabled systematic adjustment in response to new information and changing circumstances. This process has also benefitted from the three decades of lessons learned that have emerged from the biodiversity work-stream of the city (Roberts 2016).

There has also been a strong reliance on identifying and developing champions within the municipality who, with their deep sectoral knowledge, understand where it is appropriate to work with other sectors, encouraging more integrative action and overlapping circles of influence. These champions have been critical in re-casting climate change as a development issue, minimising the marginalisation associated with environmental department programmes. For example, eThekwini Municipality has contributed to establishing a multi-stakeholder, trans-municipal partnership addressing the role of ecological infrastructure to increase water security and adaptive capacity in the uMgeni River catchment. This reflects a significant shift towards a "socio-ecological systems approach" to managing water, biodiversity, climate and poverty challenges (Sutherland 2014, p. 1). Making space on the political and bureaucratic agendas for this integrative approach required the leadership of the (then) head of eThekwini Water and Sanitation Unit. A key outcome has been the commitment of a wide range of stakeholders to a 2013 agreement focused on investment in local ecological infrastructure. This strong alignment of the adaptation and biodiversity agendas has been key in helping the city's environmental champions to become early climate change adaptation adopters, and contributing to advances in the biodiversity sector; for example, a new Restoration Ecology Branch created in 2011 to help move from a "preserve and protect" model of biodiversity planning to one capable of managing novel and changing ecosystems as the impacts of global environmental change materialise.

A catchment approach has also improved understanding of the requirements of fine-scale adaptation action (as opposed to macro-level planning). In 2012 a sister-city partnership with Bremen (Germany) provided the impetus for a climate change adaptation-focused partnership in the uMhlangane River catchment with a strong focus on governance, social learning and integration between municipal line functions. Despite the benefits, there have been significant challenges in maintaining the adaptation focus – partners bring different needs to the table, and engagement is complicated by staff shortages and historically poor communication between sectors. External funding has helped maintain momentum.

Some partnerships cannot survive the complex institutional and governance challenges. In 2009, participants at Durban's first Climate Summit agreed on the desirability of a broadly representative partnership to address the city's climate change issues. Elsewhere in the world such partnerships have been convened by leadership figures like the mayor. The Durban Climate Change Partnership was established using a democratic process with advertisements, public consultation and the establishment of an advisory forum to elect a representative steering committee. But a lack of effective leadership, long-term commitment and reliable funding made this committee largely ineffective. The Municipality's involvement in the committee was restricted by financial regulations, which reduced its participation to observer status and limited its ability to fund the partnership (Roberts and O'Donoghue 2013).

Attempts at developing locally and contextually appropriate tools for climate change planning have also had mixed results in Durban (Walsh et al. 2013, Cartwright et al. 2013), often proving expensive and time consuming. The resources and constraints of local government (especially in the global South) limit what can be created, and if the process is driven by research institutes or national governments alone, tools may not address contextually specific needs. Partnerships appear to offer the best route forward on this front (Walsh et al. 2013).

Financial limitations have been an on-going challenge in Durban's adaptation work, most of it initially funded from the municipal biodiversity budget. The first dedicated local funding for the MCPP was only received in 2010/2011. Because national and international funding have supplemented municipal resources, it is difficult to ascertain the exact amount of climate change-related spending by the municipality, but for 2008–2014 it appears to have been 0.2 to 1 per cent of the municipality's total budget – a cumulative $128 million (Cartwright et al. 2015).

A further complicating factor is that local governments in South Africa have no formal climate change response obligations. This is an unfunded mandate, often dependent on strong personalities. The 2011 National Climate Change Response Policy and the National Development Plan, for example, acknowledged a role for local government but gave no guidance on that role or how it should be financed (Department of Environmental Affairs 2011, National Planning Commission 2011) A proposed amendment to the national Disaster Management Act will create the first official mandate requiring municipalities to "provide measures and indicate how it will invest in disaster risk reduction and climate change adaptation, including ecosystem and community-based adaptation approaches".[10] The risk, however, is that adaptation will become subsumed by the disaster risk reduction agenda.

The international adaptation mandate for local government is similarly unclear. South Africa's hosting of the United Nation's Framework Convention on Climate Change COP17–CMP7 in 2011 was a unique opportunity for eThekwini Municipality to work with other national and international partners, to organise and host an adaptation-focused local government convention. The key outcome was the Durban Adaptation Charter, signed by 107 mayors and officials representing more than 950 local governments worldwide, most from the Global South. In the absence of a national or international agency able to act as a short-term home for the Charter, eThekwini Municipality has continued working with the engaged members of the original local government partnership, as well as new international partners to ensure the Charter's effective implementation.

As at the local level, champions (both individual and institutional) have been pivotal in facilitating key international networking opportunities that have strengthened support for the Durban Adaptation Charter, and in securing funding to operationalise it. They have also helped clarify the role of the Charter, not as a replacement for other local initiatives, but as a co-ordination hub identifying, communicating and co-ordinating adaptation-related opportunities for Charter signatories. Beginning in 2014, the carbon*n* Climate Registry (cCR) for cities (also the reporting platform for the international Compact of Mayors) became the agreed reporting platform for the Charter. Engagement with the South African national government has also ensured that the cCR will be used for local government level reporting in the country.

A key step in advancing the Charter has been a partnership with the U.S. Agency for International Development (USAID) and the International City/County Management Association (ICMA) CityLinks programme which enabled funding to be sourced for hosting an implementation guidance workshop in Durban in 2013. This meeting drew together key Charter signatories, partners and adaptation experts to agree on the most appropriate implementation strategy. Participants highlighted the need for national support, local leadership, local institutions, resources and stakeholder input and identified measures that could be developed into programming and support for signatories, among them recognising achievements, engaging mayors, disseminating knowledge and generating funding for adaptation (EThekwini Municipality 2013c). The need for a secretariat to identify and co-ordinate adaptation-related opportunities for Charter signatories and hubs was also stressed.

Using this input, an implementation model for the Charter has been developed, focusing on establishing a "network of networks" built around regional hubs and local compacts anchored in cities that are regional climate change leaders. This operates at three scales (Figure 6.4). First, the regional hubs interact with each other to learn from one another and work together on shared climate change issues. Thus far, hubs have been established in Southern Africa

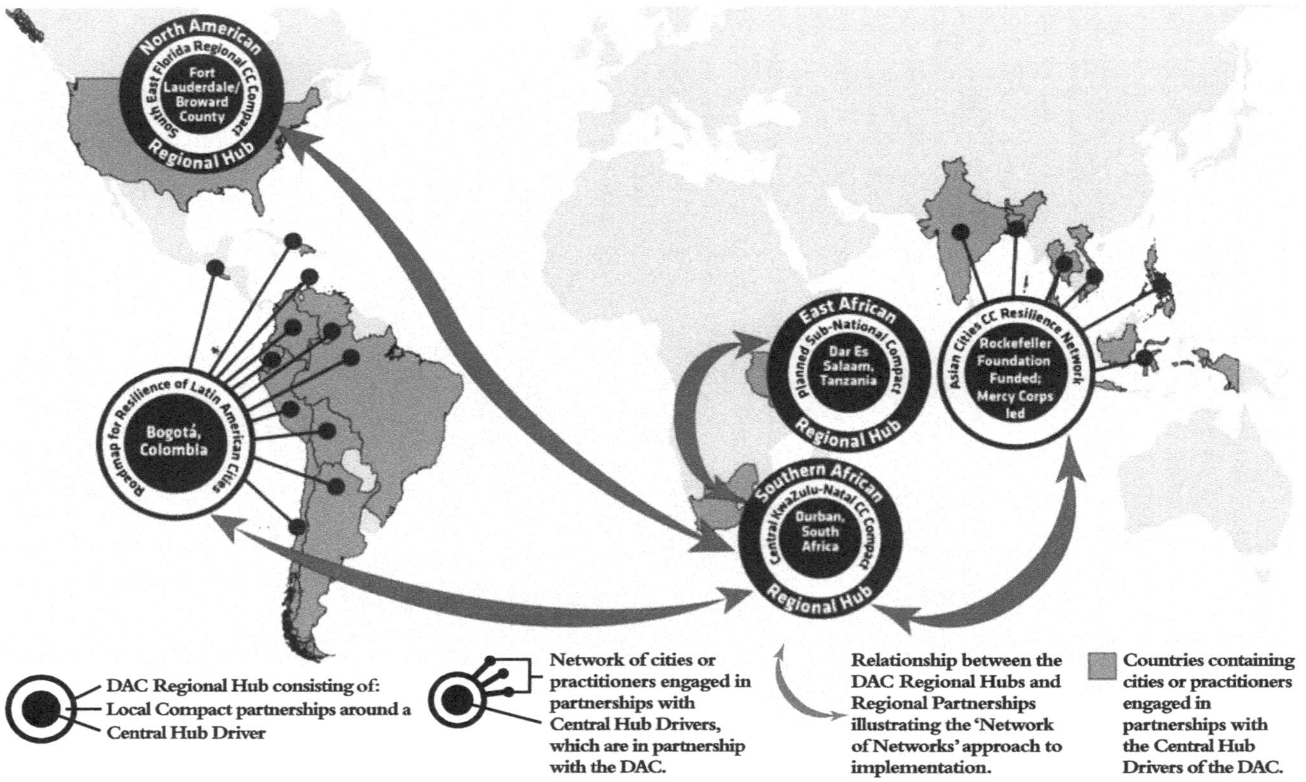

FIGURE 6.4 Global distribution of the network of networks created through partnerships within the Durban Adaptation Charter

(Durban), East Africa (Dar es Salaam) and North America (Fort Lauderdale/Broward County), and attempts are being made to establish West African, South American and South East Asian hubs. Durban has undertaken exchange visits with Fort Lauderdale/Broward County and Dar es Salaam, and in the latter case they have begun to build trans-national project teams focused on issues of common concern such as coastal erosion. Second, Regional Hubs provide a focal point for cities and local authorities in their region to interact around context-specific adaptation issues. The first regional meeting led by a hub city was in Dar es Salaam in November 2014 for East African Charter signatories. A similar Southern African regional meeting was convened at the Durban Adaptation Charter-focused Local Climate Solutions for Africa Conference hosted by eThekwini Municipality with ICLEI Africa in October 2015.

Third, sub-national networks (or local compacts) have been established around the regional hubs to provide support to smaller local authorities and secondary cities. The approach was pioneered by Fort Lauderdale/Broward County, where a local compact had been in place for six years. Using this model, the Central KwaZulu-Natal Climate Change Compact (CKZNCCC) was established between Durban and its neighbouring municipalities in 2013, with regular meetings and learning exchanges to share experiences on specific climate change themes. This local compact model is part of a growing recognition of the need to address climate change at the city region level and to increase adaptive capacity of secondary cities. Both the Regional Hubs and the local compacts are supported by the Charter secretariat currently hosted by eThekwini Municipality.

Although great progress has been made in operationalising the Charter through multi-sectoral and multi-scale (local, sub-national, regional and international) work, this has curtailed the local adaptation work of the Environmental Planning and Climate Protection Department and highlighted the difficult choices facing proactive local governments. Progress has also been limited by a growing need for knowledge and data to better inform decision making and the prioritisation of activities. In Durban, addressing this shortfall has catalysed the development of different knowledge networks, such as research partnerships with a local university, focused on climate change impacts on the city's biodiversity, and socio-ecological impacts of large-scale community reforestation initiatives. These trans-disciplinary partnerships (Cockburn et al. in press) serve a dual purpose: first, enabling the co-production of knowledge to advance evidence-based decision making and, second, helping to address the climate change and biodiversity skills shortage. Similarly, at the international level, linkages are being established and investigated with research organisations with an interest in climate protection at the local government level.

Integrating adaptation and mitigation

The Durban experience highlights the institutional complexity of local-level climate change adaptation action, necessitating a portfolio of "10 per cent solutions", often emerging from opportunistic and experimental activities that are co-ordinated, synergised and constantly re-evaluated to guard against maladaptation. The tendency to favour no-risk interventions with value across a range of climate scenarios, however, can limit consideration of more transformative interventions involving greater risk and systemic change. This is problematic, given the increasing need for more ambitious adaptation to respond to "greater risks and complexities" (Rickards and Howden 2012, p. 246) from a substantial global adaptation gap (UNEP, 2014).

In all cases the role of champions has been critical in initiating and sustaining the work. Without their sustained input, progress stalls and this accounts for the differences in the adaptation and mitigation work-streams in Durban – adaptation has less financial resources but a committed long-term champion. Driving progress is also time-consuming. It took a decade to advance in this "learning-by-doing" mode from the initiation of the MCPP to a point where it was possible to develop the city's first climate change strategy.[11]

An important first step lies in determining how local adaptation and mitigation agendas could be better co-ordinated to maximise synergies and minimise conflicts. In Durban this has necessitated deeper consideration of how the climate question itself should be framed. The developmental needs of the city, its high risk socio-ecological profile and limited human and financial resources, make adaptation a priority for the foreseeable future. But broadening the concept of adaptation to include a just transition to a low carbon future to address development, energy security and GHG reduction pressures will make mitigation key to reducing vulnerability and risk in an unpredictable, climate stressed future.

A number of activities in Durban have already explored the adaptation–mitigation interface. A carbon stock inventory (Glenday 2007) established that the city's open space system (D'MOSS) stored 6.6 ± 0.2 million tonnes of carbon (Mt C) in 2005, equivalent to 24.3 ± 0.9 million tonnes of carbon dioxide (Mt CO_2) (roughly the carbon equivalent of the city's annual emissions at the time) and sequestered 8400–9800 tonnes of carbon annually (tC/yr). The Academy of Science of South Africa also produced a report exploring how Durban could transition to a low carbon future (ASSAf 2011). This DANIDA-funded research confirmed the need to better integrate the city's adaptation and mitigation agendas but with limited impact due to the minimal involvement of municipal departments during the preparation and review of the report. Three large community reforestation projects, initiated to offset the carbon footprints of the FIFA Football World Cup in 2010 and COP17-CMP7 in 2011, serve as practical examples of such integration, having created new carbon sinks and delivered multiple adaptation co-benefits, such as biodiversity enhancement and improved supply of ecosystem services. The socio-economic co-benefits are particularly important in encouraging local climate action, as risk acceptance is greater in vulnerable communities, especially for climate change risks seen as secondary to development concerns.

Institutional restructuring has also been important to reframing the climate question in Durban. A decision in 2015 to combine the Energy Office and Environmental Planning and Climate Protection Department will connect three global change agendas at the local level: mitigation, adaptation and biodiversity (given the already strong integration of the adaptation and biodiversity agendas). These two offices have already worked together to develop the city's first climate change strategy, which opened the climate debate to wider participation, increasing the diversity of values and ideas and providing for greater equity in decision making. The strategy was approved by the City Council in 2015 and an implementation plan is being developed to maximise the co-benefits between adaptation and mitigation actions.

An important new development is the increasing political prioritisation of climate change driven by the Mayor's role as a global climate change champion. He proposed the establishment of a political committee to raise the profile of this issue amongst city leadership; the first meeting of this committee was convened in September 2015. Some politicians have also requested training to better understand the climate change challenge, suggesting a growing maturity in governance structures, which will be central in supporting the integration of the city's adaptation and mitigation agendas and fostering actions to influence systemic and potentially transformative change.

Realising this potential, however, means focusing less on maintaining an untenable status quo and more on working through the adaptive cycle to create the possibility of transition to a new and better state (Park et al. 2011, Rickards and Howden 2012, Solecki et al. in review). In Durban this means improving equity, social legitimacy and environmental sustainability (Revi et al. 2014). To achieve this outcome, transformative adaptation pathways will in some instances require reducing the resilience of systems to facilitate a state change. This has the potential to shift the choice from win-win to win-lose, and necessitates careful consideration of who or what loses in the move from the status quo. In the end, transformative adaptation will require strong leadership prepared to take difficult decisions.

Notes

1 All climate statistics obtained from Weather SA: www.weathersa.co.za/
2 2014 exchange rate $1=R10–11.
3 M. Byerley, Manager: Research and Policy, Policy and Development Department, eThekwini Municipality personal communication.
4 1994 – the first municipal Environmental Manager was appointed within the Physical Environment Service Unit (an engineering and urban design focused unit) with an operational focus on sustainable development.

1995–2003 – the appointment of additional staff created the Environmental Branch, which moved to the Development Planning Service Unit in 1997 (this was a unit focused on urban planning and development control). In 2002, the operational focus of the branch changed from sustainable development to biodiversity planning.

2003 – an institutional elevation to departmental level created the Environmental Management Department. Climate change emerged as an exploratory operational area in 2004.

2009 – the Department's name was changed to Environmental Planning and Climate Protection, as climate change emerged as a core operational function.

2014 – a Departmental name change to Climate Change, Biodiversity and Resilience was proposed, to more accurately identify its three core business areas.

5 www.dbnlandfillgas2elec.co.za/
6 http://en.wikipedia.org/wiki/Durban_Industry_Climate_Change_Partnership_Project
7 International Local Government GHG Emissions Analysis Protocol Version 1.0 and Local Government Operations Protocol for the Quantification and Reporting of Greenhouse Gas Emissions Inventories Version 1.1.
8 Conference of the Parties serving as a meeting of the Parties.
9 www.energycommunity.org/default.asp?action=47
10 http://pmg-assets.s3-website-eu-west–1.amazonaws.com/130619disastermanagementamendmentdraftbill.pdf
11 www.durban.gov.za/DCCS

References

Archer, D, F Almansi, M Digregorio, D Roberts, D Sharma and D Syam (2014), "Moving towards inclusive urban adaptation: approaches to integrating community-based adaptation to climate change at city and national scale", *Climate and Development* Vol 6, No 44, pages 345–356, DOI: 10.1080/17565529.2014.918868.

ASSAf (2011), *Towards a Low Carbon City: Focus on Durban,* Report by the Academy of Science of South Africa for eThekwini Municipality, Durban, South Africa, 265 pages.

Barnett, J, S Graham, C Mortreux, R Fincher, E Waters and A Hurlimann (2014), "A local coastal adaptation pathway", *Nature Climate Change* 4, pages 1103–1108, DOI: 10.1038/nclimate2383.

Carmin J, I Anguelovski and D Roberts (2012), "Urban climate adaptation in the global south: planning in an emergency policy domain", *Journal of Planning Education Research* 32, pages 18–32.

Cartwright, A, J Blignaut, M De Wit, K Goldberg, M Mander, S O'Donoghue and D Roberts (2013), "Economics of climate change adaptation at the local scale under conditions of uncertainty and resource constraints: the case of Durban, South Africa", *Environment and Urbanization* Vol 25, No 1, pages 1–18.

Cartwright, A, J Blignaut, M Mander and M McKenzie (2015), *EThekwini Municipality Climate Change Spend Analysis: Towards a Credible Quantification of Municipal Investment into Climate Change Mitigation and Adaptation,* Report, Durban, South Africa, 20 pages.

Cockburn, J, M Rouget, R Slotow, D Roberts, R Boon, E Douwes, S O'Donoghue, C Downs, S Mukherjee, W Musakwa, O Mutanga, T Mwabvu, J Odindi, A Odindo, S Procheş, S Ramdhani, J Ray-Mukherjee, S Naidoo, C Schoeman, A Smit, E Wale and S Willows-Munro (in press), "Implementation of a science-action partnership to manage a threatened ecosystem in an urban context", *Ecology and Society.*

DANIDA (2005), *Denmark–South Africa Urban Environmental Management Programme. Programme and Component Documents*, Report, South Africa, 98 pages.

Department of Environmental Affairs (2011), *National Climate Change Response White Paper*, Report, The National Government of the Republic of South Africa, Pretoria, South Africa, 48 pages.

Diab, R and D Roberts (2012), "Towards a low carbon city: the case of Durban", *Informationen zur Raumentwicklung Heft* 5/6, pages 1–8.

EThekwini Municipality (2008), *Energy Strategy 2008*, Report by Enviros Consulting Limited for eThekwini Municipality, 92 pages.

EThekwini Municipality (2013a), *Economic Development and Job Creation Strategy,* Report, Durban, South Africa, 78 pages.

EThekwini Municipality (2013b), *2011/12 Municipal Services and Living Conditions Survey*, Report, eThekwini Municipality Corporate Policy Unit, 75 pages.

EThekwini Municipality (2013c), *Durban Adaptation Charter: Summary Report on the Durban Adaptation Charter Implementation Guidance Workshop,* Report, Durban, South Africa, 41pages.

EThekwini Municipality (2014a), *Durban State of Biodiversity Report 2013/2014,* Report by Environmental Planning and Climate Protection Department, Durban, 26 pages.

EThekwini Municipality (2014b), *Medium Term Revenue and Expenditure Framework 2014/2015 to 2016/2017*, Report, Durban, South Africa, 259 pages.

EThekwini Municipality (2015a), *EThekwini Municipality Integrated Development Plan, 2015/2016*, Report, Durban, South Africa, 482 pages.

EThekwini Municipality (2015b), *EThekwini Municipal Services and Living Conditions Survey: Three Year Trend Report. June 2015*, Report compiled by Eureka Market Research Services, 69 pages.

EThekwini Municipality (2015c), *Draft Summary Document: eThekwini Greenhouse Gas Emissions Inventory 2013,* Report by eThekwini Municipality Energy Office, 15 pages.

Glenday, J (2007), *Carbon Storage and Sequestration Analysis of the eThekwini Environmental Services Management Plan Open Space System*, Report for the eThekwini Municipality Environmental Management Department, Durban, South Africa, 71 pages.

Golder Associates (2011), "*Community-based Adaptation to Climate Change in Durban,* Report Number 11977-10286-9, Golder Associates report prepared for eThekwini Municipality, Durban, South Africa, 140 pages.

Leck, H and D Roberts (2015), "What lies beneath: understanding the invisible aspects of municipal climate change governance", *Current Opinion in Environmental Sustainability* Vol 13, pages 61–67.

Leck, H, C Sutherland, D Scott and G Oelofse (2011), "Social and cultural barriers to adaptation implementation: The case of South Africa", in L Masters and L Duff (editors), *Overcoming Barriers to Climate Change Adaptation Implementation in Southern Africa,* Institute for Global Dialog, Pretoria, South Africa, 294 pages.

Mather, A, G Garland and D Stretch (2009), "Southern African sea levels: corrections, influences and trends", *African Journal of Marine Science* Vol 31, No 2, pages 145–156.

National Planning Commission (2011), *National Development Plan: Vision for 2030*, Report by the South African Government, Pretoria, South Africa, 429 pages.

Park, S E, N A Marshall, E Jakku, A M Dowd, S M Howden, E Mendham and A Fleming (2011), "Informing adaptation responses to climate change through theories of transformation", *Global Environmental Change* 22, pages 115–126, DOI: 10.1016/j.gloenvcha.2011.10.003.

Revi, A, D Satterthwaite, F Aragón-Durand, J Corfee-Morlot, R B Kiunsi, M Pelling, D Roberts, W Solecki, S P Gajjar and A Sverdlik (2014), "Towards transformative adaptation in cities: the IPCC's Fifth Assessment", *Environment and Urbanization* Vol 26, No 1, pages 11–28.

Rickards, L and S M Howden (2012), "Transformational adaptation: agriculture and climate change", *Crop and Pasture Science* 63, pages 240–250.

Roberts, D (2008), "Thinking globally, acting locally: institutionalizing climate change at the local government level in Durban, South Africa", *Environment and Urbanization* Vol 20, No 2, pages 521–537.

Roberts, D (2010), "Prioritizing climate change adaptation and local level resilience in Durban, South Africa", *Environment and Urbanization* Vol 22, No 2, pages 397–413.

Roberts, D (2016). "City action for global environmental change: assessment and case study of Durban, South Africa", in K C Seto, W Solecki and C Griffith (editors), *Handbook on Urbanization and Global Environmental Change*, Routledge, London.

Roberts, D and S O'Donoghue (2013), "Urban environmental challenges and climate change action in Durban, South Africa", *Environment and Urbanization* Vol 25, No 2, pages 299–319.

Roberts, D, R Boon, N Diederichs, E Douwes, N Govender, A Mcinnes, A Mclean, S O'Donoghue and M Spires (2012), "Exploring ecosystem-based adaptation in Durban, South Africa: 'learning-by-doing' at the local government coal face", *Environment and Urbanization* Vol 24, No 1, pages 167–195.

Roma, E, K Philp, C Buckley, S Xulu and D Scott (2013), "User perceptions of urine diversion dehydration toilets: experiences from a cross-sectional study in eThekwini Municipality", *Water SA* 39, pages 305–311.

Scenario Building Team (2007), *Long Term Mitigation Scenarios: Scenario Document.* Department of Environment Affairs and Tourism, Pretoria, 31 pages.

Solecki, W, M Dorsch and M Pelling (in review), Resilience and transformation in response to risk and hazards in urban coastal settings: conceptual framework for scenario and case study analysis. *Ecology and Society*.

Statistics South Africa (2012), *Census 2011 Municipal Report KwaZulu-Natal*, Report No. 03-01-53, Pretoria, South Africa, 195 pages.

Statistics South Africa (2014), *Poverty Trends in South Africa: An Examination of Absolute Poverty between 2006 and 2011*, Report No. 03-10-06, Pretoria, South Africa, 74 pages.

Sutherland, C with contributions from D Roberts (2014), *Why Leadership Matters in Water and Climate Governance, Chance To Sustain Opinion July 2014*, EADI, Bonn.

Thopil, G A and A Pouris (2013), "International positioning of South African electricity prices and commodity differentiated pricing", *South African Journal of Science* 109, pages 1–4.

UNEP (2014), *The Adaptation Gap Report 2014*, United Nations Environment Programme (UNEP), Nairobi, Kenya, 68 pages.

Walsh, C, D Roberts, R Dawson, J Hall, A Nickson and R Hounsome (2013), "Experiences of integrated assessment of climate impacts, adaptation and mitigation modelling in London and Durban", *Environment and Urbanization* Vol 25, No 2, pages 361–380.

Ziervogel, G, M New, E Archer van Garderen, G Midgley, A Taylor, R Hamann, S Stuart-Hill, J Myers and M Warburton (2014), "Climate change impacts and adaptation in South Africa", *Wiley Interdisciplinary Reviews: Climate Change* Vol 5, pages 605–620, DOI: 10.1002/wcc.295.

7

LONDON, UNITED KINGDOM

Sari Kovats, Mark Pelling, Markella Koniordou, Jörn Birkmann and Torsten Welle

Introduction

London, the capital city of the United Kingdom, is also one of the cities at the forefront of climate change research and policy. The UK Climate Change Act 2008 entails legally binding targets for emissions reductions, and also a statutory responsibility for public agencies to adapt to climate change. This means that London has a wide range of climate policies, and, in addition, an emerging evidence-base regarding the risks of climate change, effective responses, and the level of implementation of such policies.

Physical context

Greater London, located in the south-east of the United Kingdom, is one of the largest and most densely populated cities in Europe. It is divided into Inner and Outer regions. Inner London refers to the part of Greater London falling within the boundaries of the former London County, which existed from 1889 to 1965, and which includes the City of London and 13 of the London boroughs. Outer London is generally lower density and suburban.

London has a mid-latitude marine/oceanic climate with low pressure systems passing generally eastward. Owing to both its climate and an urban heat island effect, London is the warmest place in the UK, with annual mean temperatures ranging from 7.8°C to 15.3°C (mean 11°C) (Met Office 2011).

Despite the relatively moderate UK climate, London has experienced severe heatwaves, often associated with pollution episodes. The heatwave of 2003 was associated with approximately 600 deaths in London, mostly in the elderly (Johnson et al. 2005). The 2003 heatwave (which also affected most of Europe) led to the development of the Heatwave Plan for England. Heatwaves have also occurred in 2006, 2009 and 2013 (PHE 2014a).

The River Thames, the longest river in England, flows through London and is tidal until Teddington Lock in south-west London. Approximately, 15 per cent of Greater London has some extent of known tidal and/or fluvial flood risk, affecting more than 680,000 properties (GLA 2009).

For its size London is one of the greenest cities in the world, placing behind only Sydney and Singapore among world cities for the highest percentage of green cover (Mayor of London and BOP Consulting 2013). Over 40 per cent of its land cover is dedicated to green space. Protected sites include 37 Sites of Special Scientific Interest (SSSIs), in addition to two Special Protection Areas (SPAs), three Special Areas of Conservation (SACs), two National Nature Reserves (NNRs) and 142 Local Nature Reserves (LNRs) (GiGL 2013).

Social context

London's population is over 13 per cent of the total population of the United Kingdom and was estimated to be 8.4 million residents in 2013 (Nomis ONS 2015). London is a fast growing city and part of the fastest-growing region in the UK (ONS 2014). An additional 13 per cent increase in London's population is expected in the ten-year period from 2012 to 2022, and the population is likely to exceed 9 million by 2020 (GLA 2014a). The increase in population is a result of both natural change and migration, with increases in births and in-migration and declines in deaths and emigration.

London is a multi-cultural, diverse and (relatively for the UK) young city. Young adults (25–34 year olds) comprise 25 per cent of the population in Inner London and 15 per cent in Outer London, compared with 12 per cent elsewhere in England (London's Poverty Profile 2015). This age profile is partly due to the younger immigrant population (Krausova and Vargas-Silva 2013). London has received repeated and consistent waves of immigration. The majority of Londoners are White (45 per cent White British and 15 per cent Other White); Asian (18 per cent), Black (13 per cent) and Mixed or Other ethnic groups (8 per cent) also constitute a high proportion of London's working population (ONS 2013).

Today London is one of the top world financial centres. The city was affected by the recent economic crisis (2007) but has recovered faster than any other region in the United Kingdom. Historically, its economy was associated with an extended manufacturing sector. Nowadays, however, it has almost entirely moved to a service-based economy with professional, scientific and technical services leading the city, alongside strong partnerships with emerging markets such as China and India (GLA 2014a).

Despite economic recovery, economic benefits are not equally distributed between or within London areas. London's growing economy is in fact accompanied by a widening gap between the richer and poorer of its residents, and by both income and pay poverty. London's unemployment rates have decreased faster than those in the rest of the UK – with an employment sector reaching 5.2 million jobs in 2013 (GLA 2014a). However, in 2014 unemployment was slightly higher in London (7.1 per cent) than the UK average (6.3 per cent) (Nomis ONS 2015). There is persistent unequal distribution of employment opportunities among London boroughs, particularly between Inner and Outer London, with a lower concentration of local jobs in the latter (GLA 2014a).

London social inequalities are based on geographical, socio-economic, ethnic, gender, sexuality, age and disability factors. These inequalities are also reflected in the health and well-being of Londoners, with most prominent effects on life-expectancy, childhood obesity and long-term illness/disability. For example, during the period 2010–12, male residents of the London borough of Kensington and Chelsea had an average life-expectancy at birth of 82.1 years, while that of males living in Tower Hamlets was 77.1 years (PHE 2014b).

Environmental hazards such as low-quality housing, poor air quality and lack of green space exacerbate health inequalities in London. Air pollution levels, which are primarily driven by road transport, have been shown to be highest in more deprived neighbourhoods (Tonne et al. 2008). It has also been shown that low-income groups generally have less access to green space in London (Balfour and Allen 2014).

If the cost of housing is factored into the calculation, then poverty is highest in London relative to the rest of the UK (Carr et al. 2014). Approximately one out of four working adults and over 40 per cent of children in London face housing poverty (GLA 2014a). London housing includes owner-occupied housing, private rentals and social housing (including council housing). Accommodating London's growing population will be an ever-greater challenge; projections suggest that another half a million houses will be needed by 2021 and possibly 1 million by 2036 (GLA 2014a).

City governance

London is governed in a two-tier system. The Greater London Authority (GLA) was created in 2000 under the 'Greater London Authority Act 1999' and consists of the Mayor of London and the London Assembly. The Mayor is elected every four years, and plays an executive role, developing city-wide plans and strategies, while the London Assembly, consisting of 25 elected members, inspects and scrutinises the plans made by the Mayor (GLA 2016a).

London is locally governed by 33 councils, which represent the 32 London boroughs and the City of London. Councils are run by elected councillors and are responsible for day-to-day services to residents including local housing, waste and recycling, crime reduction, enterprise partnerships and health (including public health) and social care.

With regards to environmental regulation, the UK has a fairly strong record. The Environment Agency (London office) plays a dominant role, having statutory responsibility and ensuring that environmental standards are being met. Moreover, the Mayor's strategies (including the Spatial Development

Strategy for London, the most recent version of which is the 2011 'London Plan') also cover actions on improving air and water quality, waste management, and tacking climate change in London.

London's responses to climate change

London's response to climate change is guided by international and national policies, but by far the most significant body of governance is the Greater London Authority (GLA); and under the Greater London Authority Act 2007, the Mayor has statutory responsibility to address climate change mitigation and adaptation.

The Mayor has developed the following key climate change strategies: The London Plan 2011 (note that a Draft with changes was also released in December 2014), formerly known as the London Spatial Development Plan, describes all London policies and frameworks on changing infrastructure and includes a dedicated chapter (Chapter 7) on Climate Change (Policies 5.1–5.22) (Table 7.1). It has significant overlap with the two further specific strategies on tackling climate change in London (also issued in 2011), one on mitigation – 'The Mayor's Climate Change Mitigation and Energy Strategy' (GLA 2011c), and the other on adaptation – 'Managing Risks and Increasing Resilience' (GLA 2011a).

These are further complemented by the Transport Strategy, the Housing Strategy, the Mayor's Air Quality Strategy (including the creation of a Low-Emission zone), the 'All London Green Grid' framework, the London Water Strategy and the Waste Strategy. Policies are implemented as programmes via cooperation of the GLA with a large variety of functional agents such as the London Borough Councils, the Department of Energy and Climate Change, the Environmental Agency, Transport for London, Metropolitan Police Authority, the London Fire and Emergency Planning Authority and London Development Agency amongst others.

TABLE 7.1 London Plan policies on climate change mitigation and adaptation

Adaptation	*Mitigation*
• Overheating and cooling in housing • Urban greening • Green roofs and development site environs • Flood risk management • Sustainable drainage • Water quality and wastewater infrastructure • Water use and supplies	• Retrofitting homes and workplaces • New development sustainable guidelines • Low carbon transport • Decentralisation of energy systems • Renewable and alternative sources of energy (particularly from waste) • Engaging with businesses and communities

Source: GLA (2011a, 2011c).

Climate risks and adaptation policies, strategies and measures

London's adaptation strategy, developed by the GLA, is articulated in policies in the London Plan (Policies 5.9–5.15) and in the Mayor's Adaptation Strategy, both which have been formulated to tackle the climate risks identified in the first UK Climate Change Risk Assessment (Defra 2012). The key climate risks for London are considered to be flooding, drought and high temperatures (heatwaves).

The Mayor's Adaptation strategy places an emphasis on collaborating with partners and distributing tasks across different public agencies and voluntary organisations (e.g. London Resilience and the London Climate Change Partnership, Drain London, etc.). Resilience has become an important feature of national and local policy discourse in relation to both climate change adaptation and disaster risk reduction (Zaidi and Pelling 2013), and the position of the concept of resilience as a policy narrative in London is indicative of wider political priorities. However, there is also some concern about London's ability to mitigate and adapt to climate change. Although it is recognised, from the perspective of achieving sustainable urbanisation, that resilience requires pro-active, joined-up, cross-sectoral and multi-hazard approaches to risk management – as expressed, for example in the Sustainable Development Goals – this has been difficult to implement in practice for London.

The case of London highlights how slippery the concept of resilience is as a policy term for enhancing sustainability. This has played out in London through the strategic positioning of those institutions 'owning' the resilience agenda in the city. A focal point for resilience has been the London Resilience Team, hosted by the London Mayor's Office up to 2014. Even during this period, a lack of clarity and consistency existed between the centralised London Resilience Team and the 32 London Boroughs, some of which employed Resilience Officers. The London Borough concerns were local and not easily aligned with the vision of the city level Resilience Team. There was agreement that resilience required pro-active, joined-up, cross-sectoral and multi-hazard approaches to risk management. More difficult was finding political will and institutional capacity to put these ambitions into practice. Since 2014, a resolution has become even less likely. Bdget cuts in London Boroughs have seen a reduction in Resilience Officer posts and a slowing of policy discourse and weakening of capacity to mainstream resilience and sustainability into development planning at the local level. At the same time, city-wide leadership and advocacy power has arguably been diminished by the relocation of the London Resilience Team to the London Fire Brigade. The retreat of the concept of resilience as a term used in support of integrated development is also signalled by the award of a Rockerfeller 100 Resilient Cities title to London in 2015. The award was made not to the Resilience Team with its recognised agenda, but to the Mayor's Office for Policing and

Crime. Resilience is now being refashioned as a concern for public order, counter-terrorism and cyber-crime. These are important issues for London as a global financial centre, but where does this leave the everyday risks from environmental change and the global responsibility of London as a major emitter of atmospheric pollution and greenhouse gases? Certainly in the London case the idea of resilience and its champions have not been able to refocus development on sustainability. This reflects the conservative political and policy context of contemporary London and the challenge of delivering the transformational potential of resilience at the city scale without the alignment of strategic and local interests.

Heat risks: overheating and the urban heat island

Higher temperatures and an increase in the frequency and intensity of heatwaves are key risks related to climate change. Cities also experience higher temperatures that are a function of the concentration of human activity and built-up areas – so-called urban heat islands. London has a well-described heat island (Mavrogianni et al. 2015) which may be further enhanced in summer by climate change (McCarthy et al. 2010; Wilby 2008).

The effects of climate change on high indoor temperatures has important implications for health and wellbeing (thermal comfort) as people spend most of their time indoors. A large proportion of homes already experience overheating even during relatively cool summers (Mavrogianni et al. 2015; Beizaee et al. 2013). Housing characteristics are a more important determinant of indoor temperatures than the urban heat island itself (outdoor temperatures) (Taylor et al. 2015). The current adaptation strategy in London to tackle overheating in buildings and homes is in the form of guidance provided by the Chartered Institution of Building Services Engineers (CIBSE) in association with GLA and the Code for Sustainable Homes (GLA 2014a). However, there is a lack of policy from the national government on addressing overheating, and the fact that it is not fully considered in current building regulations means that the potential for future adaptation is limited.

The determinants of heat risks to health (as opposed to comfort) are complex. High temperatures are known to cause short-term increases in daily mortality, and the elderly and those with chronic diseases are most at risk (Kovats and Hajat 2008). There is currently no evidence for a socio-economic gradient in heat-related mortality in London (Hajat et al. 2007). A recent survey of heat protection behaviours showed that Londoners are less likely to have air conditioning than those in other UK regions, and younger people are more likely to undertake heat protection behaviours (Khare et al. 2015).

A number of research projects have sought to map heatwave risk in London at different spatial scales (Wolf and McGregor 2013; Taylor et al. 2015). This can help emergency planners to focus risk management efforts. However, heatwave risks in particular are challenging to identify and map using available data. This is the case even in London, which has a more comprehensive data resource than many other cities internationally.

Figure 7.1 shows how exposure, vulnerability and risk to extreme heat varies between the London boroughs. Figure 7.2 shows the variables used to generate the maps in Figure 7.1, to represent susceptibility (openness to harm), coping capacity (resources available to avoid harm) and adaptive capacity (scope to avoid future harm) (see www.bel-truc.org, Welle et al. 2013 and Birkmann et al. 2013 for more details on the methods). Deriving indicators to capture abstract concepts such as vulnerability requires interaction with key stakeholders such as emergency planners.

Figure 7.1 illustrates both the opportunities and challenges for heatwave risk mapping. The class 'very high' is represented with crosshatching and indicates those boroughs where the exposure, the vulnerability and the risk towards heat stress is the highest. An improved differentiation of hazard exposure, vulnerability and risk is important to better understand the different drivers of risk, but also to inform and improve risk management and planning at the local level. Heatwave mapping can be useful as an information base for informed decision making in different institutions. The assessment also underscores the necessity of better linking strategic spatial and urban planning and health and social care in London, and for the GLA to integrate strategies to reduce urban heat exposures on the one hand and to improve disaster risk and emergency management strategies on the other.

Modification of the outdoor environment, via enhanced urban greening for example, provides other opportunities for reducing heat risks, with additional benefits for health and wellbeing through increased access to green space. The GLA aims to increase tree cover by 5 per cent by 2025 and total green urban space by 10 per cent by 2050, as well promoting the installation of green roofs or vertical green systems. These strategies not only support city cooling but also act as natural barriers that assist flood management (GLA 2014a). Community involvement is also a significant part of greening area projects, taking the form of voluntary initiatives that encourage residents to engage with green spaces near them (e.g. communal gardening, food growing, weed-cleaning, river clean-up and other outdoor activities, such as offering exercise classes for residents in its parks). Such projects provide both training opportunities for green skill development and platforms for sustainable behaviour change that will improve mental and physical health.

Flood risk management

London is at risk of flooding from several sources: tidal (overtopping of defences by a major storm surge in the North Sea); fluvial (when the capacity of the tributary rivers is exceeded or breached); and surface water (when intense rainfall in a thunderstorm exceeds the capacity of the drainage system). Climate change is likely to increase all of these types of flooding (Defra 2012). London

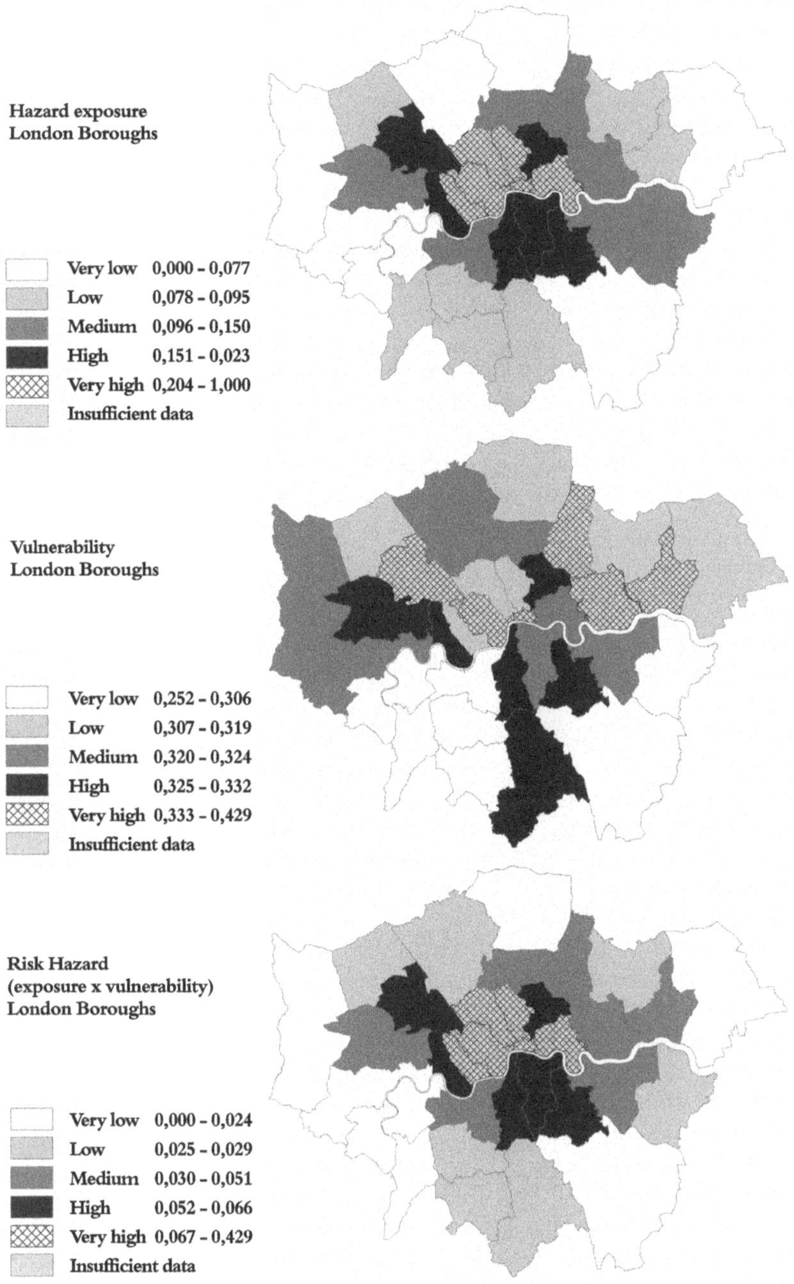

FIGURE 7.1 Maps of current vulnerability index for heat-related outcomes in London

Susceptibility	Coping capacity	Adaptive Capacity
Demography A Migrant population/ short term migrants B % of pupils whose first language is not English C Dependency ratio D % people aged 3+ whose main language is not English (2011 census) E New migrant (NINo) rates (2012/13) F One-person households >65y **Health and nutrition** G Obesity in adults H Health status **Poverty and income** I Children in poverty J Multiple deprivation rank of average score K Income Support claimant rate (Feb-2013) L % children in out-of-work families (2012) M % people on low income N ILO unemployment rate (2012/13) O Youth unemployment rate (2012/13) P % working-age population who claim benefits (May-2013) Q Employment rate **Housing and neighbourhood conditions** R Overcrowded households by borough S Median house price (£ 2013) T London Happiness Scores	**Government and authorities** A Crime rates per thousand population (2012/13) B Turnout at 2010 local elections (%) **Medical services/DRR** C % working-age with a disability (2012) **Economic coverage** D Total mean gross annual pay – income (2013) **Social networks** E Volunteering work among adults F Social isolation: % of adult social care users who have as much social contact as they would like **DRR strategies** G Internet usage	**Education and research** A Proportion of working age people with no qualification B Proportion of 16–18 years not in employment, education or training **Gender equity** C Gender parity in annual gross pay (female-male) **Environmental status / ecosystem protection** D % of people with access to open space E Environmental footprint F Net change in street trees (2009–2010) **Investment** G Life expectancy (2010–12) **Adaptation strategies/ awareness** H Household waste recycling rate (2012/13)

FIGURE 7.2 Selected indicators for the development of the vulnerability index for heat-related outcomes in London

is currently protected from tidal surges by the Thames Barrier, which has been operational since 1982 and was built in response to a major coastal flood event in 1953 that killed more than 300 people across the UK. This 30-year delay is typical for major infrastructure projects.

The UK government has developed extensive adaptation plans (TE2100) to adjust and improve flood defences for the protection of the Thames Estuary and London from future storm surges and flooding, and the increased risk from climate change and sea-level rise (TE2100 2012). The method used is iterative, with key decision points in the future, allowing for insight into the pathways for different adaptation options and decisions that depend on the eventual sea-level rise, which at present is highly uncertain. The TE2100 project is often quoted as a highly successful example of adaptation planning. However, the TE2100 plan also requires significant government investment from about 2050 for defences to be put in place by 2070.

London boroughs are being guided towards adapting to flood risks by the Flood and Water Management Act 2010 which urges the development of sustainable drainage systems (SUDs) in cooperation with private companies that own the drains (GLA 2011a). The London Drain Forum has produced a surface water management plan for each borough (GLA 2014a). SUDs will be increasingly important in adapting to changes in surface water runoff in cities. SUDs techniques include permeable paving and rainwater harvesting, as well as tree planting as discussed above, collectively becoming known as green infrastructure. Adapting existing urban drainage systems that have been designed based on historical rainfall records may require significant changes to urban landscapes (Charlesworth 2010).

Drought risks

London is also at risk of droughts. As well as rainfall variability, there is increasing demand for water, not only due to London's rising population but also as Londoners use more water per day (167 litres) than the UK average (146 litres). This further increases pressures on the public water supply (GLA 2011b).

London has not suffered a severe drought since 1976, when the loss of household water supply led to the use of standpipes. London has managed shortages in supply with emergency management measures such as bans on non-essential uses of water, including the use of hosepipes (GLA 2011a). However, the supply of water for personal and business use and, importantly, the health of green spaces and London's biodiversity, are already under threat from climate change. To date, there is no London-specific recovery from drought plan (GLA 2011a). However, under the Water Act 2003, water companies are obliged to form Drought Plans and Water Resource Management Plans (WRMPs) (GLA 2011b). WRMPs are water sufficiency plans approved by the Environmental Agency, financially supported and regulated by the water services economic regulator. They operate on the dual basis of optimising supply and demand (lowering consumption) (GLA 2011a).

Despite the lack of a London-specific drought plan, there are certain initiatives on improving water efficiency in London's Mayoral plans, including aims to integrate water efficiency into national government agendas and into the retrofitting building initiative, which is also part of London's mitigation strategy to improve energy efficiency. In order to engage consumers, water meters and informative bills are supplied, as are business incentives for tackling water leakages and looking at new water resources (GLA 2011a).

Key adaptation challenges

A recent assessment found that a lack of cross-sector impact and adaptation linkages was an important weakness in the adaptation plans of cities in general (Hunt and Watkiss 2011). Flexibility in adaptation decision making is essential for good planning. Additional barriers to adaptation in London have been identified in a gap analysis (Davoudi 2013). These include:

- institutional barriers to learning (Zaidi and Pelling 2013);
- governance issues, and a lack of regulatory frameworks or specific policies, e.g. to address overheating in housing;
- lack of integration with other policies, e.g. energy efficiency in housing;
- lack of understanding of climate risks.

A community's resources and facilities are likely to play an important part in successful adaptation. It is also clear that one of the great challenges facing London is the highly variable nature of its housing stock and other buildings. In general, buildings have not been designed to be either well insulated against cold or sufficiently well designed to prevent overheating and thereby maintain people's health and well-being during periods of cold and heat. Buildings are also not well designed to recover quickly after flooding, and there is an absence of property level protection in homes.

Low-carbon development and mitigation policies, strategies and measures

Greenhouse gas (GHG) inventory

The decade from 1990 to 2000 saw London's greenhouse gas (GHG) emissions soar from an (estimated) total of 45.05 Mt CO_2 to a (confirmed) total of 50.31 Mt CO_2 (a 12 per cent increase). GHG emissions are approximately evenly distributed over the three large sectors: residential, transport, and industrial and commercial sectors (Figure 7.3). Buildings (workplaces and housing) are responsible for the greatest proportion of GHG emissions, at almost 80 per cent (GLA 2011c). London is responsible for 8.5 per cent of UK total CO_2 emissions (GLA 2011c).

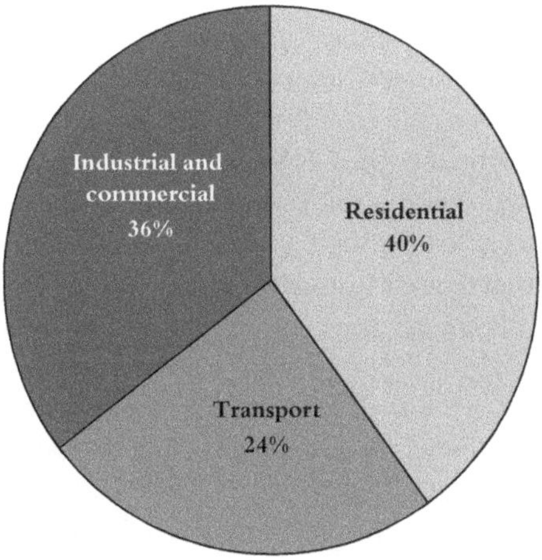

FIGURE 7.3 GHG emissions by sector for London (source: based on data from GLA 2014b)

Climate-change mitigation policies (London Plan 5.1–5.8) aim at reducing CO_2 emissions by 60 per cent in 2025 from 1990 levels. Recently, London has managed to make steady reductions in total GHG emissions, which decreased by 15 per cent between 2002 and 2009 to 42.52 Mt CO_2 and by a further 7 per cent in 2011 to 38.99 Mt CO_2e (GLA 2014b).

Energy consumption

To reduce London's energy consumption, the GLA places most emphasis on changing the built environment, both existing and new, and the transport system. Existing buildings (homes and workplaces), of which 80 per cent are expected still to be standing in 2050, contribute, as noted, the great majority of London's CO_2 emissions (GLA 2014b). As a result, existing buildings are being retrofitted with low-carbon technologies to promote energy efficiency. Retrofitting for existing commercial buildings is implemented through the 'RE:FIT' programme, and for homes through the 'RE:NEW' programme and according to the 'Housing Strategy'. RE:NEW, which operates on a borough council level, aims at retrofitting 1.2 million homes by 2015 and all homes by 2030.

With regards to new development, regulations aim to make domestic and non-domestic buildings zero carbon by 2016 and 2019, respectively. This is to be achieved by following the Mayor's energy hierarchy (1 Be lean: use less energy; 2 Be clean: supply energy efficiently; 3 Be green: use renewable energy). Building guidance is provided in the 'Mayor's supplementary planning guidance on Sustainable Design and Construction' (and the national Building Regulations), while the Government's Code for Sustainable Homes (CSH) provides guidance specifically for housing. Detailed energy assessments and design and access statements are also requested as part of the building process (GLA 2014a).

As the transport sector contributes up to 22 per cent of London's total CO_2 emissions (GLA 2014b), the GLA uses CO_2 reduction policies to encourage use of carbon-efficient modes of transport and carbon-efficient operation. This is practically achieved through an overall upgrade of the London public transport systems that maximises capacity and use of low-carbon buses and fuels, and the encouragement of use of electric and hydrogen-fuelled vehicles. Reductions in vehicular transport would lead to improvements in air quality, with benefits to human health (Haines 2012). 'Active travel' measures, which also have significant co-benefits for health, include support for cycling (a Cycle Hire scheme, Cycling Superhighways, more bike parking spaces) and walking (the Legible London scheme and walkways) (GLA 2011c). Increasing walking and cycling has the potential to save millions of pounds in health care costs for the treatment of chronic diseases (obesity, diabetes and cancer) (Woodcock et al. 2009).

Energy supply

There has been a shift in the energy supply for London to sustainable energy sources, through the uptake of low-carbon or renewable energy, re-evaluation of electricity and gas supply and the decentralisation of energy systems (DE). DE systems are a major priority of GLA climate change plans. This not only serves the purposes of energy efficiency and self-sufficiency, but also acts as a means to attract investment. Use of renewable/alternative sources of energy is encouraged across GLA plans. Along with the nation-wide targets set by the Government's Renewable Energy Strategy, 15 per cent of London's total energy is to be "generated by renewable sources by 2020" (GLA 2011c, p. 73). Another London target is to produce 25 per cent of London's energy from local sources by 2025 (GLA 2011c).

Electricity and gas is supplied by private companies. While the use of electricity is reported (by companies) to rise concomitantly with the growth of London's population, gas use is not increasing at the same rate. There is little information in the London Plan on strategies for reducing use, apart from decentralisation which aims to reduce consumption and increase renewable energy use by increasing uptake of solar schemes. To meet electricity demands, the Mayor has established the London Electricity High-level Working Group to determine that growing infrastructure is meeting decentralisation targets. It is also mentioned that the general aim is eventually to shift the supply to Combined Heat and Power (CHP) systems, from natural gas to energy from waste.

In 2014 the UK launched its first ever 'Community Energy Strategy', which outlines the government's support to community initiatives that aim at generating energy, reducing use and energy demand or improve the purchasing of energy. However, the uptake of solar panels (on homes) has been relatively low compared to other parts of the country. Only 0.5 per cent of London households have installed domestic PVs, compared with the national 2.3 per cent uptake in UK households (DECC 2015). Three barriers to a higher uptake of community energy in London have been identified. First, the lack of London-specific funds – despite the higher installation costs for London. Second, the nature and high costs of London's housing itself, with a significant proportion of the population privately renting and having to keep up with increasing rents. Third, the uncertainty in future investment and political support for the schemes.

London has adopted several nation-wide schemes that aim at changing the city's energy supply system and enhancing decentralisation further. These include the Energy Company Obligation (ECO) that obligates energy suppliers to cover the cost of energy improvements in the homes of people on low-income benefits, Feed-in Tariffs (FITs), pay energy users who invest in small-scale, low-carbon electricity generation systems for the electricity they generate and use, and for unused electricity they export back to the grid. The Renewable Heat Incentive (RHI) provides incentives for consumers to install renewable heating in place of fossil fuels. It is open to homeowners and landlords, commercial, industrial, public, not-for-profit and community generators of renewable heat (DECC EA 2015).

Low-carbon business

The UK capital has embraced the 'green economy', enabling London to lead as a low-carbon city. A report commissioned by the London Mayor found that in 2013 there were over 9,200 green businesses employing over 163,500 people (kMatrix 2013). Further, unlike other sectors, the green economy grew significantly throughout the economic downturn. The largest sectors in the 'Low-carbon and Environmental Goods and Services sector' were carbon finance, geothermal, wind, and building technologies. Overall, 97 per cent of the UK's carbon finance sector is contained within London. Business and entrepreneurial opportunities include the London Green Fund that invests in projects that lower London's carbon emissions (GLA 2016b). In addition, a booming green technology sector in 'smart city plans' for London are supported by the Mayor and national government (GLA 2014c).

Key mitigation challenges

Reducing carbon emissions remains a challenge for London, as for other cities. Companies and public agencies are obliged to produce plans but are not required or necessarily regulated to implement them. The Climate Change Committee undertakes a formal evaluation of emissions reductions by sector, as part of its remit under the Climate Change Act. Its 2014 report found that all sectors could do more to reduce emissions. The UK was on track to meet the second carbon budget (2013–2017), primarily due to the economic downturns, but also increasing energy efficiency measures (CCC 2015). However, the committee highlights the gap in achieving the emission reductions required to meet the fourth carbon budget (2023–2027).

The disbenefits of mitigation have also not been sufficiently considered. The increased proportion of diesel-fuelled traffic in London, and the failure of European emission standards for diesel cars to deliver the expected emission reductions of nitrogen oxides, have resulted in difficulties meeting EU air quality limit values for nitrogen dioxide (NO_2), prompting infraction proceedings by the European Commission against the UK.

Way forward: integrating adaptation and mitigation

London has passed through several historical moments of environmental crisis – from cholera and fire to sanitation and the great smog. Each challenge has been overcome in ways that improved the liveability of the city and the wellbeing of its citizens. The current crisis associated with the co-needs of climate change adaptation and mitigation, and wider concerns in particular of air quality and water accessibility, are not being met with the same level of resolve. Comprehensive and integrated approaches that place risk management within development and economic planning seem increasingly unlikely. This is at a time when, globally, cities are rising in prominence as environmental and development actors rivalling the ability of countries to deliver change.

Why is London shifting away from its position as a leading global city for resilience and risk management? Part of the answer lies in political choice and the underlying values and interests influencing urban policy. Even after the financial crisis, London's financial sector continues to provide a considerable contribution to the UK economy. London presents itself externally as a city fit for business and resilience is increasingly seen in these terms – resilience for business, and security for capital and physical assets, is at the fore of strategy at the city level. This is in contrast with the responsibilities for housing and urban planning which lie at the borough level, and for flood and heatwave risk management which are distributed among many, often national, agencies. All are constrained by significant budget cuts brought about by austerity policies.

Popular opinion is also yet to identify climate change as a priority when set against employment opportunities, public health priorities (obesity and chronic disease), health care demands, or crime. London is not alone in this respect. The immediate concerns of social policy make it difficult for more fundamental and longer-term planning priorities to rise up the agenda. There is no lack of scientific data and analysis presenting current and future risk, although as we have outlined, the empirical basis for such analysis has challenges. More limiting is the gap between science and policy with policy makers at the borough, GLA, and wider (national) levels having tightly defined mandates that determine their ability to act, and so the kinds of information they can act upon. The result is policy lock-in, or at best a slow drag on the evolution of policy and popular opinion.

Perhaps the central dilemma facing resilience building for London is a tension between the speed of social and environmental change on one hand and the trajectory and speed of public attitude and policy change on the other. The city is becoming increasingly diverse, with new migration from Eastern Europe and elsewhere. Cuts in funding for public services are already undermining the ability of health and social sectors to provide adequate quality housing, education and health care, with market solutions beyond the reach of the majority. Not only is the population of London increasing and becoming more diverse, its most at-risk populations – the very young (less than 5 years) and the elderly (more than 65 years) age groups – are growing. Economic change and a reduction in social protection measures are likely to exacerbate inequality so that at the very moment when vulnerability is increasing, the state has less capacity to adapt. Climate change impacts exacerbate this. The trajectory of mitigation policy is similarly under pressure with controls on vehicle emissions and on urban development less stringent than in the past. Commentators have pointed to a common blockage for adaptation and mitigation. Both require shifts in the basic drivers of established development – adaptation calls for more equity in development; mitigation for a willingness to invest in the future.

London has the potential to benefit from the synergies between adaptation and mitigation – most notably, regarding energy-efficient space cooling in housing, and increased green space and the development of its green infrastructure. The lack of integration of these policy agendas persists despite being recognised. A key recommendation by the UK Climate Change Committee is that the buildings sector 'Develop plans and policies that deliver low-carbon heat and energy efficiency, whilst also addressing the increasing risks of heat stress and flooding' (CCC 2015).

Learning from past successes and regaining a sense of international prestige through the integration of adaptation, mitigation and development will require both focused policy work and political leadership, as well as a science community that can effectively critique and support policy. London is a city of innovation with many committed actors in the public sector, business, science and civil society. The key challenge is to find the right policy environment within which to foster and project these energies so that the development co-benefits of adaptation and mitigation can be realised and London can retain its position as a leading global city for business and quality of life.

Acknowledgements

We acknowledge funding from the Belmont Forum for the grant 'Transformation and Resilience on Urban Coasts', and from the National Institute for Health Research Health Protection Research Unit (NIHR HPRU) in Environmental Change and Health at the London School of Hygiene and Tropical Medicine in partnership with Public Health England (PHE), and in collaboration with the University of Exeter, University College London, and the Met Office. The views expressed are those of the authors and not necessarily those of the NHS, the NIHR, the Department of Health or Public Health England.

References

Balfour, R and J Allen (2014), *Local Action on Health Inequalities: Improving Access to Green Spaces*, Public Health England and UCL Institute of Health Equity Report, London.

Beizaee, A, K J Lomas and S K Firth (2013), "National survey of summertime temperatures and overheating risk in English homes", *Building and Environment* Vol 65, pages 1–17.

Birkmann J, S Cutter, D Rothman, T Welle, M Garschagen, B van Ruijven et al. (2013), "Scenarios for vulnerability: opportunities and constraints in the context of climate change and disaster risk", *Climatic Change* Vol 133, No 1, pp 53–68

Carr J, R Councell, M Higgs and N Singh (2014), *Households Below Average Income. An Analysis of the Income Distribution 1994/95–2012/13*. London, UK: Department for Work and Pensions.

CCC (2015), *Reducing Emissions and Preparing for Climate Change: 2015 Progress Report to Parliament*. London: Committee on Climate Change.

Charlesworth, S M (2010), "A review of the adaptation and mitigation of global climate change using sustainable drainage in cities", *Journal of Water and Climate Change* Vol 1, No. 3, pages 165–180.

Davoudi, S, E Brooks and A Mehmood (2013), "Evolutionary resilience and strategies for climate adaptation", *Planning Practice and Research* Vol 28, No 3, pages 307–322.

DECC (2014), *Community Energy in the UK: Part 2,* Final report undertaken by Databuild Research and Solutions Ltd, supported by the Energy Saving Trust, DECC, London.

DECC (2015), *Sub-regional Feed-in Tariffs on the CFR statistics*, Data available from www.gov.uk/government/statistical-data-sets/sub-regional-feed-in-tariffs-confirmed-on-the-cfr-statistics Department of Energy and Climate Change, last updated 24 July 2015.

Defra (2012), *UK Climate Change Risk Assessment: Government Report*, Norwich, TSO.

GiGL (2013), *Key London Figures*, www.gigl.org.uk/our-data-holdings/keyfigures/

GLA (2009), London Regional Flood Risk Appraisal. www.london.gov.uk/file/1072/download?token=DJloydSf

GLA (2011a), *Managing Risks and Increasing Resilience, The Mayor's Climate Change Adaptation Strategy,* London, Greater London Authority.

GLA (2011b), *Securing London's Water Future, The Mayor's Water Strategy*, London, Greater London Authority.

GLA (2011c), *Delivering London's Energy Future, The Mayor's Climate Change Mitigation and Energy Strategy*, London, UK: Greater London Authority.

GLA (2014a), *Further Alterations to the London Plan, Consolidated With Alterations Since 2011,* Intend to publish version 15 December 2014 for submission to SOS CLG, London, Greater London Authority.

GLA (2014b), *London Energy and Greenhouse Gas Inventory (LEGGI) 2012*. http://data.london.gov.uk/dataset/leggi2012/resource/10e2d257-a8cb-4ed7-b592-fce6e1e971a3

GLA (2014c), *Mayor outlines Vision to make London the Tech Capital of the World*. www.london.gov.uk/press-releases-6094

GLA (2015a), *London Councils,* www.londoncouncils.gov.uk/londonfacts/londonlocalgovernment/onlineessentialguide/greaterlondonauthority.htm

GLA (2016a). *How London Government is Run*. www.london.gov.uk/about-us/our-role

GLA (2016b), *The London Green Fund.* www.london.gov.uk/about-us/mayor-london/london-green-fund

Haines, A (2012), "Health benefits of a low carbon economy", *Public Health* Vol 126, pages S33–S39.

Hajat, S, R S Kovats and K Lachowycz (2007), "Heat-related and cold-related deaths in England and Wales: who is at risk?" *Occupational and Environmental Medicine* Vol 64, no 2, pages 93–100.

Hunt, A and P Watkiss (2011), "Climate change impacts and adaptation in cities: a review of the literature", *Climatic Change*, Vol 104, no 1, pages 13–49.

Johnson, H, R S Kovats, G McGregor, J Stedman, M Gibbs and H Walton (2005), "The impact of the 2003 heatwave on daily mortality in England and Wales and the use of rapid weekly mortality estimates", *Eurosurveillance* Vol 10, no 7–9, pages 168–171.

Khare, S, S Hajat, S Kovats, C Lefevre, W de Bruin, S Dessai and A Bone (2015), "Heat protection behaviour in the UK: results of an online survey after the 2013 heatwave", *BMC Public Health* Vol 15, no 1, pages 1–12.

kMatrix (2013), *London's Low Carbon Market Snapshot. London's Low Carbon and Environmental Goods and Services – Updated Report.* Report Commissioned by the GLA, London.

Kovats, R S and S Hajat (2008), "Heat stress and public health: a critical review", *Annual Review of Public Health* Vol 29, no 1, pages 41–55.

Krausova, A and C Vargas-Silva (2013), *London: Census Profile*, Oxford, The Migration Observatory, University of Oxford.

London's Poverty Profile (2015), *London's Age Structure.* www.londonspovertyprofile.org.uk/london/londons-age-structure-1/

Mavrogianni, A, J Taylor, M Davies, C Thoua and J Kolm-Murray (2015), "Urban social housing resilience to excess summer heat", *Building Research and Information* Vol 43, no 3, pages 316–333.

Mayor of London and BOP Consulting (2013), *World Cities Culture Report 2013*, World Cities Culture Forum.

McCarthy, M P, M J Best and R A Betts (2010), "Climate change in cities due to global warming and urban effects", *Geophysical Research Letters* Vol 37, no 9, pages L09705.

Met Office (2011), *Climate: Observations, Projections and Impacts,* Exeter, UK: Met Office.

Nomis ONS (2015), *Labour Market Profile – London.* www.nomisweb.co.uk/reports/lmp/gor/2013265927/report.aspx

ONS (2013), *Comparison of Mid-2010 Population Estimates by Ethnic Group against the 2011 Census*, Office for National Statistics.

ONS (2014), *Mid-year Population Estimates for the UK 2013.* www.ons.gov.uk/ons/rel/pop-estimate/population-estimates-for-uk-england-and-wales-scotland-and-northern-ireland/2013/info-population-estimates.html

PHE (2014a), *Heatwave Plan for England*, London, Public Health England and Department of Health.

PHE (2014b), *Understanding Inequalities in London's Life Expectancy and Healthy Life Expectancy*, London: Public Health England.

Taylor, J, P Wilkinson, M Davies, B Armstrong, Z Chalabi, A Mavrogianni et al. (2015), "Mapping the effects of urban heat island, housing, and age on excess heat-related mortality in London", *Urban Climate* Vol 14, no 4, pages 517–528.

TE2100 (2012), *Thames Estuary 2100 (TE2100) Plan*, London, UK: Environment Agency.

Tonne, C, S Beevers, B Armstrong, F Kelly and P Wilkinson (2008), "Air pollution and mortality benefits of the London Congestion Charge: spatial and socioeconomic inequalities", *Occupational and Environmental Medicine* Vol 65, no 9, pages 620–627.

Welle, T, J Birkmann, D Krause, D C Suarez, N Setiadi and J Wolfertz (2013), "The WorldRiskIndex: A concept for the assessment of risk and vulnerability at global/ national scale", In J Birkmann, *Measuring Vulnerability to Natural Hazards: Towards Disaster Resilient Societies*, Second Edition, United Nations University Press, pages 219–251.

Wilby, RL (2008), "Constructing climate change scenarios of urban heat island intensity and air quality", *Environment and Planning B: Planning and Design* Vol 35, no 5, pages 902–919.

Wolf, T and G McGregor (2013), "The development of a heat wave vulnerability index for London, United Kingdom", *Weather and Climate Extremes* Vol 1, pages 59–68.

Woodcock, J, P Edwards, C Tonne, B Armstrong, O Ashiru, D Banister and I Roberts (2009), "Public health benefits of strategies to reduce greenhouse-gas emissions: urban land transport", *The Lancet* Vol 374, no 9705, pages 1930–1943.

Zaidi, R Z and M Pelling (2013), "Institutionally configured risk: assessing urban resilience and disaster risk reduction to heat wave risk in London", *Urban Studies* Vol 52, no 7, pages 1218–1233.

8

MANIZALES, COLOMBIA

Jorgelina Hardoy and Luz Stella Velásquez Barrero

Introduction[1]

Manizales, Colombia, because of its location and the way that it developed and expanded over the years on challengingly steep terrain, faces permanent disaster risk, which will only be exacerbated in the context of projected climate change. At the same time, responses to the challenges it has faced and continues to face have made Manizales a national and international point of reference in terms of its environmental policy and integrated risk management. The city is widely recognized for its longstanding urban environmental policy (Biomanizales) and local environmental action plan (Bioplan), and it has been integrating environmental planning with disaster risk reduction and urban development planning for over 20 years (Velásquez 1998; Velásquez Barrero 2005, 2010, 2011; Hardoy and Velásquez Barrero 2014; Marulanda 2000).

Until recently, however, these environmental issues have had no institutional home within the municipal structure. During the present administration, a new Environmental Secretariat was created to coordinate environmental projects and give environmental issues more visibility. It is also working to formulate a climate change agenda that is compatible with forward thinking regional and national plans. Local councillors also support work to strengthen links between environmental policies, disaster risk reduction and climate change. Building on the city's long history of participatory governance around environmental issues, the Environmental Secretariat has led a consensus building process and launched a participatory, strategic environmental planning process in 2015 to consolidate the environmental policy of the city and integrate it into the land use plan. The final plan[2] is expected to be approved by December 2015. It has used climate change adaptation as a nexus to further integrate environmental issues with disaster risk management.

The physical context

Manizales, a municipality as well as a city, and the capital of the Department of Caldas, is located on a high ridge in Colombia's central Andes mountain range within the coffee growing axis (*eje cafetero*), a network of urban centres and rural settlements with some of the highest quality of life in Colombia. Founded by goldminers in 1849, Manizales was originally one of several small settlements developed near mines, which explains its location in this steep inaccessible area. This location has restricted its capacity for growth, and today it has a population of 387,000.

Because of the natural topography and great variation in altitude (the municipality rises from 870 metres above sea level at the Cauca River to 4,050 metres near the volcano Nevado del Ruiz) there is an incredible diversity of eco-regions within the municipal area. Most of the urban area, where 93 per cent of the population lives, is located about 2,100 metres above sea level, where there are over 289 rainy days each year and very fragile soils.

Manizales initially occupied a narrow plateau, but as it grew it expanded over steep slopes with little consideration to the implications for disaster risk or ecological services. The costly diversion and control of runoff water, for instance, affected soil stability and overstepped the natural limits of the Chinchiná and Olivares rivers to the south and north of the city. The lack of approval for construction seldom stopped urban expansion, which has continued since the 1940s (Chardon 2006). Internal population displacements due to armed conflict and rural poverty have added pressure to the fragile mountain ecosystems. The municipality now occupies 507 square kilometres of steep and vulnerable terrain.

Now accepting the limits to its capacity to expand, Manizales is undergoing a process of densification in the central area, guided by land use zoning that takes risk into account. All construction and development now meets specific standards. Relocation of residents in high risk areas has been ongoing over recent decades, and there are plans to further reduce the number of settlements in high risk areas in the municipality by 75 per cent.

Little is left of the original ecosystem at this point – about 60 hectares remain unchanged and are protected by strict preservation by-laws – but vegetation recovers quickly in this climate, and secondary forests have a rich biodiversity. A network of ecoparks developed by the city jointly with universities helps protect the environment, improve environmental quality and promote slope stabilization, reducing landslides and floods associated both with occupation and with increases in the intensity and frequency of rainfall. The city has assigned almost 12 per cent of its budget in the last ten years to structural work and corrective measures.

Demographics

The population of Manizales, both the city and the municipality, has been growing more slowly than the average for the country's urban areas. Projected growth between 2005 and 2020 is 6 per cent, down from 15 per cent in the preceding decade, and very low compared with the projected 23 per cent growth for urban centres nationally. This is a reflection of the constraints imposed by steep topography, but it is also a function of other trends related to employment and housing opportunities.

Poverty is relatively low in Manizales municipality, where those with unsatisfied basic needs average under 10 per cent compared with a national average of 27.78 per cent (DANE 2005). On average, people in Manizales are also better off than those in nearby municipalities. One of the main equity concerns in Manizales is the situation of elderly people, almost 13 per cent of whom live in poverty.

Economy

The city's economy has always been primarily driven by coffee production. Despite a coffee crisis in the 1930s, Manizales remained politically and culturally important, hosting regional campuses of several universities. A new coffee boom in the mid-1970s contributed to a surge of economic development, but increased pressure on the fragile ecosystems (Velásquez Barrero 2010). Manizales' economy continues to depend on coffee production, and the city remains a major hub for higher education. Other activities in its more urban parts include industrial and service activities, with financial and specialized services like IT, telematics and robotics coexisting with informal and traditional activities.

Since 2010, the unemployment rate in Colombia has been declining, and in Manizales was 1.7 per cent in the last quarter of 2014 (compared with 9.2 per cent in nearby Villamaria). As of 2014, 42.4 per cent of Manizales residents were engaged in informal employment, a considerably lower proportion than in most Colombia department capitals.

Governance

Manizales is governed by a mayor and a 19-member city council, elected for four-year terms. Two independent agencies oversee government actions, and a Territorial Planning Council, with 12 members from different sectors, is appointed by the mayor from a list submitted by civil society. The 1991 Constitution mandates participation in local governance. Elected officials are required to turn their campaign proposals into development plans at municipal and departmental levels, and implementation is evaluated every year through a public accountability process.

The city is part of a sub-region which also includes four other municipalities (Neira, Villamaría, Palestina and Chinchiná). Their mayors have pledged to share knowledge, technical resources and policies on environmental, energy, health and education issues, as well as infrastructure and service provision work, with the support of the governor and the provincial council as well as CORPOCALDAS, the regional environmental authority.

Municipal autonomy, supported by Colombia's decentralization process, has been important for Manizales. Yet most decisions still involve other levels of government to finance, coordinate, support or implement policies, and there is good cooperation. Most resources transferred to municipalities are earmarked by law for areas like health, education and water management, with only a small percentage left for other responsibilities. Municipalities vary in their capacity to raise income through local taxes (Scott and Tarazona 2011).

Service delivery

Almost all the municipality's urban population have electricity, piped water and sewerage services, and regular garbage collection, a third of it treated in a recycling plant. For the small rural population, water provision (89 per cent coverage) is through a network of small independent aquaducts; sanitation needs are partly met by connection to the municipal system and alternative technologies; and almost all residents have electricity. Sewage and wastewater treatment remains an issue. Efforts to build a shared plant with neighbouring Villamaria did not succeed, since residents contested the location.

Investments in infrastructure have been continuous in the city, primarily in traditional technologies but also in bio-engineering. Aguas de Manizales, the city's water utility, recently renovated most of its water and drainage network and works steadily on slope stabilization and water drainage control methods. A huge landslide in Barrio Cervantes in 2011, triggered by heavy rains and a burst water pipe, destroyed lives and homes, and demonstrated the implications of a lack of appropriate risk reduction infrastructure.

Transport

Manizales lacks an integrated, clean, efficient public transport system, which has contributed to the use of private vehicles and congestion. The city has made some advances with networks of pedestrian and bicycle lanes and a cable service to neighbouring Villamaría, used daily by 21,000 passengers, and reducing by 63 per cent their use of traditional bus and van systems. There are plans to expand the system. Private cars and taxis will soon be prohibited in the city centre.

Climate and climate risk

The location of Manizales, near the equator, means little variation in average temperature throughout the year from the mean of 18°C. Two rainy seasons each year yield an average annual rainfall of over 2000 mm. Averages aside, the topography and extreme variation in altitude mean considerable variety in the area's weather, with a number of microclimates. There is also the climate variability associated with ENSO (El Niño, La Niña).[3]

Manizales has been experiencing more extreme precipitation events and an extended rainy season period, associated locally with the natural ENSO variability. People are slow to see global climate change as playing a role, because of the lack of both historical and consistent data. For instance, some studies show an increase in annual precipitation and extremes (Suarez 2011). Others find a declining tendency (Benavides 2009).

Projections around the impacts of climate change include the following:

- Intense rains and changing rainfall patterns, generating landslides, mudslides and, combined with loss in vegetation cover, increasing stream flow and generating more intense floods
- Rise in temperature
- Loss of ecosystems, changes in distribution of plants and animals, loss of vegetation cover which will affect the hydrologic cycle and may affect coffee growing areas.
- Glacier retreat may decrease water availability and affect the hydrologic cycle. Retreat, recorded since 1850, has increased faster in the last three decades (IDEAM et al. 2010).

Manizales has always experienced disaster risk, mainly from floods, volcanic eruptions and mudslides. The limited suitable land for settlement, combined with market pressures and initial lack of controls on expansion, resulted, as noted above, in the occupation of fragile at-risk areas. Key disaster events have shaped the city's disaster risk approach. In 1985, the eruption of the Nevado de Ruiz triggered the development of the National System for the Prevention and Attention to Disasters (SNPD). In 2012, the region was seriously affected by one of the most intense rainy seasons in recent years, associated with La Niña. Mudslides caused pipes from a water treatment plant to be washed away, and the city had to rely for ten days on local springs and water tanks. In many ways, the city's risk management had been both neglected and inappropriate, with too much focus on traditional infrastructure and emergency response and too little on prevention. Successive La Niña years made evident the flaws in the DRR approach. The new administration has taken on the challenge of re-thinking and re-organizing DR planning and action to include climate change impacts. Much the same is happening at the national level.

The larger context for climate protection action in Manizales

Since the early 1990s, Manizales, driven by its multiple risk exposure, has been integrating environmental planning, disaster risk reduction and urban development through processes involving many stakeholders, and has in many ways shaped and guided national urban environmental policy. With regard to climate change, however, it is difficult to separate what is going on at national, sub-national and local levels, as all are influenced by each other.

National level

In Colombia over recent years, especially since the IPCC's Fourth Assessment Report, more energy has been devoted to modelling climate change scenarios, collecting data (Lampis and Fraser 2011) and consolidating the national institutional framework. The Climate Change National System (SISCLIMA) was created to coordinate initiatives generated by different levels and sectors of government and by local communities.[4] There is also a new Disaster Risk Management Unit and a new DRR law. Since 2010, a number of climate change strategies have been incorporated in the National Development Plan 2010–2014, including the National Adaptation Plan (PNACC), with guidelines for governors and mayors on the drafting of land use plans (POTS) and environmental protection plans for catchment areas (PONCAS/POMAS). There are also strategies for low carbon development, for emission reduction in deforestation, and for financial protection against disasters.[5] In 2013, the Government, through the Agricultural Financial Fund, FINAGRO, assigned resources to support cultivation on 61,000 hectares in different parts of the country, so producers could better face losses related to climate change. Central to Colombia's climate change policy is the concept of sustainable environmental management which is the guiding principle of the National Development Plan, the local land use and environmental protection plans (POTS and PONCAS/POMAS), and the municipal and departmental adaptation plans (Lampis 2012).

Regional level

Regional policies and plans are in line with national mandates and policies, and with the National Development Plan. Climate change adaptation is included as a cross-cutting theme in the regional environmental policy, and efforts are focused on research and evaluation of hazard events associated with climate change, their potential impact vis-à-vis the vulnerability of communities, ecosystems and productive systems, and adaptation options.

Corpocaldas is the regional authority responsible for applying national environmental policies, managing natural resources and supporting municipal governments. For instance, it is in charge of approving the environmental aspects of the Manizales land use plan. It is actively engaged in DRR and over recent years has incorporated climate change issues in its activities. The winter emergency of 2011–2012 (during the La Niña phase of ENSO) made this more explicit – for example, land use norms have been revised according to new climate parameters. They have made progress on a Strategic Mitigation and Adaptation Plan for Climate Variability, developed within their 2013–2016 Action Plan as a response to climate changes that affect the natural environment and social and economic development. The main challenge is the many already inhabited areas that have lagged behind in prevention and are increasingly at risk.

Corpocaldas also handles river basin management, protection of catchment areas, management of water resources and protected areas, glacier retreat monitoring, and education and awareness-raising. Most activities are implemented in partnership with other stakeholders (municipal government, universities, the Chamber of Commerce, civil society groups etc.). Corpocaldas is also involved in mitigation projects related to REDD+ (Reducing Emissions from Deforestation and forest Degradation), carbon markets and CDM (Clean Development Mechanisms) and is an active member of the Inter-institutional Network on Climate Change and Food Security (RICCLISA), an initiative based in the Ministry of Agriculture and Rural Development that works through regional nodes and brings a territorial perspective to climate change issues.

Municipal level

In Manizales, while the focus over the years has been primarily on social and environmental sustainability and DRR, in recent years climate change has increasingly been accepted as a major driver of increasing climate risks. The development of Manizales' environmental policy began in 1990 with an environmental profile and assessment of disaster risks associated with urban development. A process of shared research between municipality and universities along with other stakeholders resulted in the Biomanizales (environmental policy), the Bioplan (local environmental action plan), and a local disaster risk plan, all stitched together within the city's development plan. The formulation of territorial plans (Law for Territorial Order – Ordenamiento Territorial, Law 388/97) fully integrated the environmental dimension as an organizing axis and these too were incorporated in the urban development plan. Environmental policies and community participation mechanisms were features of all related environmental programmes and projects. The process in Manizales became the basis for Colombia's urban environmental policy.

Attention in Manizales to integrating environmental planning, disaster risk reduction and urban development has had its ups and downs. At times, momentum and government support were lost, and an active civil society and academic sector continued the work. The current administration, backed by strong national policies and institutional frameworks, has begun gradually to incorporate climate change into their agenda. Environmental concerns, including disaster risk and climate change issues, are integrated within the Municipal Development Plan 2012–2016; and a Municipal Agenda on climate change (Manizales ante el Cambio Climático) in agreement with regional and national plans is being formulated. The administration is also fully committed to participatory up-dating of the Biomanizales with environmental profiles of different neighbourhoods to develop local Bioplans and contribute to the Biomanizales.

Until recently the city lacked an Environmental Secretariat, despite the importance of environmental issues within the local agenda. Prior to this it had the level of a unit, much lower in the municipal hierarchy, possibly allowing some administrations to neglect environmental issues. The creation of a secretariat with a specific budget gives stronger institutional support and visibility to environmental and climate change issues within the municipal structure.

The adaptation work-stream

The adaptation work-stream in Manizales has several components, and is based on the idea that good DRR, environmental sustainability and territorial planning all contribute to adaptation and vulnerability reduction. Many actions that contribute to adaptation, some already described, have been undertaken or incorporated into the Municipal Development Plan (Plan de Desarrollo Manizales 2012):

- The creation of the Environment Secretariat and strengthening of inter-institutional cooperation (100 per cent implemented).
- Implementation of the Municipal Environmental Management System – SIGAM (80 per cent implemented).[6]
- Formulation of a municipal climate change plan: there has been progress in drafting the risk profile, achieving inter-institutional integration and engaging with civil society, but the plan is still in process.
- Re-structuring the disaster risk management (DRM) approach in line with the new national DRR law[7] and national DRM institutional structure.[8]
- Development of the Municipal System of Protected Areas – SIMAP.
- Evaluation and updating of Manizales' environmental profile and the environmental agenda (Bioplan) to reflect potential climate change impacts. It was updated in 2014 with the participation of neighbours and community representatives, slope guardians and community environmental leaders, and climate change was incorporated as an important variable. Work was done at micro-scale (street–neighbourhood) by trained volunteers (citizens, educators, local government staff) who assessed and documented local environmental and social conditions to come up with neighbourhood agendas. The goal is to include this information in both the Biomanizales and the Bioplan. This process is funded by the Environment Secretariat, inter-institutional funds and voluntary support (75 per cent implemented).

- Strengthening environmental observatories in partnership with universities (these are hubs throughout the city for monitoring socioeconomic and environmental conditions).
- Participating in the Territorial and Management Plan of the Chinchiná River basin (Corpocaldas is responsible for Plan coordination and implementation).
- Development of the local land use plans (POTs or Plan de Ordenamiento Territorial) of Manizales. These have important adaptation implications. The plan classifies land for either development or restricted use and protection, depending on the potential for risk reduction. This determines whether construction can occur, for what uses, and what measures have to be taken during construction. For vacant areas classified as high risk, it needs to establish whether hazards can be reduced and construction allowed. For high risk areas already developed, the necessary mitigation must be established, or residents must be relocated.
- Relocation of population from at-risk areas has been going on for over 30 years with a wide variety of approaches led by different institutions and programmes, some more participatory than others. There are currently plans to reduce the number of settlements in high risk areas by 75 per cent, so the amount of relocation is likely to increase. Recent in situ relocation of the Barrio Cervantes includes social housing 100 per cent subsidized by national government.
- Slope stabilization work has transformed some hazard prone areas into areas with "mitigatable risk", where construction with restrictions is allowed.
- Strengthening the Slope Guardians (*Guardianes de Ladera*), who are part of a longstanding programme that trains women living in or near high risk zones to maintain slope vegetation, control drainage channels, monitor slope stabilization work, report problems and changes in land use, keep an updated register of families living there at high risk, and raise the awareness of their neighbours. The number of women involved has increased by 20 per cent over recent years. This is permanent employment, although with a minimal wage of USD 400 per month, and they receive ongoing training. They are highly valued within the communities they work in, and theyalso engage in building awareness.
- Development of monitoring technology that integrates traditional/ancestral and expert knowledge to develop a participatory early warning system.
- Strengthening of the ecoparks network with a coherent management plan to protect environmentally fragile areas. Two new parks have been incorporated in the network. These are integrated into the POT. Ecoparks combine recreation, environmental education and conservation while protecting areas at risk from landslides or floods.
- Renovation, improved maintenance and expansion of basic infrastructure and services, and the planned installation of a sewage treatment plant within the municipality.

The Manizales POT 2017 is a key adaptation measure. Coordinated by the Secretariats of Planning and Environment, the plan requires the participation and consensus of civil society. The process has been slow and complex, with little progress for several years. A key reason has been the use of external consultants whose draft plan involved no participation. The current administration re-launched the process with municipal government technicians and local experts, and today there is good progress in terms of reaching consensus around goals, contents and strategic projects.

The academic sector, civil society and private sector have all engaged consistently in the Biomanizales and on specific environmental projects. The Chamber of Commerce in Manizales, for instance, has been engaged in environmental education programmes and in coordinating the regional node of RICCLISA (the climate change and food security network). Universities have developed the theoretical and methodological framework for the Biomanizales, are actively engaged in the collection of environmental indicators through the environmental observatories, and have provided scientific support to the government of Manizales and Corpocaldas in defining areas to be protected. A team from the National University of Colombia in Manizales has been monitoring glacier retreat in the Nevado de Ruiz since 1997, and manages the hydro-meteorological and environmental stations that gather data for the early warning system. Most, if not all, monitoring stations, evaluation processes, indicators, and so on have been developed through a joint effort by several stakeholders. Access to good information and the generation of knowledge have been key to stakeholder involvement. Technical and academic knowledge is usually combined with lay knowledge. The case of Manizales demonstrates that knowledge is best produced locally by local technicians, researchers and citizens, at least when there is capacity for this.

Funds are usually a limitation, but Colombia and Manizales have had foresight in this regard. Colombia has a 1.0 per cent tax on property which municipalities are required to invest in solving key local environmental problems. Manizales has added a 0.5 per cent tax to this. Risk management and activities like reforestation, the ecopark network, neighbourhood parks and protection of fragile ecosystems are all in the municipal budget. The city also has a voluntary collective insurance system, charged as a percentage of local property taxes, through which higher income sectors cover the costs for low-income groups or organizations working for the public good (Fay, Ghesquiere and Solo 2003). Other mechanisms include tax breaks for those who reduce housing vulnerability in areas at risk from landslides or floods.

Often research is guided by outside funding, which can bias the research agenda to the point that it fails to be useful for local action. An important partner in this respect is the local private sector, which mostly gets involved in awareness raising activities such as those undertaken by the Chamber of Commerce. The shared work developed over the years helps to bridge the gap between useful projects with no funds and funded projects of little use, aiding the access to funds and promoting a more practical type of research and intervention.

There is always discussion of the merits of corrective vs. preventive measures, or traditional structural work vs. alternative technologies. The measures mostly funded by Manizales over recent years are sometimes questioned for being too traditional or costly, compared with alternative technologies with techniques like appropriate vegetation cover, good micro-drainage systems and water management, at a fraction of the cost of traditional infrastructure work (approximately 1:25).

National financial resources are crucial for adaptation. The Adaptation Fund (Government Decree 4819 2010) concentrated resources on recovery after the 2011 La Niña emergency. Increased political support to adaptation could bring about much needed change in this regard.

The mitigation work stream

Although mitigation has not been a direct or priority line of work in Manizales, mitigation issues are indirectly included in policies, plans and actions. Some relevant actions include:

- Protection of environmentally fragile areas and river basins, development of the ecopark network, reforestation, promotion of "green actions" in consumer education (Biociudadanos), solid waste management. This includes reforestation in the River Chinchiná basin as a DRR measure and Clean Development Mechanism.
- A workshop on the city's carbon footprint, with participation of different sectors (agriculture, industry, energy and transportation) and consensus on strategic actions to control emissions.
- Progress on knowledge sharing and training, including with community members, in climate change adaptation and mitigation. Direct mitigation goals by Corpocaldas within the Strategic Mitigation and Adaptation Plan, with projects related to REDD+, carbon markets and CDM.
- Procuenca is a programme started in 2000 by the Food and Agriculture Organization of United Nations (FAO) to promote reforestation, improve land use and fresh water quantity, quality and water flow regulation in the region. Agreements have been reached with land owners, with legal and technical support, development of a landowner's association and training courses for the community involved in the programme. Adaptation elements are also integrated, including hydrological cycle recovery, biodiversity conservation, awareness and land use change (Suarez 2011). Procuenca also participates in the Water Management Plan of Aguas de Manizales SA and the conservation of 5,500 hectares of public natural forests to protect the basin, with sustainable management and regulation of the water sources that feed into the city's water plants. These measures all help prevent future disasters like that in 2011.

Integrating adaptation and mitigation

Plans and actions in Manizales (and in Colombia more generally) look for coherence between disaster risk reduction and climate change adaptation, assuming that capacity to adapt to future changes will increase if disaster risk and emergencies are handled well now (PNACC 2013). The balance tilts towards adaptation, but the environmental and development coherence guiding plans and actions make it inevitable that the mitigation of negative environmental impacts be considered. In line with this vision of development, a low carbon future is a realistic goal.

A former mayor served as a champion for much of the early work, integrating urban environmental planning and DRR. During his term, Biomanizales and the Bioplans were first developed, as well as tools such as environmental observatories and environmental indicators used to measure environmental quality in a participatory way. The strength of the process lay in the involvement of many different, committed local stakeholders, and even when local government showed less commitment on environmental issues (as in recent administrations), work continued. A strong emphasis has been placed also on capacity building and raising awareness within the community. Today this remains a joint process with no particular champion. The creation of an Environmental Secretariat is to ensure administrative support in the future.

The academic sector has also been engaged in integrating climate change adaptation and mitigation. The University of Caldas has created a climate change office which is used by Corpocaldas and other universities to present research projects and develop inter-institutional alliances.

Changes at national level help anchor the local process. A national framework and legal support promotes integrated action, especially among municipal and regional governments that have developed good capacities. The main challenge, both at national and local level, is to focus on prevention, resilience and vulnerability reduction, when the tendency is to fall back on emergency response. Another critical goal is to move from costly structural engineering measures to a greater emphasis on softer alternatives.

Notes

1 Much of the material in this chapter was taken from interviews with municipal and state government officials and other relevant stakeholders engaged in the city's climate change efforts. A version of the chapter appeared in *Environment and Urbanization* (Hardoy and Velásquez Barrero 2014).

2 The plan is called Biomanizales – Política de Responsabilidad Ambiental y Adaptación al Cambio Climático (Biomanizales – Environmental responsibility and climate change adaptation plan).

3 ENSO (El Niño/Southern Oscillation) is the interaction between the atmosphere and ocean in the tropical Pacific that results in a somewhat periodic variation between below-normal and above-normal sea surface temperatures and dry and wet conditions over the course of a few years.

4 Article 7 of National Law1450 of 2011 cited in www.dnp.gov.co/LinkClick.aspx?file ticket=2yrDLdRTUKY%3D&tabid=1260
5 These strategies are Estrategia Colombiana de Desarrollo Bajo en Carbono – ECDBC; Estrategia Nacional para la Reducción de las Emisiones debidas a la Deforestación y la Degradación Forestal en los Países en Desarrollo- ENREDD+ and Estrategia de Protección Financiera ante Desastres; seewww.dnp.gov.co/LinkClick.aspx?fileticket=2yrDLdRTUKY%3D&tabid=1260
6 SIGAM advances the municipal environmental agenda, coordinating proposals, actions, planning etc. related to environmental management involving many different stakeholders.
7 Law No. 1523 – Ley Sistema Nacional de Gestión de Riesgos, April 2012.
8 Unidad Nacional de gestion del riesgo de desastres (UNGRD) which again operates out of the President's office, with financial and administrative autonomy.

References

Benavidez, Javier Andrés (2009), *Informe Boletín Metereológico*. Instituto de Hidrología, Metereología y Estudios Ambientales IDEAM, Colombia. (mimeo).

Chardon, A (2006), "Undesafíopara el desarrollourbano: amenazasnaturales y vulnerabilidad global asociada: El caso de la ciudad de Manizales". Paper presented at Taller Internacionalsobre la gestióndelriesgo a nivel local, Universidad Nacional de Colombia, USAID, Alcaldía de Manizales, 28–29 September, 2006.

Departamento Administrativo Nacional de Estadísticas (DANE) (2005), *Census 2005*. Available at: www.dane.gov.co/files/censo2005/PERFIL_PDF_CG2005/00000T7T000.PDF

Departamento Administrativo Nacional de Estadísticas DANE (2014a), Informe de Coyuntura Económica Regional Departamento de Caldas 2013. ICER – Banco de la República de Colombia, Bogotá.

Departamento Administrativo Nacional de Estadísticas DANE (2014b), Medición del Empleo Informal y Seguridad Social, Trimestre abril–junio de 2014, Boletín de Prensa Gobierno de Colombia Bogotá, June 2014.

Fay, M, F Ghesquiere and T Solo (2003), "Natural disasters and the urban poor", in *Breve* No. 23, October, World Bank, Washington DC, pages 1–4.

Hardoy, Jorgelina and Luz Stella Velásquez Barrero (2014), "Re-thinking 'Biomanizales': addressing climate change adaptation in Manizales, Colombia", *Environment and Urbanization* Vol 26, No 1, pages 53–68.

Instituto de Hidrología, Meteorología y Estudios Ambientales (Ed.) (IDEAM), Gobierno de Colombia, Programa de las Naciones Unidaspara el Desarrollo (PNUD) (2010). *Segunda Comunicación Nacional ante la Convención Marco de las Naciones Unidassobre Cambio Climático*, Bogotá, 2010. Available at: www.pnud.org.co/sitio.shtml?apc=aCa020011-&x=62593

Lampis, A (2012), "Bogotá Case Study", Background paper for international report of IAI funded ADAPTE project (mimeo), 23 pages.

Lampis, A and A Fraser (2011), "The impact of climate change on urban settlements in Colombia", United Nations Human Settlements Programme (UN-Habitat), Nairobi, 90 pages.

Marulanda, Liliana M (2000), El Biomanizales: Política Ambiental local. Documentación de la Experiencia de Gestión Ambiental Urbana de Manizales, Colombia. Instituto de Estudios de Vivienda y Desarrollo Urbano (IHS) dentro del marco de implementación del proyecto: Apoyo para la implementación de Planes Nacionales de Acción del Habitat II (SINPA) (mimeo), n.p.

Plan de Desarrollo Manizales 2012–2015: Gobierno en la calle, 387 pages. Available at: www.manizales.gov.co/RecursosAlcaldia/201505052131055709.pdf

Plan Nacional de Adaptacion al Cambio Climático (PNACC) (2013), prepared by DNP, MADS, IDEAM, UNGRD, published by Dirección Nacional de Planeamiento (DNP), Colombia, 74 pages. Available at: www.dnp.gov.co/LinkClick.aspx?fileticket=2yrDLdRTUKY%3D&tabid=1260

Scott, S and M Tarazona (2011), "Decentralization and disaster risk reduction". Report paper prepared for UNISDR *Global Assessment Report 2011, GAR*, Geneva, 53 pages. Available at: www.preventionweb.net/english/hyogo/gar/2011/en/bgdocs/Scott_&_Tarazona_2011.pdf

Suarez, O Dora Catalina (2011), *Disaster Risk Reduction in Latin America, Improving Tools and Methods Regarding Climate Change: The Case Study of Colombia and the City of Manizales.* United Nations University, Institute of Environment and Human Security, National University of Colombia in Manizales, Institute of Environmental Studies (IDEA). Manizales. Available at: http://idea.manizales.unal.edu.co/gestion_riesgos/descargas/DRRinLatinAmerica.pdf

Velásquez, Luz Stella (1998), "Agenda 21: a form of joint environmental management in Manizales", in *Environment and Urbanization*, Vol 10, No 2, pages 9–36.

Velásquez Barrero, Luz Stella (2005), "The Bioplan: decreasing poverty in Manizales, Colombia, through shared environmental management", (Chapter 3), in S Bass et al. (Eds.) *Reducing Poverty and Sustaining the Environment: The Politics of Local Engagement*, Earthscan, London, pages 44–77.

Velásquez Barrero, Luz Stella (2010), *El Biomanizales. Manual de Bioarquitectura y Biourbanismo*, Universidad Nacional de Colombia, Sede Manizales, Manizales, 109 pages.

Velásquez Barrero, Luz Stella (2011), "La gestión del riesgo en el contextoambientalurbano local, unretopermanente y compartido. Caso Manizales, Colombia", in *Medio Ambiente y Urbanización* No 75, pages 27–46.

9

MEXICO CITY, MEXICO

Fernando Aragón-Durand and
Gian Carlo Delgado-Ramos

Introduction

Mexico, a country exposed to a range of climate- and weather-related hazards, is considered highly vulnerable to climate change, with 15 per cent of its territory, over two-thirds of its population and 71 per cent of the national GDP exposed to adverse effects (DOF 2009). Since 1980, the economic costs of hydrometeorological extreme events have more than tripled, jeopardizing resources that could otherwise have been used for development (DOF 2013). The country's greenhouse gas (GHG) emissions are also a concern, having risen by a third between 1990 and 2010. Mexico City is central to these concerns. It is not only the most important settlement in terms of GHG emissions, but is also exposed to heatwaves, heavy rainfall and flooding in both the central city and the informal settlements spread over the city's western territory.

These problems must be seen in the context of the significant measures already undertaken. Since the 1980s, Mexico City's government has been engaged in tackling various ecological problems associated with uncontrolled urbanization, and it is well known for reducing air pollution in partnership with industry, the commercial and transportation sectors and the general population. Over the last ten years, as climate change has become a greater concern, priorities have been shifting towards the construction of a climate agenda with the political momentum to raise Mexico City's profile in the international political arena. The actual planning of actions to achieve adaptation and mitigation goals set for 2020 and 2050 remains a challenge, as does the coordination of all three government levels, the deployment of qualified monitoring capacities, and the competent, external validation of achieved goals. There are also important challenges in building adaptive capacities including weak institutions, a lack of local decentralized capacities and a general perception of the climate change agenda as primarily environmental.

Geographical context and the development of Mexico City

Mexico City, the centre of Mexico's economic, social and cultural life, is located in the country's central basin, a closed hydrological watershed of approximately 7,000 km^2 at about 2,250 m above sea level. The basin is enclosed on three sides by magnificent volcanic ranges and a series of hills, an important physical boundary that limits the expansion of urbanized areas (Ezcurra et al. 1999). Despite these limits, it is the largest city in Latin America. The Federal District of Mexico City, which covers 1,495 km^2, 41 per cent of it urbanized, has a population of almost 9 million. The larger Metropolitan Area, which covers 9,600 km^2 in both the State of Mexico and Hidalgo State, has 20 million inhabitants, a huge increase from one million in 1930.

The development of Mexico City has always been closely related to the dynamics of the hydrological basin over which it sprawls. Even in pre-Hispanic times there were severe ecological problems associated with resource depletion in the basin, but the magnitude, speed and intensity of environmental change became more extreme after the Spanish Conquest, when the imposition of European urbanism on a fragile ecosystem led to the desiccation of the Mexico valley lake and a reduction in its ecological productivity (Aragón-Durand 2007). The city's rapid development has continued to have significant environmental consequences, including air pollution, a loss of biodiversity, the generation of considerable waste and the ongoing transformation of the basin's hydrological cycle, which has led to water depletion and increased the vulnerability of poor households, mainly in the peri-urban interface.

Socio-economic context

The intensive exploitation of natural resources within the central basin facilitated a great expansion in economic activity. Throughout the second half of the 20th century, the city experienced rapid economic growth based on import-substitution industrialization, to the detriment of agriculture. Investment was particularly drawn to the agglomeration economies provided by Mexico City. This economic growth, together with political and administrative centralization and the supply of various kinds of services, attracted large numbers of rural migrants, and between 1940 and 1960 the population tripled (Aragón-Durand 2007).

The city did not, however, provide adequate living and working conditions for all its inhabitants. Reductions in available space promoted land speculation, and demographic growth resulted in a housing deficit that the state could not manage. As of 1999, as much as 60 per cent of the city's spatial growth was the result of people building their own dwellings on unserviced peripheral land,

and informal subsistence work has always accounted for a large proportion of total employment (Connolly 1999 p. 56) and this trend continues. The growth of low-income settlements on the city's peripheries has represented the prevailing phenomenon of urban space transformation (Banzo 2000, quoted in Aragón-Durand 2007) and still contributes to the generation of vulnerability to hydrometeorological and climate-related hazards. This has paradoxically been underdocumented, let alone being a concern for policy makers.

The expansion of the built environment has impacted Mexico City's conservation land where most of urban ecological services take place, such as water infiltration and carbon sequestration (GDF 2012). From 1970 to 2005, about 8,590 hectares experienced drastic land use changes, including the location of 867 illegal settlements. Between 2010 and 2030 it is expected that a further 219 hectares of forestland will be lost every year (GDF 2012).

Governance

Mexico City, which houses both the federal and local administrative and political powers, is governed by the Chief of Government, who, along with his cabinet, is in charge of policy and planning of the city's development and oversees the sectoral implementation of plans. The elected Representative Assembly (Local Congress) designs laws, norms and regulations and exerts a great deal of political power. Good governance depends to a great extent on agreement between the Chief of Government and the Assembly. In political and administrative terms, Mexico City is subdivided into sixteen boroughs (*delegaciones*) which are not fully autonomous, but are meant to be the smallest governance unit to which inhabitants relate. Most city services are provided by the Government of Mexico City, not by the boroughs themselves. By the end of 2015 a reform was carried out in order to transform the Federal District into the state No 32. By January 2017 a political local constitution will have to be approved while the legal figure of "delegación" (borough) will change to "local districts". Thus, local policy is expected to be more autonomous in the near future.

Climate, projected climate change and climate risk

Mexico City's average annual temperature is 15°C, varying 8°C between summer and winter. Its annual rainfall varies from 600 to 1,200 mm from north to south, occurring mostly between May and September. Over the last 600 years, annual averages aside, wet and dry years have tended to alternate, and Mexico City has suffered from floods and droughts which have been aggravated by the socio-environmental transformation of the hydrological cycle along with land use changes. Climate change is expected to amplify these floods and droughts (Romero-Lankao 2010; Aragón-Durand 2007). Temperatures in the short term are expected to rise between 0.5°C and 1.5°C and up to 2.25°C in the long term (SEDEMA, 2014b p.94). Precipitation reductions in the short term are expected to be between 5 and 10 per cent in the rainiest months (June and July), and far more than that during the relatively dry month of December, and with a somewhat greater decrease in the longer term (SEDEMA 2014b p.64).

Despite these reductions in precipitation, the greatest climate change risk is associated with heavy rainfall and flooding (SEDEMA 2014b). Intense precipitation events have already taken place 180 times in the last 30 years and have flooded various vulnerable areas in Mexico City's boroughs, with more extreme effects for poor unserviced settlements. The situation is expected to worsen as climate change intensifies and as deforestation increases, especially given the inadequate management of the city's drainage system. Moreover, the expected decrease in precipitation during the dry season may result in a greater water service disruption than that already experienced in certain urban areas (SEDEMA 2014b).

There is, however, little knowledge about the city's vulnerability and the potential impacts of climate change. Comparatively little research has been carried out to inform policy choices and to explain the extent to which certain populations, neighbourhoods and sectors will be put at risk in the coming decades. There has also been little research to assess the vulnerability of strategic sectors such as water conservation and provision (Escolero et al. 2009), the economic costs of climate change (Estrada y Martínez 2010) and the relationship between poverty and climate change (Sánchez Vargas et al. 2012). According to Escolero et al. (2009), water provision is key to the sustainability of Mexico City and it is of paramount importance to evaluate the vulnerability of drinking water sources. Infrastructural and institutional management factors have been found to play a central role in generating this vulnerability, and the impact of climate change on water provision should be assessed in the context of increasing demand, deterioration of catchment areas, degradation of water quality and reduction of recharging areas.

Sánchez Vargas et al. (2012) attempted to determine the impact of climate change on poverty indicators in the Federal District and noted the following consequences for the poor: less access to water and food, deteriorating health, increasing migration, decreasing income and deteriorating quality of life. Some policy recommendations include rainfall harvesting in deprived zones and the adequate maintenance of the drainage system to better cope with floods. With regard to the impact of climate change on Mexico City's public financing, Estrada and Martínez (2010) developed a stochastic model that integrates the city's basic factors such as the effects of heat islands, microclimates, and socio-economic and demographic differences amongst the different boroughs. This study estimates the accumulated costs of climate change under a no-action scenario and suggests that during the 21st century they could reach 46 times the current local GDP, and, without additional policy responses, could drag more than a million people into poverty.

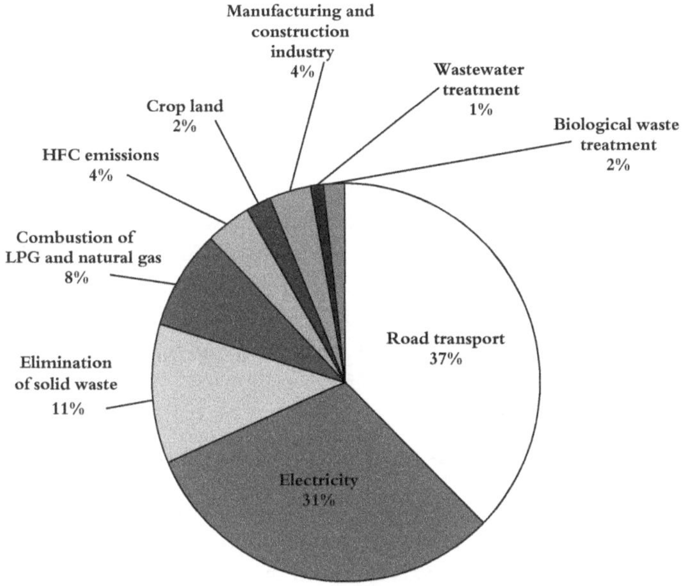

FIGURE 9.1 Mexico City's main GHG emission sources, 2012

GHG and black carbon emissions

Industrial activity and the pursuits of a massive population have been reflected in the extent of Mexico City's greenhouse gas (GHG) and black carbon emissions. GHG emissions were estimated to reach 31 million tons of CO_2e in 2012, a substantial share of the Metropolitan Area's emissions, which in 2010 reached 54.7 million tons of CO_2e, or 9 per cent of national emissions (SEDEMA 2012). Of Mexico City emissions, 80 per cent came from fossil energy, and the transport and energy sectors were the main source (see Figure 9.1). Black carbon emissions in 2012 were calculated at about 1,200 tons, 97 per cent attributable to the transport sector, with 84 per cent of the total from diesel vehicles (SEDEMA 2014b).

Over recent decades, as will be more fully discussed below, there have been concerted efforts to address the emissions problem. As a signatory of the Kyoto Protocol, Mexico is committed to reducing its emissions by 30 per cent by 2020 and 50 per cent by 2050 (partially conditioned by international financial support and technology transfer), and is focused on renewable energy and the creation of a National Emissions Registry, among other general goals specified in the *National Strategy on Climate Change. Vision 10-20-40* (DOF 2013). Within Mexico City, there has been considerable progress and between 2008 and 2012, when the Climate Change Action Plan of Mexico City (CCAPMC) was active, 5.8 million tons of CO_2e were mitigated, and the expected increase of GHG emissions for that period was neutralized (SEDEMA 2014b p.93). It is worth highlighting, however, that the data are for direct emissions. If indirect emissions are taken into account, GHG mitigation efforts since 2008 are without question overshadowed. It should also be pointed out that the absolute reduction of GHG emissions has not yet been achieved; in fact they have recently increased, since no mitigation actions were taken in 2013. Estimates of emissions for 2020 are 34.5 million tCO_2e and for 2015, 37 million tCO_2e. If the 2013 emissions are included in the reckoning, accumulated reductions from 2013 to 2020 would be only 3.5 per cent, while accumulated emissions would be about 5.5 per cent. Clearly, mitigation efforts are not yet adequate to address the actual problem.

With regard to black carbon emissions, current CCAPMC goals are to reduce these by 360 tons between 2014 and 2020 through freight transport regulation. Black carbon emissions will increase to 1,370 tons by 2020 and 1,570 tons by 2025; accumulated mitigation will then be about 8.2 per cent, while the accumulated increase of emissions is 7.5 per cent.[1]

Climate change policy: the planning and legal framework

Climate change policy for Mexico generally and Mexico City in particular is heavily slanted towards mitigation. The first National Climate Change Strategy 2009–2012, developed in 2007, was followed by approval of a General Climate Change Act in 2012, the second National Climate Change Strategy (DOF 2013) and the second Special Program on Climate Change 2014–2018 (DOF 2013). Mexico's national climate change system involves the integrated action of 13 federal ministries, the National Institute of Ecology and Climate Change, the Climate Change Council, the association of the municipal authorities and the Congress. A number of federal and state policies apply at the local level, and urban authorities are key to addressing climate change, since they are responsible for land planning, transport, waste management and natural resource management – including water and building codes (SEDEMA 2014b p.34).

Mexico City's attention to climate change actually precedes that of the federal government. In 2008, the Local Climate Change Strategy of Mexico City (LCCSMC) was set in motion for 2008–2012, as well as the corresponding Climate Change Action Program of Mexico City (CCAPMC) ,[2] and in 2010 the Mexico City Pact was signed at the World Mayors Summit on Climate Change. In 2011, the approval of a General Climate Change Act meant Mexico City was already in compliance with the federal legal framework. By 2014, there were a new LCCSMC and CCAPMC for 2014–2020. These extend beyond 2018, when a new government will come into power, so that this government will have time to prepare a new strategy and programme without interrupting climate change mitigation and adaptation actions, as had happened in 2013. This legal framework applies only to Mexico City – that is to the 16 boroughs of the Federal District, not to the rest of the metropolitan region.

In addition to the current LCCSMC and the CCAPMC, other local policy instruments put in place by the city's General Climate Change Act include the Inter-institutional Climate Change Commission, the GHG emissions inventory, Mexico City's Atlas of Risk, the Emissions Register, the Local System of Carbon

Credits, the Mexico City Virtual Center of Climate Change (MCVCCC) and the Environmental Fund for Climate Change (SEDEMA 2014a p.40).

The creation of this Fund is an important step forward. Investing in climate change actions was previously negotiated between responsible authorities in charge of CCAPMC implementation, and conflicts and troubled or contradictory operations abounded. Sectoral authorities operated as usual because climate related agreements or considerations were not always or fully achieved, and many of their conventional urban solutions contradicted mitigation and ecological objectives (for instance, the construction of several kilometres of elevated urban highway that disturbed urban ravines of important ecological value as well as locking the city into future GHG emissions associated with private vehicle use).

The Fund, part of the Public Environmental Fund of the city's Ministry of Environment, is made up of public funds allocated yearly, donations and transactions of Certified Emission Reductions, among other sources (SEDEMA 2014a and b). The existence of the Fund does not mean that climate change issues will be mainstreamed into sectoral practices, but the CCAPMC will have dedicated resources for pushing these issues, mainly with regard to construction and management of infrastructure and urban utilities. It is relevant, therefore, to fully coordinate the CCAPMC and the LCCSMC objectives with a range of government development programmes.

An assessment of mitigation policy actions[3]

Although there are obvious links between the 2000–2012 LCCSMC and CCAPMC and those of 2014–2020 as a continuation of local climate change policy, there are some discrepancies regarding the GHG emissions inventory used in each CCAPMC (SEDEMA 2014a p.146),[4] as well as some contradictions between existing environmental programmes and climate change mitigation actions. Responsibility for both continues to be allocated to the same authority: the Ministry of Environment.

Some other issues also emerge in the current CCAPMC, such as the need for integration between adaptation and mitigation actions. This need is recognized, but in practical terms the implications of this integration are not elaborated. The document even acknowledges the absence of an adaptation baseline, which results in an unclear vision of adaptation goals and thus in a limited integration of these goals with mitigation goals within a specific timeframe. The LCCSMC also concedes that: "…although orientation measures seem to focus only on adaptation or mitigation [within the CCAPMC], it is believed that the interrelationship between the two helps to reduce more efficiently climate change risks for nature and society, therefore whenever it may be possible, synergies between the two type of actions should be pursued" (SEDEMA 2014a p.141). Although co-benefits and eventual trade-offs are usually not identified or explicitly described, such interplay between mitigation and adaptation is, in practice, assumed to be an automatic given, once individual actions are proposed in each adaptation or mitigation axis (SEDEMA 2014b p.99).

No coordination thus far has been achieved between Mexico City's government and the governments of the municipalities that comprise the Metropolitan Area; in fact, only two municipalities of the Metropolitan Area have developed their climate change action plan. This is without doubt one of the deepest prevailing policy-making gaps. It was supposed to be resolved with the establishment in 2013 of the Environmental Megalopolitan Commission, but this is yet to happen.

The CCAPMC (both 2008–2012 and 2014–2020) supposedly focuses on mitigation actions of the sectors that emit the most GHG. Transport should be most relevant, as it accounts for about half of Mexico City emissions. However, measures are contradictory as noted; expansion of infrastructure for private vehicles overshadows the still limited efforts towards public and non-motorized mobility. Both CCAPMCs focus on expanding the subway system, regulating the public bus service while expanding the BRT system, establishing cycle roads, and, more recently, promoting energy efficiency in public transportation. Meanwhile, the latest subway line, built during the government of 2008–2012 and surrounded by allegations of corruption, does not fully operate due to defects in design and construction; and increased investment in private vehicle infrastructure permits existing asymmetries to remain undaunted: 42 per cent of urbanized land is dedicated to motorized transportation (mostly private) which serves only 30 per cent of passengers, and private infrastructure maintenance and expansion absorbs about 70 per cent of the public budget (Delgado-Ramos 2012). This is despite the fact that the General Development Program of the city states the need to reduce the private vehicle fleet.

The CCAPMC 2014–2020 is making progress in certain key aspects, at least at the level of discourse. It introduces a metabolic urban approach, backs a mixed and compact city, acknowledges the need to limit urban expansion and to coordinate urban and conservation land regulation, and also recognizes gender and human rights, among other aspects described in Table 9.1.

The theoretical and methodological limitations, however, remain evident in the LCCSMC and CCAPMC 2014–2020 approaches, as well as on related actions and regulations. The opacity of the methodologies used for the following are especially troubling:

- Estimating the mitigation potential of actions proposed by CCAPMC 2014–2020
- Estimating Mexico City's vulnerability, including the assumptions, criteria or weighting values and the consequent adaptation measures and options
- Modelling macroeconomic data used for estimating the GHG emissions base line
- Defining a proposed education and social communication agenda that reflects an understanding of social empowerment and active participation. The current vision of citizen involvement in local climate change policy and decision-making is restricted to top-down consultancy processes.

TABLE 9.1 Specific actions of CCAPMC 2014–2018 and their estimated cost and mitigation potential

Specific actions	*Cost ($, pesos)★★*	*Mitigation potential by 2020 (tCO_2e)*
Energy transition		
Energy efficiency		
Modernization, energy efficiency of subway system	$370 million	438,615 – 439,524★
HFC emissions reduction and efficiency increase through refrigerator decommissioning (cost per refrigerator)	$1,000	1,240,552 – 1,242,424★
Energy consumption cutback in institutional buildings (–15% per employee; currently estimated at 1,039 kw/h-year)	$2.7 million	5,695 – 6,664★
Energy efficiency services sector (kw/m^2): illumination systems, air conditioning, motors, pumps and heaters	to be determined	159,352
Electricity saving in water-pump governmental facilities	$94,000 million	54,700 – 94,083★
Modernizing illumination of the electric transport system (light train and trolleybus service)	$9.5 million	1,408
Restoration of street lighting within city's primary road network (54,600 lamps up to 45% more efficient)	$628 million	87,995 – 88,188★
Renewable energies		
Amend regulations to harmonize with international sustainability criteria	$500,000 (§)	150,207★
Harnessing renewable energy in government facilities	–	60,078
Incorporation of photovoltaic panels at BRT stations	$50 million	2,831 – 2,837★
Energy efficiency and renewable energy access programme to improve women's health (fuels for cooking and heating water)	–	–
Public solar street lighting in urban forests (Chapultepec, San Juan de Aragón) and at environmental education centres	$28.2 million	261

continued…

Table 9.1 continued

Specific actions	*Cost ($, pesos)***	*Mitigation potential by 2020 (tCO_2e)*
Urban sprawl containment		
Urban planning		
Zoning programme for integrating environmental and urban land use policies with a gender approach and a metropolitan vision	$3.5 million	–
Study to identify strategy for the efficient urban land use; initially zoning the "central city"*	$10 million	–
Study of potential intensity building capacity of urban land	–	–
Identification of under-utilized land for urban densification	$100 million	–
Guidelines manual for TOD sustainable corridors	$800,000	–
Reformulation of guidelines manual for systemic analysis of the impacts of real estate developments in strategic areas	$800,000	–
Transport infrastructure and mobility		
Urban equipment placement near modal-transfer-centres (CETRAMs), including its regulation	$200,000	–
Intra-urban green spaces		
Rehabilitation and increase of intra-urban green spaces to achieve OMS standard of 9 m2/h	$16 million	3,300
Development and incorporation of management programs of urban ravines (including definition of land uses allowed)	$285 million	–
Environmental improvement		
Reduction of air pollutant emissions		
Subway extension (4 km of Line 12, with operational problems mostly since its inauguration)	$19,500 million	280,000 – 281,582*
Microbus decommissioning, creation of public bus corridors with exclusive stops and pre-paid systems	$2,000 million	930,000 – 933,506*
Standard for regulating heavy construction machinery (diesel) aimed at reducing black carbon emissions	$500,000	–

Standards for emergency and standby power systems	$1 million	–
Regulation for reducing LP gas leakages	$300,000	52
Expansion of cycle routes (117 km), bicycle-parking lots and parking pay systems	$1,605 million	2,000,000
New BRTs corridors (5 Metrobús lines adding 100 km, substituting 800 microbuses) + selling of carbon credits	$11,000 million	875,000
Regulating air pollutants through enhanced industry inspection	$20 million	–
Green purchasing (potential savings)	$15 million	–
Integrated water management		
Water savings and rainwater harvesting in public buildings	$700,000	–
Suppression of water leaks and pipe rehabilitation	$30 million	17 Gwh/year
Integrated waste management		
Sludge stabilization systems for wastewater treatment plants	$11 million	101,180
Wastewater treatment efficiency and capacity increase	$771 million	8,931
Technologies to seize waste (e.g. biodigestion, energy recovery)	$1,000 million	2,361,934 – 2.4 million*
Sustainable management of natural resources and biodiversity conservation		
Conservation land		
Food producer training to meet safety standards	$40 million	All actions: 146,879
Impact assessment of logging ban	$1 million	
Local food producers as suppliers of governments' green procurement system	$500,000	
Management of micro-basins for conservation and rural development	$300,000	
Monitoring GM ban to protect native maize	$130 million	
Soil and water preservation within city's conservation land	$450 million	
Protection and recovery of native crops and herbs to support agrosystem resilience	$150 million	
Recovery of vacant land for reforestation or conversion into agroforestry land	$400 million	
Rainwater harvesting for crop irrigation	$200 million	

continued…

Table 9.1 continued

Specific actions	*Cost (\$, pesos)***	*Mitigation potential by 2020 (tCO_2e)*
Native species and wildlife		
Elaboration of the Protection, Conservation and Sustainable Use of Biodiversity in the Federal District Act	\$6 million	–
Creation of Biodiversity and Sustainable Development Directorate	\$300 million	–
Implementation of management programmes for natural protected areas	\$200 million	–
Renewal of the molecular diagnostics laboratory and expansion of existing germplasm bank	\$12 million	–
Payment for environmental services (creation/expansion of communal ecological reserves or conservation areas)	\$300 million	–
Resilience building		
Prevention and mitigation of risks		
Preventive programme for hydrometeorological risks	\$8,000 million	–
Atlas of Natural Hazards and Risks update every 5 years	\$7.5 million	–
Revaluation and relocation of human settlements from risk areas	\$600 million	–
Expansion and modernization of Valley's hydrometeorological monitoring and early warning system	\$100 million	–
Preventive actions for hydrometeorological extreme events	\$200 million	–
Training of strategic sectors on prevention and detection of diseases related to climate change	\$7 million	–
Monitoring and prevention of vector-borne diseases through awareness	\$20 million	–
Prevention of diseases caused by extreme events	\$90 million	–
Creation of Environmental Fund for Climate Change (creation cost)	\$390 million	–

Education & communication		
Citizens empowerment		
Climate Change Observatory in Museum of Natural History, Chapultepec	$15 million	–
Education campaigns for protection of the environment	$50 million	–
Officials' training on climate change issues	$20 million	–
Publication of material related to climate change in tax, water and electricity bills	$3 million	–
Mobile schools to promote bicycle use	$35 million	–
Programme to encourage low carbon and sustainable schools	$10 million	–
Adequacy of process and contents		
Homogenization concepts in environmental education and public information	$1 million	–
Development of education guideline for sustainable and pro-climate individual choices	$1 million	–
Research & development		
Strengthening phase implementation		
Study public perceptions of environmental and climate change education with a gender equity perspective and human rights protection	$1.2 million	–
Climate change effects metrics with gender perspective	$1 million	–
Regulation of freight transport	$2 million	1,165,151
Action plan for infrastructure for mobility and transport		
Coordination action for urban planning	$1 million	–
Strengthening monitoring & evaluation		
Improvement of adaptation metrics	$1 million	–
Development of indirect mitigation metrics	$1 million	–
Totals:	$143,202 million	10,074,121 –10,160,617*

Notes

* CCAPMC's data inconsistency range.

** Exchange rate by the end of 2013 was about 13 MX-pesos per US-dollar.

§ Besides the cost of the amendment itself, an additional cost per solar water heating system incorporated is considered; from $3,000 to 2.8 million pesos, depending on the size and user.

Source: author's own elaboration based on SEDEMA (2014b).

The introduction of the urban metabolism approach into the CCAPMC 2014–2020 would certainly be positive if it were fully understood and integrated into policy and decision-making, which seems not to be the case. This approach analyses urban settlements as open systems, accounting for in-flows of energy and materials and out-flows of degraded energy and materials (GHG, waste and wastewater mostly). The first such analyses developed a *linear material and energy flow* accounting. Later analyses included flows of recycled materials and energy recovery, a methodology known as *circular metabolic analysis*. More recently, the study of urban stock (materials and energy embedded in infrastructure and vehicle fleet) has been added into circular metabolic analyses. All modalities have developed a range of scenarios modelling techniques for policy and decision-making (Kennedy et al. 2011; Zhang 2013).

The analysis of urban flows and stocks and their interactions allows current and future policy design to keep pace with reasonable future metabolic scenarios, while considering eventual uncertainties and challenges (e.g. resource availability/depletion, environmental pollution, climate change) in and out of city limits. However, to be more useful, metabolic planning needs to be integrated with land use planning, infrastructure design, operation and renewal, and planned material recovery from expected urban stock decommissioning. The key challenge is to find better forms of organization and more efficient and integrated modes of human settlements to establish a trend towards reducing biophysical metabolism, both in per capita and total terms. This is relevant from both adaptation and mitigation perspectives. Planning material and energy dynamics of settlements is not a minor issue, mostly because minimizing biophysical metabolism and thus direct and indirect emissions will be crucial, especially in relation to newer infrastructure which will have to be designed for livable, inclusive low-carbon settlements considering such aspects as climate conditions, weather resilience and GHG emissions.

None of these aspects has been explicitly considered in the LCCSMC 2014–2020 or the 69 actions comprising the CCAPMC 2014–2020. Nor have preliminary metabolic data for Mexico City and policy recommendations following from it been taken into account (Delgado-Ramos 2012, 2013 and 2014). The recommendations related to the political ecology of urban water metabolism in the Metropolitan Area are particularly relevant (Delgado-Ramos 2014 and 2015a). Among them are:

- A "new water culture" centred around moderate, responsible, socially fair consumption
- Addressing the issue of leakage in present and future systems
- Protecting conservation land and restoring vegetation there and in the city to increase evapotranspiration capacity and reduce city temperature, among other things

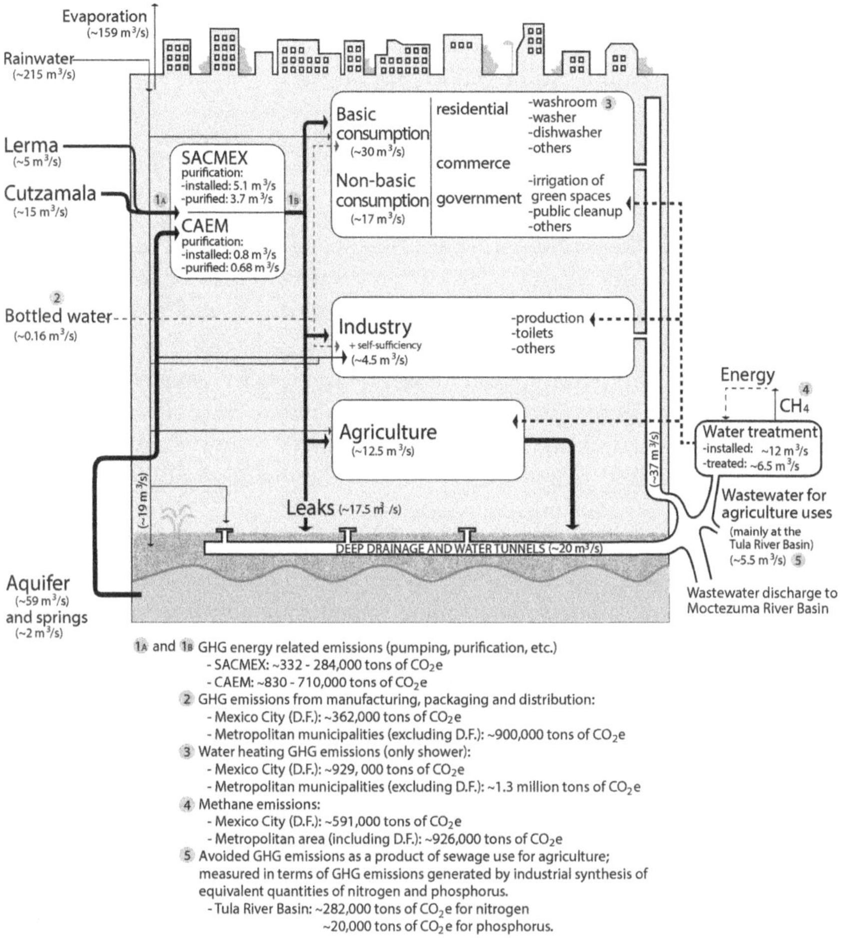

FIGURE 9.2 Urban water metabolism of Mexico City Metropolitan Area (source Delgado-Ramos 2015a)

- Attempting to effectively plan land use, especially peripheral urban land
- Decentralizing water infrastructure to increase flexibility, resilience and transformation by adding small local water reuse/treatment systems or rainwater-harvesting locations.

A synthesis of Mexico City's current water metabolic arrangements (a reasonable base line for policy), is offered in Figure 9.2. Note that direct and indirect energy consumption related to bottled water production is similar to or greater than the energy consumption of utility service companies in serving the entire Metropolitan Area.

This brief qualitative assessment, taken from another detailed exercise (Delgado-Ramos, 2015b), clarifies that even the most advanced climate change action plan in the country still requires major efforts.

Adaptation policy and planning

As mentioned earlier, Mexico City is prone to extreme weather-related events and even though the city is rather well equipped with water and sanitation infrastructure, chronic flooding disrupts several boroughs on a yearly basis. Heat islands and droughts are also being identified as issues of policy and social concern. Unlike mitigation policy, however, adaptation is still an open question. Social and political awareness on the need for adaptive capacity is lacking and the few proposed actions and measures are disconnected from the urban development agenda. This section is intended to unpack the few policy references on climate change adaptation with the intention of identifying the main gaps, challenges and current obstacles.

The lack of development of the adaptation agenda is clearly evident in both the LCCSMC and CCAPMC 2014–2020. The LCCSMC 2014–2020 acknowledges that around 5.6 million people are vulnerable to climate change and that supporting resilience is crucial. But no concrete measures are proposed to achieve that goal. The LCCSMC includes a superficial diagnosis of vulnerability at borough level, but is not detailed enough to define concrete adaptation actions, although it does claim that conservation of green areas and densification of the built environment are key to fostering resilience.

The CCAPMC 2014–2020 addresses resilience building as one of its seven axes, and it includes three lines of action: updating the Hazards and Risk Atlas, implementing the programme of Hydrometeorological Risk Prevention and promoting the Environmental Fund. No vulnerability analysis of key sectors was undertaken, and the conceptual underpinnings for adaptation focus on identification of meteorological risks posed by extreme events with no clear distinction between the adaptation agenda and the existing civil protection agenda. No connection is identified with climate change scenarios, and there are no explicit linkages between the proposed resilience-building actions and the existing and future environmental, water resources, and soil conservation and urbanization regulation actions.

The National Strategy on Climate Change (DOF 2013) and the Special Program on Climate Change (2013–2018) show some progress towards setting up an adaptation agenda. The former recognizes that 1,380 municipalities, among a national total of 2,440, are highly vulnerable to climate change-related disasters (DOF 2013). The document "Climate change adaptation in Mexico: vision, tools and criteria for decision-making" (INECC/SEMARNAT 2012) and the disposition of the General Law on Climate Change to elaborate adaptation plans at state level are also proof of progress. In parallel, the Civil Protection General Law has already vaguely alluded to adaptation as a mechanism to protect "…the person, society and the environment to face the risk posed by climate change" (DOF 2012). It is worth noting, however, that while the word "adaptation" is becoming part of the policy discourse in the environment sector, there are no concrete references to adaptation when it comes to "non-environmental" sectors such as transport and communications or energy. The National Strategy on Climate Change acknowledges that since adaptation takes place at the local level, more detailed information on regional and local conditions and impacts is still needed, as well as the involvement of municipalities in this effort (DOF 2013). Proposed measures include, among others, sustainable resource use, land use planning and the protection of strategic infrastructure and productive systems. However, all of them are pointed out only in generic terms. Therefore, a great deal still needs to be done around adaptation strategies and options in the light of increasing urban vulnerability and potential climate change impacts.

Civil protection policy as a disaster prevention agenda

Before concluding, the last policy pillar to analyse is the disaster prevention policy (DPP) for several reasons: 1) in Mexico City, DPP has influenced the way policy makers, scientists and lay people perceive weather and climate-related events as mainly natural extreme events that can be tackled through civil engineering infrastructure, education and behavioural change; 2) DPP has been mainstreamed and institutionalized as a civil protection agenda that is focused on emergency, restoration and damage mitigation actions; and 3) DPP has played a very important role in shaping the national disaster prevention system as a reactive policy framework that is socially insensitive to the vulnerability and climate sensitivity of people and sectors (Aragón-Durand 2011).

In terms of coping with weather-related risks, the government of Mexico City is rather well equipped with plans, programmes, regulations and staff whose main goal is to protect people, livelihoods and infrastructure from the impact of heavy rainfall and the resultant run-off water that may inundate streets, houses and public equipment. The rationale behind the civil protection tools and intervention is to act once flooding has occurred, not to address the underlying causes that put people at risk. This has made for a reactive civil protection system that is not fully integrated with the development agenda of the city in terms of long-term climate risk reduction. This has had severe and negative manifestations and implications in the land use planning of vulnerable areas and the lack of conservation of surrounding ecosystems that may provide risk reduction services. Each of the 16 administrative boroughs has a civil protection unit that in practice functions to only put out fires, and to assist people once an earthquake strikes or a flood creates havoc. As it happens, at national level, the Mexico City Risk Atlas is in fact an atlas of dangers that does not take into account social participation and therefore fails to inform people and institutions about the potential impact of hydrometeorological events.

For a disaster prevention system to function as a real disaster reduction policy, it has to shift from a reactive perspective towards a more preventive one that considers vulnerability reduction as the main goal. It is worth mentioning that a reactive civil protection system is necessary to manage disaster situations and alleviate damage and losses but it may well also function as the basis for adaptation to climate change if important changes are implemented, such as mainstreaming disaster risk reduction into sectoral policies including climate adaptation responses.

Conclusions

The purpose of identifying problems, contradictions and inconsistencies in Mexico City's climate change adaptation and mitigation strategy and action plan, far from discrediting what so far has been achieved, is to show that in fact local policy is still going through a steep learning curve with regard to design and actual implementation and evaluation mechanisms (a national assessment that corroborates this has been published by Delgado et al, 2015). Thus, a mandatory guideline for climate change action plans at every level of government, but mostly at the local level, is urgently needed. It should include issues of basic components, criteria, technical aspects, goals and mechanisms for active citizen participation and accountability. The same applies for the purposes of analysis and action experiences, both successful and undesirable. In that sense, the experience of Mexico City is relevant for other national (or even some international) climate change policy efforts at the local level, as they might have lesser capacities and expertise.

A successful policy must be sensitive enough to the different values and even beliefs that various stakeholders assign to what is agreed to be a shared common objective. Thus, climate change implementation is not a linear mechanistic process but an incremental, complex and sometimes messy one. What is clear is that adaptation and mitigation measures demand an imaginative and integrated policy framework with novel paths for reinventing decision-making and public participation. Such an improved governance framework is crucial for coping with urban climate change challenges, which demand a profound transformation of present trends in planning, building, operating, managing and living in urban settlements. It is the sum of multiple actions, if these actions are rooted in an integrated planning process for urban territories and their uses, that will be decisive in enabling synergies and co-benefits of different kinds. As just pointed out, this includes a more comprehensive and proactive approach to disaster prevention, one that is integrated with land use planning and development as well as serving as a basis for longer term adaptation. This is why traditional management by sectors is neither sufficient nor viable and seems still to be a limitation in current modes of executing climate change policy. In a similar way, mitigation and adaptation agendas need to be integrated in order to develop original modes of governance that actually take advantage of potential synergies and co-benefits. At the same time, such modes of governance need to be socially robust, building on genuine bottom-up citizen participation and inclusiveness, responsive to realities on the ground. Apart from being more socially fair and inclusive, sustainable cities, in a broad sense, should be seen as territorial spaces that need to be progressively less greedy for land, materials and energy, more livable, with a greater capacity for reacting in the face of climate change and the environmental crisis.

Notes

1 Based on an emission rate of 1,285 tons, obtained from the average between the initial year (2014: 1,200 tons) and the last year (2020: 1,370 tons) of official estimations.
2 The CCAPMC derives from the LCCAMC. The latter is considered a guiding instrument of Mexico City's government policy as it "...establishes the scientific, technical and institutional framework for climate change mitigation and adaptation" (SEDEMA 2014a p 10). Thus, the CCAPMC delineates the climate actions within the framework established by the LCCAMC.
3 Based on Delgado (2015b).
4 Mexico City's environmental authority recognizes that the LCCSMC of 2004 did not rely on documented local data on GHG emissions, certainly a challenge and a limitation when "...designing a climate action plan fitted to the necessities of the Federal District" (SEDEMA 2014a p.146). The current LCCSMC is now supposed to be custom designed.

References

Aragón-Durand, Fernando (2007) "Urbanisation and flood vulnerability in the peri-urban interface of Mexico City", *Disasters* Vol. 31, No4, pages 477–494.

Aragón-Durand, Fernando (2011) *Disaster Discourses, Policy Values and Responses: The Social Construction of Urban Floods in the Peri-Urban Interface of Mexico City.* Lambert Academic Publishing, Germany, 353 pages.

Banzo, M. (2000) "Franja peri-urbana y proceso de urbanización: La formación de la megalópolis de México" in D. Hiernaux, A. Lindón and J. Loyola (coord) *La construcción social de un territorio emergente: El Valle de Chalco*, El Colegio' Mexiquense, pages 137–166.

Connolly, Priscilla (1999) "Mexico City: Our common future", *Environment and Urbanization* Vol 11, No 1, pages 53–78.

Delgado-Ramos, Gian Carlo (2012). "Metabolismo urbano y transporte" in G. C. Delgado-Ramos (coord) *Transporte, ciudad y cambio climático*, CEIICH, UNAM, Mexico, pages 129–167.

Delgado-Ramos, Gian Carlo (2013) "Climate change and metabolic dynamics in Latin American major cities" in S. S. Zubir and C. A. Brebbia (editors) *Sustainable City VIII. Urban Regeneration and Sustainability*, Southampton: WIT Press, pages 39–56.

Delgado-Ramos, Gian Carlo (2014) "Ciudad, agua y cambio climático. Una aproximación desde el metabolismo urbano", *Medio Ambiente y Urbanización* Vol. 80, No 1, pages 95–123.

Delgado-Ramos, Gian Carlo (2015a) "Water and the political ecology of urban metabolism: the case of Mexico City". *Journal of Political Ecology* Vol. 22, pages 98–114.

Delgado-Ramos, Gian Carlo (2015b) "Adaptación y Mitigación del cambio climático en la Ciudad de México: análisis de la estrategia, programa y avances alcanzados". *Revista Científica Monfragüe. Desarrollo Resiliente.* Vol. V, No 1 pages 1–24.

Delgado-Ramos, Gian Carlo, Ana De Luca Zuria and Verónica Vázquez Zentella (2015) *Adaptación y mitigación urbana del cambio climático*. Mexico: CEIICH / PINCC, UNAM.

Available online: http://computo.ceiich.unam.mx/webceiich/docs/libro/Adaptacion-web1.pd

DOF – Diario Oficial de la Federación (2009) “Programa Especial de Cambio Climático 2009–2012”. Diario Oficial de la Federación, Secretaria de Gobernación, Mexico, 28 de agosto.

DOF – Diario Oficial de la Federación (2012) “Ley General de Protección Civil. México.” Diario Oficial de la Federación. Secretaría de Gobernación. Available online: www.diputados.gob.mx/LeyesBiblio/pdf/LGPC_030614.pdf

DOF – Diario Oficial de la Federación (2013) “Estrategia Nacional de Cambio Climático. Visión 10-20-40”. Diario Oficial de la Federación, Secretaría de Gobernación, Mexico, 6 de junio. Available online: www.dof.gob.mx/nota_detalle.php?codigo=5301093&fecha=03/06/2013

Escolero, Óscar, Sandra Martínez, Stefanie Kralisch and Maria Perevochtchikova (2009) *Vulnerabilidad de las fuentes de abastecimiento de agua potable de la ciudad de México en el contexto del cambio climático.* Informe final, Instituto de Geología, Centro de Ciencias de la Atmósfera, UNAM e Instituto de Ciencia y Tecnología del DF. Available online: www.cvcccm-atmosfera.unam.mx/resumen_proyectos.php?id=3, fecha 20/04/2015

Estrada, Francisco and Benjamín Martínez (2010) *Economía del cambio climático en la ciudad de México.* Instituto de Ciencia y Tecnología del Distrito federal y Centro Virtual de Cambio Climático de la Ciudad de México. Available online: www.cvcccm-atmosfera.unam.mx/sis_admin/archivos/informe.pdf, fecha 15/03/2015.

Ezcurra, E., A. Aguilar, T. Garcia, M. Mazari and I. Pisanty (1999) *The Basin of Mexico: Critical Environmental Issues and Sustainability*, United Nations University Press, New York, 216 pages.

GDF – Gobierno del Distrito Federal (2012) *Atlas geográfico del suelo de conservación del Distrito Federal.* Procuraduría Ambiental y del Ordenamiento Territorial del Distrito Federal, Mexico.

INECC/SEMARNAT (2012) “Adaptación al cambio climático en México: visión, elementos y criterios para la toma de decisiones”, Instituto Nacional de Ecología y Cambio Climático – Secretaria de Medio Ambiente y Recursos Naturales, Mexico. Available online: www.inecc.gob.mx/descargas/dgipea/ine-ecc-pc-01-2012.pdf

Kennedy, Christopher, Stephanie Pincetl and Paul Bunje (2011) “The study of urban metabolism and its applications to urban planning and design”, *Environmental Pollution*. Vol. 159, No 8–9, pages 1965–1973.

Romero-Lankao, Patricia (2010) “Water in Mexico City: What will climate change to its history of water-related hazards and vulnerabilities”, *Environment and Urbanization*, Vol. 22, No 1, pages 157–178.

Sánchez Vargas, Armando, Francisco Estrada and Carlos Gay (2012) E*l cambio climático y la pobreza en el Distrito Federal. Gobierno del Distrito Federal*, Instituto de Ciencia y Tecnología del DF y CCA-UNAM, 47 pages. Available online: www.cvcccm-atmosfera.unam.mx/sis_admin/archivos/ccypobreza.pdf, fecha 12/03/2015.

SEDEMA – Secretaría de Medio Ambiente del Distrito Federal (2012) *Inventario de Emsiones de la Zona Metropolitana del Valle de Mexico, 2010,* Gobierno del Distrito Federal, Mexico.

SEDEMA – Secretaría de Medio Ambiente del Distrito Federal (2014a) *Estrategia Local de Acción Climática: Ciudad de México 2014–2020,* México, 158 pages.

SEDEMA – Secretaría de Medio Ambiente del Distrito Federal (2014b) *Programa de Acción Climática de la Ciudad de México 2014–2020.* México, 388 pages.

Zhang, Yan (2013). “Urban metabolism: a review of research methodologies.” *Environmental Pollution*. Vol. 178, pages 463–473.

10

NEW YORK, USA

William Solecki, Cynthia Rosenzweig, Stephen Solecki, Lesley Patrick, Radley Horton and Michael Dorsch

Introduction

New York City, one of the most populous and ethnically diverse cities in the world, has responded to a variety of environmental challenges in its history. The most recent is climate change, which is projected to have wide impacts on the city's critical infrastructure and population through higher temperatures, more intense flooding events and sea level rise. The city recognized the risks early and has become a national and international leader in responding to this new challenge, illustrating how this is possible for a large city. As part of a mature urban region, it is an excellent bellwether for the impacts that may be experienced by other cities, especially those in emerging metropolitan conurbations.

The physical setting

The New York Statistical Area, which includes the five boroughs of New York City (the primary focus of this chapter) and 25 adjacent counties in the states of New York, New Jersey, and Connecticut, is the quintessential urban agglomeration. Approximately 8.4 million people live in the high density urban core of the city and another 15 million in smaller cities, towns, and villages nearby (US Census 2014). Urban and suburban land uses have increased dramatically and continue to increase, but 60 per cent of the land is still covered by farms and forests (Cox 2014).

With over 2,400 kilometers of coastline, the region's development is intimately connected to the ocean. Four of the five city boroughs are on islands and waterways cut deeply into the land area. The Hudson–Raritan River watershed encompasses about half the region, including some of the most densely settled parts. Much of the land is at low elevation, about 1 per cent of it below 3 meters, including heavily developed land and important infrastructure, such as lower Manhattan, the three major airports, and the Hackensack Meadowlands area.

Some exurban areas still maintain extensive wildlife habitat but most has been heavily degraded. Surface water and groundwater supplies in more urbanized areas typically exceed federal water pollution standards and there are more than 100,000 known or potential toxic sites (including leaking underground fuel tanks), many where coastal wetlands were used as landfills.

The large, relatively wealthy population of the region consumes more goods and resources than most low and medium income countries, placing demands on locales distant from its borders and watershed. The water supply system, for example, supplies 1,500 million gallons per day to the region, drawing from upland reservoirs. Almost all food must be imported, because remaining farmland is continuously converted to suburban land uses.

Socio-economic context and governance

The city's population grew rapidly in the 19th and early 20th centuries, then slowed, and since 1980 has grown steadily again. Density is about 27,000 inhabitants per square mile. The population, a third of it foreign born, is astonishingly diverse, and includes Caucasian (including Hispanic), African American, Asian, and other groups. The income gap between the rich and poor has grown and continues to increase. The poorest 20 per cent, which earns 88 times less than the top 5 per cent, has been below the national poverty line in recent years (Roberts 2014). Hispanics have the lowest median income, at USD 36,196 (U.S. Census Bureau 2013). By global standards this number seems high, but the high cost of housing in New York City is a serious constraint (USD 3,000 per month is the average for one bedroom). In 2013, almost a third of renter households paid more than half their income on rent, a situation that has worsened as incomes remain stagnant while rents continue to rise (Furman Center 2015). Despite the significant disparities, almost all residents live in formal housing with uninterrupted access to fresh drinking water, safe sanitation services, solid waste collection, and electricity.

A leading national and global economic center, New York City has a GDP of $1,403 billion, 9 per cent of national GDP (Brookings Institute 2014). Its thriving economy is concentrated in banking, finance and communication, as well as retail, trade, transportation, tourism, real estate, education, the arts, and new media. Professional and business services, health, social, and educational sectors have added the most jobs in recent years and helped lower unemployment rates. As of 2013, 63 per cent of residents over 16 were employed (U.S. Census Bureau 2013).

New York City is governed jointly by an elected city council and mayor, and city government oversees public education, correctional institutions, libraries, public safety, recreational facilities, sanitation, water supply, and welfare services within the city and in locations throughout the metropolitan region where the city maintains facilities and infrastructure such as the drinking water supply reservoirs and watersheds. Lands vulnerable to coastal flooding are managed through complex multiple jurisdictions including the City of New York, State of New York, and US federal government. Agencies and departments in each entity have their own mandates regarding land management which must also be coordinated.

Climate and climate risk

Over recent decades, the metropolitan region has experienced higher temperatures, more frequent intense rainfalls, and rising sea levels (Rosenzweig and Solecki 2010; Rosenzweig et al. 2011). While this comparatively wealthy region has limited vulnerability to environmental hazards compared with some of the cities described in this volume, it still faces serious threats. Key climate risks include coastal and inland flooding, heat waves, coastal storm surges, extreme wind events, urban heat islands, and primary and secondary air pollutants, all expected to be exacerbated by climate change. Given the region's density, extreme storm events could cause damage in excess of several hundred billion USD.

No single event can be attributed to climate change, but recent history highlights potential climate change risks. A downpour in August 2007 crippled the subway system, and in 2011, Hurricane Irene caused the city government for the first time to implement its storm surge evacuation plan and risk reduction activities on a broad scale, shutting down public transit and authorizing mandatory evacuation of some areas. In the fall of 2012, Hurricane Sandy brought widespread devastation to the region via coastal flooding and record storm surge. Other major climate events have included:

- 2010 and 2011: very hot stormy summers;
- 1999: Hurricane/Tropical Storm Floyd – widespread flooding following massive rainfall;
- 1992: December Nor'easter – extensive flooding of regional transportation systems;
- 1985: Hurricane Gloria – storm surge causes extensive coastal damage and flooding;
- 1960s: mid-decade drought of record;
- 1947: Nor'easter – extensive flooding of regional transportation infrastructure systems;
- 1938: Long Island Express hurricane – extensive damage on Long Island;
- 1888: March blizzard cripples new electricity and telephone wiring.

Sea level rise, increased probability of storm surge, and associated coastal flooding are seen as the most significant future challenge to the city, with its extensive shoreline (NPCC 2010). Sea level rise since 1900 has averaged 1.2 inches per decade, about twice the global average, due to regional land subsidence (NPCC 2015). Climate change will foster further sea level rise through increased glacial melting and thermal expansion of upper layers of the ocean (Table 10.1). The resulting heightened flood potential during future hurricane and nor'easters (extra-tropical cyclonic winter storms) will cause the most significant damage. Under a worst-case scenario, by the 2080s, a 100-year coastal flooding event could occur every 8 years (in the best case, every 25 to 30 years). More extreme estimates show a 500-year event every 50 years (NPCC 2015).

As demonstrated by Hurricane Sandy and other recent storms (Table 10.2), much significant infrastructure will be at increased risk from sea level rise and storm surges (Figure 10.1). The policy of placing necessary yet locally unwanted land uses (LULUs) on marginal lands has had some unintended consequences. Hurricane Sandy, for instance, caused several hundred million dollars of flood damage in the Hackensack Meadowlands in northern New Jersey, criss-crossed by major ship, train, air, road, and pipeline infrastructure features (Leichenko and Solecki 2013). Storm surge flooding also revealed the complex geography of development along the coastline, with both high-end commercial and residential development and modest, working, and middle class housing pockmarking the vast network of infrastructure.

The region's few remaining coastal wetlands, which provide critical habitat to local and migratory animals, protect inland development and act as water purifiers, are also vulnerable. Under natural conditions, these wetlands could respond to sea level rise; but extensive land development has meant severe wetland loss. Future scenarios show that the rate of sea level rise will likely exceed the wetland accretion rate by mid-century, which, along with increasing evapotranspiration and projected water deficits, will mean further wetland loss (Wolfe et al. 2011).

Water supply

Many scenarios for the region show the potential for extended rainy periods followed by drought. While changes in precipitation are less certain than for temperature, there will likely be greater variability (Rosenzweig and Solecki 2010). Recent weather illustrates the implications. For example, water supply systems with no capacity to store heavy early-year rains in 1999 began to call for drought emergencies after a dry spring and mid-summer, only to switch abruptly to emergency flood measures after mid-September Tropical Storm Floyd dumped up to 12 inches of rain.

Expected sea level rise will also affect the water supply infrastructure. Pumping stations, treatment facilities, and intake and outflow sites will be subject to more frequent flooding. Still under investigation is the threat of saltwater intrusion into regional groundwater supplies and surface water withdrawal sites (Major and Goldberg 2000). New York City's huge water supply system

TABLE 10.1 Sea level rise projections over the coming century for New York City (NPCC, 2015)

Baseline	*2020s*	*2050s*	*2080s*	*Year 2100*
0 inches 2000–2004	+4 to +8 in	+11 to +21 in	+18 to +39 in	+22 to +50 in

TABLE 10.2 Extreme coastal storm events in New York City from 1999 to 2014

Hurricane Floyd
September 16–17, 1999
- Category: TS-1; Central pressure: 974 mb; Wind speed: 70 mph
- Major inland riverine flooding; 24-hour rainfall totals 10 to 15 inches (Pasch et al. 1999 updated 2014; US National Weather Service, ND)

Hurricane Irene
August 27–29, 2011
- Category: TS (Avila & Cagialosi 2011)
- Central pressure: 959 mb (Avila & Cagialosi 2011)
- Wind speed: 65 mph (Dolnick 2011)
- 3–6 foot storm surge (Avila & Cagialosi 2011)
- First mandatory evacuation of coastal areas, 370,000 residents (New York City Office of Emergency Management 2015)
- First natural disaster to shut down the NYC Subway system (National Oceanic and Atmospheric Association & National Weather Service 2012)
- Estimated $100 million in damage (New York City Office of Emergency Management 2015)
- 1 death (Avila & Cagialosi 2011)

Hurricane Sandy
October 29–30, 2012
- Category: TS (Blake et al. 2012)
- Central pressure: 965 mb (Blake et al. 2012)
- Wind speed: 74 mph (Blake et al. 2012)
- Storm surge reached 9.4 feet and storm tide reached 14.06 feet at the Battery, flooding lower Manhattan (Blake et al. 2012)
- Second-ever mandatory evacuation of coastal areas (New York City Office of Emergency Management 2015)
- Estimated $19 billion in damage to the city (Blake et al. 2012)
- Estimated 43 deaths in NYC (Keller 2012)
- 800,000 customers lost power in NYC (Gibbs & Holloway 2013)

November 2012 Nor'easter
November 7–10, 2012
- Strong winds and downed power lines to areas recovering from the effects of Hurricane Sandy
- 2.8 inches of snow in Central Park, new daily record (Raftery 2012), affecting those in temporary shelters due to Hurricane Sandy

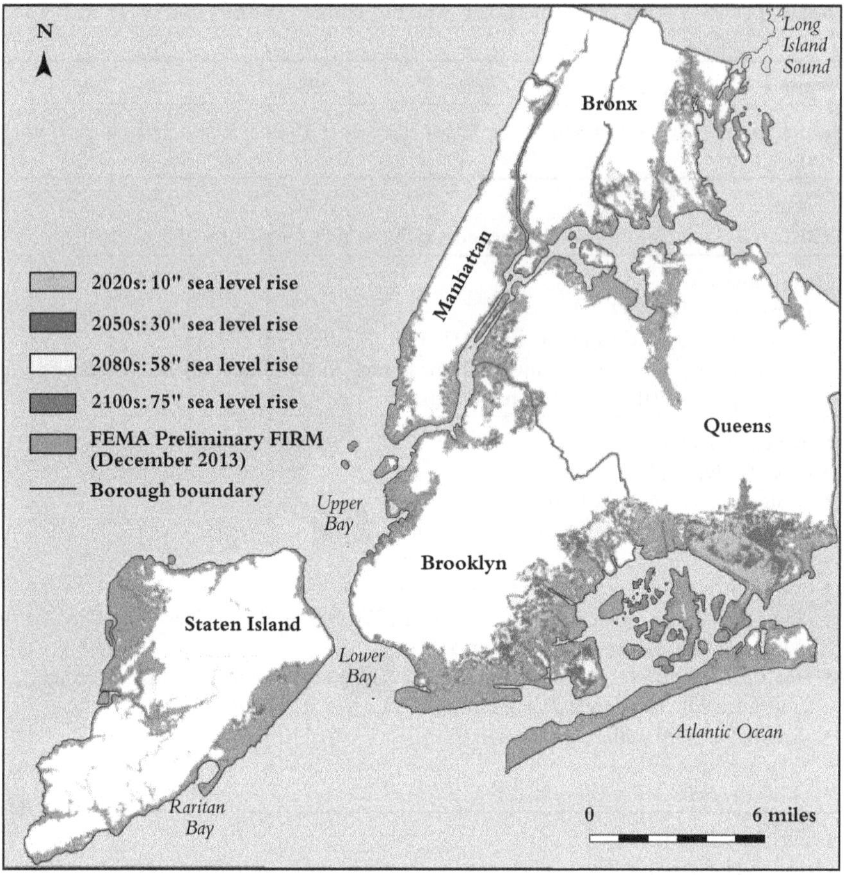

FIGURE 10.1 Future 100-year flood zones (source: based on a map drawn by L. Partrick and W. Solecki)

should be able to respond to increased temperatures and rainfall variability but the shifts might overwhelm smaller regional systems. Experts have called for evaluation of enhanced intra-regional water distribution protocols to reduce overall vulnerability to drought (Hansler and Major 1999). Interdependent vulnerabilities between the water supply system and other critical infrastructure systems are also being studied (Zimmerman and Faris 2010).

Energy demand

Climate change will have direct impacts on energy demand. Lower winter fuel demand will be far offset by the summer increase with the average number of days exceeding 90°F projected to increase three- to four-fold by 2080 (NPCC 2015). During a 1999 heat wave, the region experienced a record peak for electrical power that precipitated brownouts and an extended blackout in largely minority sections of the City. Residents and local politicians argued that the local power authority had not properly maintained the equipment serving these neighborhoods, and demands were made to ensure that disadvantaged communities not be disproportionately affected by future events. Such events foreshadow the inequities that might arise in the face of intensified environmental risk exposure.

Public health

The spatial and demographic inequities of climate change impacts are well expressed in the public health risks. Urban populations will experience increased heat stress, greater potential of water-borne or vector-related disease outbreaks, and higher concentrations of secondary air pollutants (Kinney et al. 2011). The poor, elderly, very young, and immuno-compromised will be at greatest risk. Recent studies of the effects of Hurricane Sandy highlighted the vulnerability of impoverished populations in critical flood zones around New York City, who were less able to evacuate during or after the storm, or remediate the long-term health implications such as exposure to mold resulting from the storm water flood damage (Lane et al. 2013). Populations at heightened risk of heat stress will be those without access to air conditioning, which will in any case become problematic with the increased cooling demands. Risk of morbidity and mortality becomes severe if blackouts occur during an extreme heat event. Heat waves also will exacerbate air pollution problems associated with respiratory-related health attacks. As an indirect effect, the increased number of mosquitos with a warmer, wetter climate also potentially means an increasing risk of West-Nile virus in New York, as demonstrated in summer 1999 when heavy rains, preceded by drought, were followed by a small outbreak with several deaths (Kinney et al. 2011).

Infrastructure

New York City maintains some of the densest, most complex infrastructure in the world, much of it rapidly aging and increasingly vulnerable to the projected stresses from a changing climate (Zimmerman and Faris 2010). Much of the large-scale infrastructure (energy, transportation, water, and waste) was built during the early and mid-twentieth century, when most available sites were on or near remnant wetlands or derelict industrial sites; for example, the three major international airports, built on low elevation or landfill sites.

The city's infrastructure also includes thousands of miles of underground electrical distribution lines, sewer piping, water distribution piping, and transit system tracks along with almost 100 sewerage pumping stations, 14 water pollution control plants, two dozen major electricity generating facilities, a million buildings, and a vast network of fixed and mobile telecommunication networks. These systems are tightly coupled, leading to the possibility of a cascade of failures and secondary and tertiary impacts. The intense rainstorm and flash flooding in August 2007, for instance, rendered almost the entire subway system inoperable, causing significant economic losses.

The origins of climate protection action in New York

Concern about climate change impacts precipitated the 1994 conference *Metropolitan New York in the Greenhouse: The Baked Apple?*, convened as a first step in encouraging direct action (Hill 1996). The first major, scenario-based scientific assessment of regional climate impacts was developed only in the late 1990s as part of the first comprehensive national climate assessment. In 2001, a report on potential climate change consequences was produced for the U.S. Global Change Research Program (Rosenzweig and Solecki 2001). While widely cited, the report was not immediately translated into significant policy changes or management actions.

Mayor Bloomberg, elected in November 2001 in the aftermath of the September attack, brought a technocratic approach to governance, focused on immediate security threats but also longer-term challenges. In 2005, he joined 131 other mayors to embrace the Kyoto Protocol for GHG reduction. In the following year, he announced the creation of the Office of Long-Term Planning and Sustainability (OLTPS), tasked with developing and implementing a comprehensive plan for a greener, more sustainable city. The 2007, PlaNYC 2030 aimed for 30 per cent reduction in emissions by 2030, creation of a climate change adaptation taskforce, the development of adaptation plans, and the consideration of highly vulnerable communities. Later that year, on August 8, a severe thunderstorm swept through the city, resulting in major service disruptions of the Metropolitan Transportation Authority (MTA) transit system, causing significant economic losses and marking a real transition in awareness and in the city's climate action. The state governor directed the MTA to assess the system's vulnerability to future storms, and recommendations included the creation of an Emergency Response Center and Inter/Intra-Agency Flooding Task Force.

Development of the adaptation work-stream

The primary adaptation focus in New York City has been on ensuring the continued function of the city's critical infrastructure (roads, subways, communication services, energy, water and public parks and open space), and the city has described its own efforts in this regard as "...one of the most comprehensive and inclusive strategies ever launched to secure a City's critical infrastructure against the effects of climate change" (NYC Office of the Mayor 2008).

Current climate change adaptation efforts in New York City build on previous assessments and lessons from experience. The region's issues have been studied for almost 15 years. The 2001 MEC report (Rosenzweig and Solecki 2001) was an important benchmark, introducing new climate and sea level rise model results. In 2004, the New York City Department of Environmental Protection launched an adaptation initiative that included creation of a task force to ensure that potential climate risks to the city's water supply, drainage, and wastewater management systems were taken into account in planning, integrating GHG emissions management to the greatest extent possible. It identified adaptations to increase the robustness of current systems, and immediately improved responses, for instance by managing intense precipitation events in upstate reservoirs. This became an exemplar for work soon to be carried out by other New York City agencies.

PlaNYC 2030, initially focused most heavily on mitigation, was later expanded to include additional adaptation measures, especially in response to the 8 August 2007 extreme precipitation event. A new goal was the creation of an interagency Climate Change Adaptation Task Force, charged with identifying risks, opportunities, and adaptation strategies for the city's critical infrastructure. This body provides a forum for middle level administrators and officials from relevant city and regional public authorities and private companies to discuss and debate new information about climate change impacts and adaptation opportunities. It also allows for discussion to include representatives of such regional organizations as commuter rail authorities and communications companies to facilitate regional coordination.

To support the work of this task force, the city convened the New York City Panel on Climate Change (NPCC), a group of experts (climate scientists and legal, insurance, and risk management experts) to advise on climate change science, potential impacts, adaptation pathways, and climate protection levels specific to the city's vital infrastructure, taking an objective role in ensuring that efforts were based on sound science, and contributing to the development of the city's adaptation planning framework (NPCC 2010, 2015). A critical task was to address regulations and design standards related to sea level rise and storm surge, heat waves and inland flooding in the context of future climate change. To maintain current risk levels, the city will have to adjust building codes, establishing guidelines on building for increased frequency and intensity of precipitation, flooding, heat waves and extreme wind events. A 2010 Green Codes Task Force Report included recommendations for building code adjustments for resilence.

The *Adaptation Assessment Guidebook* (AAG), another NPCC product, describes a detailed process to help the agencies that manage critical infrastructure with guidelines for ongoing risk management, maintenance and operation, and capital planning (Major and Grady 2010). It includes infrastructure questionnaires, a risk matrix and a prioritization framework, and defines the adaptation process as a dynamic cycle of analysis and action followed by evaluation, further analysis and policy refinement.

The NPCC fosters a "flexible adaptation pathways" approach, originally developed by the London TE2100 (Lowe et al. 2009), encouraging strategies that can be adjusted and modified over time to reflect evolving climate change understanding. Adaptation planning was initially focused on critical infrastructure, but the approach can also be helpful in other sectors, as well as other cities and metropolitan regions. Other initiatives have since emerged to promote adaptation of assets and populations in high risk locations (e.g. coastal sites) or of high risk populations (e.g. the elderly and young, institutionalized, and immune-compromised).

Many challenges remain. The Bloomberg administration worked actively to institutionalize regulations; future administrations will need to maintain the focus, updating urban sustainability efforts and periodically reviewing progress towards stated goals and objectives, while incorporating new climate science and findings on adaptation planning and implementation. The de Blasio administration is continuing to address climate change mitigation and adaptation while also introducing increased concern and focus on inequities and injustice (NPCC 2015; NYC Mayor's Office of Sustainability 2015). Other challenges include larger scale cultural norms and practices. For example, it is very difficult to generate the institutional and legal capacity to change the development pathway on the city's waterfront – almost all the land in the city has already been developed, and there is little opportunity to steer new development from highly exposed coastal sites. Private property rights in the US are heavily protected, making it difficult to limit use of locations at risk from flooding or other climate-related hazards.

Synergies with disaster risk reduction

The city's disaster risk reduction strategies were largely developed by the city's Office of Emergency Management which has extensively expanded its capacity in the last decade to include integrated GIS data products, vulnerability mapping efforts and emergency response materials in a range of languages. Revised climate risk assessments have facilitated more active engagement by the city's disaster risk community, especially with the recent emergence of climate resilience as a dominant policy discourse. Planning activities to enhance resilience include a focus on heat stress reduction, stormwater management via green infrastructure techniques, updates of flood and storm surge mapping efforts with high resolution elevation data, a re-mapping of the flood hazard zones (FEMA FIRM – Flood Insurance Rate Maps), funding the next generation of storm surge modeling, and a new natural hazards risk model for the city (Botzen and Aerts 2012). Disaster risk reduction (DRR) efforts focus on reducing vulnerability to extreme events, rather than on larger-scale planning efforts or economic development goals. Mechanisms to support DDR and adaptation include rising insurance premiums for flood protection and building codes to limit exposure, for instance, requiring elevated construction to reduce storm surge damage.

Several key flood mitigation projects have been taken on by the city and the MTA to help reduce the impacts of future floods on the massive transit networks. Plans for flood mitigation projects exist for three subway yards and 12 ventilation plants in low-lying parts of the city, and flood mitigation equipment is to be installed near low-lying subway entrances. As a major economic hub, it is crucial that the city safeguard its assets; resiliency for the business sector is being augmented by protecting inventory and equipment (i.e. transit or utility related), financing means to provide heat and power during and after extreme events, and having data backup investments.

Funding

Initial funding for climate change action in New York City was largely provided by the city itself. NPCC funding, however, came from the Rockefeller Foundation, with additional resources from the PlaNYC 2030 effort. Other funding has been drawn from various general revenue fund and capital investment sources for the maintenance of critical infrastructure. The city has also created a USD 1.5 billion green infrastructure initiative to foster development of alternative stormwater management strategies (e.g. structures that can hold flood waters but drain soon after the event).

The mitigation work-stream

The focus on climate mitigation pre-dates activities to address climate impacts and adaptation by several years, and mitigation was a primary initial element of the PlaNYC process. Of the city's total GHG emissions in 2012 (47.9 million tCO_2e), buildings (heating fuel, natural gas, electricity, and steam) contributed 71 per cent and the transportation sector 20 per cent. The remaining 3 per cent is from fugitive emissions from the management of solid waste, treatment of wastewater, and distribution of natural gas and electricity (City of New York 2013). Overall emissions decreased by 19 per cent between 2005 and 2012, close to two-thirds of the 30 per cent reduction aimed for by 2030 under the goals of PlaNYC. Much of the reduction is due to the 11 per cent decrease in carbon intensity of the electrical supply system (City of New York 2013), but total energy consumption (electricity and heating fuels), per capita vehicle use, and solid waste generation have also decreased. The city's multi-faceted approach responded to emissions reduction opportunities in several sectors, including action by the city focused on infrastructure (e.g. government buildings and vehicles) and by leading edge educational institutions (e.g. pledging to voluntarily reduce GHG emissions).

Energy efficiency

The city's Greener, Greater Buildings Plan (GGBP) provides information for integrating economical and efficient energy practices in large buildings, along with job training and a financing body (New York City Energy Efficiency

Corporation – NYCEEC) to help individual building owners choose the most suitable energy efficiency retrofit financing program. A local energy code has also been established under the GGBP, and regulations requiring the benchmarking of energy and water consumption, energy audits and retro-commissioning every ten years, and lighting that meets code by 2025 in non-residential space. These laws seek to decrease GHG emissions by 5 per cent, save the city billions of dollars, and establish around 18,000 new jobs in the construction sector. Several hundred energy efficiency reports have been obtained to date from landlords, allowing information on best practices to be made accessible. Currently, the Mayor's Office and the New York State Energy Research and Development Authority (NYSERDA) are pooling resources to convey how buildings can economically integrate energy efficiency upgrades and retrofits. The numerous transit options provided by the MTA also help reduce emissions. A typical MTA trip saves an average of 10 lbs of carbon dioxide emissions over an equivalent private vehicle trip (MTA, 2012). The MTA has been gradually switching to cleaner fuels and integrating more efficient engines into its fleet. Numerous bike lanes and the Citi Bike program encourage bicycle use. The City is also highly walkable, with everyday necessities often within just a few blocks of people's homes.

Renewable energy

Renewable energy use is increasingly popular in New York. Solar photovoltaic (PV) energy use has expanded from 1 MW to 20 MW since publication of PlaNYC. SunEdison is creating a PV system at a former Staten Island landfill with the potential to increase renewable energy usage by over 50 per cent. The city has also been finding ways to use renewable biogas from anaerobic bacteria at wastewater treatment facilities, for instance at Newtown Creek, where gases are captured and rerouted via the national grid system for city customers. There are also plans with the Department of Interior for wind turbines offshore which can generate a massive 500 megawatts.

Climate change reporting

In addition to the routinely updated PlaNYC, which provides the likely outlook for millions of residents on changing climate conditions, an evolving economy, and aging infrastructure, the City has also released several works related to low carbon building practices, and reports on GHG emissions inventory.

Networking

An important contribution to the development of the mitigation and adaptation activities in NYC has been the professional and personal connections between the New York City participants and their counterparts in other cities (e.g., Chicago, San Francisco, Boston, Tokyo, London). Networking played an important role in promoting climate change mitigation and adaptation in European cities in the early 2000s, and in the latter part of the decade networks began to emerge across North American cities, as well as within international organizations such as C20 (later renamed C40) and the World Mayors Council on Climate Change. There have been significant connections with the city of London and the work of the Greater London Authority. Close collaborations resulted from the ongoing discussions between the groups in both cities.

Integrating adaptation and mitigation

The connections between climate change adaptation and mitigation in New York City have been present since the issues first emerged on the policy agenda, but most often have run on parallel tracks. As mitigation and adaption activities have continued to develop and expand, links between the two have been made in broad policy terms – for instance, the NPCC recommended that the migitation consequences of adaptation action should be considered whenever possible. While some adaptation actions have negative implications for GHG reduction efforts (such as an increase in air conditioning use in response to heightened summer heat stress), the promotion of mitigation and adaptation strategies more generally have followed many of the same development routes. Both have largely taken a flexible approach to policy specification and implementation in the face of climate change demands, emerging best practices, and new science. As of 2015, the migitation and adaptation policies and initiatives of New York City remain largely separate yet connected by a variety of soft linkages, for example both are highlighted as key goals of the new de Blasio administration.

Recent developments

In April 2015, the new administration of Mayor Bill de Blasio released its version of a comprehensive sustainability plan for the City, entitled *OneNYC* as opposed to *PlaNYC*. The approach is designed to highlight the connections between sustainability, justice, and equity. *OneNYC* includes four broad vision areas: 1) Our Growing, Thriving City; 2) Our Just and Equitable City; 3) Our Sustainable City; and 4) Our Resilient City. Within visions 3 and 4, the administration explicitly states its mitigation and adaptation goals with a corresponding set of initatives, empirical targets, and associated funding sources (NYC Mayor's Office of Sustainability 2015).

The de Blasio administration is attempting to build on the aggressive recent history of climate action in the city while broadening its approach and appeal to a larger set of New Yorkers. Previous efforts had been critiqued as too elitist, overly focused on the wealthiest borough (Manhattan) and too technocratic and top down, with limited opportunities for public involvement. These efforts, which combine a climate change agenda and equity and justice concerns with an openness to broader civic society engagement, could provide a foundation for more transformative climate action.

For emissions reduction, *OneNYC* has promoted a very aggressive goal of 80 per cent GHG emissions reduction (from the 2005 levels) by 2050. Guiding strategies include the need to empower New Yorkers to take action, hold buildings to the highest energy performance standards, ensure benefits are shared in every neighborhood, and use data, analysis, and stakeholder feedback to drive the approach. For adaptation, the *OneNYC* effort is largely focused on making the city more resilient – eliminating by 2050 disaster-related long-term displacement (i.e. more than 1 year), reducing social vulnerability of neighborhoods, and reducing the average annual economic losses from climate related events, with strategies targeted at neighborhoods, buildings, infrastructure, and coastal defenses. In order to press forward on planning, de Blasio reconstituted the NPCC in June 2015 with a remit of providing new science and knowledge to help implement *OneNYC* goals.

While the achievements of the new administration remain to be developed, *OneNYC* and its initiatives establish the precedent that the focus on climate change mitigation and adaptation can be successfully passed from one mayoral administration to another and that, as envisioned, this planning effort will be part of a regular, ongoing, flexible response to climate change. The city has begun to meet the requirements of creating a non-stationary climate policy in the face of an ever more dynamic and threat-rich climate (NPCC 2015).

References

Avila, Lixion A and John Cangialosi (2011) *Tropical Cyclone, Report Hurricane Irene* Miami, FL, National Hurricane Center.

Blake, E S, C W Landsea and E J Gibney (2011) "The deadliest, costliest, and most intense United States tropical cyclones from 1851 to 2010 (and other frequently requested hurricane facts)". NOAA Tech. Memo. NWS NHC-6, National Hurricane Center, Miami, FL, 49 pp. available at www.nhc.noaa.gov/pdf/nws-nhc-6.pdf.

Botzen, W and J Aerts (2012) "The National Flood Insurance Programme (NFIP) and climate resilient waterfront development in New York City", in J Aerts, W Botzen, M J Bowman, P J Ward and P Dircke (editors), *Climate Adaptation and Flood Risk in Coastal Cities*, Earthscan, New York, pages 165–196.

Brookings Institute (2014) "2014 Global Metro Monitor Map", *Global Metro Monitor 2014*, available at www.brookings.edu/research/reports2/2015/01/22-global-metro-monitor

City of New York (2013) *Inventory of New York City Greenhouse Gas Emissions, December 2013*, by J Dickinson, J Khan and M Amar, Mayor's Office of Long-Term Planning and Sustainability, New York, available at www.nyc.gov/html/planyc/downloads/pdf/publications/NYC_GHG_Inventory_2013.pdf

Cox, J R (2014) "Suburban Heat Islands: The influence of residential minimum lot size zoning on surface heat islands in Somerset County, New Jersey". PhD Dissertation, City University of New York, available at http://academicworks.cuny.edu/gc_etds/28/

Dolnick, S (2011) "Damage from Irene largely spares New York", *New York Times,* August 28, available at www.nytimes.com/2011/08/29/nyregion/wind-and-rain-from-hurricane-irene-lash-new-york.html?pagewanted=all

Furman Center (2015) *State of Renters and Their Homes,* NYU Furman Center Report. available at http://furmancenter.org/files/sotc/SOC2014_Renters.pdf

Gibbs, Linda, and Caswell Holloway (2013) *Hurricane Sandy After Action: Report and Recommendations to Mayor Michael R. Bloomberg*, New York, The City of New York.

Hansler, Gerald, and David C Major (1999) "Climate change and the water supply systems of New York City and the Delaware Basin: planning and action considerations for water managers", in American Water Resources Association, Extended Abstracts Proceedings: Specialty Conference on "Potential Consequences of Climate Variability and Change to Water Resources of the United States" Atlanta GA. May 10–12, 1999, pages 327–330.

Hill, D (1996) "The baked apple?: Metropolitan New York in the greenhouse", *Annals of the New York Academy of Sciences,* 221 pages.

Keller, Josh (2012) "Mapping Hurricane Sandy's deadly toll", *New York Times*, November 17, available at www. nytimes. com/interactive/2012/11/17/nyregion/hurricane sandy-map. html

Kinney, P, P Sheffield, R Ostfeld, J Carr, R Leichenko and P Vancura (2011) "Public health", in C Rosenzweig, W Solecki, A deGaetano et al. (editors), *Responding to Climate Change in New York State: The ClimAID Integrated Assessment for Effective Climate Change Adaptation in New York State* (November 2011), 87, available at www.nyserda.ny.gov/climaid

Lane, K, K Charles-Guzman, K Wheeler, Z Abid, N Graber, and T Matte (2013) "Health effects of coastal storms and flooding in urban areas: a review and vulnerability assessment", *Journal of Environmental and Public Health,* doi: 10.1155/2013/913064

Leichenko, R, and W Solecki (2013) "Climate change in suburbs: an exploration of key impacts and vulnerabilities", *Urban Climate* Vol 6, pages 82–97.

Lowe, J, T Reeder, K Horsburgh and V Bell (2009) *Using the New TE2100 Science Scenarios, City of London – The Thames Estuary 2100 Plan*, UK Environment Agency.

Major, D, and M Grady (2010) "Adaptation assessment guidebook – appendix B", in C Rosenzweig and W Solecki (editors), *Climate Change Adaptation in New York City: Building a Risk Management Response: New York City Panel on Climate Change 2010 Report. Annals of the New York Academy of Sciences*, pages 229–292.

Major, D and R Goldberg (2000) *Metro East Coast Study Water Sector Report*, available at http://metroeast_climate.ciesin.columbia.edu/reports/water.pdf

Metropolitan Transportation Authority (MTA) (2012) "An average MTA trip saves over 10 pounds of greenhouse gas emissions", available at http://web.mta.info/sustainability/pdf/2012Report.pdf

National Oceanic and Atmospheric Association and National Weather Service (2012) Weather Extremes: Central Park, New York 1869 to Present. New York, National Weather Service. available at www.weather.gov/media/okx/Climate/CentralPark/extremes.pdf

New York City Mayor's Office of Sustainability (2015) *One New York: The Plan for a Strong and Just City*, available at www.nyc.gov/html/onenyc/downloads/pdf/publications/OneNYC.pdf

New York City Office of Emergency Management (2015) "NNYC hazards: extreme heat basics" available at www1.nyc.gov/site/em/ready/extreme-heat.page

New York City, Office of the Mayor (2008), "Mayor Bloomberg launches task force to adapt critical infrastructure to environmental effects of climate change", Press release PR-3008, August 12, available at www.nyc.gov/portal/site/nycgov/menuitem.c0935b9a57bb4ef3daf2f1c701c789a0/index.jsp?pageID=mayor_press_ release&catID=1194&doc_name=www.nyc.gov/html/om/html/2008b/pr308-08.html &cc=unused1978&rc=1194&ndi=1

New York City Panel on Climate Change (NPCC) (2010) "Climate change adaptation in New York City: building a risk management response", *Annals of the New York Academy of Sciences* Vol 1196, pages 1–354, available at http://onlinelibrary.wiley.com/doi/10.1111/nyas.2010.1196.issue-1/issuetoc

New York City Panel on Climate Change (NPCC) (2015) "Building the knowledge base for climate resiliency: New York City Panel on Climate Change 2015 Report," *Annals of the New York Academy of Sciences* Vol 1336, pages 1–150, available at http://onlinelibrary.wiley.com/doi/10.1111/nyas.2015.1336.issue-1/issuetoc

Pasch, Richard J and Lixion A Avila (1999) "Atlantic hurricane season of 1996", *Monthly Weather Review* 127, pages 581–610 available at www.aoml.noaa.gov/hrd/hurdat/mwr_pdf/1996.pdf

Raftery, Isolde (2012) "Water surges into lower Manhattan as superstorm Sandy blasts through", NBC News, October 29, available at http://usnews.nbcnews.com/_news/2012/10/29/14789362-water-surges-into-lower-manhattan-as-superstorm-sandy-blasts-through?lite

Roberts S (2014) "Gap between Manhattan's rich and poor is greatest in U.S., census finds", *The New York Times,* available at www.nytimes.com/2014/09/18/nyregion/gap-between-manhattans-rich-and-poor-is-greatest-in-us-census-finds.html?_r=14

Rosenzweig, C and W Solecki (editors) (2001) *Climate Change and a Global City: The Potential Consequences of Climate Variability and Change, Metro East Coast,* Report for the US Global Change Research Programme, National Assessment of Potential Consequences of Climate Variability and Change for the United States Columbia Earth Institute, 201 pages.

Rosenzweig, C and W Solecki (editors) (2010) *Climate Change Adaptation in New York City: Building a Risk Management Response*" Report of New York City Panel on Climate Change, Annals of New York Academy of Sciences Vol 1196, 354 pages.

Rosenzweig, C, W D Solecki, R Blake, M Bowman, C Faris, V Gornitz, R Horton, K Jacob, A LeBlanc, R Leichenko, M Linkin, D Major, M O'Grady, L Patrick, E Sussman, G.Yohe and R Zimmerman (2011) "Developing coastal adaptation to climate change in the New York City infrastructure-shed: process, approach, tools, and strategies". *Climatic Change* Vol 106, pages 93–127, doi:10.1007/s10584-010-0002-8

U.S. Census Bureau (2013) *2009–2013 5-Year American Community Survey*, available at http://factfinder.census.gov/faces/tableservices/jsf/pages/productview.xhtml?src=CF

U.S. Census Bureau (2014) "New York City, New York", *American Fact Finder,* available at http://factfinder.census.gov/faces/nav/jsf/pages/community_facts.xhtml

Wolfe, D, J Comstock, H Menninger, D Weinstein, K Sullivan, C Kraft, B Chabot, P Curtis, R Leichenko and P Vancura (2011) "Responding to climate change in New York State: The ClimAID integrated assessment for effective climate change adaptation in New York State", available at www.nyserda.ny.gov/climaid

Zimmerman, R and C Faris (2010) "Infrastructure impacts and adaptation challenges", in C. Rosenzweig and W. Solecki (eds) *New York City Panel on Climate Change 2010 Report, Climate Change Adaptation in New York City: Building a Risk Management Response*, New York: Annals of the New York Academy of Sciences.

11

ROSARIO, ARGENTINA

Jorgelina Hardoy, Vanessa Herrera and Daniela Mastrángelo

Introduction[1]

The city of Rosario is not an international frontrunner or recognized leader in the field of climate change. It has no explicit climate change strategy or programme, nor any office coordinating initiatives that contribute to mitigation or adaptation. Climate change is quite new on the agenda and still limited to certain programmes and actions. Rosario has a strong coherent governance system, however, and a commitment to decentralization, transparency, accountability and participation. Its long tradition of urban planning has evolved to include a broad vision of urban challenges and responses, a commitment to environmental sustainability and a strategic plan that involves multiple stakeholders and encompasses the whole metropolitan area (Hardoy and Ruete 2013). Gradually, within this conducive context, initiatives that address mitigation and adaptation are growing in number and scope, and the city is working to find the best way to develop an integrated response to climate change and disaster.

Physical setting and urban dynamics

Rosario, on the Paraná River in central Argentina, is the third largest city in the country and the largest in Santa Fe province, with a population of about 960,000 and land area of 179 square kilometres, two-thirds of it built up. Average density is 5,300 inhabitants per square kilometre.[2] The city is the core of Metropolitan Rosario, population 1.3 million, and covering an area of 1,770 square kilometres. It falls within the wetlands of the Río Paraná bioregion, an ecosystem shared by three provinces (Buenos Aires, Entre Ríos and Santa Fe). Little is left of the original natural habitat, the *pampa húmeda* (humid pampas), since this is one of the most heavily populated areas of Argentina and has been extensively used for agriculture and cattle rearing.

As a regional centre that attracts migration, Rosario faces accelerated urban growth – between 2001 and 2010 its population grew by 4.3 per cent a year.[3] Keeping up with housing stock, infrastructure and land for development has been a challenge and informal settlements have grown rapidly towards the west (expansion is blocked in other directions by the river and neighbouring cities).

Approximately 155,000 people currently live in some 91 informal settlements in the city.

Social context

Rosario used to be an immigrant city, but now 98 per cent of its inhabitants were born in Argentina, and over 70 per cent here in the city. The rest of the city's residents come mostly from the northeast of Argentina or other parts of the province.

Rosario's poverty levels were among the highest in the country during the 2001–2002 socio-economic crisis, but between 2003 and 2011, the percentage of people below the poverty line dropped from 42 to 7 per cent. When poverty is measured instead in terms of Unsatisfied Basic Needs (UBN) the number is 9.2 per cent (IPEC 2015).[4] Even during the high poverty years, Rosario did better than the national average on basic needs because housing quality and access to health, education and basic services were relatively good (Almansi 2009). However, despite a recovering economy, high levels of poverty and unemployment persist in some areas (Table 11.1). On the whole, Rosario's citizens are well educated and well trained. Over 98 per cent are literate and 90 per cent have completed at least primary school. Of those between 18 and 24 years of age, 44 per cent attend some form of tertiary education.

Economy

Rosario is the centre of the main agricultural and cattle producing region of the country, as well as a centre for industry and trade and an important financial hub. There is also a strong service sector. The metropolitan area produces half

TABLE 11.1 Proportion of households and individuals below poverty and extreme poverty lines in Rosario, 2003 to 2011 (%)

		2003		*2006*		*2008*		*2010*		*2011*
		1	*2*	*1*	*2*	*1*	*2*	*1*	*2*	*1*
Poverty	Households	42.4	37.5	20.4	16.6	8.0	9.6	9.4	7.5	6.7
	Individuals	54.6	47.9	27.4	22.9	12.0	13.7	14.7	11.5	9.0
Extreme poverty	Households	20.7	16.5	7.7	6.2	2.9	4.9	3.9	3.6	4.2
	Individuals	29.3	23.9	10.2	7.5	3.9	6.6	6.2	3.8	4.5

Source: based on data from INDEC-IPEC, Permanent Household Survey.

the total GDP for the province, generates more than half its employment and has 62 per cent of its industry. Industrial development started slowly in the 1930s with the farming industry, and consolidated in the 1960s when a mix of metal, mechanical, chemical, petrochemical and other industries settled in the area, taking advantage of its river port and railway and highway systems. In the mid-1970s, the city's economy went into steep decline until immediately after the socioeconomic crisis of 2001. With the boom in production and the export of agricultural goods following the crisis, the city's economy quickly recovered.

Rosario is also a node of national and international transportation, located strategically for trading within the *Mercosur* (*Southern Common Market*) trading bloc comprising Argentina, Brazil, Paraguay, Uruguay and Venezuela. Regional ports are extremely active, exporting 80 per cent of the country's oilseed, grain and by-products. There is a plan to develop the Hidrovía, an industrial waterway that would reduce regional export costs. It is still uncertain what effect this would have on natural ecosystems such as the Pantanal and the Río de la Plata basin.

Governance and planning

Governed by the Socialist party since 1989, Rosario is characterized by its long-term policies and governance system. Despite national economic and political turmoil, there has been political continuity and institutional stability, with a long-term vision and each successive administration building on past work. The elected mayor has a four-year term, and half of the legislative council of 22 members is replaced every two years. Ideals about inclusion and transparency, and about the social, economic and environmental benefits that the city should deliver, are shared within government and among residents.

One objective of this administration is to integrate social dimensions into urban planning and development,[5] as seen in the restoration of riverbanks and public spaces, infrastructure and service provision in peri-urban areas, public health services and the participation process. Municipal decentralization is more than just administrative. Since the 1980s, Rosario has been actively implementing different participatory experiences including in neighbourhood planning and decision-making and the development of different city plans and strategies.

The two main urban planning tools are the Urban Plan of Rosario 2007–2017 (*Plan Urbano de Rosario* – PUR) and the Metropolitan Strategic Plan (PERM + 10), which includes neighbouring areas and cities. Together they integrate social, environmental, economic and territorial planning (Hardoy and Ruete 2013). The city also has a transportation plan (*Plan Integral de Movilidad Rosario* – PIM), and is working on an environmental city plan to identify and develop local policies and strategies through different work-streams: climate change, energy, air and water quality, wastes, sanitation and biodiversity.

The city works incrementally in this regard. Previous plans took a long time to be approved by the local council, always too late to actually guide development.

The PUR, divided into master plans and plans for specific areas of intervention, made it possible to move ahead even before approval of the complete plan (Plan Urbano Rosario 2011). The city code (*Normas Urbanísticas de la Ciudad de Rosario*) is also progressively updated with an eye to disaster risk and the need to steer development away from hazardous areas. The PUR is considered "realistic and implementable" because of its clear rules, innovative mechanisms for accessing funds, establishment of public and public–private partnerships and a reliance on *concertación* (or agreement) among different stakeholders. By establishing mechanisms for compensation that is then used to buy more land, construct trunk services, public housing or public spaces, the city captures investments with clear public benefits (Levin 2011).

The planning process developed over the years has an important learning component which has contributed to flexibility in addressing challenges – for instance last year's work on the city's environmental plan started with seven participatory workshops and citizen agreement on strategies for integrating environmental concerns into the planning and management of the city. These approaches come with risks, as there are many vested interests in land and property development. What sustains everything is the strong, long-term political support by successive administrations.

Service provision

Water, sanitation, drainage, utilities

Rosario faces critical infrastructure challenges, both around much-needed expansion and the maintenance of what currently exists. The sewerage and drainage system in the city centre has never been updated. In parts of the city with backlogs, there are clandestine sewer connections to the drainage system, and in the periphery of the city, open-air sewage channels. The public sewage network reaches 73 per cent of households at this point and drainage reaches 85 per cent (ECOM 2014). However, the city has an integrated sanitation plan and is working with the provincial service provider to expand the sewerage network to peripheral and low-income neighbourhoods through different programmes. Almost all (98.8 per cent) have access to the public water network provided by public utility; all have electricity provided by a state-run electricity company; and 73 per cent are connected to the natural gas network (ECOM 2014) (Table 11.2).

Solid waste management

City households generate a monthly average of 24,000 tons of solid waste, and the construction sector, basic production, services and maintenance of public spaces generate another 20,000 tons that are not easily biodegradable. The *programme of solid waste management and reduction* (SEPARE) has been running for over 20 years, and the city has a daily collection and street cleaning service and

TABLE 11.2 Energy consumption by category

Category	*Users*	*Consumption (kwh)*	*Consumption %*
Residential	301,568	616,254,777	34.04
Commercial	37,923	258,980,152	14.30
Industrial	4,297	55,809,509	3.08
Authorities	2,724	39,227,114	2.17
Street light	2,726	82,912,348	4.58
Big clients	887	592,480,397	32.73
GUMA/E	19	163,803,793	9.05
Other	2	1,049,070	0.06
Total	350,146	1,810,517,160	100

Note: GUMA/E are clients that buy in bulk from Electricity Wholesalers. The Provincial utility (Empresa Provincial de Energía – EPE) charges a fee.
Source: drawing on information provided by Empresa Provincial de la Energía (EPE), 2010.

has been a pioneer in the introduction of street containers. Waste is recovered and recycled, and the city works with three co-operatives. In line with its *Basura Cero* (Zero Waste) by-law to be met by the end of 2015, the city inaugurated in 2013 a composting plant that at full capacity will be able to treat 250 tons per day, 25 per cent of the total of solid waste generated in the city. Half of it is organic, which reduces the amount that goes to the three sanitary landfills in the metropolitan area.

Low-income housing and neighbourhoods

The city's Public Housing Service (SPV) which oversees all public housing issues, has realized the need to go beyond a focus on missing services (water, sewers, paved roads, trees, parks, community centres) to incorporating unserved settlements socially and functionally into the city.[6] The Rosario Hábitat Program for informal settlements, which ended in 2012, promoted integrated intervention in informal settlements and has been followed by an Integrated Neighborhood Improvement Program (*Intervención Integral en Barrios*), which includes work on infrastructure (streets, housing, sanitation, re-location, public areas), training (especially for youth who have not finished school) and public security. Also, since 2014 the city, with the provincial government, has developed an initiative called My Land My House (*Mi Tierra Mi Casa*), to facilitate access to land and housing at below market cost for those with economic difficulties, supplementing it with other tools such as improvement and titling of former housing projects.

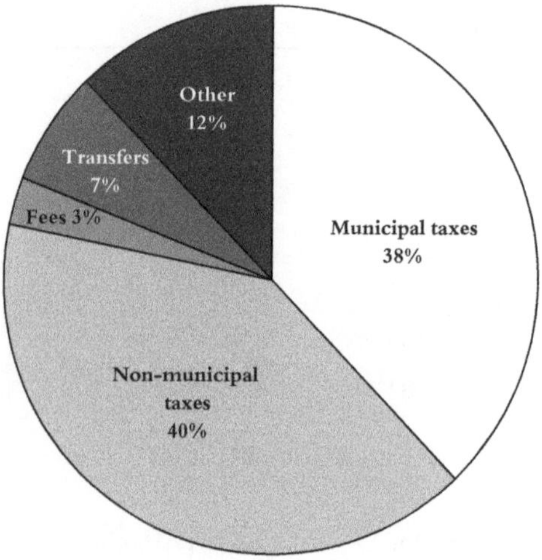

FIGURE 11.1 Breakdown of municipal resources in 2014 (source: based on data from the Office of Resource Management (Dirección General de Recursos), Municipality of Rosario)

Health

Health, considered a basic human right and a public good in Rosario, has been a top priority for many years, accounting for 25 per cent of the budget, even though responsibility falls technically on the province (Hardoy and Ruete 2013). The city has expanded its prevention and promotion work with a decentralized network of community health centres, hospitals and emergency services.

Municipal resources

Municipal government funds come from a range of taxes and fees. Direct municipal taxes and registrar fees represent 38 per cent, with the remainder from non-municipal taxes, fees and transfers. Only 7 per cent of funds come from outside sources (Figure 11.1).

GHG inventory

A GHG inventory emerged as a priority when the city started developing its climate strategy, but there have been insufficient resources to complete it. In 2013, the city signed an agreement with the national Secretariat of Environment and Sustainable Development to develop and implement a methodology to evaluate the public sector's carbon footprint. The city has also been monitoring air quality (in collaboration with the Regional Office of the *Universidad Tecnológica Nacional*), and plans to develop air quality control policies and set up controls based on this data. A network of 25 operating stations[7] makes it possible

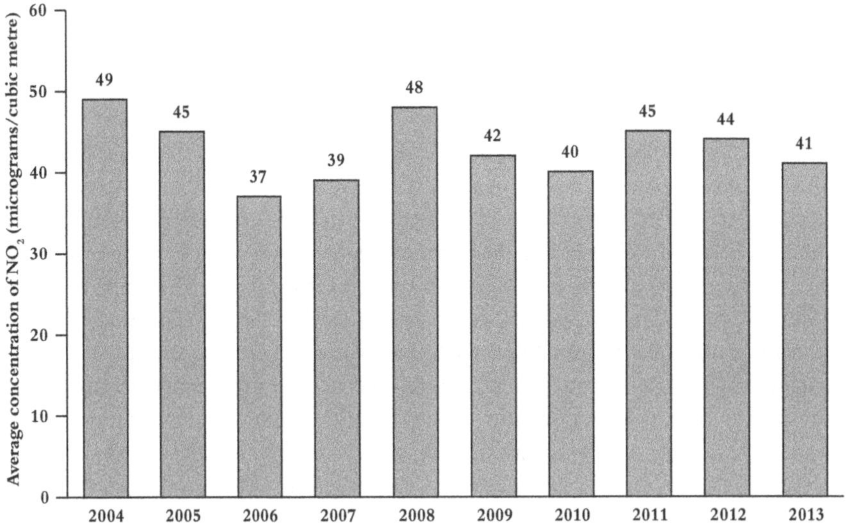

FIGURE 11.2. Average NO_2 concentrations in the Municipality of Rosario (source: drawn from data provided by the Municipality of Rosario)

to measure current trends, especially of NO_2 related to vehicle transportation (Figure 11.2), and to evaluate impacts of different transportation decisions and integrate them into the city's mobility plan (PIM). Records suggest that despite an increase in the number of private cars, emission levels are tending to decrease, even with adverse meteorological conditions. The results are averages, so major emission sources cannot be identified.

Climate and climate risk

Rosario has a temperate climate, with temperatures of between 8.1 and 40.7°C and annual rainfall between 800 and 1,200 mm. Like many cities, it is affected by both climate variability and climate change. A recent report points to increases in both average temperature and precipitation since 1950 (Secretaría de Ambiente y Desarrollo Sustentable y Cima 2015). Average median temperature has increased by 0.4°C in the province, with by far the greatest increase in minimum temperatures. (Maximum temperatures in summer and autumn have actually decreased as a result of increased precipitation.) Average annual precipitation has increased between 100 and 200 mm in the region, among the greatest increases in the world. There is also an increase in intensity and frequency, and the duration of dry periods is getting shorter. These increases in precipitation are not expected to revert back, and warming is expected to accelerate over the 21st century.

The main climate-related risk for this riverside city is flooding, from both intense rainfall and overflow of local streams and rivers. In 2007, 300–400 mm of rain fell in 5 days;[8] there were more than 3,000 evacuees and 5 square kilometres of flooded area. In 2012, 179 mm fell in only 6.5 hours, flooding different areas than before, causing significant damage to infrastructure and housing (almost USD 2 million), and affecting 1,000 families, half of which had to evacuate. Increased development, especially near the Ludueña stream, has increased water runoff, stream overflow and the saturation of drainage capacity, placing some low-income areas at particular risk, especially where construction has occurred on the flood plains of streams or on dry stream beds, as in barrios Ludueña, Nuevo Alberdi and Mangrullo. Farming practices upstream have also contributed to increased water runoff, resulting in the flooding even of neighbourhoods already risk-proofed or considered not at risk. Extreme hazards combine with social vulnerability to create risk and disasters especially where there are backlogs in such risk-reducing infrastructure as sewerage and drainage systems and solid waste collection. Despite the city's constant work to mitigate floods and reduce vulnerability, the capacity of protective measures can be overwhelmed, as in the case of the 2012 floods. Piecemeal measures can also have unintended consequences. Zoning restrictions on flood-prone areas, for instance, have resulted in the informal occupation of intentionally vacant land.

The origins of climate protection actions

Rosario has no official mitigation or adaptation plans, and still struggles to complete GHG inventories. But its coordinated, integrated planning strategy includes a strong sustainable and social development component, and as they advance, adaptation and mitigation goals become clearer. For example, new building norms take wind patterns and energy efficiency into account; and the urban plan aims to reduce density in the central district and redistribute population to other areas, taking into account flood risks, mobility, and access to basic infrastructure and services.

So far, specific work on climate change has been mostly the sum of isolated actions responding to particular concerns. This has mostly been led by the Sub-Secretariat of Environment although offices of planning, water management, civil defence, health, habitat and housing are all actively involved in programmes and strategies that enhance climate protection and resilience. This Sub-Secretariat, created during Mayor Lifschitz's first term from an Environment Department, reflected the need for environment to be a cross-cutting issue addressed in coordination with a general environmental policy. In practice, this has been harder than initially expected. Despite the acknowledgement of former Mayor Lifschitz and today's Mayor Fein of the need for a climate strategy, the city is still finding its way, developing the means and capacity. The lack of an institutional umbrella slows down full engagement in climate work, and there are distinct budgetary limitations (the city of Buenos Aires has three times Rosario's population, but a budget 15 times larger).

In 2009, the Sub-Secretariat for the Environment, a local NGO (*Taller Ecologista*) and the Universidad Tecnológica Nacional signed an agreement to develop a climate strategy for the city. A series of workshops and awareness-raising campaigns was planned and a meeting was convened with students to present projects related to climate change. An advisory board, with members from the local administration and academia, concentrated on knowledge production, but progressed slowly on a subject that was new to many. The process had ups and downs but managed to keep climate change issues on the agenda.

In 2010, Rosario signed the Global Cities Covenant on Climate – Mexico City Pact together with other cities committed to reducing GHG emissions and working on adaptation. In April 2012, the city held a series of workshops and activities to prepare for Rio+20, with climate change as a prioritized theme. Since then, the city has held events, such as the environmental fair *Feria Ambiental Rosario*, to promote awareness and education on recycling, biodiversity and renewable energy among other things. The city is also an active member of different city networks, including the Argentine Network of Municipalities for Climate Change (RAMCC), Network of Mercociudades (*Red de Mercociudades*), United Cities and Local Governments (UCLG), Metropolis, Iberoamerican Centre of Urban Development (CIDEU), International Association of Educating Cities (AICE), Cities against Urban Poverty, and the URB-AL Program, among others. The city has also been part of the recent city colloquium convened by Pope Francis to reflect on how cities can implement the sustainable development agenda, focusing on modern slavery and climate change. Participating in the colloquium means a recognition of work done and has mobilized the mayor to strengthen this line of work, looking into the Sustainable Development Goals discussions and COP21.

Meanwhile, there has been practical progress on the ground in a number of areas, as described below. These initiatives have helped build the articulation between different departments and secretariats, making it possible to address complex issues such as those related to climate change.

The adaptation work-stream

As in Durban, the adaptation work-stream has been phased and opportunistic, taking advantage of opportunities and learning from setbacks (Roberts and O'Donoghue 2013). Unlike in Durban, the work has not been a conscious climate strategy, but emerged as a by-product of a concern with vulnerability and good planning. The city's adaptation strategy is in effect a set of responses to other city needs, planned in an integrated way, but not labelled as climate change adaptation.

1 *Plans and regulations:* Rosario, as noted, has a number of plans in place or in preparation – the PUR, PERM+10, an environmental plan and a transportation plan (PIM) – which together provide an integrated, comprehensive approach to guiding the city's actions in ways that also support sustainable development

and the reduction of climate risks. The city has also participated twice in strategic planning projects for the bioregion; the three provinces (Santa Fe, Entre Ríons and Buenos Aires) have signed a letter of agreement recognizing the importance of their shared resource and committing to its sustainable use. Under this framework they developed a strategic plan for the conservation and sustainable use of the Paraná Delta (PIECAS-DP).

2 *City and provincial laws and by-laws* have established land use restrictions based on flood risk, drawing on precipitation records to re-define flood areas and establish restrictions on construction and measures to increase permeability. Specific regulations for the areas around the Saladillo and Ludueña streams, for example, were modified and approved in 2011. Flood risk maps for the city take into account the latest climate-related information and hydraulic works. Land use codes in flood-prone areas establish three categories of restrictions based on past trends, recent events, climate projections and such variables as water absorption capacity.

3 *Several redevelopment processes* have moved low-income communities away from flood-prone areas (sometimes with mixed results when cleared lands are resettled). All new proposals for housing development and informal settlement upgrading are assessed for conformity to flood prevention. Many interests are at play, for instance when private developers seek to displace informal settlers on land that has become more desirable after being protected from flooding.

4 *The creation or restoration of parks and green spaces* in riverside and flood-prone areas limits use, creates a buffer and promotes social inclusion. There is now a 7.5 km linear space intersected with parks and recreational areas within the 17 km of the city's Paraná river shore. Borders of streams defined as environmental protection areas are also being recovered for public use, promoting restoration of the basin within the metropolitan area, and creating a green corridor. The creation of a green belt around the city, used for urban agriculture, also contributes both to adaptation and mitigation. The city, together with civil society organizations and a multisectorial commission, is also working on the recuperation and appropriate use of a donated portion of land on the delta known as the *Legado Deliot.*

5 *Dams, reservoirs and alleviation channels* within the city and region control peak stream flows, taking into account potential future levels of the Paraná River. These are coordinated between different municipal areas and, over the last few years, with the province. Strong partnerships are being developed with water basin committees (*comités de cuenca*), wards and other stakeholders, aiming to avoid improvised piecemeal measures as in the past. There is also continuous work to maintain open drain channels along streets. As floods cannot be totally prevented, the city has strengthened early warning and emergency systems and education campaigns for risk prevention. Emergency actions are coordinated by COEM (Municipal Emergency Operations Centre) and Civil Defence. A staff of over 100, as

well as machinery, trucks and portable power plants, show its increasing importance within the municipal system. Information on water levels and meteorological variables is exchanged with the province in real time, and the network of weather stations, deteriorated over the years, is being restored. Participatory planning towards a Local Disaster Risk Reduction Plan aims to improve local resources to better manage and prevent disaster risk.

6 *Rosario's strong municipal health system* is fundamental to reducing vulnerability. Activities have included prevention of dengue and other diseases, and the prevention of heat strokes and heat stress through research, awareness campaigns and adequate treatment protocols.
7 *Data remains a challenge*. Adaptation requires specific local knowledge and an updated, comprehensive database. Information sharing and the documentation and evaluation of current efforts can also be valuable. While Rosario is producing good information on flood risks, so far it has made no attempt to model local climate change impacts. Nor are there good historical records. External consultants often undertake programme evaluations with little participation of local government staff, resulting in reports of little practical use.

The mitigation work-stream

Rosario's lack of a GHG inventory, noted above, constrains the development of a mitigation strategy (Hardoy and Ruete 2013). Neither the city nor the country have any obligation regarding GHG emissions. Different environmental policies, however, contribute to lowering emissions. SEPARE, the 20-year solid waste management and reduction programme, has been working by trial and error to make recycling more sociably and economically sustainable. More recently there has been a focus on efficient energy and water use and development of solar energy and alternative energy sources.

The city created a sustainable construction and energy efficiency programme, now under the planning secretariat, which provides training for the construction sector, with the aim of passing construction norms and by-laws, developing tools and sharing good practices. For the first time, mitigation is part of an evolving public policy, not just an isolated initiative. The approach is to go slowly, incorporating the proposed measures and seeing the advantages in the context of disappearing energy subsidies. The effort has the support of the province, universities, research centres and NGOs. Some results to date are a by-law on the use of solar energy on public buildings, developed with academic and institutional stakeholders, establishing that all new or upgraded public buildings and sports and social centres use solar water heaters. Another by-law regulates the thermal and energy demand of new buildings. The city has also passed guidelines on urban green terraces, which help slow down water flow and reduce peaks during intensive rains. A challenge is of course the funding to implement these actions and make a difference.

Believing that change comes through concerted efforts, the administration is also developing environmental workshops with schools, the private sector and citizens, focused on solid waste separation and recycling, trees in public spaces, rational use of water and energy (and alternative sources), noise pollution, air quality, and mobility. Some of the programmes are:

- *Rosario 10 per cent less (Rosario 10 per cent menos)* aiming to reduce energy use in public buildings;
- *Green households (Hogares verdes)* offering two workshops a week to raise awareness and train households in efficient energy and water use and reducing the carbon footprint;
- *Green schools (Escuelas verdes)* which train teachers to work with students;
- *Sustainable neighbourhoods (Barrios sustentables)* which engage neighbours in projects that address their local economic, social and environmental needs in inclusive ways;
- *Cleaner Rosario (Rosario MásLimpia)* aiming for a changed culture around solid waste management and the use of public resources;
- *Programme of Good Environmental Practices (Programa de Buenas Prácticas Ambientales)* aiming for clean production and the use of less polluting technologies;
- *Everything starts one day (Todoempieza un día)* promoting new habits around use of public transport and bicycles, care of public parks and green areas, hygiene and responsible management of solid wastes.

Other efforts include plans for a new sanitary landfill for non-recyclables and compostable organics. A compost plant started this year currently receives a third of the city's organic waste and when fully operational will process 250 tons daily with reduced GHG. The city also promotes workshops for household composting. There has also been work on converting public lighting and traffic lights to more efficient technologies such as LEDs, as well as work on public forestation.

The PIM is important to mitigation, with its measures to reduce congestion, promote the use of non-motorized vehicles, develop exclusive lanes for public transportation and bicycles and improve mobility in general, with new technologies that improve sustainability, connectivity and efficient circulation within the metropolitan area. One measure is the development of a tram system, efficient in terms of emissions, noise levels and energy use. The PIM integrates transportation and mobility policies with land use and environmental planning. Drafted in a participatory way, it includes a signed pact (*Pacto de Movilidad*) that states the programme's goals, and was signed by over 100 local institutions.

Among mitigation efforts that incorporate adaptation measures are activities developed as part of an international project to monitor impacts of urban and peri-urban agriculture. Developed by the city's Urban Agriculture Program with international organizations and local academic centres, the project monitors and evaluates the multiple benefits of urban agriculture, including reduction of transportation costs and emissions, reduction in pesticide and fertilizer use, recycling of organic materials and residual water, reduced competition for water use, improved water infiltration, reduced urban heat island effect, improved GHG absorption, food security, employment options and income generation. By developing indicators and data collection relevant to climate change challenges, the project makes urban agriculture and forestry practices an essential component of the city's climate change strategy. At provincial level, the *Un sol para mi techo* (Sun for my roof) programme has promoted solar energy use since 2013 through a preferential credit line.

Integrating adaptation and mitigation

All these plans and programmes in Rosario have been designed for their multiple environmental benefits, not just because they are climate smart. They are all anticipatory however, not just reactive. Critically, the various lines of work – urban planning, social development and health, environmental planning, education and solid waste management, flood prevention and emergency response – have also been integrated, at least in principle, because the city administration recognizes the complexity and multi-dimensional quality of the challenges. Despite ups and downs, there has been significant progress in the policies developed. Today one of the main goals is to develop an institutional umbrella to coordinate all this climate-related work, while continuing to strengthen the good work done so far.

The city faces three main challenges in developing its climate work:

1 *Access to funds:* Rosario has been creative in finding partners and practical strategies; but every action also needs financial resources, whether it is managing the health service or maintaining green areas and solid waste collection. Funds are also needed to develop a GHG inventory, support development of a disaster risk-coordinating body, and promote sustainable construction technologies and energy efficiency. But they all have to compete with pressing routine needs. For a city like Rosario with no obligations in this regard, it is difficult to access mitigation funds. Adaptation work, meanwhile, is a city management obligation, especially since it is not a climate risk hot spot. Funds obtained for particular projects are not sustainable and reliable in the long run.
2 *Coordination:* This work needs to be coordinated across jurisdictions, stakeholders and government levels, and this demands constant negotiations. National level support is scarce – climate change is not a top issue in the national agenda. The access to national funds or support to develop local capacities has been insignificant.
3 *Skills and time:* Climate change and disaster risk management are relatively new for the city administration. Despite strong local political commitment

and continuity, institutional capacity still needs to be developed further to address new goals and challenges. Developing new skills takes time from regular work, and when funds are a constraint this is even more challenging.

Rosario does not yet qualify as a city doing radical or transformative adaptation, addressing the root causes of climate risks and developing a low carbon economy that meets everyone's needs, now and in the future. But it has certain critical pre-conditions that simplify the path to radical adaptation and it shares the underlying vision that can sustain such a process.

Notes

1 Much of the material in this chapter was taken from interviews with municipal and state government officials and other relevant stakeholders engaged in the city's climate change efforts. A version of the chapter appeared in *Environment and Urbanization* (Hardoy and Ruete 2013).
2 www.rosario.gov.ar/web/ciudad/caracteristicas/territorio
3 www.santafe.gov.ar/index.php/web/content/view/full/165361/(subtema)/93664 accessed January 2, 2015.
4 UBN; this measure uses a set of indicators of deprivation (overcrowding, housing conditions, access to sanitary services, education and stable employment) recorded by the National Housing and Population Census. A household is poor if it experiences at least one deprivation.
5 Interview with former mayor of Rosario, in Almansi (2009).
6 The SPV manages its own funds (from taxes to the gas service and the repayment of housing credits), and receives financial help from the local government and the provincial government to complement infrastructure works when needed in different neighbourhoods. The SPV also receives national and international financial aid for the development and implementation of specific programmes, such as the Rosario Hábitat programme, for which the city received a loan from the Inter-American Development Bank (IDB).
7 Twenty-four stations are passive, making it possible to monitor spatial distribution of monthly average concentrations; one is active and monitors average concentrations of NO_x in 24-hour periods.
8 Dr. Ing. Civil Gerardo Riccardi de la Universidad Nacional de Rosario. www.rosario.gov.ar/ArchivosWeb/pluvial/eventos_extremos.pdf

References

Almansi, F (2009), "Rosario's development: interview with Miguel Lifschitz, mayor of Rosario, Argentina", *Environment and Urbanization* Vol 21, No 1, pages 19–35.

Ente de Coordinación Metropolitana – ECOM (2014), Unidad de Planificación y Gestión Estratégica Rosario. Estructura Institucional y Caracterización Territorial. El Área Metropolitana de Rosario, Cuaderno 1.

Hardoy, Jorgelina and Regina Ruete (2013), "Incorporating climate change adaptation into planning for a livable city in Rosario, Argentina", in *Environment and Urbanization* Vol 25, No 2, pages 339–360.

Instituto Provincial de Estadísticas y Censos (IPEC) 2015. Based on data from 2010 Censo Nacional de Población y Vivienda, Instituto Nacional de Estadísticas y

Censos (INDEC), Buenos Aires. www.santafe.gov.ar/index.php/web/content/view/full/163622/(subtema)/93664

Levin, Mirta (2011), Plan urbano Rosario 2007–2017, Jornada Rosario y Buenos Aires, Dos Ciudades, sus Planes y Conflictos, 12 October.

Plan Urbano Rosario (PUR) 2007–2017 (2011), Municipality of Rosario, 339 pages. www.rosario.gov.ar/sitio/arquitectura/urbanismo/plan_urbano4.jsp

Roberts, Debra and Sean O'Donoghue (2013), "Urban environmental challenges and climate change action in Durban, South Africa", *Environment and Urbanization* Vol. 25 No 2, pages 299–319.

Secretaría de Ambiente y Desarrollo Sustentable y Centro de Investigaciones del Mar y la Atmósfera (CIMA) (2015), Cambio Climático en Argentina: Tendencias y Proyecciones (Climate change in Argentina: tendencies and projections) prepared as part of the Third National Communication to UNFCCC, 339 pages.

12

CROSS-CITY ANALYSIS

Sheridan Bartlett, David Satterthwaite, Debra Roberts, Jan Corfee-Morlot, David Dodman and Jorgelina Hardoy

Introduction

This chapter considers what we can learn from the nine cities whose experience with climate change adaptation and mitigation are described in previous chapters. These chapters look at how the scientific assessment of climate change and its implications can be translated into local action. They look in particular at four local agendas – human development, disaster risk reduction, climate change adaptation and climate change mitigation – and at how coherence can be achieved across them. The first two are usually accepted as local government responsibilities, although these responsibilities are often not fully met. National or provincial/state agencies may have key roles in disaster response but most of the actions needed for disaster risk reduction fall within local government responsibilities.

Resilience, an objective at the forefront of much discussion these days, can be viewed as a synthesis of the first three of these agendas. It also supports the fourth agenda, climate change mitigation, since ultimately even the most resilient cities will not be able to protect themselves from climate change impacts without global reductions in anthropogenic greenhouse gas emissions.

These nine cities are at quite different points on each of the four agendas and in their integration into city planning and management. As we pointed out in the preface, every city's experience is unique, formed or shaped by local economic, social and political forces, and environmental circumstances as well as external forces. Table 12.1 summarizes some basic data for each city, but caution is needed in drawing comparisons – for instance most large cities have two or more boundaries (built-up area, city government jurisdiction, metropolitan area, larger planning region, commuter belt added) which have different land areas, densities, populations and population growth. But all these cities are faced

TABLE 12.1 The nine cities

	Population	*Land area*	*Density*	*Population growth rate per annum*
Bangalore	11 million (2015 estimate)	741 km^2 metro area	11,371/km^2	4–5%
Bangkok	8.2 million Bangkok Metropolis 14.5 million Bangkok Metropolitan Region (2010 census)	1568.7 km^2 7761.6 km^2	5300/km^2 1900/km^2	2%
Dar es Salaam	4.6 million (2012)	1691 km^2 only 22% built up	2400/km^2 near centre almost 3000/km^2	4.4% (changed urban boundaries)
Durban	3.4 million	2297 km^2	1500/km^2 municipality	1.1%
London	8. 4 million Greater London (2014)	1583 km^2 Greater London	4542/km^2	1.2 % 2001–2011
Manizales	0.4 million city 0.45 million plus municipality	507 km^2 municipality	770/km^2	15% 1995–2005 6% p.a. projected to 2020
Mexico City	9 million Federal District 20 million metro area	1495 km^2 Federal District	9800/km^2	1.2%
New York	8.4 million New York City 15 million (or 20.1 million in metro statistical area; estimate for 2013)	786 km^2 (land only NYC)	27,000/km^2	$< 1\%$
Rosario	0.96 million city 1.3 million metro area	179 km^2 1770 km^2 metro area	5300 /km^2	4.2% 2001–2010

with addressing these four agendas, and a critical assessment of their responses yields some interesting insights.

Not only is the experience of each city unique, but each case study is written from the particular perspective of the authors and their engagement with the city. All the authors are experts in this topic, but they bring different forms of experience and expertise to what are already unique experiences. A key question is how local governments are engaging with relevant stakeholders at different levels, from the local to the international and trans-national levels, to create platforms for action. The authors of the case studies represent a range of stakeholders across civil society, the research community and practitioners. Durban is unusual in bringing a strong insider perspective on the complex processes of city government and in its commitment to recording problems as well as achievements (Box 12.1). The efforts of city governments need to be critically assessed, which implies the need for this kind of openness.

Box 12.1 How we have learnt from Durban and its commitment to documenting progress

We can learn from Durban on a number of fronts: the institutional changes that brought more attention to climate change issues and the policies adopted; the tools used to do this; the identification of different options and their benefits and costs; the integration of concern for climate change across the urban, peri-urban and rural areas within the local government boundaries; the assessment of the contributions of ecosystem services to adaptation, mitigation and disaster risk reduction and measures needed to protect and enhance these; the demonstration that local innovators, not national policies or international initiatives, are providing the knowledge on what needs to be done; the success of the environmental sector in getting the attention of city government by drawing issues of job creation (within the restoration economy) and improved living conditions into climate change policy discussions; the encouragement and recognition of local innovation (the interest in green roofs was started by one enthusiastic student); and in the honesty around what is not yet achieved, such as building firm political support for climate action. The experience in Durban has also produced some surprises, for instance on what best builds support for climate change adaptation within local governments, what measures work and where lessons can be drawn. Durban's government has far more capacity to act than the local government in Dar es Salaam, for instance; it has developed more capacity even than some better-resourced cities, but it also has other pressing development priorities that can make the necessary commitment to adaptation and mitigation difficult (Roberts 2008, 2010; Roberts, Boon, Diederichs et al. 2012; Cartwright et al. 2013; Roberts and O'Donoghue 2013).

We start by exploring some of the forces that shape these cities' experiences – in particular the climate-related risks and changes that they all face and the political and governance contexts from which they respond to these challenges. Then we consider the four agendas, one by one, looking at the links among them, and comparing the ways they have been tackled by these cities.

Changes in climate and climate-related risks

All nine cities have basic information on variations and extremes in climate that they have faced in recent years and the risks that they are currently experiencing, but there are considerable differences in the information they have available about projected changes in climate and projected risks. Even cities that are mounting strong responses to current trends may have comparatively little information about what they are likely to face in the future. New York and Durban, for instance, both forward thinking and proactive in terms of adaptation, are operating based on quite different levels of information. In New York, there had been a major scenario-based assessment by the early 1990s, and a report on potential climate change consequences by 2001. For Durban, there are projections – but the uncertainty increases as you downscale.

What comes through clearly, with or without sophisticated projections, is how many of these cities are experiencing an increase in the intensity and frequency of extreme events. Most of the cities have been getting warmer – in most cases, relatively minor changes over recent decades, but in Bangalore, for instance, average temperatures have increased by 2 to 2.5°C over the last decade and in Bangkok, there has been an average increase of 0.06°C per year since the 1980s. Temperatures are expected to continue to increase everywhere – by 2080, Dar es Salaam's temperatures are projected to have increased by 2.5 to 4.5°C and in New York, the average number of days exceeding 90°F (32°C) is expected by then to have increased three- to four-fold. Heat island effects associated with the extent of the built-up area contribute, of course, to these increases. London, for instance, is the warmest place in the United Kingdom, due to climate as well as a heat island effect, despite the fact that over 40 per cent of its land cover is green space. The heat island effect here is expected to be intensified by climate change, and several heat waves have occurred in recent years. The one in 2003 was associated with around 600 deaths. In Bangkok, a 5°C difference was found between the city and an outlying part of the metropolitan region, and here a rise of 1°C in the average ambient temperature is calculated to result in a 7.5 per cent increase in average monthly electricity consumption.

Changes in precipitation, both those experienced and those projected, are more varied – up in some places, down in others. Either way, however, a general increase in intensity has meant more flooding in all of these cities, a trend projected to continue. Rosario has experienced the most dramatic increase in average annual precipitation – between 100 and 200 mm, with an increase in both frequency and intensity, and there has been flooding over extensive areas, causing significant damage and displacing thousands of people. In 2012, for instance, 179 mm of rain fell in only 6.5 hours. In Bangalore, too, increasing rainfall since about 1900 has been accompanied by increases in both frequency and intensity, and the incidence of urban flooding has increased substantially in recent years, causing damage to low lying areas of the city and severely affecting transportation systems. Recently, over 1000 areas in the city were identified as flood prone, 85 per cent of them categorized as critical. In Manizales, more intense rainfalls have made landslides and serious flooding increasingly common.

In Mexico City, the greatest climate change-related risk is also associated with heavy rainfalls and flooding, even with an overall decline in precipitation. Over the last thirty years, 180 intense precipitation events have flooded vulnerable parts of the city, with more extreme effects in informal settlements, and this is projected to become worse. Bangkok has prolonged periods of no precipitation, but at the same time, rainfall events have increased in intensity and frequency, and rainfall is expected to increase by 2 to 3 per cent by 2050. Here too floods are an increasingly severe problem – approximately 900,000 people are currently at risk, and this will likely increase to more than 5 million by 2070. Dar es Salaam, despite predictions for higher rainfall, has also experienced decreased precipitation over the last four decades, yet here too increased intensity has contributed to flooding. Those most at risk are in unplanned settlements along rivers and on the coast, where flooding is exacerbated by poor planning, poor drainage and housing conditions, and lack of local capacity to adapt to flooding. In New York, flash floods from intensive rainstorms are increasingly common. In August 2007, an intense rainstorm rendered almost the entire 1352 kilometres of the subway system inoperable.

Flooding in New York, as in other coastal cities, is exacerbated by rising sea level and storm surges. Sea level rise has averaged 3 cm per decade since 1900, about twice the global average, and it is expected to rise by another 30 to 60 cm by 2050. So far this has been caused primarily by land subsidence, but is expected to intensify with climate change, and is considered the most significant future challenge to this city with its very extensive coastline (2400 km). In Bangkok, too, the combination of subsidence and sea level rise is expected to result in an overall rise of over 30 cm by 2050. With a 50 cm rise, 55 per cent of the city would experience flooding. Durban faces especially extreme sea level rise, calculated in 2009 at 2.7 mm a year. Dar es Salaam is also coping with sea level rise and storm surges; more than 31,000 people are currently at risk from a 100-year storm surge, and this is expected to increase to 100,000 by 2030. London is at risk of flooding from several sources: tidal (overtopping of defences with a major storm surge in the North Sea); fluvial (when the capacity of tributary rivers is exceeded or breached); surface water (when intense rainfall in a summer thunderstorm exceeds the capacity of the drainage system). Climate change is likely to increase all of these types of flooding. As already noted, water shortages paired with flooding are an increasingly common phenomenon. At the same time that London faces flooding, it is also at risk of droughts, as rainfall and the volume of available water decreases due to lower river flow, groundwater replenishment and water evaporation. The pressure on diminishing water supplies has been intensified by increased demand in the context of rising temperatures.

Just as flooding can happen even where rainfall is decreasing, water shortages can happen even where rainfall is increasing – in both cases partly a function of increased intensity. In New York for example, water supply systems lacked the capacity to store heavy early-year rains in 1999, and drought emergencies were called for after a dry spring and mid-summer, only to switch abruptly to emergency flood measures after Tropical Storm Floyd dropped up to 12 inches of rain (304 mm) in September. Bangalore is an especially notable example of water shortages in the face of increased rainfall. Poorly managed urbanization has dramatically changed the drainage potential of natural catchments and man-made lakes, increasing the volume and rate of surface run-off and progressively lowering the water table.

Bangalore is not alone in contributing, through its development patterns, to the severity of the risk to which residents, infrastructure and property are exposed. Land subsidence in Bangkok, for instance, which has reached the alarming rate of 3 cm per year in some outlying areas of the city, adding to the threat of flooding, is partly due to the over-pumping of groundwater. Manizales is a most dramatic example – its development and expansion over steep and ecologically fragile slopes has contributed to repeated disaster events even with the resettlement of those on slopes most at risk. In 2012, for instance, an intense rainy season associated with La Niña resulted in mudslides that caused pipes from the water treatment plant to be washed away, and the city had to rely on springs and water tanks for ten days. In Rosario, too, urban development near the Ludueña stream has increased water run-off and affected many urban residents, especially those in low-income settlements that are within the flood plain.

The risks associated with higher temperatures, more intense rainfall, rising sea levels and other features of a changing climate are seldom distributed equally. While everyone may be affected by rising temperatures, those who live in poorly ventilated shacks in densely built informal settlements are clearly at greater risk. Even in cities like New York without such settlements, those who cannot afford air conditioning are disproportionately vulnerable to heat waves, especially the elderly. Flooding also can affect both the rich and the poor, as is clear in London, where adequate infrastructure protects everyone equally. But those who squat alongside canals in Bangkok or who have not yet been relocated from high-risk slopes in Manizales or who live in settlements without proper drainage in Mexico City are far more likely to be affected. Even in New York, where storm drains and proper zoning limit the risks, Hurricane Sandy hit the poorest residents the hardest. They were not the only people living in high-risk areas, but they were less able to evacuate during the storm and far less able to cope with damage to their homes or with the health implications of mould resulting from inundation.

Coordination issues: boundaries, jurisdictions and governance responsibilities

All these cities exist within a complex web of relationships, both with higher levels of government and with surrounding areas that may lie within the same larger river basin or ecosystem. The implications for governance can be complex and challenging. There is also the matter of coordination among departments and agencies within these city governments and of the relationship with local communities and civil society.

National level

Policies and programmes at national level should ideally help to anchor and support local processes. In some of the cities, climate-related action is driven by or has been catalysed by a national agenda on this front, in other cases local action has been more the outcome of local decisions and planning. Bangalore lies at the first extreme here – attention to climate change, as it affects this city, is almost totally framed by national level policies and programmes. According to the Bangalore chapter's authors, the capacity of the municipal team to tackle climate change is limited by their lack of capacity and understanding of the issues, as well as their focus on economic growth. Most of the climate change agenda is driven by centrally sponsored schemes, or managed at the state level through programmes, coordinated with the national agenda, which for the most part transcend city boundaries. Most relevant city-level actions have been conceived primarily as development interventions, driven by the National Urban Renewal Mission and aimed at upgrading city-level infrastructure.

In South Africa too, national policies and plans do not include clear directives for local action. Local governments have no formal climate change response obligations, and although national plans acknowledge a role for local government, they give no guidance on this role or how it should be financed. A proposed amendment to the national Disaster Management Act will create the first official mandate requiring municipalities to specify their measures and investments in disaster risk reduction and climate change adaptation, and to include ecosystem and community-based adaptation approaches. The risk, say the Durban authors, is that adaptation will become subsumed into the disaster risk reduction agenda. In contrast to Bangalore, however, action in Durban has not waited for national directives or support. As this team puts it, "This is an unfunded mandate, often dependent on strong personalities." Rather than following the national lead, Durban has stepped out in front of it.

In Mexico City, local attention to climate change also preceded that at the national level. The same is true in Manizales, although national level changes helped anchor this. Manizales has a long history of responding to disaster risk, and over time has developed policies related to adaptation that have helped to shape the national framework for action. There are, however, both national and sub-national policies that support integrated action; coordination is good and it can be difficult to separate out what is happening at these various levels. The Climate Change National System (SISCLIMA) was created specifically to coordinate initiatives by different levels and sectors of government and by local communities, and the National Adaptation plan includes guidelines for local planning and environmental protection, well coordinated with regional policies and plans.

In some cases, there has been little or no national agenda to respond to. In Rosario, despite a high level of coordination at the local level, support from the national level is scarce and neither funds nor capacity building support have been significant. This is not surprising given that climate change is not a top issue on the national agenda. But it is also linked to the fact that the city has long been governed by a political party different from the one in power nationally. In Tanzania, a 2012 draft National Climate Change Strategy and Action Plan has highlighted adaptation actions to be taken by different sectors, and the National Climate Change Committee now provides overall guidance on climate change issues and on mitigation and adaptation measures, working together with sector ministries, research institutions and NGOs.

New York, London and Bangkok have to a large extent crafted their own responses. In New York, the PlaNYC 2030 (first adopted in 2007, with new versions in 2011 and 2013 and annual updates) initially focused on mitigation, but rapidly expanded to take adaptation into account after extreme rainfall in August 2007. More recently, the new OneNYC under Mayor de Blasio has expanded the focus to include equity. In London, responses are guided and supported by national policies, but the key climate change strategies for both adaptation and mitigation have come from the mayor's office, and are complemented by the city's strategies for transport, housing, waste and water. In Bangkok too, the municipal authority, which is responsible for formulating policies regarding transport, urban planning, waste management, environment and security, developed a mitigation action plan for 2007 to 2012, and is currently formulating a ten-year master plan on climate change which includes adaptation and mitigation.

Coordination with surrounding areas

City governments need to understand city-region interactions, in part because many interventions for adaptation and mitigation depend on changing these. This is much easier when city boundaries are wide enough to allow them to address these issues – for instance where watersheds and large areas of forest and farmland are within their jurisdictions. This is the case in Durban, where the municipal boundaries encompass 2297 km^2 and where the local government recognizes the importance of the city region. Manizales municipality also extends well beyond the built-up centre to include the more peri-urban or rural surroundings.

In other cases, such as New York or Mexico City, many municipalities are included in the extended metropolitan area, and there are numerous, often overlapping, municipal and state jurisdictions that need to be coordinated to manage contiguous areas. The New York Statistical Area, for instance, includes not only the five boroughs of New York City, already a complex governance unit, but also 25 adjacent counties in three different states, with several thousand jurisdictions. Most are small municipalities whose boundaries do not overlap. But many have overlapping jurisdictional boundaries – for instance counties, school boards, water management districts and flood control districts. Coordination is a critical challenge for meaningful climate action, and there can be tensions on a number of fronts, especially around environmental and social equity, as some areas become externality sinks while others concentrate amenities.

In Mexico City, there is no real mechanism for coordination between the Federal District and the other municipalities that make up the Metropolitan Area. The legal framework for mitigation and adaptation actions does not apply beyond the Federal District, and only two of the municipalities of the Metropolitan Area have developed a climate change action plan. According to the authors, "This [lack of coordination] is without doubt one of the deepest prevailing policy-making gaps. It was supposed to be resolved with the establishment in 2013 of the *Environmental Megalopolitan Commission*, but this is yet to happen."

This kind of cross-boundary coordination is important even where there is not a complex metropolitan area to deal with. The city of Rosario, for instance, falls within an ecosystem (the wetlands of the Río Paraná bioregion) shared by three provinces. Here, planning takes these overlaps into account – the Metropolitan Strategic Plan (PERM + 10) includes neighbouring areas and cities, integrating social, economic, environmental and territorial planning. Rosario has twice participated in strategic planning projects for the bioregion; the three provinces have signed an agreement recognizing the importance of their shared resource and committing to its sustainable use, and a strategic plan has been developed for the conservation and sustainable use of the Paraná Delta (PIECAS-DP). This kind of coordination demands constant negotiations however, and here too, the authors list this as one of the major challenges in developing their climate work.

This kind of cross-boundary coordination can be focused on learning as well as planning. In Durban, the Central KwaZulu-Natal Climate Change Compact, part of a growing recognition of the need to address climate change at the city region level, was established between Durban and its neighbouring municipalities in 2013, with regular meetings and learning exchanges to share experiences on specific climate change themes.

Integration within local government

Internal coordination between different sectors and departments within local government is always challenging, not least because they usually compete for funding and attention. The absence of this coordination can be costly however. In Dar es Salaam, for instance, the December 2011 floods that hit the city, causing 20 deaths and displacing 10,000, clearly showed the need for links between adaptation and disaster risk reduction efforts, which currently operate under the oversight of different national departments, but also the importance of links between disaster risk reduction and physical planning and infrastructure development. In Bangalore too, although there is some recognition of the vulnerability of different sectors to climate change, no structured institutional response has emerged at city level.

Experience shows the need for a local coordinating body with sufficient status to lead the way. In Manizales, for instance, the establishment of an Environmental Secretariat has promoted stronger institutional support and visibility for environmental and climate change issues within the municipal structure. Prior to this, this unit had a far lower rank within the institutional hierarchy, which allowed some administrations to neglect environmental issues. In Rosario, by contrast, although there is an integrated planning strategy, the lack of this kind of institutional umbrella still slows things up.

In larger cities, several bodies may provide aspects of this coordinating function. In New York for instance, an interagency Climate Change Adaptation Task Force has been supported by the New York City Panel on Climate Change, a group of scientific, legal, insurance and risk management experts who can ensure that decisions are soundly based. In London, the London Climate Change Partnership brings together public and private sector organizations, and its work is supplemented by that of the London Resilience Partnership, with its focus on emergency, and the Climate Change Committee, which deals with mitigation issues. In Mexico City, several mechanisms ensure, if not fully coordinated action among sectoral authorities, at least an integrated mandate for attention to climate change. The local climate change strategy is accompanied by an Action Plan, an Inter-institutional Climate Change Commission and an Environmental Fund for Climate Change, which provides dedicated resources for pushing climate change actions within sectoral practices. Prior to this, the more conventional approaches of various city authorities often ran counter to environmental concerns (for instance with new highways crossing ravines of ecological value and locking the city into private vehicle use).

Even where there is the political will, some partnerships have trouble surviving the complex political and institutional challenges. In Durban, for instance, there was a felt need for a broadly representative partnership to address climate change issues, and a committee was established using a democratic process. But according to the Durban authors, "a lack of effective leadership, long-term commitment and reliable funding made this committee largely ineffective. The Municipality's involvement in the committee was restricted by financial regulations, which reduced its participation to observer status and limited its ability to fund the partnership." On the other hand, consistent efforts over the years on the part of the Environmental Planning and Climate Protection Department have resulted in growing coordination among city government sectors.

There is also the matter of continuity from one city administration to the next. Rosario's good fortune in being governed by the same party for over 25 years has allowed for sustained political support for important initiatives. In the absence of this political continuity, pet projects of a previous administration can easily fall between the cracks. New York's new de Blasio administration is to be credited for building on the important climate change achievements of the Bloomberg years, adding a social justice perspective to what has already been effective. In Durban, strong leadership within the civil service has carried climate-related and relevant policies forward over the years to provide a foundation for a broader strategy today. And in Manizales, a strong, decentralized territorial and local planning mandate – which recognizes the link between development, environmental and disaster risk – combined with active engagement of civil society, has provided a stable platform to address climate change in spite of shifts in political or formal government leadership.

The role of champions

In any city that is innovating on climate change (or most other fronts) there are likely to be people, often only known locally, who are critical in catalysing, supporting or defending these innovations. The most obvious champions in these cases are high-profile mayors like Bloomberg in New York and Livingstone in London, who managed to get their city government to take climate change more seriously. The current mayor of Rosario, as well as the previous two, has also been important, as has the current Durban mayor. In Manizales, the engagement with environmental issues that then developed into attention to climate change relied on the positive leadership role of some mayors, one of whom built a strong local constituency for the early work integrating urban environmental planning and DRR.

But there are other champions too – they may be politicians, civil servants, community leaders, staff from local NGOs or other stakeholders. London has many committed actors in the public sector, business, science and civil society, even if the current administration (and national government) provide little support. As Chapter 7 notes, the key challenge is to find the right policy environment within which to foster and project these energies so that the development co-benefits of adaptation and mitigation can be realized.

In Manizales, a research group at the National University kept climate change issues alive during periods when mayors were not responsive. Occasionally case studies identify these champions but there is not much of a literature on this phenomenon – or at least not with regard to climate change. In a very different sphere, documentation on the work of the federations of slum/shack dwellers identifies the champions that have supported them – typically politicians and senior civil servants – and how the federations then engage with and support these champions.

The Durban chapter sheds an unusual amount of light on the work of multiple champions within the municipality who, with their deep sectoral knowledge, have understood where it is appropriate to work with other sectors. They have also encouraged more integrated action and overlapping circles of influence, re-casting climate change as a development issue, and minimizing the marginalization more often associated with environmental department programmes. An important new development in Durban is the increasing political prioritization of climate change, driven by the Mayor's role as a global climate change champion, with his proposed establishment of a political committee to raise the profile of this issue. Politicians here have also requested training to better understand the climate change challenge, suggesting a growing maturity in governance structures which will be central in supporting the integration of the city's adaptation and mitigation agendas and fostering actions to influence systemic and potentially transformative change.

Citizen engagement and local community involvement

One of the most important yet difficult issues is how to engage with civil society – especially those groups formed or represented by low-income urban dwellers. In most of the nine cities, a substantial proportion of the population lives in informal settlements and works in the informal economy. These residents are often among those at highest risk from disasters and climate change – yet they are often seen by local and national governments as illegal and detrimental to urban development. They need to be engaged not only because they are "at risk" by virtue of both the hazards they face and their status, but also because they can bring knowledge, capacity and innovation to adaptation (and mitigation).

Of course, even in high-income nations there are still particular groups, settlements or buildings that are not adequately protected, but they generally represent a small proportion of the urban population. Although the risk of death from extreme weather has decreased substantially in high-income nations, there are still examples each year of disasters in some cities, often caused by extreme weather with unusual or even unprecedented intensity, and often especially devastating for low-income communities, as in the case of Hurricane Sandy in New York. In high-income nations, though, there are more often channels through which citizens who are excluded or inadequately served can complain – through the courts, through ombudsmen, through their local politicians. Even here, though, the input of local citizens is an important way to build knowledge of risks and capacity to act at the local level.

This engagement by local government, especially with those most at risk in low- and middle-income countries, has to involve more than inviting representatives to meetings. It also important to support the documentation of "good practice" by local citizens and their organizations – perhaps most critically in the partnerships they form with local governments. The case studies suggest that the most effective engagement emerges when there are ongoing participatory processes to help set the agenda for local action. While local champions for action can make a difference, other elements for success often include a lasting national mandate for local engagement, which in turn can provide entry-points, resources and a legal framework to support local action.

Manizales is an inspiring example on this front. Colombia has a strong decentralized approach to planning and policy and this pertains also to the environment; it has also mandated attention to disaster risk management alongside climate change. Manizales has shown leadership with early action that builds on a foundation of community-based engagement and agenda-setting. When its environmental agenda was updated in 2014 to reflect potential climate change impacts, assessment was conducted at a street and neighbourhood level by trained local volunteers and government staff who documented local conditions, both environmental and social, to come up with neighbourhood agendas. Another important innovation here is the longstanding Slope Guardian programme that trains women in high-risk zones not only to control drainage channels and report problems and changes in land use, but to keep registers of families at high risk, and raise their neighbours' awareness of their situations.

By contrast, the current vision of citizen participation in Mexico City's climate-related decisions and actions is limited to top-down consultancy processes, a far more common response that fails to take account of the value of local knowledge and input.

Networks, alliances and partnerships

The role of inter-city networks focusing on climate change was recognized relatively early as an important component of individual city climate planning and action. Inter-city networking played an important role in promoting climate change mitigation and adaptation in European cities in the early 2000s (Kern and Bulkeley 2009). So too did ICLEI Local Governments for Sustainable Development through its local government members. Later in the decade, networks began to emerge across North American cities, as well as within international organizations such as C20 (later renamed C40) and the World Mayors Council on Climate Change (Rosenzweig et al. 2010; Gore and Robinson 2009; Rutland and Aylett 2008; Toly 2008).

All the case study cities are members of international city networks. New York has had significant connections with the city of London and the Greater London Authority. Close collaborations resulted from ongoing discussions between groups in both cities. The New York chapter also notes the important contribution to the development of the mitigation and adaptation activities in New York from the professional and personal connections with counterparts in other cities (e.g., Chicago, San Francisco, Boston, Tokyo and London) who were also developing their own climate action efforts.

The city of Rosario is an active member of the Argentine Network of Municipalities for Climate Change (RAMCC), Network of Mercociudades (Red de Mercociudades), United Cities and Local Governments (UCLG), Metropolis, Iberoamerican Centre of Urban Development (CIDEU), International Association of Educating Cities (AICE), Cities against Urban Poverty, and the URB-AL Program, among others. In Mexico City, the signing of the Mexico City Pact in 2010 at the World Mayors Summit on Climate Change became a spur to local action. Rosario has also been part of a city colloquium recently convened by Pope Francis, focused in large part on climate change – a recognition of work done and a source of mobilization for future action.

Dar es Salaam's attention to climate change has been supported by a number of international alliances including the Mayors' Task Force on Climate Change, Disaster Risk and Urban Poor; the ICLEI Local Governments for Sustainable Development; and the World Bank. Under the auspices of the Mayors' Task Force, a study on urban poverty and climate change in the city was conducted and, under ICLEI, a capacity-building programme on adaptation was implemented in the Temeke municipality.

Durban (eThekwini) is an especially important example here, not only for what it has gained from these networks but also for what it has contributed. In the absence of an international agency to serve as an institutional home for the Durban Adaptation Charter, which was signed by representatives of over 900 local governments at COP17-CMP7,[1] the eThekwini Municipality took on the task of ensuring the Charter's effective implementation, continuing to work with members of the original local government partnership and new international partners (we return to this Charter in Chapter 13).

Research alliances and partnerships between city governments, universities and local stakeholders also emerge as a key support to local climate action and its integration with disaster risk and development planning. Across cities as diverse as Dar es Salaam, Manizales and New York, the role of on-going partnerships with local universities is cited as a way to generate place-based information and knowledge to help build capacity and inform decision-making. Dar es Salaam was also part of the Climate Change and Urban Vulnerability in Africa (CLUVA) programme, funded by the European Union, and partnering with five universities in Africa and a number of European and African research institutions.[2] In Durban, trans-disciplinary research partnerships with a local university focus on the interface between biodiversity and climate change (Cockburn et al. in prep); they serve the dual purpose of enabling the co-production of knowledge to advance evidence-based decision-making and helping to address the skills shortage to support local decision-making.

The role of such partnerships may be greatest when funding and research partners are local and the research is tailored to local challenges and informed by local knowledge. The case of Manizales shows that research guided solely by outside funding may bias the research agenda such that it fails to be useful for local action. There, the local private sector, namely the Chamber of Commerce, has been engaged to help fund locally-tailored and targeted research that can directly support local decisions. Experience in both Durban and Manizales highlights the critical role that local universities and research institutes can play in delivering sound monitoring and indicators of progress to support on-going engagement with stakeholders and local government. In Manizales, formal knowledge is combined with local knowledge to strengthen insights and the foundation for decision-making.

Finance

Some of the city case studies document the sources of finance to support urban government and attention to climate change within the broad range of priorities managed at this level. The extent to which a city has authority over local fiscal policy and the ability to raise its own revenues and align these policies to reflect environmental risks and goals is typically determined through national-level institutional frameworks. Where the national-level frameworks set out a clear role for local authorities in planning for and managing urban development, including environmental risks and disaster, this can empower and support local action on climate change within the development. The case study findings confirm that internal sources of finance – whether locally or nationally generated – are the most stable foundation for action (e.g. as shown in the cases of Manizales and New York).

There are also cases of unfunded urban mandates on climate change, as for instance in the case of Dar es Salaam, where increased financial capacity in city government staff and institutions is highlighted as a key need to enable climate action. Often there is a mix of funded and unfunded urban mandates on climate change, driven by multiple actors with varied motivations, with a wider goal of responding to risks in the city – as seen in the Bangalore case. Clearly, municipalities vary widely in their capacity and authority to raise income through local taxes (UCLG 2010; Scott and Tarazona 2011).

Strengthened partnerships between city and national governments, and with international urban initiatives, could help to fill this urban funding and financial capacity gap. Particularly when coupled with decentralized authority on fiscal policies, such dedicated revenue transfers from the national government can help city governments to weave climate change into urban development. In Colombia, a 1.0 per cent tax on property is used to require municipalities to invest in solving key local environmental problems, and in the case of Manizales, local action added a 0.5 per cent tax to strengthen the funding for such action. In Durban, an important share of the municipality's budget is grants and subsidies (from the national government) and in the case of urban infrastructure investment this will comprise roughly half of what is needed, followed by internal (local) sources and then external sources. The challenge of depending on external sources is a lack of predictability and transaction costs, which are difficult to manage for urban governments that are already struggling to build institutional capacity and the expertise to manage climate change. However, the case of Durban shows that external funding can be catalytic is supporting early stage action – DANIDA funded the Urban Environmental Management Programme in South Africa in 2006, and funding from the United States Environmental Protection Agency made it possible to kick off implementation of the Durban Adaptation Charter following COP17 the year before. Mexico City established a stable source of financing for climate action through a dedicated fund for urban action on climate change, made up of local public funds allocated yearly, donations, and Clean Development Mechanism (CDM) revenues among other sources. In Rosario, only a small share (roughly 7 per cent) of the urban budget is composed of transfers from the national government, and climate change still competes with many other local priorities to find a place on the policy agenda (as in Bangalore and Dar es Salaam). All the case studies highlight that financial constraints are a key barrier to action; grants and subsidies (external or from the central government) can be critical or catalytic in supplementing local funding, especially in early stages of programme development, particularly if they are predictable and locally governed with respect to allocation.

Human development

The first of the four agendas that we are reviewing for these nine cities is human development – used here to mean reduction in the deprivations caused or exacerbated by the many dimensions of poverty – or more broadly, the effort to work towards and ensure the common good, which has to include those who are most excluded. This effort includes the universal provision for infrastructure (piped water, all-weather roads and paths, storm and surface drainage, infrastructure for good sanitation), services (solid waste collection, health care, schools and child-care, emergency services, safety nets, policing), secure housing that meets health and safety standards, a rule of law that includes policing and voice (so pressure can be brought on local government). As noted in Chapter 1, these objectives can all be found within the Sustainable Development Goals. The realization of all these combined by 2030 would represent a transformation in the health, living conditions and level of risk for very large sections of the world's current and future urban populations, and would go a long way towards realizing the ideal of the common good.

City governments are fundamental to addressing most of these concerns. This might sound obvious. But much of the discussion on "development" has actually ignored the needs and priorities of low-income dwellers and the importance for development of good city government and governance. Even now, with a rising interest from governments and international agencies in urban issues, the focus tends to be on the role of cities in economic growth, which is assumed to underpin development. What is less evident is an understanding of the basic responsibility of city governments for social development, poverty reduction and the improvement of health, not to mention the other three agendas of disaster risk reduction, climate change adaptation and mitigation. Part of this responsibility means responding to changing circumstances, often not foreseen. New investments come in, migrants move in and out, enterprises boom, decline and move, prices for food, fuel and other necessities change (often influenced by national or global changes). It falls to city government to guide city expansion and new developments, and to ensure provision for the infrastructure and services on which citizens and enterprises depend.

The extent to which all these needs are met has enormous implications for disaster risk reduction and climate change adaptation, discussion of which must, in effect, start from the footing that the city's development provides. Many of these case study cities have the infrastructure and services to ensure that all or most residents live in buildings that meet health and safety standards, with water piped to their homes, sewer connections, electricity, solid waste collection, paved roads and storm drains. But even where their local governments have the power and resources to ensure these systems are maintained and expanded, this does not mean that these systems will be able to cope with more intense extreme weather events. New York City, for instance, may be among the world's wealthiest and most powerful cities, but upgrading its infrastructure and services to cope with climate change risks will be very costly. As Chapter 10 describes, New York's infrastructure includes thousands of miles of underground electricity distribution lines, sewer pipes, water distribution pipes and transit system tracks, along with almost 100 sewerage pumping stations, 14 water pollution control plants, two dozen major electricity generating facilities, a million buildings and a vast network of fixed and mobile telecommunication networks. These systems are tightly coupled, leading to the possibility of a cascade of failures with secondary and tertiary impacts.

Dar es Salaam is at the other end of the development spectrum. Most of its residents live in homes that do not meet building standards in neighbourhoods without risk-reducing infrastructure and services. It is much the wealthiest city in Tanzania, yet its three municipalities depend on central government for most of their budget. Dar faces a large development deficit as well as climate change impacts, current and future, that need to be addressed. Although there have been measures to address the concerns, the backlog remains huge in provision for water, sanitation, drainage, solid waste collection and paved roads.

There is little question that the level of development in a city has a major impact on its capacity to respond to risk. Settlements in flood zones, for instance, can obviously not respond adequately to the risks posed by extreme precipitation if they have no storm drains. Table 1.2 in Chapter 1, drawn from the urban chapter in the IPCC's Fifth Assessment, illustrates the very large differences between cities in adaptive capacity and their position relative to four key factors that influence this – local government capacity; the proportion of residents served with risk-reducing infrastructure and services; the proportion living in housing built to appropriate health and safety standards; and the levels of risk from direct and indirect impacts of climate change. Some of these differences in adaptive capacity are difficult to quantify.

City governments with development deficits need to give priority to these, although this in part can act as a stimulus and focus for adaptation and disaster risk reduction, and to some degree for mitigation too. Upgrading of informal settlements, for instance, can include identifying and acting on disaster risks and on low carbon energy provision. Both energy and transport policies can contribute to meeting basic needs and reducing the often very large health burden from indoor and outdoor air pollution – as well as contributing to mitigation. But these responses need a carefully constructed, locally-rooted and sustained political narrative, and this requires organizations and individuals who are capable of acting as the bridge between climate change science and political processes.

An issue to which we return constantly is that three of the four agendas are about identifying and acting on local risks – and much of the responsibility falls to local government. Development, disaster risk reduction and climate change adaptation share the common goal of safeguarding city resident's lives, health, homes, livelihoods and assets, even if they see risk through different lenses. The capacity to respond to and reduce risk, from whatever perspective, is a fundamental aspect of the common good.

The case studies of Rosario and Manizales, in particular, draw attention to the great distance that attention to development can go towards meeting both disaster reduction and adaptation needs. Rosario is particularly interesting here. It has no explicit climate change strategy or programme, nor any office coordinating initiatives that contribute to mitigation or adaptation. Its adaptation strategy is simply a set of isolated responses to other city needs. But Rosario has had a strong coherent governance system that includes a commitment to development, decentralization, transparency, accountability and participation. It has a long tradition of urban planning and land-use management, with a commitment to environmental sustainability and a strategic plan that involves multiple stakeholders and encompasses the whole metropolitan area. Many of the city's development programmes and initiatives contribute to disaster risk reduction and to adaptation – improved provision for infrastructure, upgrading of informal settlements, a much admired municipal health care service with focus on prevention, the expansion of public space, initiatives for energy efficiency – initiatives, in short, that have enhanced the common good in Rosario. All of these contribute to a city that is more resilient to disasters and climate change impacts.

In Manizales too, local government investment in development, along with disaster risk reduction, has built a strong base for adaptation. Almost all the urban population has electricity, piped water and sewerage services, and regular collection of garbage. Many of those who lived on unstable slopes have been rehoused and there are slope protection systems in place that include community-managed parks.

Durban has not progressed as far in development terms. While there have been very impressive gains, considerable backlogs remain in housing, infrastructure and basic services. For instance, although over 183,000 houses have been built since 1994, 390,000 are still needed, as are more piped water connections, electrical connections and proper sanitation. There are also tensions here in more remote parts of the municipality between environmentally sound solutions and people's felt needs. Despite its impressive record on climate change, Durban's climate-related hazards still combine with social vulnerability to create high levels of risk and a challenge in terms of meeting adaptation needs.

The remaining development deficiencies in Durban highlight an important paradox that was raised in the Preface. Those of us at a distance can focus on the city's very real achievements around climate change. But those who live there, struggling to find work and still living in informal settlements or lacking adequate services, have little interest in the international performance of their city – they want their needs addressed now. To some degree the same can be said of Rosario and Manizales. And even in New York City, with its reputation as a climate change leader and its high level of development and attention to the common good, there are many low-income residents who continue to feel seriously neglected by their city and its policies.

The development goals espoused by the SDGs are not limited to those primarily focused on poverty reduction, but also include development that is environmentally sound and sustainable, that respects "our common home". Although our focus here has been on the human side of this, there is no question that land and land-use management are critical to this. As noted in the climate risk section, in cities where a focus on growth has taken precedence over sound land-use management, there can be distinct implications for levels of risk. In Bangkok, for instance, rapid changes in land use over recent decades have affected water courses, ponds, canals, with impacts for drainage and the effectiveness of flood protection. Over-pumping of groundwater has lowered the water table and contributed to dramatic land subsidence and flood risk. Groundwater extraction is also a concern in Bangalore where the lowering of the water table adds to an impending water supply crisis, and where rapid unplanned development has contributed among other things to the disappearance of a critical system of lakes, ponds and water tanks. Despite its generally rather dismal record with regard to effective land management and allocation, Bangalore has recently responded to legal concerns around encroachment on a dry lake bed (including 30 commercial complexes, a private dental college and a municipal roadway) by initiating eviction proceedings.

Environmental and land-use planning have been an important entry point for climate-related attention in several of the cities. Durban in particular has integrated attention to biodiversity and environmental planning with its evolving adaptation agenda. Manizales too, after an earlier history of uncontrolled expansion, is now recognized for its environmental policies, and the Environmental Secretariat serves now as the umbrella institution for climate-related issues. Rosario's long tradition of urban planning has included a strong focus on environmental sustainability, which underpins its evolving climate-related strategies. In New York, one of the very earliest adaptation initiatives (2004) included creation by the Department of Environmental Protection of a task force to take into account potential climate risks to the city's water supply. London's adaptation measures include an "All Green Grid" to increase tree cover and total green urban space, and Sustainable Drainage Systems to help manage surface water run-off.

Disaster risk reduction

The first issue to consider here is a city's institutional capacity for disaster or emergency response, and for coordination with disaster response agencies. The second is whether there is recognition of the need also to reduce disaster risk and the capacity for key sectors to develop this. Disaster risk reduction should be fully integrated into urban development planning and thus go far beyond just emergency response. The third issue is whether disaster risk reduction, disaster preparedness and disaster response begin to assess how climate change may change the risks in question and the exposure to these risks, and to act on this.

These nine cities are very different in terms of the foundation they present from which to build disaster risk reduction. A city government focused on the common good in a broad sense, with the power, resources and will to ensure universal provision for risk-reducing infrastructure and services and to manage land-use changes, has the necessary groundwork for disaster risk reduction and by extension for climate change adaptation. Many of the measures that reduce disaster risk in these cities were installed to supply everyday needs, not to prevent disasters. But sewer and drainage systems that serve daily requirements can also be upgraded to cope with storms. Good quality health care services and emergency services that meet everyday needs also form a critical component of disaster risk reduction and rapid, effective post-disaster response. One gets a sense of their effectiveness by looking at the decline in disaster-related deaths and injuries over time, and by comparing these numbers in cities in high-income nations with those in low- or middle-income nations with comparable levels of exposure to extreme weather (United Nations 2009).

In London and New York, this foundation of resilience was built incrementally over more than 150 years, mostly in response to some disastrous epidemics (especially cholera), fires and other local disasters and environmental health risks including those associated with inadequate solid waste collection, air pollution, and inadequate and polluted water supplies (see also Solecki 2012). Little over a century ago, cities in what were then the highest income countries had worse health conditions than most cities in low-income nations today (Bairoch 1988). What we see in New York and London is a long, complex and contested history of city government being pressed to act on everyday risks and on disaster impacts. This gradually resulted in today's universal provision of risk-reducing infrastructure and services, although the wealthier more powerful groups are generally better served. Government institutions ensure that these are provided, but also that buildings and enterprises meet health and safety standards that take into account extreme weather and hazard events. Urban populations in all cities in high-income and some middle-income nations take it for granted that such institutions, infrastructure, services and regulations will protect them from disasters, and that this protection is a key component of attention to their common good. These provisions in most situations prevent extreme events from turning into disasters – for instance heavy rainfall and high winds generally result in no major losses or fatalities. London, for instance, invested heavily in a barrier across the Thames to protect against tidal surges; this has been in place since 1982 and was built in response to a major coastal flood event in 1953 that killed more than 300 people across the UK. This investment has paid for itself many times over in terms of lives and property saved. But Chapter 7 on London notes that a record of innovation in the past in response to environmental crises does not mean that this will continue, especially in a larger context of budget cuts for local governments.

Sometimes these approaches can involve trade-offs, as in Bangkok, where there has been substantial investment in flood prevention and measures to divert flood waters away from the central city to what are judged to be less important and investment-intensive districts and provinces (Boonyabancha and Archer 2011). This was the case, for instance, in the severe floods of 2011. Although much of the city was inundated and damages were in excess of USD 9 billion, the inner downtown area of Bangkok was largely spared. The city's systems struggle, nevertheless, to keep up with intense rainfall and massive run-off.

In other cities too, coping with current disasters remains a considerable challenge. In Bangalore for instance, where there has been increasing incidence of flooding, the 2009 city development plan recognizes the critical need for disaster management, and an early warning system is in the works; but there is still no comprehensive response to DRR, nor even any policies to safeguard areas at risk from flooding or to protect water bodies from encroachment. The state's disaster management plan, however, provides the framework for a progressive response. Dar es Salaam is currently reported to be preparing a disaster resilience action plan, which will include a disaster centre to respond to the need for shelter and other basics after floods. The need for disaster management policy is also recognized however, and the fact that this should ideally include climate change impacts.

Even in cities with strong disaster prevention capacity, there can be considerable differences in how this is framed. In Mexico City, for example, the response to disaster is explicitly framed as a reactive civil protection agenda, focused on emergencies and on restoration and damage mitigation, with little attention to underlying causes or to social vulnerabilities. It is poorly integrated with the city's development agenda and with the longer-term reduction of climate related risk and vulnerability.

In other cities, the evolving DRR agenda includes an increasing acknowledgement of the need for preventive responses, and for expanding this focus to include climate change adaptation. Chapter 10, for instance, describes how New York's disaster risk reduction strategies were largely developed by the city's Office of Emergency Management, which has expanded its capacity in the last decade for vulnerability mapping and emergency responses, and is moving towards integrating climate change as a concern, with new modelling, remapping flood zones, rethinking flood insurance and a general focus on climate resilience. But the chapter also notes that disaster risk reduction efforts still focus on reducing vulnerability to extreme events, rather than on larger-scale economic development goals, or enhancing livelihoods and other aspects of quality of life that are essential to the common good. The link between DRR and economic development can be hard to make, except in cases where climate resiliency is seen as an added benefit for gentrification-oriented development, as in a proposed seaport city project.

A refocusing of disaster risk reduction is under discussion in Manizales too. The city, originally accommodated on a narrow plateau, expanded onto steep slopes without municipal approval. The city's risk management had focused too much on traditional infrastructure and emergency response and too little on prevention, a problem made evident in successive la Niña years. The new administration is re-thinking and re-organizing disaster risk planning and action to include climate change impacts, and to focus on prevention, resilience and vulnerability reduction, rather than falling back on emergency response. There is also a recognized need to move from costly structural engineering measures to a greater emphasis on soft alternatives. Here, as noted, community action and partnerships with local government are central not just to minimizing risk but also in responding to impact and shaping recovery in ways that can strengthen local livelihoods and quality of life.

In Rosario, disaster risk management and climate change are both relatively new for the city administration. Despite strong local political commitment and continuity, institutional capacity still needs to be developed to address the new goals and challenges these bring.

Durban's experience is of particular interest. The city's Environmental Planning and Climate Protection Department tried to encourage other city departments, including the disaster response group, to focus on climate change. While the Disaster Management Unit recognized that climate change was a significant risk, they lacked the powers and funding to address the challenges facing the city (Roberts 2010). As in many cities, disaster management was regarded as a relief and welfare response, not a key influence on the city's development plans. However, the national Municipal Systems Act (2000) and Disaster Management Act (2002) required local governments to develop a disaster management plan that shifted the focus from post-event response to disaster risk reduction, providing the mandate for Durban's Disaster Management Unit to establish an advisory forum, chaired by the city manager, that included a technical task team on adaptation. A city-wide risk assessment, currently underway, will include a consideration of climate change risk towards the development of the Disaster Management Plan.

Climate change adaptation: getting buy-in and continuity

A sequence of steps can be used as benchmarks for progress on climate change adaptation:

1 a formal recognition by local government of the need for adaptation;
2 the commissioning of studies on this (a local institution with the capacity usually has more influence than a non-local institution);
3 a policy, which might be outlined within a larger framework, such as an environmental or disaster risk reduction policy;
4 an institutional home for adaptation (the level within the municipal hierarchy makes a difference);
5 the assignment of responsibilities and budgets;
6 the interaction of those responsible with all the conventional infrastructure and development-oriented departments, including those responsible for disaster risk reduction and climate change mitigation;
7 the interaction of this whole city process with neighbouring local governments and the wider region and with regional authorities;
8 the provision or modification by national government of legal frameworks and funding – this includes supporting a stronger financial basis for local government responsibilities.

Logical as this progression is, when we look at actual cases, we find there are different starting points, different routes and considerable differences in what has been achieved and what still needs to happen. Of course, in each case, complex and very city-specific politics help explain these variations.

It is perhaps surprising that some cities' engagement with climate change began with mitigation, not adaptation. This was the case for Durban, Bangkok and Mexico City, for instance, although in these cases it was linked to the initiatives that external agencies supported. It was also the case for London and New York, in part because much of the initial interest in climate change was in cities in high-income nations, whose large contribution to global anthropogenic greenhouse gas emissions was recognized.

In most of the case study cities, local attention to adaptation has taken place within the context of national frameworks. In some cases it has developed in tandem with these frameworks, or has actually led the way, as in Durban or

Manizales. In Bangalore, by contrast, there has been very limited local initiative in response to the centrally driven climate change agenda. The authors offer several reasons, including the lack of technical capacity, fragmented governance structures and a continued focus on economic growth as the city's main priority.

As noted before, attention to adaptation in some of these cities has been expressed primarily as a response to more general development needs – especially in Rosario, where an evolving adaptation strategy was actually built on its attention to a variety of other local needs, and in Manizales, where adaptation evolved out of its history of responding to disaster and its strong environmental focus. In Bangalore again, although both flooding and environmental degradation have been significant problems, the city has not developed a strategic response. As the authors describe it, climate change "has failed to capture the local government imagination".

For Durban, adaptation grew initially out of an exposure to and interest in the science and its implications on the part of environment sector staff. There is a long history here of interest in climate change within the environmental department and there has been a gradual evolution in both policy and capacity, as links with other sectors were developed, as the institutional base for adaptation was strengthened and as strong support was received from the Mayor. The city's important international role (as in the Durban Charter described earlier) also helped legitimate local attention to climate change adaptation and mitigation. So for Durban, there is evidence of progress on all the benchmarks suggested above. This can be contrasted with both Dar es Salaam and Bangalore where there is no formal institutional arrangement for climate change management in urban areas and where almost all official discussions on adaptation and mitigation are at national level.

In Mexico City, where the climate change policy, both nationally and for the Federal District, is heavily slanted towards mitigation, with ambitious commitments to reducing GHG emissions, the need for attention to adaptation is acknowledged, but this has not led to specific measures to actually address adaptation. While the local climate change strategy and action plan include a diagnosis of vulnerability, this is too superficial to drive concrete action in, for instance, transport, energy, water conservation or even the clarification of who is most at risk. There is little research on climate change impacts and vulnerabilities, and what action there has been on adaptation is mostly on extreme weather events. The National Strategy recognizes, for instance, that 1380 of the country's 2440 municipalities are highly vulnerable to climate change-related disasters, but adaptation is still seen as an environmental issue and much needs to be done to get detailed local analyses and actions.

Bangkok, too, is coming late to an adaptation focus. By 2007, the city had a five-year plan on mitigation. A new master plan aims to expand the focus to include adaptation, with measures to address the huge risks the city faces from flooding, coastal erosion and drought, but this has yet to be approved. Meanwhile there are numerous practical measures in place, as noted, to minimize flood impacts and address coastal erosion.

New York was one of the first cities with a city government (and Mayor) that recognized the importance of adaptation for the city's economy and future success. Early attention to mitigation in the PlaNYC 2030 plan quickly expanded to include adaptation in the face of an extreme precipitation event in August 2007 storms that threatened to incapacitate vital systems. The primary focus has been on the continued functioning of the city's very extensive and critical infrastructure (i.e., roads, subways, communication services, energy, water, and public parks and open space). The creation of an interagency Climate Change Adaptation Task Force in 2008, the convening of the New York City Panel on Climate Change (NPCC), the 2010 Green Codes Task Force Report which included recommendations for building code adjustments for resilience, and a regulatory framework have all contributed to the institutionalization of attention to adaptation during the Bloomberg administration. The de Blasio administration is continuing the legacy of addressing climate change mitigation and adaptation while also introducing a sharper focus on inequities and injustice, a particular concern in the extended aftermath of Hurricane Sandy, and one that is helping to expand the understanding there of the common good.

London was one of the cities at the forefront of climate change research and policy on adaptation and mitigation. The UK Climate Change Act 2008 entails legally binding targets for emissions reductions, and a statutory responsibility for public agencies to adapt to climate change. London has a wide range of climate policies, strategies and measures for adaptation and mitigation in order to meet national targets specified by this 2008 Act and, in addition, an emerging evidence-base regarding the risks of climate change, effective responses, and the level of implementation of such policies.

However, there are still several barriers to effective adaptation including institutional barriers and governance issues (for instance, the lack of specific policies to address over-heating housing); lack of integration with other policies, e.g. needed links between energy efficiency in housing, health and addressing heat stress; and a lack of understanding of climate risks. Although London is reducing its carbon footprint, there have been some mis-steps – most notably in the increased use of diesel in cars, with negative effects for air quality. The population of London is growing after many decades of decline, leading to conflicting demands for land for housing, green space and flood defence measures. More also needs to be done to address higher risk levels across the whole population including those for low-income groups related to low quality housing, poor air quality and lack of green space. London also faces the fact that a large part of its housing stock is old and was not designed to be well insulated against cold, to prevent overheating or to cope with flooding.

Resilience as a framework connecting development, DRR and adaptation

Discussions within cities on responses to climate change have increasingly turned to the term resilience. As discussed in Chapter 2, resilience for any city is the capacity to act, cope with and adapt to climate change as part of the larger context of risk, including non-climate risks, economic shocks and perhaps conflict, as well as the after-shocks from these challenges. Beyond the ability to respond to a specific event or impact, resilience also implies being able to reorganize to reduce risk and exposure to risk, and to "bounce forward" after a shock to greater resilience in relation to these risks.

Considering resilience encourages us to think about all the risks that cities or specific city populations, enterprises or groups face and what makes them resilient to these risks. For most cities, this clearly has strong development components. It also has strong disaster risk reduction components; indeed, one of the central goals of disaster risk reduction is a capacity to build greater resilience. So many different aspects of cities need to be resilient – housing stocks, industries, networked infrastructure and services (transport, communications, electricity, water, waste water) as well as their ecosystems, which need to be protected and managed to deliver a sustained supply of ecosystem services. Several city chapters highlight how so many of these systems are interconnected. For infrastructure networks, resilience means the capacity to withstand external shocks and to have alternative paths of provision while also being designed to recover quickly and cheaply (Vugrin and Turnquist 2012).

Thinking about resilience also encourages us to think about the larger systems within which risks and vulnerabilities are generated. This includes the larger urban area and the wider region. New York, Manizales and Durban, for instance, all look for more resilient water supplies and waste water management by working at spatial scales that include surrounding regions. In London, the boroughs are being guided towards adapting to flood risks through the development of sustainable drainage systems that slow run-off – for instance through green roofs, rain gardens, tree planting, permeable paving and rainwater harvesting, collectively known as green infrastructure.

We are also reminded of the other complexities of large cities and their surrounding regions, with their interdependent social, economic and environmental systems, as well as their roles within national and global systems and supply chains.

The framing of resilience can be pulled away from the four agendas. As Chapter 7 explains, London is increasingly presented in terms of resilience for business, and security for capital and physical assets. Meanwhile, large budget cuts for local governments limit needed responses on housing and urban planning and on flood and heat wave risk management. They also undermine the capacity of health system and that of other social services and thus also undermining their contribution to resilience.

Cities that are resilient to climate change need city governments with the knowledge and capacity to act across the development/DRR/climate change adaptation agendas, genuinely responsive to the common good, and to the priorities and needs of all residents. But in the end, resilience also has to include climate change mitigation – as even the most resilient city cannot protect itself against all disruptions within the global production system and against ever more dangerous climate change.

Climate change mitigation

Mitigation is different from the other three agendas:

- It is not concerned with local risks but with reducing the global risk of dangerous climate change, although this global risk will increase local risks in almost all locations, and there are some co-benefits between mitigation and adaptation.
- It usually falls outside the formal responsibilities of city governments (although this may apply to adaptation too – and it may change).
- In most cities it brings no immediate benefits to the common good of the local populations, and may rather impose unwanted costs or restrict desired activities. For that reason, it may face local opposition in a way that the other three agendas do not. It may also compete with other city or city-region uses for land. However, it should be noted that many measures to improve conditions or reduce health risks also have strong co-benefits with mitigation – including lower air pollution, improved public transport and provision for walking and bicycles, energy conservation and solid-waste management.
- For cities with high greenhouse gas emissions per person, addressing mitigation seriously requires transformative change. The needed reduction in emissions cannot be achieved within a conventional "priority to economic growth" or business as usual agenda. But the need for reduction is so pressing that even cities with relatively low GHG emissions per person need to move towards still lower emissions and lower carbon development. This is especially the case for cities in low- and middle-income nations with rapid economic growth which will join the high greenhouse gas emission/person cities unless they build mitigation into their development.

These case study cities vary considerably in terms of both their GHG emissions and their mitigation efforts. Emissions range from a low of less than half a ton of carbon dioxide equivalent per person each year in Dar es Salaam to 8.5 tons per person in Durban in 2012 – higher than Mexico City (about 3.4 tons in 2012), higher than London (about 4.6 tons in 2011) and New York (about 5.7 tons in 2012), and higher than Bangkok (about 7.1 tons per person in 2007) – see Table 12.2 (p. 228). Not all these cities have formal GHG inventories. In

Bangalore and Dar es Salaam, for instance, the estimates are not from formal inventories, and in Rosario and Manizales there are not even estimates of overall emissions. Most cities are not yet mandated by national policy or international expectations to deliver on this front.

Caution is needed about any comparison between cities' greenhouse gas emissions for at least two reasons. The first relates to differences in the proportion of urban area and rural surrounds within the bounds of the city – as explained in Chapter 1. The second is the differences in the assumptions made and the methodology used – the figure for total emissions may for instance refer to just the emissions generated within city boundaries or may also include emissions from electricity consumed in the city but generated elsewhere. If it is the latter, cities that draw their electricity supply from hydro power will have lower emissions figures than cities that draw from fossil fuel power stations. Do city boundaries include suburbs with a high proportion of their workforce commuting to the central city? There is also the issue of whether emissions from fuel used for international airports or ports should be ascribed to the city where they are located (and the further complication when one or more of a city's international airports are outside its boundaries). Another methodology for assessing a city's greenhouse gas emissions for cities is based on the consumption of its inhabitants and so would include the emissions their consumption generates when they are outside their home city. This produces very different figures – for instance per capita emissions for London from this consumption-based accounting are twice that of the more conventional production-based accounting (Bioregional and London Sustainable Development Commission 2010; see also Seto, Dhakal et al. 2014 for detailed discussions of these issues).

In the case study cities with inventories or estimates, the transport sector is in most cases responsible for the largest share of emissions – almost half in Bangkok, Bangalore and Dar es Salaam; over a third in Mexico City and Durban. In New York City and London, transportation contributes only about one fifth, and the great majority of emissions are from heating, cooling and electrifying buildings (industrial, commercial, service, institutional and residential). But the transport share in both would be higher if the wider urban area was included.

In some of these cities, there has been fairly longstanding attention to mitigation, which in New York, Mexico City, Durban and Bangkok preceded formal work on adaptation. Only New York and London appear to have been successful at this point in lowering emissions in an absolute sense. In London they were reduced by 22 per cent between 2002 and 2011; and in New York by 19 per cent between 2005 and 2012 – although this was mostly from acting on the easy win-wins, as in the shift from oil to natural gas for space heating. In London, there is a commitment that 15 per cent of total energy will be generated by renewable sources by 2020 and that carbon dioxide emissions will be reduced by 60 per cent of their 1990 level by 2025. Mexico City has also succeeded in mitigating considerable amounts (about 5.8 million tons of CO_2e between 2008 and 2012, in great part by reducing the number of vehicles on the road) but

TABLE 12.2 Greenhouse gas emissions from the case study cities

City	*Information source*	*Amount*	*Tons per capita*	*Source by sector*
Bangalore	No official GHG inventory Ramachandra and Aithal (2015) estimated	19.79 million tCO_2e for 2009	2.23 expected to double between 2007–2030	Road transport 44% Domestic 37% Industry 12%
Bangkok		42.65 million tCO_2e	7.1	Transport 49% Electricity 33% Waste 20%
Dar es Salaam	No formal inventory – these are estimates	1.6 million tCO^2e 0.5 tCO_2e per capita	0.36	Transportation 49% Waste 32% Electricity 7%
Durban	GHG inventory 2012	29.36 million tCO_2e in 2012 8.3% increase since 2010 (because of greater rigour)	8.5	Transport 37% Industry 32%
London	GHG inventory 2011	38.99 million tCO_2e	4.6	Industrial/ commercial 42% Residential 36% Transport 22%
Manizales	No inventory	No information available		
Mexico City	GHG inventory 2012	GHG 31 million tCO_2e in 2012 Black carbon 1200 tons in 2012	3.4	Road transport 37% Electricity 31% Transport 97%

New York	GHG inventory 2012	47.9 million tCO2e 2012 Down by 19% since 2005	5.7	Buildings 71% Transportation 20%
Rosario	Insufficient resources to complete a GHG inventory	But they estimate that emission levels are decreasing		By far the highest electricity use is residential – about 85%. Nothing on other fuels

Note: In reporting on the sources of GHG, different cities report in different ways, some including the generation of electricity, but others the uses towards which it is put.

Source: information from case studies.

this amount only neutralized the ongoing increase in emissions, and if indirect emissions are also considered, it did not even manage this. Precise figures on mitigation are unavailable for most cities. Bangkok, for instance, had a five-year action plan to reduce emissions by 15 per cent between 2007 and 2012 by expanding mass transit, promoting more efficient and renewable energy use and improving solid waste management, but it is not clear with what success; nor are the targets for the current action plan formalized.

Work on mitigation, however, is clearly not wholly dependent on either GHG inventories or national or international obligations with regard to mitigation. In Rosario for instance, a number of environmental policies contribute to lowering emissions, and mitigation is becoming part of an evolving public policy, especially practical in the context of disappearing energy subsidies. There are bylaws for instance on energy efficiency and sustainability in construction and the use of solar power in public buildings, there is a 20-year solid waste reduction programme, plans for a new sanitary landfill, programmes to train households in efficient energy use, support for clean and less polluting technologies and for public forestation.

In Manizales, work on mitigation is more a fringe benefit of national and local policies on sustainable environmental management, with the effect of increasing carbon sinks, than it is a specific effort to lower emissions. Considerable work here has gone into reforestation, the protection of environmentally fragile areas, and improving land use through national and regional policies and plans, as well as into local commitment to the environment as expressed in the Biomanizales environmental policy and accompanying plans. But even here, where mitigation is not the priority that adaptation is, there has been a workshop on the city's carbon footprint, an effort to gain consensus among different municipal sectors on strategic actions to control emissions.

The potential local co-benefits of mitigation are highlighted by a study from Bangkok, which estimated the health damage costs from particulate matter (PM) emissions in 2011 to equal USD 2678 million, or 2.4 per cent of the country's GDP that year. A 25 per cent reduction in PM_{10}, on the other hand, was calculated to yield a potential health benefit of USD 1484 million.

Looking for synergies: integrating the four agendas

There has already been a good deal of discussion here about the natural synergies between the first three agendas, and the degree to which both adaptation and disaster risk reduction build on development as well as contributing to it. Adaptation, by the same token, can build on a strong DRR agenda as well as adding another dimension to disaster preparedness. Where these synergies are actively explored and exploited, there is notable progress, as in Durban for instance, where the long-time integration of biodiversity and climate protection concerns has been a productive partnership, and in Manizales, where the coherence between environmental and development concerns, along with a history of disaster preparedness, has laid a strong foundation for adaptation. In Bangalore, by contrast, it appears to be precisely the fragmented governance and lack of institutional coherence that has prevented the kinds of positive synergies that one finds in Durban, Manizales or New York. The extremely rapid and poorly planned growth of the city, the degradation of the local environment, the extent of the water problems, the large disparities in living conditions, added to the threats of a changing climate, call for integrated responses, which have failed to emerge.

If the synergies between these first three agendas are obvious, the potential for integration between adaptation and mitigation is less immediately clear. At a global level, both are clearly essential to preserving and protecting "our common home". But more locally, if mitigation is seen as requiring expensive investments that draw away from the other three agendas, it will face strong opposition. This is less likely to be the case if it is seen as a way to contribute to making "big" sectors such as transport, electricity/energy, water, waste management and infrastructure investments more efficient and resilient.

Given the focus of mitigation on reducing disruption to global systems (often with no immediate local benefits), it is surprising how many city governments have made commitments to reducing greenhouse gas emissions and other mitigation measures – as described in the city chapters for Durban, Bangkok, New York and London. A very tentative conclusion here is that city governments (and often city mayors) that are liked and trusted by their residents, and that do well on other fronts, are able to initiate and support mitigation measures bundled into other work. The chapter on Durban notes that there will be losers in the move to integrate adaptation and mitigation and it will require strong leadership that is prepared to take difficult decisions. Reasonable solutions, as these authors point out, cannot always be "win-win". There will be winners and losers.

Chapter 6 describes various activities already taken in Durban to explore the adaptation–mitigation interface including three large-scale community reforestation projects. These have delivered multiple adaptation co-benefits, including biodiversity enhancement and the improved supply of ecosystem services. The socio-economic co-benefits are particularly important in encouraging and sustaining local climate action. A carbon stock inventory established the contribution of the city's open space system (D'MOSS) to carbon storage and sequestration. A report exploring how Durban could transition to a low carbon future was produced by the Academy of Science of South Africa and confirmed the need to better integrate the city's adaptation and mitigation agendas. Institutional restructuring has also been important to the broader reframing of the climate question in Durban. A decision was taken in 2015 to combine the Energy Office and Environmental Planning and Climate Protection Department. Given the already strong integration of the adaptation and biodiversity agendas, this will connect three global change agendas at the local level: mitigation, adaptation and biodiversity.

Chapter 11 on Rosario notes how the various lines of work – urban planning, social development and health, environmental planning, education and solid waste management, flood prevention and emergency response – have also been integrated, at least in principle, because the city administration recognizes the necessity to do so. Despite ups and downs, there has been significant progress in the policies developed. Now one of the main goals is to develop an institutional umbrella to coordinate all climate-related work across sectors, jurisdictions, stakeholders and government levels. The city government works in increasingly coordinated ways within the metropolitan region and the province. But as the Rosario chapter notes, this demands constant negotiation. Here, there has been little support from national level. Without external funding, mitigation is especially difficult as it lies outside the formal responsibilities of local government. If there is no external funding for this, it will always have to compete with pressing routine needs (and this is an issue also highlighted in the Durban chapter).

Manizales differs from Rosario in having a more supportive national government. Urban plans and actions in Manizales (and in Colombia more generally) look for coherence between disaster risk reduction and climate change adaptation and assume that capacity to adapt to future changes will increase if disaster risk and emergencies are handled well. But the long history of environmental innovation (that includes engaging communities and publicly monitoring environmental performance – see Velasquez 1998) has also helped get attention to mitigation and to the idea of a lower carbon future. The idea of creating an Environmental Secretariat within local government is to ensure administrative support in the future.

As the chapter on Mexico City explains, the need for integration between adaptation and mitigation is recognized by government, but in practical terms the implications of this integration are not acted on. The current CCAPMC has no integration between adaptation and mitigation actions. Official documentation acknowledges the synergies between adaptation and mitigation but it does not explore co-benefits and eventual trade-offs. In Bangkok as well, while adaptation has now been included in the draft master plan on climate change, these are still relatively early days on the adaptation front, and integration between these agendas has yet to be explored.

In New York, the strong focus on adaptation and resilience does seek to take into account GHG emissions reduction to the greatest extent possible. PlaNYC 2030 initially focused on mitigation and later, after the 8 August 2007 extreme precipitation event, expanded to include adaptation measures, including the creation of an interagency Climate Change Adaptation Task Force. The connections between climate change adaptation and mitigation have been present since the issues first emerged on the policy agenda but most often on parallel tracks. But as mitigation and adaptation activities have continued to develop and expand, the links between them are evident in broad policy terms. While some adaptation actions have negative implications for GHG reduction efforts (such as an increase in air conditioning use in response to heightened summer heat stress), the promotion of mitigation and adaptation strategies have followed many of the same development routes. As of 2015, the mitigation and adaptation policies and initiatives of New York City remain largely separate yet connected by a variety of soft linkages, for example both are highlighted as key goals of the de Blasio administration.

For Dar es Salaam, planning and implementation of direct climate change mitigation (and adaptation) still receives very low priority and, to date, there are no significant city level climate change mitigation and adaptation activities. Because institutional arrangements provide no direct links between disaster management and climate change adaptation, there has been little coordination in these areas among the key institutions in Dar es Salaam. The same holds true in Bangalore – the city can hardly achieve integration in areas that currently receive little or no explicit attention at the local level.

We noted earlier the commitment by London to greenhouse gas emission reduction. There is a recognition here of synergies between different agendas – perhaps most especially for health from less air pollution (associated with reduced motor vehicle use and cleaner fuels), more walking and bicycling, and buildings better equipped to maintain thermal comfort and prevent heat stress, although Chapter 7 also notes the lack of integration of these policy agendas.

Moving to transformational adaptation

The final section in this cross-city discussion is on transformative adaptation. As Chapter 2 discussed, this goes beyond climate change adaptation and resilience to consider the system changes needed to produce a more encompassing resilience that includes mitigation to avoid dangerous climate change. This transition has implications for development, for city and national politics, and for international funding. When this kind of transformation becomes the goal, our lens on urban vulnerability and adaptation expands from its local and proximate causes to wider and less easily visible root causes.

The IPCC's 5th Assessment defines transformation as "a change in the fundamental attributes of natural and human systems". When discussing climate change adaptation, it refers to transformational adaptation as "adaptation that changes the fundamental attributes of a system in response to climate and its effects". This is contrasted with "incremental adaptation" which is defined to mean "adaptation actions where the central aim is to maintain the essence and integrity of a system or process at a given scale". Although this language is value free in social terms, it implies attention to the common good, in the sense that it means a move away from the structures and processes that are primarily geared to support economic growth at whatever cost. Drawing again from Chapter 2, the word transformation conveys an occurrence of profound system change, which entails not only structural and behavioural changes but also a realignment of the values and goals espoused by collective and individual actors within a system.

As noted in Table 1.2, transformative adaptation for an urban centre combines the needed adaptation with changes in the urban centre's fundamental attributes – for instance, finding ways to delink prosperity and a high quality of life from high greenhouse gas emissions. For any city to successfully realize Goal 11 of the SDGs ("Make cities and human settlements inclusive, safe, resilient and sustainable") certainly requires transformational change. For most cities, transformational change is needed for each of these individually (i.e. for inclusiveness, safety, resilience and sustainability) as well as in combination.

There are examples of transformational change in cities that fall outside discussions of climate change, yet are highly relevant to this issue. One of the most profound transformations can be seen in many cities in some Latin American nations over recent decades – the transformation in city governments and city governance when mayors and city governments were elected for the first time. In some cities where this happened, it was strongly supported by the decentralization of revenues or powers to raise revenues locally.

This transformation was also present in the relationship between local governments and low-income groups in informal settlements, a change that helps explain how the upgrading of informal settlements became a conventional local government policy response – unlike the bulldozing or the disregard for citizen needs that had previously dominated city politics. Rosario and Manizales, each in its own particular way, have seen transformational change on this front.

The many innovations in Latin American local government have included participatory budgeting, which increased the influence of citizens and civil society organizations in setting priorities within each district of the city, and made the allocation and spending of the government budget more transparent (Cabannes 2004). This process is far from universal in the region's cities and smaller urban centres, and remains a work on progress where it exists. But it is certainly a profound and transformative system change, underpinned by citizen and civil society pressure. It is linked to local politicians and civil servants with commitments to local development, local populations and a different way of doing business that includes learning, leadership and partnership with low-income groups, all with a view to enhancing the common good in its most inclusive sense.

Over a longer time horizon, the changes in city governance in high-income nations can be judged to be transformational, at least in the spheres of development and disaster risk reduction, if we compare the current day to the late 19th century. As noted earlier, the extent to which London and New York are able to address climate change issues is rooted in transformative change in their city governments and governance that started in the late 19th or early 20th centuries.

Most cities and urban centres in low- and middle-income nations need transformational change in the first of the four agendas – human development/

poverty reduction. Changes in their "fundamental attributes" will be needed if they are to deliver on the full range of poverty reduction measures promised in the SDGs (as discussed in Chapter 1). Perhaps the most fundamental change required is in the relationship between local government and low-income groups and their organizations. Recognizing and supporting the agency of these groups may even be seen as a pre-condition for integrating the climate change mitigation and adaptation agendas with the development agenda.

The changes in how disasters are conceived and acted on can also be seen as transformational – and both Rosario and Manizales are examples of cities operating within an understanding of the social construction of disaster ("there is no such thing as a natural disaster")[3] and how much disaster risk can be reduced by interventions.

We can see the beginnings of needed transformation in the many systems that make up functioning cities – for instance in water-use, waste water management, solid waste collection and management, rural–urban linkages, transport and energy. Some of the city chapters point to progress in some of these aspects – for instance in Durban, in the understanding of how to integrate productive and protective ecosystem services into water and land-use management and mitigation. Other chapters point to the need for transformative change – for instance in Mexico City in how water and waste water is managed. One obvious transformative change is in the provision of electricity through a grid that draws on renewable sources.

Transformation is also needed in production, consumption and waste generation. A most challenging transformation is the creation or expansion of a low carbon economic and employment base, in keeping with finite local and global resources and sinks, and consistent with the SDG goal of decent work and adequate remuneration. This includes the necessity to develop buildings and infrastructure with much lower levels of embedded carbon (see Seto, Dhakal et al. 2014). Another much needed but difficult transformation is the management of land-use and land-use changes within a coherent plan for managing transport and infrastructure expansion – to support all four agendas. The case studies of New York, Rosario and Durban show that transformative adaptation calls for rethinking urban planning and land-use management – although what is needed will never prove easy.

The fact that the first three agendas are all focused on local risks means considerable overlap between them. But seeing this clearly can require a much stronger local data base that makes evident the scale, nature, location and detail of local risk and vulnerability, and this is often lacking.

Achieving the political vision at city level for resilience and transformation is critical, and raises numerous questions. What political regimes and what distribution of rights and responsibilities among different actors will deliver transformative adaptation? How can local actors be supported to acquire the knowledge and capacity to become drivers of urban transformation within the context of adaptation? How can we change the way national and city governments see their urban future and their accountability to their citizens? An exclusive focus on economic growth and fantasies of creating "world-class cities" (see Watson 2014; Bhan 2014) will not address development needs or disaster risk reduction or climate change adaptation or mitigation, and however much the public good is invoked in creating these cities, this is not being framed as an inclusive vision.

One way to be able to envisage cities that address the four agendas is to explore the success of some cities in addressing some of them, and to consider the politics that underpinned this success. Rosario, for instance, shows the importance of an accountable, resourced city government, competent in the areas of development and disaster risk reduction, beginning to address climate change adaptation and beginning to consider its contribution to mitigation. Manizales shows how initial commitments to disaster risk reduction and good environmental management provide the basis for advancing on all four agendas. Durban shows us a city where climate change adaptation and mitigation are being taken seriously, along with a global championing of the role of cities in these critical endeavours. In New York, we can see the current mayor's strengthening of measures to benefit low-income groups as part of planning for climate change – an important example of building constructively on the achievements of an earlier administration.

This does not mean that these cities have developed complete "solutions". There are disgruntled residents in New York, whose marginalization was only highlighted following Hurricane Sandy; Durban has a long way to go in realizing basic provision for all its citizens; Manizales and Rosario have yet even to undertake a GHG inventory. More is clearly needed from each and much of this is not easy politically or financially. The chapter on Durban noted the tendency to favour no-risk interventions in adaptation and mitigation with value across a range of climate scenarios, and explained that this tendency can limit consideration of more transformative interventions that involve greater risk and more systemic change. The Durban chapter notes that transformative adaptation pathways will in some instances require actually reducing the resilience of some systems to facilitate a state change, necessitating careful consideration of who or what loses in the move away from the status quo. In the end, transformative adaptation will require strong leadership with the capacity to build local support for needed change and to be prepared to make difficult decisions.

The chapters on New York and London could be taken as examples of (very wealthy) cities that are moving towards transformative adaptation – in their commitments to adaptation and to mitigation. But these cities house very large concentrations of wealthy residents whose carbon footprints need to come down dramatically if dangerous climate change is to be avoided. London and New York are better at reducing greenhouse gas emissions within their boundaries than addressing the greenhouse gas emissions generated by high-consumption lifestyles from among their populations. Both cities are beginning to address this – for instance in the target that 15 per cent of London's total energy will be generated by renewable sources by 2020. In both cities, many measures have been taken that directly or indirectly reduce greenhouse gas emissions. But the measures currently taken (and what seem today to be ambitious targets for GHG reduction) will not be enough.

It is easier to envisage a city that is inclusive, safe, resilient and sustainable than it is to imagine the political changes and the funding sources that can take it there. We can applaud the few cities that have made substantial progress in realizing this expanded vision of the common good. But they need to go a lot further. And how do we make the achievements of these outliers the norm?

Notes

1 The 17th session of the Conference of the Parties (COP17) to the United Nations Framework Convention on Climate Change (UNFCCC) and the 7th session of the Conference of the Parties (CMP7) to the Kyoto Protocol.
2 www.cluva.eu
3 It is difficult to unpick attribution for this. This has been evident in discussions in Latin America for many decades – and elements of this were discussed in the 18th century after disasters (United Nations 2011). One of the earliest references for this is O'Keefe et al. (1976).

References

Bairoch, Paul (1988), *Cities and Economic Development: From the Dawn of History to the Present*, Mansell, London, 574 pages.

Bhan, Gautam (2014), "The real lives of urban fantasies", *Environment and Urbanization*, 26(1), 232–235.

Bioregional and London Sustainable Development Commission (2010), *Capital Consumption: The Transition to Sustainable Consumption and Production in London*, London: Greater London Authority, 76 pages. Available from www.londonsdc.org.uk and www.bioregional.com

Boonyabancha, Somsook and Diane Archer (2011), "Thailand's floods: complex political and geographical factors behind the crisis", www.iied.org/thailands-floods-complex-political-geographical-factors-behind-crisis, IIED, London.

Cabannes, Yves (2004), "Participatory budgeting: a significant contribution to participatory democracy", *Environment and Urbanization*, 16(1), 27–46.

Cartwright, A., J. Blignaut, M. De Wit, K. Goldberg, M. Mander, S. O'Donoghue, and D. Roberts (2013), "Economics of climate change adaptation at the local scale under conditions of uncertainty and resource constraints: the case of Durban, South Africa", *Environment and Urbanization*, 25(1), 139–156.

Cockburn J., M. Rouget, R. Slotow, D. Roberts, R. Boon, E. Douwes, S. O'Donoghue, C. Downs, S. Mukherjee, W. Musakwa, O. Mutanga, T. Mwabvu, J. Odindi, A. Odindo, S. Procheş, S. Ramdhani, J. Ray-Mukherjee, S. Naidoo, C. Schoeman, A. Smit, E. Wale and S. Willows-Munro (in prep), "Implementation of a science-action partnership to manage a threatened ecosystem in an urban context".

Gore, C. and P. Robinson (2009). "Local government response to climate change: our last, best hope", in *Changing Climates in North American Politics: Institutions, Policymaking, and*

Multilevel Governance, eds. Henrik Selin and Stacy D. VanDeveer, Cambridge, MA: MIT Press, 137–158.

Kern, K. and H. Bulkeley (2009), "Cities, Europeanization and multi-level governance: governing climate change through transnational municipal networks". *JCMS: Journal of Common Market Studies*, 47(2), 309–332.

O'Keefe , P., K. Westgate and B. Wisner,(1976), "Taking the naturalness out of natural disaster". *Nature* 260 (15 April): 566–567.

Roberts, D. (2008), "Thinking globally, acting locally – institutionalizing climate change at the local government level in Durban, South Africa", *Environment and Urbanization*, 20(2), 521–537.

Roberts, D. (2010), "Prioritizing climate change adaptation and local level resilience in Durban, South Africa", *Environment and Urbanization*, 22(2), 397–413.

Roberts, D. and S. O'Donoghue (2013), "Urban environmental challenges and climate change action in Durban, South Africa", *Environment and Urbanization*, 25(2), 299–319.

Roberts, D., R. Boon, N. Diederichs, E. Douwes, N. Govender, A. Mcinnes, C. Mclean, S. O'Donoghue, and M. Spires (2012), "Exploring ecosystem-based adaptation in Durban, South Africa: 'learning-by-doing' at the local government coal face", *Environment and Urbanization*, 24(1), 167–195.

Rosenzweig, C., W. Solecki, S. A. Hammer, and S. Mehrotra, (2010) "Cities lead the way in climate-change action". *Nature*, 467(7318), 909–911.

Rutland, T., and A. Aylett (2008), "The work of policy: actor networks, governmentality, and local action on climate change in Portland, Oregon", *Environment and Planning D Society and Space*, 26, 627–646.

Scott, Z. and M. Tarazona (2011), "Decentralization and disaster risk reduction", study on disaster risk reduction, decentralization and political economy analysis for UNDP contribution to the *2011 Global Assessment Report on Disaster Risk Reduction.* Geneva, Switzerland: UNISDR.

Seto, Karen C., S. Dhakal, A. Bigio, H. Blanco, G. C. Delgado, D. Dewar, L. Huang, A. Inaba, A. Kansal, S. Lwasa, J. E. McMahon, D. B. Müller, J. Murakami, H. Nagendra, and A. Ramaswami (2014), "Human Settlements, Infrastructure, and Spatial Planning" in A. Edenhofer, O. R. Pichs-Madruga, Y. Sokona, E. Farahani, S. Kadner, K. Seyboth, A. Adler, I. Baum, S. Brunner, P. Eickemeier, B. Kriemann, J. Savolainen, S. Schlömer, C. von Stechow, T. Zwickel and J. C. Minx (eds), *Climate Change 2014: Mitigation of Climate Change.* Contribution of Working Group III to the Fifth Assessment Report of the Intergovernmental Panel on Climate Change, Cambridge University Press, Cambridge and New York, pages 923–1000.

Solecki, William (2012), "Urban environmental challenges and climate change action in New York City", *Environment and Urbanization* 24(2), pages 557–573.

Toly, N. J. (2008), "Transnational municipal networks in climate politics: from global governance to global politics". *Globalizations*, *5*(3), 341–356.

UCLG: United Cities and Local Governments (2010), *GOLD II: Local Government Finance; The Challenges of the 21st Century*, Cheltenham: Edward Elgar, 374 pages.

United Nations (2009), *Global Assessment Report on Disaster Risk Reduction: Risk and Poverty in a Changing Climate*, ISDR, United Nations, Geneva, 207 pages.

United Nations (2011), *Revealing Risk, Redefining Development: The 2011 Global Assessment Report on Disaster Risk Reduction*, Geneva: United Nations International Strategy for Disaster Reduction, 178 pages.

Velasquez, Luz Stella (1998), "Agenda 21; a form of joint environmental management in Manizales, Colombia", *Environment and Urbanization*, 10(2), 9–36.

Vugrin, Eric D. and Mark A. Turnquist (2012), *Design for Resilience in Infrastructure Distribution Networks*, SANDIA REPORT: SAND2012–6050, Albuqueque, NM: Sandia National Laboratories, 39 pages.

Watson, Vanessa (2014), "African urban fantasies: dreams or nightmares?", *Environment and Urbanization*, 26(1), 215–231.

13

CONCLUSIONS ON WAYS FORWARD

David Satterthwaite, Sheridan Bartlett, Debra Roberts, David Dodman, William Solecki, Alice Sverdlik and Mark Pelling

Introduction

This final chapter discusses what is needed to realize the four agendas within each urban centre, and collectively for the planet. These are not conclusions directly related to the case study cities. What we can learn from the experience of these cities was the focus of Chapter 12. This chapter could be read as a discussion of what more might still be done – approaches that would help Rosario and Manizales develop a mitigation strategy that does not detract from their attention to the other three agendas; that would support Durban's leadership on biodiversity and poverty reduction within a lower-carbon economy; or encourage New York to go beyond what it has already achieved, especially in mitigation; or help London return to being a global leader on the integration of adaptation, mitigation and development. These approaches could also galvanize Bangalore to address the local, regional and global implications of its growth-oriented development path, and Dar es Salaam its massive deficit in basic infrastructure; they would direct more attention to those most at risk and most vulnerable in Bangkok and Mexico City, and encourage both to act on their emerging adaptation policies.

Governments from all over the world, including those from the countries where the case study cities are located, have committed to long lists of goals as members of the United Nations. If fulfilled, these goals would eliminate poverty and avoid dangerous climate change. They would dramatically reduce the occurrence and impacts of disasters and the unsustainable draw on planetary resources. Many of these goals are included in the new, comprehensive and very ambitious Sustainable Development Goals (SDGs) endorsed by over 190 governments in September 2015. This is supported by the new Sendai framework for disaster risk reduction. In October 2016, we are to get a "new urban agenda" agreed by national governments through which to fulfil the urban components of all of these commitments. And as we send this book to publication, there is the hope that in December 2015, a much needed global agreement on climate change migitation will be reached at the Conference of Parties to the UN Framework Convention on Climate Change (COP21). But will all these commitments actually spur governments into action? Will the policies and practices of international agencies change to support this? Who has to act in each locality to fulfill the commitments and are they committed to doing so? Do they have the resources and capacities to act? What else is needed? How is progress to be monitored in each locality? These are the questions this chapter seeks to address.

Now that we have a more substantial literature on urban adaptation and mitigation, how do we get the necessary attention to climate change on the part of all those who influence urban development? This includes attention to where urban development takes place, its form and spatial structure, provision for housing, infrastructure and services, management and incentives, and regulations and connections to the wider region. Those who influence urban development include government officials and politicians at all levels, from national down to local wards, but also residents and workers, civil society in all its diversity, the private sector from street vendors to multinational corporations. What needs to be done to make sure these actors contribute to (or at least align with) the commitments?

Part of the answer is that we badly need a shift in the global discourse towards a better understanding of the importance of local action and local institutions. There are signs of hope here. As noted earlier, the IPCC's Fifth Assessment coverage of adaptation and mitigation in urban centres was more substantial than in previous Assessments. A much expanded literature on these topics since 2006 made this possible. There is also a rich literature on household and community adaptation in urban contexts and its constraints and limitations, as well as on what city or municipal governments are doing in response to climate change. There is a vast literature now on resilience as it applies to cities, and a growing literature on urban disaster risk reduction and the need to integrate this with development and with climate change adaptation. It is also more common now to see mayors or ex-mayors speak at international conferences on climate change and disaster risk reduction and development – not to mention a "Compact of Mayors" for addressing these issues collectively.[1] The strong inclusion of urban issues in the Technical Examination Process of the UNFCCC also suggests a growing awareness of cities as key to the global climate change agenda.

The UN Secretary General set up a high-level panel of "Eminent Persons" to advise him on the Post-2015 Development Agenda. Unlike most high-level documents on development, the report of this panel gave serious attention to urban areas and local governments. It states that: "The post-2015 agenda must be relevant for urban dwellers. Cities are where the battle for sustainable development will be won or lost" (United Nations 2013, page 17). As described in Chapter 1, the SDGs include strong commitments to our four agendas: addressing almost all aspects of poverty reduction, disaster risk reduction, climate change adaptation and climate change mitigation. But these commitments need to be integrated in ways that maximize the positive overlaps and minimize the conflicts – as illustrated in Figure 13.1. This too is recognized by the SDGs: "By 2020, substantially increase the number of cities and human settlements adopting and implementing integrated policies and plans towards inclusion, resource efficiency, mitigation and adaptation to climate change, resilience to disasters, and develop and implement, in line with Sendai Framework for Disaster Risk Reduction 2015–2030, holistic disaster risk management at all levels" (United Nations 2015a, paragraph 11b). There is also what is termed the "city goal" in the SDGs – Make cities and human settlements inclusive, safe, resilient and sustainable (Goal 11). A large network of institutions (including the Sustainable Development Solutions Network SDSN, United Cities and Local Governments UCLG, C40 and ICLEI – Local Governments for Sustainability) worked hard to get this city goal included and then to keep it from being dropped.[2] The SDGs also state that "We look forward to the upcoming United Nations Conference on Housing and Sustainable Urban Development in Quito, Ecuador" (ibid., paragraph 34); also known as Habitat III, this is where a "new urban agenda" is to be agreed upon.

At the same time, a growing number of researchers and research institutions with competence on urban issues and on climate change issues are choosing to work and publish together through different types of networks. Local governments are also mobilizing through transnational networks (like the Local Government Climate Roadmap) to influence global climate debates and to ensure they are ready for action if a global deal is struck in Paris at COP21 in December 2015.

This growing network, along with the huge growth in literature and the critical supporting context of the SDGs, raises the hope that we might in fact be seeing a fundamental or even transformative change in global discussions. What might this change involve? It would recognize, to start with, the need for more space and support for urban local governments. It would mean national and provincial governments acknowledging that their achievements in meeting global goals and targets are mostly the aggregation of local achievements. The success of many national government policies and initiatives would be acknowledged to depend on the competence and capacity of local governments. Global goals and targets in an urbanizing world would be seen to depend on city and municipal government support. Innovative cities would be viewed as tangible evidence that the most pressing global concerns can be combined with good local development/poverty reduction. The four agendas would be developed with the full engagement of citizens and local civil society. Urban governments would have the legitimacy to represent their citizens in global discussions and commitments. Local governments would commit to the implementation of the SDGs and also monitor and report on their progress. Reports on progress would be discussed in each neighbourhood and city.

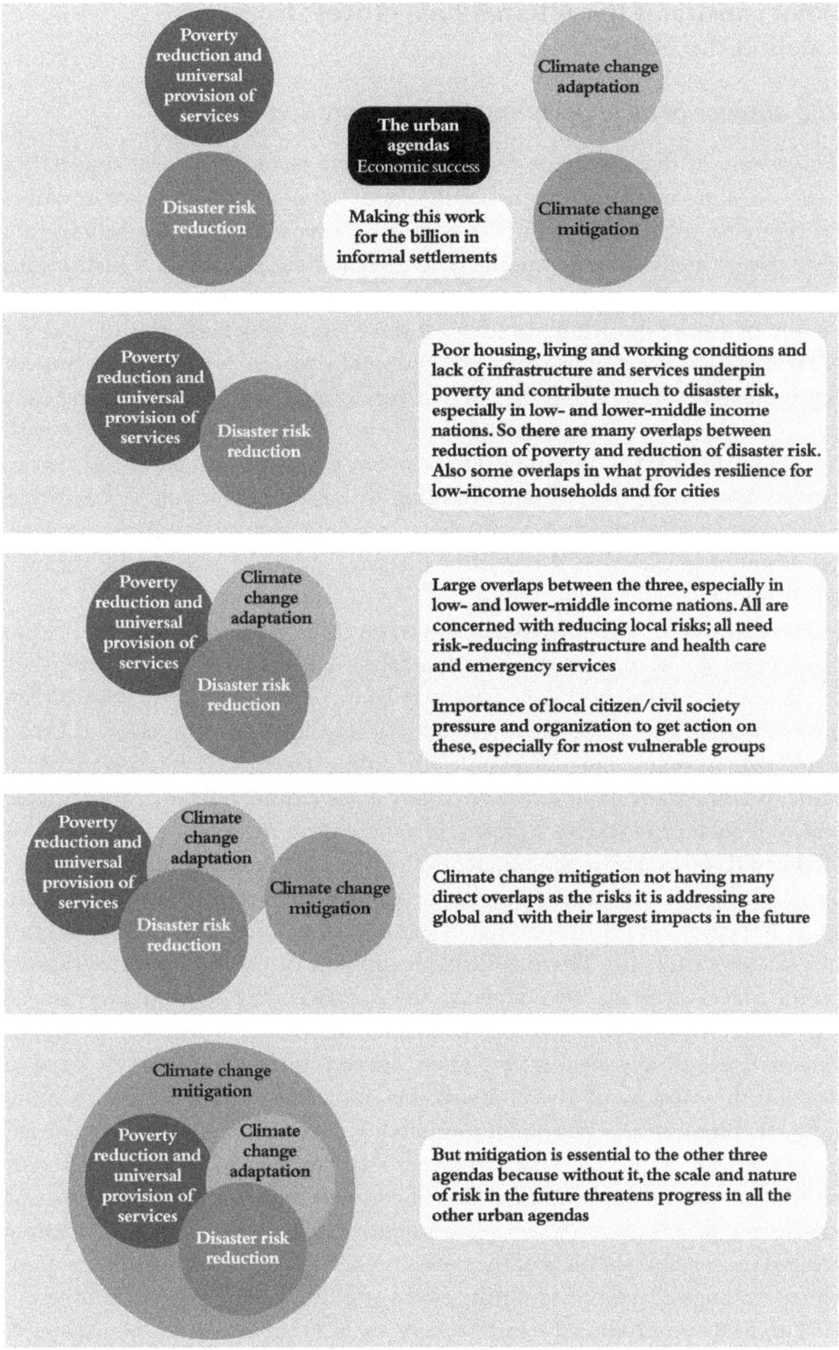

Poverty reduction and universal provision of services
The urban agendas
Economic success
Climate change adaptation
Disaster risk reduction
Making this work for the billion in informal settlements
Climate change mitigation
Poverty reduction and universal provision of services
Disaster risk reduction
Poor housing, living and working conditions and lack of infrastructure and services underpin poverty and contribute much to disaster risk, especially in low- and lower-middle income nations. So there are many overlaps between reduction of poverty and reduction of disaster risk. Also some overlaps in what provides resilience for low-income households and for cities
Poverty reduction and universal provision of services
Climate change adaptation
Disaster risk reduction
Large overlaps between the three, especially in low- and lower-middle income nations. All are concerned with reducing local risks; all need risk-reducing infrastructure and health care and emergency services
Importance of local citizen/civil society pressure and organization to get action on these, especially for most vulnerable groups
Poverty reduction and universal provision of services
Climate change adaptation
Climate change mitigation
Disaster risk reduction
Climate change mitigation not having many direct overlaps as the risks it is addressing are global and with their largest impacts in the future
Climate change mitigation
Poverty reduction and universal provision of services
Climate change adaptation
Disaster risk reduction
But mitigation is essential to the other three agendas because without it, the scale and nature of risk in the future threatens progress in all the other urban agendas

FIGURE 13.1 The four urban agendas and their overlaps

What constrains this international process from meeting the SDGs

The absence of local government representation

This vision of the possibility for transformative change has great appeal, but there are long-established constraints. National government representatives currently represent their countries within UN processes and institutions, not local governments. They form the governing bodies of many UN institutions – including multilateral development banks and UN-Habitat. They are the people that have drafted and redrafted the SDGs, which say so much about what should be done and so little on how and by whom. National government representatives are drafting "the new urban agenda" for Habitat III, and they compose the Inter-Governmental Panel on Climate Change and view with horror any draft IPCC text judged to be policy prescriptive. Almost all national governments want international funding to local governments to be within their control and to go through their accounts, especially when the local government in question is not from the same political party as the national government.

In Chapter 1, we discussed the relevance of the SDGs for urban challenges. We need to clarify here that, although the goals are relevant, they too are unaccompanied by an acknowledgement of the roles of local urban governments. The SDGs pay more attention to local government and urban issues than most previous discussions (including the MDGs), but this attention remains comparatively minimal. So many goals require effective, accountable and well-financed local institutions, but there is no mention of these. Almost all the SDGs that deal with human development and poverty reduction are set as national goals and targets, despite the fact the actions needed to meet these goals and targets in urban areas fall in so many cases within the responsibilities of local governments. There is little recognition of just how much progress on the SDGs in urban areas depends on the relationship of local government with local civil society. There is considerable discussion of finance, but not of finance for these key local actors. There are recommendations on the need to develop the capacity of governments, but for national plans. Accountability is briefly mentioned – but not accountability to those who lack the promised basic services. Many national targets also fail to elaborate on the different targets that should apply in the different contexts of urban and rural areas (for instance in provision for water and sanitation). City or sub-city governments are also responsible for most of the measures needed for disaster risk reduction, climate change adaptation and mitigation, and this too is hardly mentioned.

The SDGs' introductory text recognizes local governments in paragraph 34: "We recognize that sustainable urban development and management are crucial to the quality of life of our people. We will work with local authorities and communities to renew and plan our cities and human settlements so as to foster community cohesion and personal security and to stimulate innovation and employment." But there are no goals and targets in place to ensure that this cooperation is addressed.

Paragraph 45 states that "Governments and public institutions will also work closely on implementation with regional and local authorities, sub-regional institutions, international institutions, academia, philanthropic organisations, volunteer groups and others." By implication, regional and local authorities are relegated to the list of implementing "stakeholders" rather than being included in "governments and public institutions".

We are faced with the fact that it will fall to urban governments, municipal, city and metropolitan, to plan and manage much of the adaptation to climate change and much of the mitigation, along with the necessary integration with disaster risk reduction and poverty reduction, including the universal provision of basic services. Urban governments do not have to implement and fund all of this but they do have to provide the framework – the regulations, incentives, management and monitoring of coverage and quality – that supports relevant investments. If the planning and land use management framework is right, new residential areas and new investments can align better with adaptation and mitigation. It can help keep down the costs of land for housing, provide legal alternatives to informal settlements for low-income households, avoid low-density urban sprawl with its high infrastructure costs and dependence on private automobile use, expand and enhance public spaces, and protect and enhance critical ecosystem services. But the sheer number of cities where none of this is taking place points to the scale of change that is needed.

How do we ensure that global SDG goals and targets are translated into national government frameworks that support local action? Discussions of "good governance" focus on the national level, when it is local governance failures that account for so much disaster risk and vulnerability to climate change. And in post-disaster actions, national governments typically fail to understand the political, institutional and regulatory roadblocks that urban authorities can put in the way of effective relief and rebuilding. Perhaps in many countries, national governments feel threatened by the economic importance and power of their more successful cities (and their global connections).

The incapacity to support locally driven agendas

Then there is the incapacity of most official aid agencies, development banks and international NGOs to support locally driven agendas – something they were not set up to do. It is difficult for them to imagine a funding architecture that could support locally driven change and an increase in local capacity to plan and act in hundreds or thousands of locations. As Debra Roberts of the Durban chapter team commented, climate change is not something local government can fix like a broken pipe. It needs a constant capacity within each local government to learn, to know and to act.

In July 2015, the Third International Conference on Financing for Development produced the Addis Ababa Action Agenda, focused on financing the fulfilment of the SDGs (United Nations 2015b). This endorses the SDGs and their ambitious commitments, and acknowledges that "… expenditures and investments in sustainable development are being devolved to the subnational level, which often lacks adequate technical and technological capacity, financing and support" (paragraph 34). It makes a commitment to scaling up international cooperation to strengthen the capacities of local authorities to implement resilient and environmentally sound infrastructure "...including energy, transport, water and sanitation, and sustainable and resilient buildings" (paragraph 34) and to mobilize the appropriate revenues. This could be seen as a fine introduction to the specific measures needed to make this happen – but there is none of this. The document mentions work to strengthen debt management, and (where appropriate) "…to establish or strengthen municipal bond markets, to help subnational authorities to finance necessary investments" (paragraph 34). It also seeks to promote lending from financial institutions and development banks. But this does not amount to an action plan for delivering the finance needed to support local action. The Agenda gives us 61 pages on the importance of finance with no discussion of the changes needed to deliver it (United Nations 2015b). Will the Habitat III conference in October 2016 go beyond repeating SDG commitments and work on an international funding architecture that supports local actions to address the goals?

There are two revealing tests that gauge the interest of national governments and international agencies in urban areas. The first is to search reports on disaster risk reduction or climate change adaptation for the words "city" or "urban" – these words frequently do not even show up. The second is to search for references to "local", to see whether the roles and responsibilities of city and municipal governments are mentioned – and again, this reveals little or no discussion. The Sendai Framework demonstrates that national parties are finding it a challenge to raise the profiles of city and local actors – or perhaps they are just unwilling to do so. The framework is clear about the need to tackle disaster risk as a development concern, and is strong on the role of data and evidence as well as technology for shaping policy, but it has not managed to reposition urban and local actors at the forefront of action (Pearson and Pelling 2015). There is a policy for urban disaster risk management and reduction by donors, civil society or government, but it tends to be narrowly conceived and presented as an issue of local land use planning or enhanced infrastructure management. These are critical concerns but they are not sufficient to address the root causes of urban risk, which often lie in broader governance processes that take place at the local scale – for example, the exclusion of low-income groups from official (and often informal) land markets and from access to risk-reducing infrastructure. They also lie in an urban development model that values built capital over natural capital.

If the SGD goals are acted on by all the national governments that have endorsed them, the world will quickly become a much safer, healthier, more inclusive and resilient place. But national governments have been making and breaking these commitments for decades – there are examples of this in Box 13.1.

Box 13.1 The failure to meet the commitments of Habitat 1

At the first UN Conference on Human Settlements (Habitat) in 1976, all government delegations made commitments that most failed to act on. "Safe water supply and hygienic waste disposal should receive priority with a view to achieving measurable qualitative and quantitative targets serving all the population by a certain date" (Recommendation C12). The UN Water Conference in 1977 recommended that 1981–1990 be designated the "International Water Supply and Sanitation Decade" and that national plans should aim to provide safe drinking water and basic sanitation to all by 1990 if possible. But by 1990, 32 per cent of the urban population in low- and middle-income nations and 89 per cent of their rural population lacked water piped to premises. In this same year, 31 per cent of their urban population and 71 per cent of their rural population lacked basic sanitation. By 2015, the percentage of the urban population lacking water piped on premises in low- and middle-income nations had not fallen much. It was 28 per cent in 2015 compared with 32 per cent in 1990. And in many nations, the percentage of the urban population with water piped to premises was actually lower in 2015 than it had been in 1990. So what happened to the 1976 and 1977 commitments? Why didn't these commitments make national government more responsive to provision for water and sanitation? Why didn't aid agencies and development banks respond to these commitments (most did not increase the funding for water and sanitation and some reduced it)? Habitat I's Recommendations for National Action also included many other commitments that most governments failed to act on – including the provision of health, nutrition, education, security, recreation and other essential services (Recommendation C15), the recapture by public bodies of the unearned increment in land values (Recommendation D3) and government policies that "concentrate on the provision of services and on the physical and spatial reorganization of spontaneous settlements in ways that encourage community initiative and link 'marginal' groups to the national development process" (Recommendation C17).

Source: Hardoy and Satterthwaite 1981; UNICEF and WHO 2015. The full text of the Recommendations for National Action that came out of the 1976 UN Conference on Human Settlements can be read at http://habitat.igc.org/vancouver/vp-intr.htm.

The priority given to economic growth

A final constraint on getting action on the four agendas is the drive by many city governments to prioritize economic growth above all, along with the infrastructure to support it. Many city governments have ambitious plans to become "world cities", plans that often defy all four agendas. These cities often claim to be "eco" cities, although it is difficult to see how they will actually contribute to lowering greenhouse gas emissions. They include many of sub-Saharan Africa's larger cities, which are being "revisioned" in the image of cities such as Dubai, Shanghai and Singapore, despite the fact that most of their populations live in deep poverty with minimal urban services (Watson 2014). The most likely outcome of these plans is a steady worsening of the marginalization and inequalities that already beset these cities. As noted by Bhan (2014), these plans seem in part to be a yearning by elites for a controlled and orderly city, free of the messiness of democratic politics and guided by authoritarian city states. If these visions are implemented, they would further disconnect city plans from the actual citizens of the cities they seek to reshape.

The SDGs are also full of promises and commitments about decent work, adequate incomes and universal provision for safety nets – for instance, "We resolve also to create conditions for sustainable, inclusive and sustained economic growth, shared prosperity and decent work for all." Target 8.5 frames this in explicit terms: "By 2030, achieve full and productive employment and decent work for all women and men, including for young people and persons with disabilities, and equal pay for work of equal value." There is no disagreement with the goal, but how will this be achieved and by whom?

Similarly, while the SDGs indicate the need for sustainable development, they do not acknowledge that this is a time of global environmental crisis when the planetary boundaries of key earth systems are being exceeded (Steffen et al. 2015). The recognition that you cannot have infinite growth in a finite world must be accompanied by the realization that negotiating the tough trade-offs that will allow us to return to a low risk and resilient development path will take place, in many cases, during the day-to-day decision making of local governments and the citizens of the world's cities. As the centres of global consumption, production and waste generation, cities lie at the heart of the transition to the Anthropocene (the geological period during which human activity has been the dominant influence on climate and other environmental systems). The potential for a "good" Anthropocene also lies in cities. We need, with their cooperation, to shrink the global urban ecological footprint to make more room for nature and for the poor and vulnerable members of society who are directly dependent on natural ecosystems for their survival.

Addressing global goals through local action

National governments may still consider their departments and agencies to have the central role in disaster risk reduction (especially regarding the big infrastructure) and in post-disaster response. When they are taking action on the climate change front, they also consider that adaptation and mitigation fall within their jurisdiction. But disaster risk reduction in urban areas has always been most successful where local governments have the knowledge and capacities to understand and act on local disaster risks, and where they are accountable to those most at risk, thus ensuring that risk reduction measures serve them (Johnson and Blackburn 2014).

Our focus on the importance of local action and locally driven agendas is not an attempt to deny the role and importance of national governments. The key role of national governments is to provide the framework of legislation, the funding and support for local capacities and institutions capable of responding to disaster risk, with the links to meeting everyday needs, and, increasingly, the likely changes in risk from climate change. National governments are of course also critical in responding rapidly and effectively when natural hazards overwhelm local capacities. But development, disaster risk reduction, post-disaster response and climate change adaptation, historically tackled in isolation, need to be brought into coherence with one another around local concerns, and only local governments can provide this coherence.

How can we make progress across the vast and diverse set of cities and smaller urban centres in all four agendas in ways that are rooted in the needs, priorities and capacities of each urban centre and its population? More importantly, how does local government acquire the capacity to address these issues? It requires a permanent capacity to get all sectors in local government to learn and to act together and to engage citizens and civil society and all other stakeholders, with local contributions proposed and discussed. This has to be rooted in *local* democracy, good local governance and the rule of law (the SDGs include this as a recommendation but without the word local). It needs to recognize and support the potential in each locality for change towards meeting the four agendas. Scale is achieved by the multiplication of local (small and large) initiatives, not by ever-larger single top-down initiatives.

There is also a powerful force that unites the four agendas – all are acting to reduce risk to life, health, livelihoods and assets. This point has been made repeatedly in this book, but it cannot be stressed enough that it is key to our efforts here. Three of these agendas act to reduce these local risks; although they see these risks through different lenses. The very fact that their focus is local risks, affecting local populations, brings them into local political discussions. Of course there are locally specific trade-offs between different risks, the different groups exposed, the different time scales, but these complexities should be discussed and resolved within local jurisdictions. City-region issues will have to be addressed and these too need discussion and resolution within the region.

All four agendas include as a priority attention to vulnerable populations and reducing or removing the risks they face. There are also many overlaps here across the four agendas. For instance, for those living in poor quality housing with no sanitation in flood-prone areas, reducing disaster risks and increasing resilience to climate change impacts must of necessity also mean dealing with the deficiencies in provision for sanitation. Addressing their needs can also be done in ways that reduce greenhouse gas emissions and that protect and enhance the remaining natural ecosystems in and around the world's cities. In fact, many of the everyday decisions and practices of city governments can contribute to reducing greenhouse gas emissions (Box 13.2).

Box 13.2 Measures city governments can take that can reduce greenhouse gas emissions

Cross-sectoral

- In land use planning and management – more compact cities or city clusters, well served by public transport in peripheral and existing low density areas. Through this, avoidance of low density private-automobile dependent sprawl;
- Provision and expansion of green spaces (including planting of trees) that may be integrated with protection of eco-system services/watershed management;
- Green procurement policies;
- Environmental education and awareness programmes to encourage behavioural change in line with the measures listed here;
- Air pollution control that is associated with lower GHG emissions – for instance as industries switch to cleaner fuels to meet regulations, and through the reduction in emissions of black carbon particles;
- Reducing energy use in water provision and the waste water treatment and disposal (in many cities, this is very energy intensive).

Buildings

- Building standards and regulatory frameworks requiring high energy efficiency and encouragement for tapping renewable energy (e.g. building orientation, appropriate wall-to-window ratios, high albedo, rooftop solar PV);
- Support for building retrofits to reduce energy use for heating and cooling (e.g. insulation, double glazing, ventilation) and demonstration of this within government buildings;
- Support for fuel switching for space heating (coal and fuel oils to LPG);
- District heating and cooling systems;
- More efficient appliances and lighting.

continued ...

Box 13.2 continued

Industry

- Substantial efficiency opportunities usually available from industry-specific actions, e.g. improved maintenance, more efficient furnaces and boilers.

Transport

- Improved public transport (e.g. safety, reliability, frequency) and expanded public transport network;
- Fuel switching of public transport (e.g. deployment of hybrid or hydrogen buses);
- Encouragement for a high proportion of daily trips to be made on foot or bicycle, through adequate provision for cyclists and for pedestrians;
- Disincentives or regulations to cut private car use (parking demand management, licence plate permit days, congestion pricing);
- Incentives or regulations to support private and commercial vehicle efficiency and fuel switching (e.g. subsidies for hybrid/electric vehicles, introduction of European carbon emission standards).

Energy-efficient street lighting

- Solid waste management, including support for waste reduction, waste recycling and composting, and the management of waste dumps (e.g. methane capture/use); energy-from-waste (combined heat and power or electricity generation);
- Electricity generation (often outside municipal authority control, with notable exceptions, e.g. Germany and South Africa);
- Electricity supply drawing more on renewables or lower emission fuels (e.g. gas for coal); power plant retrofit; encouragement for customers to reduce use and integrate solar PV into their electricity supply.

What is more difficult than identifying effective measures is assessing and ranking priorities. In some cities, the demands of those most at risk have been well served by elected mayors and other local politicians or civil servants who have supported this four-fold agenda. Here, a focus on addressing these most pressing local risks can now be integrated with measures that help reduce local risks in the future (adaptation and disaster risk reduction) and global risks (mitigation). If we look only at a few innovative cities, all of this makes sense and appears to be do-able. But the daily reality of governance in most cities and smaller urban centres can make it seem totally unrealistic.

It is easy to say that all local government sectors and departments need to work together, but this is very difficult in practice. Every local government reflects complex local histories with vested interests that often have too much power and too little accountability. It is easy (and correct) to say that each local government needs to manage changes in land use, ensure sufficient supplies of land for housing and for public space, protect ecosystem services and manage urban expansion in ways that contribute to all four agendas – but much harder to say how this can be achieved in the face of powerful real estate interests (see Hasan 2015). We need strong local representative democracies where every inhabitant has an elected politician to whom they can turn if needed, as well as ready access to information and data to promote informed and evidence-based decision-making.

There are good examples of city and municipal governments driving positive change – but given the range of need and existing obligation, most of them look with horror at new obligations to address climate change adaptation and mitigation. Most can claim, with good reason, that they lack the funding, resources, knowledge and capacities to take this on, on top of addressing poverty reduction and disaster risk reduction. They can also point out that these are not within their defined responsibilities.

Who can help drive the change? The role of civil society

As the London chapter highlights, popular opinion in high-income nations has yet to identify climate change adaptation or mitigation as a priority when set against worries about employment, public health priorities, health care demands or crime. Implementing the four agendas can bring new employment opportunities, lower risks and better health. Building a green economy that includes greenhouse gas emission reduction will provide new employment opportunities; so too will addressing the SDGs and building resilience to disaster risk and climate change. But the means by which they can do so needs attention.

We have many examples of innovation in cities that are moving in the right direction in regard to some or all of the four agendas. What would it take to make these kinds of practices the norm rather than the outliers?

Some suggest that international civil society will drive the needed change – the connected planet, global campaigns, crowd-source funding, global social movements, big data. But if we accept that constructive action usually has to be locally rooted, serving, involving and getting support from local citizens and their organizations, this suggests a different route, grounded in each locality. Participatory budgeting, for instance, cannot be done globally or even nationally; it is all about local discussions with a range of very local stakeholders about the generation and use of local resources in their locality. Drivers of local change, including individuals and local civil society, become essential. So too do local politicians and civil servants that can and do work with them. They so often work below the radar of the international agencies and national governments. These agents of change are usually profoundly local – about very particular local needs and priorities, using available (public) resources to address or protect local interests.

We often underestimate the extent to which community action can generate local benefits and reconcile the different agendas, often joining together across neighbourhoods to negotiate with local government (Boonyabancha and Mitlin 2012; Boonyabancha, Carcellar and Kerr 2012; ACHR 2015; Simon 2014). These groups often tend to include those who face the greatest risks and who are particularly vulnerable. As we have noted, they need to be engaged not only because they are "at risk" but also because they can bring knowledge, capacity and innovation to adaptation and mitigation.

This local involvement is also critical around issues of accountability. Many local governments are hardly icons of accountability and transparency. The massive development deficits so evident in most cities in low- and middle-income nations cannot be blamed only on the lack of funding and of support from higher levels of government. Much of it is rooted in local decisions not to address needs in informal settlements and also in corrupt practices. Unaccountable local governments need to be pushed, and it falls to local civil society to do this – to community organizations, local NGOs and perhaps academics. Involved citizens are also important for opposing inappropriate initiatives – especially relocation projects that force them to move to peripheral locations or to housing units that fail to serve their needs, even as these are justified by their apparent contribution to risk reduction and climate change adaptation.

If we recognize that grassroots organizations and the civil society groups that support them are key drivers of change, we also need to consider the forms of external support that can serve them. Here we are faced with the gap between what international funders can do and what is needed on the ground in tens of thousands of localities. It is very difficult for an international funder to assess which local initiatives deserve support and which local partners can implement change well. There are two strong and well-established international funds that show another way: the Urban Poor Fund International (UPFI) and the Asian Coalition for Community Action. Both channel funding directly to community organizations, to support them in addressing their priorities. Both do so on a considerable scale. Neither is doing so for climate change – although many of the initiatives they fund reduce risks from extreme weather events. But what we have is a demonstration that it is possible to get funding down to grassroots organizations. These two international funds also support grassroots organizations to come together, to work with each other and to try to work with local governments (see Satterthwaite and Mitlin 2014).

But it is also important not to overstate the role of community organizations, which are limited in what they can do in the absence of adequate government support. Communities have shown their capacities to contribute – as they build bridges across drainage canals, make schools safer, improve drainage systems, collect solid wastes, map risks and vulnerabilities, and increase local awareness of evacuation procedures. But they cannot design and build the large-scale citywide infrastructure that is essential to resilience in the face of storms and heavy rainfall. They cannot ensure constructive land use and land management for expanding cities, so that new developments avoid dangerous sites and are served with infrastructure; nor can they put into place the building codes that help ensure buildings can withstand extreme weather or, where needed, earthquakes.

Partnerships with local governments

One of the most important yet difficult issues is how local authorities engage with civil society – especially those groups representing low-income urban dwellers who live in informal settlements and work in the informal economy. These are often seen by local and national governments as illegal and detrimental to urban development. Some of the most interesting, innovative and cost-effective responses to local risks in urban areas have come from partnerships between local government and civil society organizations (Anguelovski et al. 2014; Chu et al. 2015). The scale and scope of what community organizations can do increases considerably when they are supported by local authorities. This works in the other direction too.

But partnerships need partners who want to work together and to learn from each other. Often, local governments view their community organization partners only as implementers. They should, rather, recognize and support these organizations to influence what is prioritized and how priorities are addressed. In most cases, these partnerships depend on the initiative of grassroots organizations and their networks or federations, which demonstrate to local government their capacities and their willingness to work together. Ideally, senior civil servants or politicians then respond positively. Most such partnerships are not focused on climate change adaptation or disaster risk reduction but on development needs – although the development needs often coincide with disaster risk reduction and resilience to extreme weather. They also include many examples of the co-production of knowledge – for instance through the enumerations and mapping of informal settlements undertaken by their residents and supporting community organizations and federations (see the next section on local data for more details).

When there is a local university or technical college with competence to provide technical support on climate change issues, that is an added advantage (Molnar et al. 2010). Science also has a role to play in this emerging agenda – or really three roles. It is not only an originator of ideas and information; it also offers a convening space, providing legitimacy and a degree of neutrality for new conversations among urban actors about these ideas and information, and scope for influence based on evidence; but also, science can be used to hold these actors to account, through monitoring and evaluation, and independent assessments of progress made. A network of local, independent actors and academic institutions has a role to play here, which can be augmented by new data collection tools including those from social media.

Local data

As we move to a far greater engagement with adaptation and mitigation in each urban centre, within a commitment to meeting development and disaster risk reduction needs, so the key importance of changes in urban planning, management and governance becomes obvious. There is a pressing need to build knowledge, capacity and learning in each urban centre and to generate the local data needed to support this.

But how can relevant local data be generated? At present, most data gathered on development issues (including progress on the SDGs) are through national sample surveys. These are no use to local governments as their sample size is too small to produce statistics for each urban centre (let alone for each ward or neighbourhood). Censuses should be able to do this, but at best they happen every ten years and census authorities often fail to provide the data to local governments in a form that is useful for them to address needs (for example, which streets and wards do not have water piped to homes, toilets connected to sewers, all-weather roads).

Where local democracy works well, democratic processes can fill some of the data gaps. Local governments can find out about the need for water, sanitation, drainage and health care through the demands of those with inadequate provision. This can be supported by such democratic mechanisms as participatory budgeting where the needs for funds are defined, prioritized and acted on by representatives elected in each district of a city, where all details of local government revenues and expenditures are made public (see Cabannes 2004, 2015). This process becomes particularly powerful when local governments work with grassroots organizations and federations formed by residents of informal settlements (Appadurai 2001; ACHR 2015).

The current response to the lack of data on many of the SDGs is a recommendation for heavy investment in more data gathering by national governments and international agencies. But this fails to address the data needs of the local governments who are responsible for meeting these goals, and the civil society organizations that are ideally their partners. What we need is far more attention to recording the needs and priorities of those facing deprivations in each locality, in ways that are accountable to them. We have rich experience to draw on – the surveys, maps and enumerations of informal settlements done by their residents with support from federations of slum or shack dwellers in over 200 cities (Patel, Baptist and d'Cruz 2012; Makau, Dobson and Samia 2012; Butcher and Frediani 2014, Livengood and Kunte 2012, Chitekwe-Biti et al. 2002; Muller and Mbanga 2012). Although these focus on development needs, they also provide valuable information on risks and vulnerabilities for each informal settlement. For instance, the documentation and mapping of over 300 informal settlements in the city of Cuttack included the mapping and documentation of flood risk, flood impact and household responses (Livengood and Kunte 2012). These city-wide surveys of informal settlements also make clear the differences in needs and priorities.

There are many cities where local governments, NGOs or research groups have created detailed databases and maps of risk by reviewing all recorded events where people were killed or injured or houses destroyed or damaged, sometimes integrating into these data from local hospitals and emergency services (see United Nations 2009, 2011, 2015c). Other initiatives bring together all data sources within a locality from the different sectors of local government and from utilities (see Navarro 2001). There is also a need for attention to accurate and comprehensive vital registration systems (that record causes of death) and disease surveillance systems; the need for these is now more widely recognized but their importance for local decision making is often overlooked.

Every initiative to improve data collection or mine existing datasets has to ask whether this will benefit those with unmet needs, increasing their influence and their capacity to act and to hold government and international agencies to account.

Building a local and global knowledge base on urban areas

The links between local data and the global knowledge base are critical. Despite the rapid growth in the literature on climate change and cities, the knowledge base on urban issues remains woefully thin, especially for most low- and many middle-income nations. Encouragement and support is needed for relevant research in each nation and city that can be drawn on for shared learning. The learning has to be strongly connected to what is being done in particular urban centres, large and small. It needs to become more specific and useful to local actors so that they can understand the particular local implications of climate change for heat stress and heat islands within cities, for example, or for coastal flooding, sea level rise and storm surges. As several of the city case studies make clear, local universities can help ensure this key connection between knowledge of climate change and local context by producing the steady stream of data and skills that cities need to deal with the uncertainties being faced in the 21st century.

What is needed here is an expanding global network of researchers and research institutions with competence on urban issues and climate change issues who choose to work together, bringing in all universities or research centres committed to working on these issues within their own localities. They can collectively focus on and update the literature on each identified climate change-related risk and its implications for urban economies, populations and governments. This does not have to be built from scratch.

There is also the issue of how the rapidly expanding knowledge base on cities and climate change can influence government policies and practice. Will representatives from national governments who form the IPCC be willing to engage with local governments and civil society and share their accumulating knowledge? And how will governments react to an engagement by researchers with representative organizations formed by the residents of informal settlements, who absolutely have the right to influence government responses and to take action themselves?

Another concern is how the future IPCC assessments can fully cover the rapidly expanding knowledge about urban issues. Is it possible to continue relying on a small team of urban specialists, most of them working with no financial support except for transport and accommodation costs when attending meetings? Are urban areas (and urban governments) so important for adaptation and mitigation that they need a special report of their own, with mechanisms to ensure this is updated regularly? The power of IPCC special reports to bring together academic communities and to influence wider international agendas has been proven. The Special Report on Managing the Risks of Extreme Events and Disasters to Advance Climate Change Adaptation (SREX) (IPCC 2012), for example, brought the disaster risk management, climate change adaptation and climate change modelling communities together, changing the direction of the adaptation discourse and policy by introducing transformation and climate change as part of a risk agenda. If urban areas are the context within which climate change adaptation and mitigation will be won or lost, a special report seems overdue. How can this then best influence governments? Should there be chapters for each of the world's regions on urban adaptation and mitigation?

International and local plans

The UN Framework Convention on Climate Change (UNFCCC) has started to support the development of National Adaptation Plans, beginning with the Least Developed Countries. These are meant to be more operational than the existing National Adaptation Programmes of Action, where a role for sub-national stakeholders (e.g. city governments) is rarely recognized. It will be important to find ways to support the implementation of these plans and to ensure that they are developed by drawing on input from Local Adaptation Plans.

There are also international meetings and networks that are supporting cities taking action on climate change. These include the Cities Climate Registry[3] under which more than 500 cities and regions have committed to more than 1 billion tonnes of GHG emissions reductions by 2020. In relation to adaptation, the Durban Adaptation Charter, which the city of Durban helped establish during the Conference of Parties meeting in Durban in 2011, commits its more than 1,000 local government signatories to climate change adaptation action at a local level with the aim of helping communities to respond effectively to climate change.[4]

By what process can city governments be held to account for commitments made and then not acted on – in ways that encourage positive action rather than international censure? National governments can provide incentives for local authorities to develop and implement effective plans, or can legislate for certain budgetary proportions to be spent on risk-reducing activities. At the same time, international programmes (such as the UN-ISDR's "My City is Getting Ready" campaign) can provide opportunities for leading cities to be recognized and rewarded for achieving progress on this agenda. But these contributions will not provide the scale of funding needed. How can external funds increase the scale and scope of what the innovating local governments are doing and multiply the number of innovator cities? What about matching funding offered on concessional terms to city governments that meet some strong conditions on poverty reduction, transparency and accountability to their citizens? This should be serious funding within a long-term investment framework for each city for meeting development, disaster risk reduction and climate change adaptation – with mitigation woven into this wherever relevant. To what extent can the Green Climate Fund enable this change through its commitment to facilitating a paradigm shift towards low-emission and climate-resilient development pathways by providing appropriate support to local governments in low- and middle-income countries?

Cities and the common good

As noted in Chapter 1, the dominant processes that drive economic success in cities do not of themselves produce healthy cities, or sustainable or inclusive cities, or cities that adapt well to climate change or manage to keep their greenhouse gas emissions low. When the focus of governments or international agencies is only on a city's economic growth, these other things can easily be forgotten. Economic growth is of course critical to low- and middle-income countries. It provides jobs and innovation and income, usually with many local multipliers. It also usually increases revenues for city governments. And this makes it possible, in theory, for local governments to attend more seriously to their primary function – attending to the common good of all their citizens. But for this to remain in focus, economic growth must be accompanied by other essentials, as well as a concern for low carbon growth.

There is a substantial list of things that serve the public or common good, as has been discussed repeatedly throughout this book – safe working conditions and clean air, unpolluted waterways and healthy ecosystems, universal provision for piped water, sanitation, drainage and solid waste collection systems that serve everyone, social safety nets, good health care, emergency services, street lighting, schools, public transportation, effective and accountable policing, measures to reduce disaster risk etc. In most cities, local governments figure prominently in having responsibility for providing most of this, as well as implementing regulations that control air and water pollution and ensure occupational health and safety. In cities where much of the population have inadequate incomes, the importance of local government accountability is that much greater.

This substantial list needs to be expanded now to take account of the growing risks facing most cities from the current and future impacts of a changing climate. The risks to life, health, homes and assets that urban inhabitants face are not just an externality of global economic growth, to be moderated by various incremental changes. They are an instrumental component of contemporary development and need to be addressed as such. To respond to these burdens in more than a piecemeal way calls for deep structural changes informed by a commitment to our common home and our common good.

As Chapter 2 emphasized, transformative adaptation that unites development and climate change adaptation and mitigation calls for a deepening of the effort to build new solutions and new capacities. It needs a shift in attention from proximate causes to root causes. There needs, for example, to be a shift from social safety nets that support the vulnerable to community development that can reorient the distribution of power in cities. This kind of redistribution is a prerequisite to shifting development away from its contemporary pathways, where inequality and high greenhouse gas emissions are seen as acceptable, if unfortunate, "externalities".

There may be concerns within any city that too many demands, taxes and regulations implemented "in the public or common good" will cause new investments (and maybe existing businesses) to go elsewhere. But most private businesses and their employees benefit from a well-governed city with healthy citizens, good provision for infrastructure and services, and a city that is able to anticipate and cope with the risks that come its way. This means more than protecting assets. A city's large and successful enterprises, well served with risk-reducing infrastructure, are still only as resilient as their workforce and suppliers – just as the public health of a city is only as dependable as the sanitation that serves its poorest citizens. Private capital investments are increasingly likely to avoid cities at risk from climate change that are not addressing adaptation and its developmental underpinnings.

Of course, in every location, there are debates and disagreements about what is in the common good and how this is best protected or funded. Those who use public transport and those with private vehicles may have very different visions of what would best serve the general need. Those living in informal settlements at the edge of a peripheral canal in Bangkok may see flood control differently from those needing to protect valuable assets in the city centre. In every neighbourhood, municipality, city and region, the common good must be forged in debate and discussion, open to criticism and responsive to change (Calhoun 1998). This can be a rarity. A review of planning in the UK notes that it has become increasingly characterized by democratic failure "... with the wishes of local communities entirely disregarded, and sham public consultations an everyday occurrence. Meanwhile, the rise of lobbying in contentious development decisions and the revolving door between local government, developers and lobbying companies – who carry out public consultations on behalf of the private sector and local government – emerged as a defining feature of a system in which abuses are routine and as characteristic of local democracy as elections themselves" (Minton, no date, page 6). These fundamental failings are clearly not confined only to the UK. Addressing all the SDGs that relate to healthy, sustainable and inclusive cities requires institutions acting in the common good and accountable to "the public". How can they be met in a world where there has been a decisive shift towards private interests at the expense of the public good and democratic rights (see Minton, no date)?

Success in acting on the four agendas and their integration is inconceivable without local institutions and networks capable of defining and defending the common good – in ways that are acceptable to their citizens and that engage them, including the more marginalized groups. The need for this engagement is still not widely recognized by many international agencies and national governments. This helps explain the massive deficit in urban areas in low- and most middle-income countries in most of the elements that we consider to be part of the common good.

Climate change adds to the urgency. Within an urbanizing planet, we need city and municipal governments that can act in the common good – where the common good is understood as something to be achieved for each locality and for everyone in it. We also need attention to wider regions and to national and global goals, and success here also depends on national governments acting in what is so clearly both the global and the local common good – the avoidance of dangerous climate change. All the authors of this book are holding their breath hoping that this first essential underpinning, agreement on needed emissions reduction, is achieved in Paris in December 2015. This needs to be followed by a recognition of how much success depends on city governments working with their populations to act in the common good for present and future generations.

Notes

1 www.compactofmayors.org/
2 http://urbansdg.org/
3 http://carbonn.org/
4 www.durbanadaptationcharter.org/news/durban-joins-c40-cities-climate-leadership-group-as-an-innovator-city

References

ACHR (2015), *215 Cities in Asia*: Fifth yearly report of the Asian Coalition for Community Action Programme, Bangkok: Asian Coalition for Housing Rights, 75 pages.

Anguelovski, I., E. Chu and J. Carmin, (2014), "Variations in approaches to urban climate adaptation: experiences and experimentation from the global South". *Global Environmental Change*, 27, 156–167.

Appadurai, Arjun (2001), "Deep democracy: urban governmentality and the horizon of politics", *Environment and Urbanization,* 13:2, 23–43.

Bhan, Gautam (2014), "The real lives of urban fantasies", *Environment and Urbanization,* 26:1, 232–235.

Boonyabancha, Somsook and Diana Mitlin (2012), "Urban poverty reduction: learning by doing in Asia", *Environment and Urbanization*, 24:2, 403–422.

Boonyabancha, Somsook, Fr. Norberto Carcellar and Thomas Kerr (2012), "How poor communities are paving their own pathways to freedom", *Environment and Urbanization*, 24:2, 441–462.

Butcher, S. and A. Apsan Frediani (2014), "Insurgent citizenship practices: the case of Muungano wa Wanavijiji in Nairobi, Kenya", *City*, 18:2, 119–133.

Cabannes, Yves (2004), "Participatory budgeting: a significant contribution to participatory democracy", *Environment and Urbanization*, 16:1, 27–46.

Cabannes, Yves (2015), "The impact of participatory budgeting on basic services; municipal practices and evidence from the field", *Environment and Urbanization*, 27:1, 257–284.

Calhoun, Craig (1998), "The public good as a social and cultural project", in Walter W. Powell and Elisabeth S. Clemens (editors), *Private Action and the Public Good*, Yale University Press, New Haven and London, pages 20–35.

Chitekwe-Biti, Beth, Patience Mudimu, George Masimba Nyama and Takudzwa Jera (2012), "Developing an informal settlement upgrading protocol in Zimbabwe - the Epworth story", *Environment and Urbanization* 24:1, 131–148.

Chu, E., I. Anguelovski and J. Carmin, (2015) "Inclusive approaches to urban climate adaptation planning and implementation in the Global South", *Climate Policy*, DOI: 10.1080/14693062.2015.1019822.

Hardoy, Jorge E. and David Satterthwaite (1981), *Shelter: Need and Response; Housing, Land and Settlement Policies in Seventeen Third World Nations*, Chichester: John Wiley and Sons.

Hasan, Arif (2015), "Land contestation in Karachi and the impact on housing and urban development", *Environment and Urbanization*, 26:1, 217–230.

IPCC (2012), *Managing the Risks of Extreme Events and Disasters to Advance Climate Change Adaptation*, A Special Report of Working Groups I and II of the Intergovernmental Panel on Climate Change, C. B. Field, V. Barros, T. F. Stocker, D. Qin, D. J. Dokken, K. L. Ebi, M. D. Mastrandrea, K. J. Mach, G.-K. Plattner, S. K. Allen, M. Tignor and P. M. Midgley (eds), Cambridge University Press, Cambridge, UK and New York, USA, 582 pp.

Johnson, C. and Blackburn, S. (2014), "Advocacy for urban resilience: UNISDR's Making Cities Resilient campaign", *Environment and Urbanization*, 26:1, 29–52.

Livengood, Avery and Keya Kunte (2012), "Enabling participatory planning with GIS: a case study of settlement mapping in Cuttack, India", *Environment and Urbanization*, 24:1, 77–97.

Makau, J., S. Dobson and E. Samia (2012), "The five-city enumeration: the role of participatory enumerations in developing community capacity and partnerships with government in Uganda" *Environment and Urbanization*, 24:1, 31–46.

Minton, Anna (no date), *Common Good(s); Redefining the public interest and the common good*, http://howtoworktogether.org/think-tank/anna-minton-common-goods-redefining-the-public-interest-and-the-common-good/.

Molnar, C., T. Ritz, B. Heller, and W. Solecki (2010) "Using higher education-community partnerships to promote urban sustainability" *Environment: Science and Policy for Sustainable Development* 53:1, 18–28.

Muller, Anna and Edith Mbanga (2012), "Participatory enumerations at the national level in Namibia: the Community Land Information Programme (CLIP)", *Environment and Urbanization*, 24:1, 67–75.

Navarro, Lia (2001), "Exploring the environmental and political dimensions of poverty: the cases of the cities of Mar del Plata and Necochea-Quequén" *Environment and Urbanization*, 13:1, 185–199.

Patel, S., C. Baptist and C. d'Cruz (2012) "Knowledge is power – informal communities assert their right to the city through SDI and community-led enumerations", *Environment and Urbanization*, 24:1, 13–26.

Pearson, L. and M. Pelling (2015). "The UN Sendai Framework for Disaster Risk Reduction 2015–30: negotiation process and prospects for science and practice", *Journal of Extreme Events*. DOI: 10.1142/S2345737615710013.

Satterthwaite, David and Diana Mitlin (2014), *Reducing Urban Poverty in the Global South*, London: Routledge.

Simon, D. (2014) "New evidence and thinking on urban environmental change challenges", *International Development Planning Review*, 36:2, v–xi.

Steffen, Will, Katherine Richardson, Johan Rockström, Sarah E. Cornell, Ingo Fetzer, Elena M. Bennett, Reinette Biggs, Stephen R. Carpenter, Wim de Vries, Cynthia A. de Wit, Carl Folke, Dieter Gerten, Jens Heinke, Georgina M. Mace, Linn M. Persson, Veerabhadran Ramanathan, Belinda Reyers and Sverker Sörlin (2015), "Planetary boundaries: Guiding human development" *Science* 347: 6223.

UNICEF and WHO (2015), *25 Years Progress on Sanitation and Drinking Water; 2015 Update and MDG Assessment*, UNICEF and WHO, 80 pages.

United Nations (2009), *Global Assessment Report on Disaster Risk Reduction: Risk and Poverty in a Changing Climate*, UNISDR, United Nations, Geneva, 207 pages.

United Nations (2011), *Revealing Risk, Redefining Development: The 2011 Global Assessment Report on Disaster Risk Reduction*, United Nations International Strategy for Disaster Reduction, Geneva, 178 pages.

United Nations (2013), *A New Global Partnership: Eradicate Poverty and Transform Economies through Sustainable Development*, Report of the High-Level Panel of Eminent Persons on the Post-2015 Development Agenda, New York: United Nations, 60 pages.

United Nations (2015a), *Transforming our World; The 2030 Agenda for Sustainable Development*, Draft outcome document of the United Nations Summit for the adoption of the post-2015 development agenda was agreed by consensus by the member States on Sunday 2 August 2015, New York: United Nations, 29 pages.

United Nations (2015b), *Addis Ababa Action Agenda* of the Third International Conference on Financing for Development, The final text of the outcome document adopted at the Third International Conference on Financing for Development (Addis Ababa, Ethiopia, 13–16 July 2015) and endorsed by the General Assembly in its resolution 69/313 of 27 July 2015, United Nations, New York, 61 pages.

United Nations (2015c), *Making Development Sustainable: The Future of Disaster Risk Management*, Global Assessment Report on Disaster Risk Reduction, United Nations Office for Disaster Risk Reduction (UNISDR), Geneva.

Watson, Vanessa (2014), "African urban fantasies: dreams or nightmares?", *Environment and Urbanization*, 26:1, 215–231.

POSTSCRIPT

This book was completed in October 2015, two months before the Paris Agreement was reached at the Conference of Parties of the UN Framework Convention on Climate Change. This Agreement is so much more than was feared (or even expected), even if in some aspects it was less than what was desired (and less than what is needed to avoid dangerous climate change). It recognizes on its opening page that

> ...climate change represents an urgent and potentially irreversible threat to human societies and the planet and thus requires the widest possible cooperation by all countries, and their participation in an effective and appropriate international response, with a view to accelerating the reduction of global greenhouse gas emissions.

The Paris Agreement aims to hold the increase in global average temperature to well below two degrees centrigrade above pre-industrial levels – even if it does not guarantee that this will be achieved. It also lays out a framework for reporting, transparency and reviews of implementation for each nation. It emphasizes the urgent need to address the significant gap between the aggregate effect of Parties' mitigation pledges (seen in their INDCs – Intended Nationally Determined Contributions) and what is needed to keep below the 2°C limit. And it commits to pursuing efforts to achieve a much more ambitious goal,

> ...to limit the temperature increase to 1.5 °C above pre-industrial levels, recognizing that this would significantly reduce the risks and impacts of climate change.
>
> (Article 2)

The importance of adaptation as a critical and stand-alone element of the response to climate change (and more broadly to the goal of sustainable development) is recognized.

> Parties hereby establish the global goal on adaptation of enhancing adaptive capacity, strengthening resilience and reducing vulnerability to climate change, with a view to contributing to sustainable development and ensuring an adequate adaptation response in the context of the temperature goal referred to in Article 2.
>
> (Article 7)

The Agreement recognizes the key role of what it terms Non Party Stakeholders in adaptation and mitigation. These include civil society and city, municipal and other subnational authorities as well as the private sector and financial institutions. These stakeholders are encouraged to make their commitments to scale up climate actions and register these in a new Non-State Actor Zone for Climate Action platform (http://climateaction.unfccc.int/). Christiana Figueres, Executive Secretary of the UN Framework Convention on Climate Change, noted that

> The Paris Agreement also sends a powerful signal to the many thousands of cities, regions, businesses and citizens across the world already committed to climate action that their vision of a low-carbon, resilient future is now the chosen course for humanity this century.
>
> (http://newsroom.unfccc.int/unfccc-newsroom/finale-cop21/)

So, in relation to this book, the Paris Agreement shows that national governments recognize adaptation as a global challenge "faced by all with local, subnational, national, regional and international dimensions" (Article 7). Local governments here mentioned for their importance for adaptation and mitigation (which is good). But their importance for transformative adaptation and the national and international support they need to realize this still gets too little attention. *So much of what the Paris Agreement commits to depends on city and municipal governments with the willingness, competence and capacity to act on adaptation and mitigation and its developmental underpinnings* – but the agreement's promotion of capacity building is focused on national governments. When in Article 7, Parties are urged to share information, good practices, experiences and lessons learned, including, "…as these relate to science, planning, policies and implementation in relation to adaptation actions'" (Article 7), this has to include city and municipal governments and local civil society. National governments need to recognize how much their INDC ambitions for adaptation and for accurate emissions accounting depend on urban governments and effective (national) INDCs need (urban) IUDCs and (city) ICDCs.

INDEX